TRANSFORMING
LEADERSHIP

Also by James MacGregor Burns

Congress on Trial

Roosevelt: The Lion and the Fox

Roosevelt: The Soldier of Freedom

John Kennedy: A Political Profile

The Deadlock of Democracy

Presidential Government: The Crucible of Leadership

Uncommon Sense

Leadership

The American Experiment (3 vols.)
The Vineyard of Liberty
The Workshop of Democracy
The Crosswinds of Freedom

Cobblestone Leadership: Majority Rule, Minority Power

A People's Charter: The Pursuit of Rights in America
(with Stewart Burns)

Dead Center: Clinton–Gore Leadership and the Perils of Moderation
(with Georgia J. Sorenson)

The Three Roosevelts: Patrician Leaders Who Transformed America
(with Susan Dunn)

TRANSFORMING LEADERSHIP

A New Pursuit of Happiness

JAMES MacGREGOR BURNS

Atlantic Monthly Press
New York

Published simultaneously in Canada
Printed in the United States of America

FIRST EDITION

Library of Congress Cataloging-in-Publication Data

Burns, James MacGregor.
    Transforming leadership : a new pursuit of happiness / James MacGregor Burns.
        p. cm.
    Includes bibliographical references and index.
    ISBN 0-87113-866-2
    1. Leadership. 2. Leadership—History. I. Title.
HM1261 .B87 2003
    303.3'4—dc21   2002033258

Atlantic Monthly Press
841 Broadway
New York, NY 10003

03 04 05 06   10 9 8 7 6 5 4 3 2 1

For Milton Djuric,
a scholar's scholar

CONTENTS

PART FOUR *PEOPLE*

PART FIVE *TRANSFORMATION*

PROLOGUE
EMPOWERING HAPPINESS

How smoothly Thomas Jefferson's pen glided across the parchment: ". . . Life, Liberty and the pursuit of Happiness." And how deeply were these words of the Declaration of Independence—expressing the common stock of human rights—etched into the American consciousness.

But what did this gleaming passage mean? Surely *Life* must have stood for the survival of people, and of whole peoples, for their security against threats foreign and domestic. *Liberty* was clear to all in that time of rebellion against King George: protection from tyrannical and arbitrary rule, the freedoms later written into the Bill of Rights. And the *pursuit of Happiness?* This was not so clear. Enlightenment thinkers had philosophized about it during the eighteenth century; to Jefferson it represented down-to-earth needs. He would urge friends traveling in Europe to look into the "happiness of the people" by taking "every possible occasion of entering into the hovels of the labourers . . . see what they eat, how they are cloathed, whether they are obliged to labour too hard; whether the government or the landlord takes from them an unjust proportion of their labour."

Thus the pursuit of happiness was not trivial pleasure seeking. It was fundamental to the conditions of people's lives and to their efforts to change and to improve them. It was one of the great public values that took new form and urgency from the creative thinkers of the Enlightenment. Along with life, liberty, equality, justice, community—and intertwined with them—the pursuit of happiness was grounded in the most basic wants of human beings. Francis Hutcheson, the great Scottish Enlightenment philosopher, wrote that "pursuing happiness and eschewing misery" was the chief drive and purpose of the human will. And John Locke saw transformational potential in the pursuit of happiness, as human beings struggled to change themselves and their world.

Yet in the time of the Enlightenment, as also in ours today, many of the world's people—perhaps most of them—were unable to "eschew misery." It was not only that they lacked happiness. They lacked the opportunity and means to pursue it. They lacked, I will argue, the most potent agent for change, for unlocking the transformational capacities needed to make the pursuit of happiness more than a phrase on parchment.

Leadership is an expanding field of study that some day may join the traditional disciplines of history, philosophy, and the social sciences in scholarly recognition. Today, however, it remains in its growing stages; it has as yet no grand, unifying theory to provide common direction to thinkers and researchers. Even the meaning of the term itself remains controversial. Some will use it neutrally, dispassionately, to analyze qualities of both, say, a Gandhi and a Hitler.

I believe leadership is not only a descriptive term but a prescriptive one, embracing a moral, even a passionate, dimension. Consider our common usage. We don't call for *good* leadership—we expect, or at least hope, that it will be good. "Bad" leadership implies *no* leadership. I contend that there is nothing neutral about leadership; it is valued as a moral necessity.

Summoned forth by human wants, the task of leadership is to accomplish some change in the world that responds to those wants. Its actions and achievements are measured by the supreme public values that themselves are the profoundest expressions of human wants: liberty and equality, justice and opportunity, the pursuit of happiness.

And if leadership is, as I believe, a moral undertaking, a response to the human wants expressed in public values, then surely its greatest task— the task, even, of a global leadership—must be to respond to the billions of the world's people in the direst want, people whose pursuits of happiness might begin with a little food or medicine, a pair of shoes, a school within walking distance. They might seek some respect and dignity, some understanding of the interlocked burdens and frustrations of poverty as they, the poor, understand them. They might become followers of those who hear their wants and whose responsive leadership in turn empowers them, in the initial steps of a leadership process that might break the vicious circle of poverty.

Hence I would call for the protection and nourishing of happiness, for extending the opportunity to pursue happiness to all people, as the core agenda of transforming leadership.

Because leadership must be tested by results, I propose in this book's epilogue a leadership strategy to combat global poverty in this century. In millennia past, the most potent act of the rulers of nations has been the recruitment and deployment into battle of great armies of their people. Can we, in coming decades, mobilize throughout the world a new, militant, but peaceful army—tens of thousands of leaders who would in turn recruit fresh leaders at the grass roots, in villages and neighborhoods, from among the poor themselves, to *fight and win* a worldwide war against desperation?

Leaders working as partners with the dispossessed people of the world to secure life, liberty, and the pursuit of happiness—happiness empowered with transforming purpose—could become the greatest act of united leadership the world has ever known.

Part One

CHANGE

1

THE MYSTERIES
OF LEADERSHIP

Leader. *The ancient Egyptians had a word for it:* seshmi.
They also had a word for followers: shemsu.
And, remarkably, they had a word for leadership: seshem-t.

Over the millennia, we have heard far more about leaders than followers, and more about followers than leadership. Chroniclers, priests, and poets have told stories of God-anointed leaders like Moses and Muhammad, of adventuring warrior-kings like Gilgamesh and Odysseus, of great founders like Alexander the Great, Shi Huangdi, and George Washington.

The ancient Greeks raised the right questions. In Plato's *Republic,* Socrates thought that "there might be a reform of the State if only one change was made, which is not a slight or easy one." What was that? he was asked. When "philosophers are kings, or the kings and princes of this world have the spirit and power of philosophy, and political greatness and wisdom meet in one." Aristotle, too, appeared to be talking about leadership when he wrote: "Since every political society is composed of rulers and subjects let us consider whether the relations of one to the other should interchange or be permanent. For the education of the citizens will necessarily vary with the answer given to this question."

From Hesiod, who wrote of the rise and fall of a race of heroes in the eighth century B.C.E., through the writings of Polybius, Plutarch, Augustine,

Voltaire, Kant, Hegel, and a host of other celebrated thinkers, philosophers and theologians and politicians, with some striking exceptions, wrote less about change itself than about cycles and laws of history or the fickleness of fate. Certainly they never referred explicitly to what today we call leadership, but they wrote of popes and potentates, rulers and rebels, heroes and infidels in penetrating ways that some day would help us frame theories of change through leadership.

CLEOPATRA'S NOSE

The most commonly recognized "leadership" qualities in the ancient world were passed down in folk sagas and biblical stories. Men were admired for their physical strength and their fighting prowess, women for their beauty. Many centuries later men were still equating women's importance with their sex appeal. To Pascal in his *Pensées,* history had turned on "Cleopatra's nose: had it been shorter, the whole aspect of the world would have been altered."

But physical appeal was not Cleopatra's trump card. "For her actual beauty, it is said, was not in itself so remarkable that none could be compared with her," Plutarch reported, "or that no one could see her without being struck by it, but the contact of her presence, if you lived with her, was irresistible." Yet Cleopatra's charisma was in the service of her greater strengths of rulership—her intelligence, militancy, ambition—and all these qualities were harnessed in a steadfast pursuit of her supreme goal: the empowerment of her throne and empire.

Through the millennia philosophers and practical thinkers posed questions that have puzzled us to this day. Is there any meaning in the flow of history or is it just a jumble of chaotic events? Could humankind ever control the course of events or even understand it? Can laws of historical causation be drawn from the story of humanity? Can humans plan change or must they simply react to it?

If the great thinkers made no final breakthroughs on such questions, at least they posed them with clarity and panache. Still, by the start of the twentieth century—an era that would desperately need answers to some of these questions—many issues remained in vexing obscurity. More and more the search for solutions fell to the great universities that came into their own with the turn of the century. This meant that they were claimed by disciplines—history, politics, sociology, philosophy, and the rest—that had fenced off their various feudal turfs.

In my own corner of academe I typified this problem. Teaching political science at a small college, Williams, in Massachusetts, I loved analyzing the ideas and talents of the great constitution makers of the world, but I felt unable to penetrate to the moral and psychological forces that drove these leaders. To an honors class in leadership I posed lofty questions of historical causation, but I was better at raising problems than analyzing the swirl of forces that powered the transformation of cultures. Some of our most engaging classes dealt with life stories of great men and women, but I rarely felt satisfied that we had gotten to the heart of the interplay of environmental and personal forces that shaped the actions of leaders and rulers.

Something was lacking in my own intellectual background, I realized, and I began to see what it was: psychology. I had read books that used psychological concepts to explain crucial aspects of human behavior. But I lacked a disciplinary foundation. What to do? I had heard that Al Goethals in Williams's psychology department was interested in leadership. Soon I was sitting in his office and hearing of work in his field, including that of a psychologist named Abraham Maslow, who had developed a striking theory of human wants and needs that held fascinating potential for understanding leadership and change.

I have come to see leadership not only as a field of study but as a master discipline that illuminates some of the toughest problems of human needs and social change, and in the process exploits the findings of political science, history, sociology, philosophy, theology, literature, and psychology. I have come to see, too, the contributions that the study of leadership can make to those disciplines.

The extraordinary aspect of the Egyptian distinction between leader and leadership lies in its helping us to frame theories of change through leadership. Some writers contend that we can learn about leadership only by relating the "life and times" of individual leaders, especially the heroic ones. Others argue that we must construct a general theory of leadership in order that we grasp the role of individual leaders and their traits. I hope to prove in this book that both approaches are necessary and that we can do both.

* * *

From the days of Homer, the simplest way of understanding leaders and rulers was to examine their distinguishing characteristics. It is the same today. When a Russian president takes office or a European premier loses her parliamentary majority or an Asian dictator seizes power or an American presidential candidate wins his party's nomination, our first questions tend to be about their reported traits. What does he look like? Is she a good orator? Is he gay or Catholic or elderly or childless? Is she tough, compassionate, experienced, moralistic? If these are the kinds of questions that you consider most crucial, you are taking a "traits" approach to leadership. If instead you emphasize the political environment the leader faces, the economic or ideological context, the attitudes and expectations of followers, then you probably are a "situationist."

You may be a traits analyst without knowing it. When you apply for a job you expect to answer questions about your background, experience, and skills while being evaluated for such intangibles as dependability, empathy, initiative, fortitude, ambition, and the like—traits you assume relate to the tasks you would be taking on. This seems just a matter of common sense. Why should an employer not want someone with such traits? Uncommon sense suggests that some of these qualities may be irrelevant to what you will be doing, but a good deal of quantitative research backs up the usefulness of this kind of traits approach in predicting performance at school or work.

How does traits research help us to understand the sources of leadership? Much of the work on traits was done by analysts ferreting out qualities that undergird leadership skills. "The leader is characterized," leadership scholar Bernard Bass, for example, concluded, "by a strong drive for responsibility and completion of tasks, vigor and persistence in the pursuit of goals, venturesomeness and originality in problem solving," self-confidence, willingness to accept consequences, tolerance for stress, frustration, and delay.

These traits are heavily management-oriented because they were drawn mainly from extensive studies of corporations. A comparable study of political leadership might be less comprehensive, more guarded and nuanced, and subject to greater cultural differences.

The long and restless research for common traits of leadership rises from the most basic of explanations of change in history: the dynamic, decisive role of the "Great Man" who bends history's course to his own will. Humans have always needed heroes to deify or destroy, as all-powerful causes for success or as scapegoats for failure. Children are brought up on tales of warriors, outlaws, martyrs. Bookstores are filled with glossy accounts of corporate titans, military geniuses, political giants. A century and a half ago, Thomas Carlyle had baldly proclaimed on behalf of heroes that "Universal History, the history of what man has accomplished in this world, is at bottom the History of the Great Men who have worked here."

The American philosopher Sidney Hook distinguished between the "eventful" man who happened to be involved in an historic situation but without really determining its course, and the "event-making" man whose "actions influenced subsequent developments along a quite different course than would have been followed if these actions had not been taken," actions that were "the consequences of outstanding capacities of intelligence, will, and character rather than accidents of position." Hook's distinction, as he noted, recognized the general belief that a hero is great not only because of what he does but because of what he is—because of his traits.

Just as Great Men often stumble, so did the Great Man theory. The noble achievements of history's heroes were often shown to be morally flawed, or in fact the product of myriad others who shared little of the glory, or simply the result of accidents or miscalculations or "contingency." Napoleon, who won heroic status and a library of adulatory biographies after a career of brilliant victories, lost much of his luster after Waterloo, though visitors still flock to his tomb in Paris. Adolf Hitler, with his "heroic" posturings and boasts to the German people that he would establish the Greater Reich for a thousand years, brought his country to utter ruin in little more than a decade.

SLAVES OF HISTORY

It is comforting to take the Great Man approach when we reflect on our own "life and times." We can remember the good decisions we made, choosing one college or career over another, moving to the best place to live, finding the right person as our spouse. We may see those choices as our own, drawn from needs and hopes in turn drawn from years of thought and growth. If in our youth we were controlled by family and peer and school pressures, we may feel that increasingly we were able to take our lives into our own hands.

Is it so simple as that? Each of us is born in a certain place, of certain parents, in a certain neighborhood, into a particular social class, religion, belief system. Whatever choices we had fell within a relatively narrow frame. Experience may have stunted our life-chances and alternatives rather than broadened them. And if we enjoyed a sense of freedom or even self-esteem in having decided to be, say, a leader, an activist, a change maker, in school or workplace or community, how much latitude did we actually have?

To respond to situations seems as inevitable as making use of one's traits. But a theory of "situationism" is no less elusive. We exist in multiple situations—which ones are more important? Can one situation, such as living in an affluent family, override another, such as belonging to a discriminated-against race? Can dire poverty overcome high intelligence, or vice versa? We may be able to change a particular situation, such as a job, more readily than we can change a particular trait, such as sociability, but in changing jobs are we not still controlled by broader environmental factors?

If these are unsettling questions in our private lives, imagine how complex and urgent they can be in society as a whole, and how potent in their implications for leadership. Vast numbers of people exist in common circumstances of geography, race, religion, class, illiteracy, ill health, ignorance. Dire conditions create dire wants that in turn create opportunities for political leaders to mobilize those in need for the cause of transformational change—or, alternatively, to exploit them.

The potential for real, intended change that addresses the deepest human needs turns crucially on the extent to which humans are able to separate themselves from their confining social roots and growth experiences and thus manage to control their destinies, to act creatively in pursuit of real change. How far can we free ourselves from becoming pawns of situations and "slaves of history"? How far are we able to act as free agents in pursuing liberty, opportunity, happiness, for ourselves and for others?

Few in all of history have done more both to clarify and to confuse these issues than Karl Marx. Both a philosopher of change and a revolutionary strategist and activist, Marx dramatically embodied, on a grand scale, the age-old debate over the roles of individuals and situations.

Marx's intellectual "situation" was marked by myriad efforts to discern the laws governing the development of societies. His predecessor Hegel had contended that "great men" had "no consciousness of the general Idea they were unfolding," but enacted "the will of the World-Spirit." Hegel called such men the "clear-sighted ones" but, though they embodied the "Truth for their age," they had but a dim insight into it. The difference was that those who followed and obeyed them had none. The great were one-eyed men in a land of the blind.

The young Marx turned Hegel's idealism on its head. While agreeing that history was driven by impersonal forces, Marx insisted that these were not spiritual but material, grounded in human needs.

Marx pushed situationism to its most extreme form. Humankind moved through repeated and determined stages of class formation, class deprivation, class struggle. No need to search for leaders because the dialectical process of class struggle was ineluctable, invulnerable to conscious human shaping. No need to look for fancy theories of causation in history; to Marx, epochal changes lay in the unfulfilled needs of the masses.

Given Marx's belief in the dialectic of class struggle, it was both ironic and appropriate that another brilliant thinker would arise to oppose his revolutionary teachings with a different idea of struggle. This was the British social philosopher Herbert Spencer. Living in the age of Darwin, Spencer applied the exciting new ideas of evolution to the marketplace. The Great Man, he contended, was the result only of a "long series of complex influences which has produced the race in which he appears, and the social state into which that race has slowly grown." Social change was the product of economic struggle, with evolution invariably favoring the most fit. Unlike Marx, who saw tooth-and-claw capitalism as merely the prerequisite for the revolutionary birth of communism, Spencer celebrated capitalist society as a highly evolved "social organism" where "fitness" was proven by accumulations of wealth and power. He showed how the ruthless application of nature's law not only controlled economic development but militated against any intervention by the state—or by rulers wishing to use government to interfere with the automatic workings of the marketplace, say, to relieve the miseries of the "undeserving poor."

The most eloquent—and most savage—rebuttal to determinists on the left and the right came not from another philosopher but from a writer who had long pondered the question of historical causation, Leo Tolstoy.

But while he rejected as frauds all theories that claimed to disclose history's inner mechanics, Tolstoy poured equal scorn on the pretensions of Great Men. Free will was no less a delusion than simple determinism. In his masterpiece, *War and Peace,* after noting that "millions of Christian men killed and tortured each other" in Napoleon's invasion of Russia, Tolstoy asked what were the causes of this extraordinary occurrence. Not Napoleon's ambition, he replied, nor Tsar Alexander's tenacious resistance, nor any other single thing, but rather "an incalculable number of causes present themselves. The deeper we delve in search of these causes the more of them we find; and each separate cause or whole series of causes appears to us equally valid in itself and equally false by its insignificance compared to the magnitude of the events."

In some ways, Tolstoy's idea of history as an inexhaustible universe of minute causes was an admission of intellectual despair over the dilemma of the human role in causation. He recognized the explanatory attractiveness of "scientific" determinism and also of human free will, but he could not justify faith in either. Instead he sought to accommodate both: men *felt* that they were acting freely—making history—because the causes that in fact determined their actions were infinitesimal and infinite, forever beyond their comprehension.

Of one thing, however, Tolstoy was certain: none of us, no general, no leader, could control events. Indeed, even the greatest king was only "history's slave."

WHAT LEADERSHIP ANALYSIS CAN DO

All of us, in our own way, are theorists of causation. We try to figure out why certain things happen and other things don't—and then generalize about them. We wonder whether our "situations" in life unduly control us, whether we can break free of them if we wish to, whether we can gain control of our lives. Perhaps we ask ourselves whether or not our traits—our initiative, creativity, self-esteem—can free us from situations we abhor.

What you and I might consider a passing reflection or occasional puzzlement was for Karl Marx a momentous intellectual and political problem that echoed Tolstoy's. Throughout his life Marx stuck to his deterministic theory of historical materialism. But he also had to recognize the central role of activist human beings in forging their own history. After all, as early as 1848, Marx, not yet thirty years old, and Friedrich Engels, twenty-seven, had issued a momentous and ringing call to arms, concluding, "The proletarians have nothing to lose but their chains. They have a world to win. WORKING MEN OF ALL COUNTRIES, UNITE!"

Evidently this Marx was not waiting for history's inexorable logic of change; rather he would seize history by the collar and give it a shove. Historian Alan Swingewood has pointed to the contradiction between Marx's humanist conception that "change evolves through the collective, democratic actions of ordinary individuals seeking to develop their own social, political and cultural institutions" and his description of the social and economic order as "a systemic structure of collectivist and historically necessary forces." Marx remained equivocal. "Men make their own history," he wrote in 1859, "but they do not make it just as they please; they do not make it under circumstances chosen by themselves, but under circumstances directly encountered, given and transmitted from the past."

In the century and a half since Marx, no theorist, no practicing revolutionary, has eclipsed him in grasping the fundamental social and historical forces underlying change and causation in history. Even radicals and conservatives who have no use for Marx's political agenda grant that he remains the towering figure in the reach and depth of his analysis of social processes. Yet no one has solved the fundamental problem that Marx developed so well but did not resolve. Scholars have brilliantly defined the questions but, isolated in their own disciplines, they have failed to distinguish conclusively the roles played in social change by individual and situation, by human volition and inexorable social processes, by the "agency" of actors and the "structure" of systems.

What kind of new exploration of leadership might begin to reconcile these dualisms or contradictions?

First and foremost, such an exploration must delve into the anatomy of intended change. It would see humans as motivated by wants and needs that are not only material but a rich and complex mix of physical, psychological, social, sexual—wants and needs that are both inward, for self-fulfillment, self-actualization, and that also look outward for their satisfaction, through the achievement of some change in the world. It would see that change is caused by a host of forces, personal and impersonal, rational and emotional, material and psychological.

Such an exploration would also see leadership as a vital form of power, but would understand power as a relationship based not simply on the possession of resources by those who wield power, but on the creative, dynamic interplay of wants and needs, motives, values, and capacities of both would-be leaders and their potential followers.

It would view the qualities or traits of leaders as enabling them not only to cope with dire circumstances or situations but to transcend and even to transform them, transforming the people they lead in the process.

Finally, such an approach would give full recognition to the central place in leaders' acts and aims of the great public values—life, liberty, equality, justice, opportunity—that empower pursuits of happiness.

2

SEARCHING FOR
THE X FACTOR

Of all the tasks on the work agenda of leadership analysis, first and fore-most is an understanding of human change, because its nature is the key to the rest.

The stentorian cry, "We live in an age of change" comes all too readily to the lips of orators, but they are right. We need only to recall the twen-tieth century, when revolutions in thought, science, culture, technology, population, religion, and migration swept the globe. And the change that humans make is not dwindling as we move deeper into the twenty-first century, but broadening and speeding up.

Every human change begins with someone having an intention, tak-ing an initiative. This could range from planning a military invasion to setting up a university, inventing electricity to electrifying a political cam-paign, creating a new government to investing in a new business venture. At the heart of the matter lies the question of who initiates a change, in what circumstances, for what reason, proceeding by what means toward what outcome. What is the human role in human change? Tolstoy's struggles and Marx's two-mindedness exemplified the dilemma in the apparent con-traries of free will and determinism as causal explanations. Can a course toward meaningful change be plotted that will give due weight both to the intentions and actions of people and to the situations they confront, to their wants and aspirations, their values, and to the conditions of their lives?

THE QUEST FOR CAUSALITY

If happy is the nation that has no history, happy too, perhaps, are people who accept their existence as it is. They may do so out of passivity, or out of a philosophy of fatalism or a belief in a God who rules all things. They do not deny change; thus they plan for changes in the weather just as nonhuman creatures dig burrows or build nests in preparation for winter. Somehow they cope with disasters but mainly they adjust to little changes in their lives so that they might go on unperturbed. They adjust and readjust.

People's lives might have continued without end in this day-to-day existence, according to one school of thought, except for the tinkerers who invented new goods and cheaper ways of producing them. They built better machines that in turn transformed the nature of work and created a new marketplace for their products. Such changes undergirded the quickening industrialization of the eighteenth and nineteenth centuries.

According to another school of thought it was not tinkering but *thinking* that initiated broad changes in that era, beginning with a huge first step: people imagining and envisioning things that did not yet exist. For creative thinkers this might have meant a wholly different way of doing things, such as substituting steam for horse power or the telegram for the post. For those who sought to understand human society and social change, it meant a radically new way of thinking about causation in history.

To delve into Western intellectual history between the early eighteenth century and the mid-nineteenth is to find new ideas that were as exhilarating as they were intimidating. There was the Italian philosopher Giambattista Vico, who dismissed the idea that human society was static, fixed by God or by unchanging human nature. It was instead dynamic, changing in time, and, above all, the creative product of human intentions and actions: "the world of civil society has certainly been made by men." There was Montesquieu, called by Alan Swingewood "the first, and greatest sociologist of the Enlightenment," who held that "the world is not ruled by fortune" but by human actions, as evidenced by Rome's decline when its leaders adopted "usages which were exactly the reverse of those which had rendered them masters of the world." There were the extraordinary Scottish philosophers, notably David Hume, Adam Smith, and Adam Ferguson, who, rejecting a divine origin for society, wrote powerfully of human experience and sentiment—"the mutual dependence of man"—shaped by and shaping the material world, driving social change.

The keystone of philosophy's ancient régime had been the assumption that human nature was fixed and universal. From the time of the Greeks, this assumption had supported others: about the nature of human society, of social change, and of the human potential for self-development and creative thought and action. Vico had been among the first to strike a crucial blow. Others followed, insisting that the understanding of human nature could no longer be based in dogmas, but had to be approached scientifically, with conclusions drawn, in Hume's words, "from a cautious observation of human life." As explorers and colonists from Europe encountered an astonishing diversity of societies and cultures in the rest of the world, as the West itself experienced stunningly rapid changes through industrialization, the belief that human nature and human society could be God-given and unchanging collapsed. What was to take its place? Based on what "cautious observations"?

Charles Darwin had made cautious observations—five years' worth while aboard the *Beagle* in the 1830s, sailing the seas to far reaches of the earth. In huge piles of handwritten notes, he had recorded his observations of coral reefs and a tremendous variety of other natural phenomena and had begun to search for more than just data. He began to look, gropingly, for *causes*. It was evident, he later wrote, "that neither the action of the surrounding conditions, nor the will of the organisms (especially in the case of plants), could account for the innumerable cases in which organisms of every kind are beautifully adapted to their habits of life—for instance, a woodpecker or tree-frog to climb trees, or a seed for dispersal by hooks or plumes." After his return to England, he concluded that "by collecting all facts that bore in any way on the variation" of animals and plants, "some light" might be thrown on the mystery of adaptation.

Even so, he was still more a practical scientist than a theorist. It was only in 1838 after reading economist Thomas Malthus, who described a world in which the pressures of population growth and limited food supplies bred a constant struggle for survival, was Darwin able to begin to formulate his grand theory. Applying his reams of data to his new insight, he came to see how organisms were stabilized and balanced, even if ruthlessly, and that adaptation indeed was the product of an endless struggle for survival, of conflict within species as well as between them. Darwin built his theory step by step, concept by concept, as he searched for causes of heritable variations. Countering Malthus's pessimism, though, Darwin realized that natural selection was a positive process, generating better-adapted variations in species. Thus death itself was a creative force.

Darwin's theory of evolution gradually emerged as one of the grandest causation theories of all time. Among his crucial contributions, according to philosopher Daniel C. Dennett, was to show us "a new way to make sense of 'why' questions. Like it or not, Darwin's idea offers one way—a clear, cogent, astonishingly versatile way—of dissolving" the old conundrums. Believers in religion had found the ultimate source of causation in God's purposes; now biology offered a different primal force.

Darwin had become more than a creative scholar; his influence on thought was so profound that he was himself a transforming leader. Biologist Ernst Mayr wrote that he had "caused a greater upheaval in man's thinking than any other scientific advance since the rebirth of science in the Renaissance."

Darwin's theory of the struggle for existence had nearly as great an impact on thought about human society as about animal life. His ideas on evolution shaped one of the most politically potent ideas of the nineteenth century, social Darwinism. This creed, with Herbert Spencer as its greatest evangel, extended the struggle for survival to the economic and political world, culminating in the idea that only in economic conflict and competition lies the hope for progressive human change.

Paradoxically, however, Darwinism denied that evolutionary change was *intentional,* or for that matter positive. There was only an instinctive drive to survive. Species did not intend adaptation—it happened naturally. Thus Darwinism, at least as narrowly interpreted, threatened the most powerful idea that had grown out of the Enlightenment, *that human beings could control their future through intended change, that people could make causal forces work for their own well-being.*

Darwin—and Marx—brought to a climax an approach to historical causation with roots in the Enlightenment. Having rejected divine law as controlling history, historians found varieties of new laws in the course of history itself, arguing that events must be seen as caught in patterns of flux and development, part of an ongoing scheme of history. Events that did not fit the pattern were dismissed as "accidents."

It was on the whole a rational and optimistic view of history, reflecting a time in the nineteenth century of relative prosperity and peace and outwardly serene politics in the Western democracies. Still, in longer retrospect, historians continued to grope for ways to resolve the mysteries of causation, just as their predecessors had. "Laws" of history had by definition to be verifiable, predictive—but *proofs* of their truth were elusive. Untidy actual history—industrialization, urbanization, population growth and movement, class conflict, colonialism, human deprivation—was galloping ahead with relentless momentum. History's "flow" turned into a raging torrent in economic crises, local conflicts, and then World War I. In the aftermath of the deaths of millions, Bolsheviks came to power in Russia, Fascists in Italy, and Nazis in Germany. Historical laws could hardly express the irrationalism and xenophobia that had been unleashed on the world.

The effort by historians and sociologists to put causation on a strict scientific footing, to develop universal laws that reduced history to physics was bound to fail, wrote philosopher Morton White, because it excluded in favor of "regularities" the "vast, mysterious, impersonal forces which dominate men."

Mysterious causes? After millennia of religious and philosophical speculation, after Hume and Vico and Marx and Darwin and all the rest, was causation still a mystery? Yes. But why?

Partly because the variables in the process of causation—human motivations such as people's wants and needs; the ambitions of leaders and rulers; the nature and interaction of agency and of situation; the mysteries of creativity, conflict, and power—are too complex and variegated to lend themselves to simplistic explanations or monocausal analyses. Explanations of single acts taken in isolation, such as an assassination, might be relatively easy and perhaps valid, but events such as war or social transformations inevitably involve a wide array of complex causes that our conventional intellectual resources have been incapable of analyzing.

No single discipline—philosophy, psychology, history, political science—alone can deal adequately with the phenomenon of causation because the subject lies outside as well as inside every discipline. A multidiscipline is necessary to borrow from and synthesize existing intellectual resources, and to generate new ones in the process, a discipline that can approach causation using the widest array of conceptual and empirical tools.

That discipline is leadership—the X factor in historic causation.

WHAT IS TRANSFORMING LEADERSHIP?

My own uncertainty over the anatomy of causation spurred me to explore Franklin D. Roosevelt's presidency as a case study in change. I did so not as a theoretician of change but as a biographer of a man who had enormously affected the lives of millions of Americans, including my own. He was the president my college dormitory friends and I had listened to raptly over the radio. In the fall of 1940, I had looked down on him from the balcony of the Boston Garden as he painfully inched his way to the rostrum to assure "the mothers and fathers of America" that "your boys are not going to be sent into any foreign wars." Soon he would become my commander in chief in World War II.

FDR was most intent on producing change—from the campaign days of 1932 and throughout his years in the White House. "The country needs and, unless I mistake its temper, the country demands bold, persistent experimentation. It is common sense to take a method and try it: If it fails, admit it frankly and try another."

Striving to understand his pursuit of change, I found his first two years in office puzzling. He alternated between the bold steps he had promised and a baffling conservative caution. Thus he pressed for economizing in the budget even while proposing large and costly changes in dozens of policy areas. Even more puzzling were his rousing appeals to the voters coupled with endless wheeling and dealing with Democratic congressmen, progressive Republicans, city bosses, western agrarians, southern conservatives. To reflect his doublesidedness, I decided to subtitle my 1956 book, with a steal from Machiavelli, *The Lion and the Fox*.

I found FDR's second term still more fascinating than his first, because in 1937–38 he pursued institutional as well as policy changes. The reason was clear: he had been frustrated by a fragmented Congress, a rising Republican opposition, and the ancient checks and balances of the Constitution, notably the vetoes of key New Deal bills by a reactionary Supreme Court. He proposed a "court-packing" bill that aroused bitter feeling, and later he tried to "purge" Congress of several anti–New Deal

Democrats. Yet the closer I studied these "bold moves," the more they struck me as expedient, high-level brokerage. Thus he sought to manipulate the membership of the Supreme Court rather than alter its constitutional mandate, and he tried to oust his congressional foes without a broad-reaching grassroots strategy that might have mobilized Democrats to fight for a more decisively liberal party. The best word for this practical, give-and-take leadership was "transactional."

It was only years later, when I came to study FDR's war presidency for a second volume of my biography, that I found "transactional" leadership an inadequate tool of analysis for the broader and deeper dimensions of his actions. The foundation for leadership had markedly changed during—and because of—the war. After Pearl Harbor, FDR had the backing of an aroused and united people. Goals were now clear—beat the Axis—and they were set in defense of the great public values threatened by the Nazis and their allies. Change, planned and unplanned, was so pervasive that it reached into every sector of the nation. Arguing that a healthy, well-housed, properly trained, and well-paid population was vital to the war effort, the president engineered social programs far broader than anything he had achieved with the New Deal. He proclaimed an "Economic Bill of Rights" that in effect laid out the domestic programs of Democratic presidencies over the next quarter century.

Of course behind the façade of war unity politicians conducted the same old transactional leadership. But it seemed clear to me that FDR, driven by the new situation, was following a governing strategy significantly different from that of the prewar years. It was not simply a souped-up version of transactional leadership. He boasted that he was shifting from Dr. New Deal to Dr. Win-the-War. He—and the war effort he conducted—was fundamentally changing the country. He had become what his example inspired me to call a *transforming* leader, just as Lincoln had midway through the Civil War. He had been both a lion and a fox, but now the lion prevailed.

This realization—this new analytical tool of transforming leadership—made me take another look at episodes earlier in FDR's presidency where the lion might have outpaced the fox. Perhaps they were not as marked as during the war, but were there not strong strands of transforming leadership in the extraordinary outpouring of legislation in the "Second Hundred Days" of 1935? And could they not be found even amid the ill-planned effort to transform the Democratic party into a reliable vehicle for "continuous liberal government"?

* * *

Historians of ideas have long noted the element of simultaneity in the advent of theories and concepts. Thinkers taking different paths converge at almost the same moment on a problem and even on its solution. While I was groping toward a theory of transforming leadership in order to understand the process of change, psychologists and other behavioral scientists were headed in that direction too. Most notable was a group of scholars at the Center for Leadership Studies at the State University of New York at Binghamton. The transforming leadership that I was approaching biographically they were studying psychologically.

During the past two decades both transactional and transformational leadership have become a focus of research and of controversy. Transactional leadership seemed fairly easy to define, if only because it was the basic, daily stuff of politics, the pursuit of change in measured and often reluctant doses. The transactional leader functioned as a broker and, especially when the stakes were low, his role could be relatively minor, even automatic. But what did it mean to *transform*? Was there a decisive difference between transactional and transforming leadership or were they variations on a spectrum?

We must distinguish here between the verbs "change" and "transform," using exacting definitions. To change is to substitute one thing for another, to give and take, to exchange places, to pass from one place to another. These are the kinds of changes I attribute to transactional leadership. But to transform something cuts much more profoundly. It is to cause a metamorphosis in form or structure, a change in the very condition or nature of a thing, a change into another substance, a radical change in outward form or inner character, as when a frog is transformed into a prince or a carriage maker into an auto factory. It is change of this breadth and depth that is fostered by transforming leadership.

In broad social and political terms, transformation means basic alterations in entire systems—revolutions that replace one structure of power with another, or the constitutional changes America achieved in the late eighteenth century. Bernard Bass of the Binghamton group has distinguished between the "first order of change," or changes of degree, and a "higher order of change," constituting alterations in "attitudes, beliefs, values, and needs." Quantitative changes are not enough; they must be qualitative too. All this does not mean total change, which is impossible in human life. It does mean alterations so comprehensive and pervasive, and perhaps accelerated, that new cultures and value systems take the places of the old.

Is transforming leadership measured simply by the number of alterations achieved? The more transactions, in short, the more transformational change? No, the issue is the nature of change and not merely the degree, as when the temperature in a pot of water is gradually raised to produce a transformation, boiling. Time—timing—can be crucial. Continual transactions over a long period can produce transformation. If such incremental changes take lifetimes, how long should people wait?

Is transforming leadership simply a new version of the Great Man theory, thinly disguised in academic clothing? Work on transforming leadership did occur during the "age of the titans"—from Churchill and Attlee in Britain to Margaret Thatcher, from FDR and Truman to JFK and LBJ, from Stalin to Khrushchev and Gorbachev, from Mao to a host of remarkable postcolonial leaders in the Third World. But for leadership students the rise and fall of luminaries—many of them, indeed, more rulers and tyrants than leaders—dramatized the basic leadership issue of *agency* versus *structure,* the relation between the leaders' character and qualities and the social and political context in which they operated, and the role of each in change. FDR, we noted, was a prime example. Winston Churchill was another. Despite his long-honed political skills, the British leader was a much-frustrated politician in peacetime who flowered in the demanding circumstances of two world wars. Charles de Gaulle could not have assumed leadership in 1940 and 1958 without the collapse of transactional politics-as-usual. And the limited transactional skills of Mao Tse-tung were nearly irrelevant to the dire needs of the followers who instead put their trust in his transforming powers.

Vigorous interaction between transforming leaders and their followers is itself a powerful causal force for change. By the 1990s almost all leadership scholars emphasized the role of *followers;* a few even argued that leaders and followers merged in interdependent collectivities in which it was difficult to discern the differences between the roles—in effect, denying a distinct leadership function. But this was a mistake. Leaders take the initiative in mobilizing people for participation in the processes of change, encouraging a sense of collective identity and collective efficacy, which in turn brings stronger feelings of self-worth and self-efficacy, described by Bernard Bass as an enhanced "sense of 'meaningfulness' in their work and lives." By pursuing transformational change, people can transform themselves.

The word for this process is *empowerment*. Instead of exercising power over people, transforming leaders champion and inspire followers. Tension can develop in this process. As leaders encourage followers to rise above narrow interests and work together for transcending goals, leaders can come into conflict with followers' rising sense of efficacy and purpose. Followers might outstrip leaders. They might become leaders themselves. That is what makes transforming leadership participatory and democratic.

The use of such subjective terms as "self-worth" and "meaningfulness" in leadership analysis poses the question of the place of emotions in the relationship between leaders and followers. This side of it has usually been identified with charisma, and studies of this phenomenon burgeoned in the twentieth century, in part from the urgency to understand the recurrence of demagogues who goaded their "masses" to extremes of racial and ethnic hatred, ideological extremism, religious fanaticism. Early in the century, Max Weber described charisma as "the greatest revolutionary force," capable of producing "a completely new orientation" through followers' "complete personal devotion" to leaders they perceived as endowed with almost magical—"supernatural, superhuman"—qualities and powers.

Following Weber, leadership scholar Ann Ruth Willner viewed charisma as based in worshipful emotions of "devotion, awe, reverence, and blind faith," while Robert Tucker, another student of leadership, saw followers responding to charismatic leaders with "fervent loyalty" because the "promise of salvation from distress" fulfilled urgently felt needs. Indeed, psychoanalyst Erik Erikson recognized that people might become "charisma hungry" in times of fear and crisis, when the old values that had upheld social structures and personal identity dissolved.

So the crucial elements of emotion and faith, as well as mysticism, irrationality, and psychological need, in the bond between leaders and followers have long been recognized. Yet hard questions arise. How much weight is to be put on these factors, among all those that define leadership? Weber and others sought to isolate a "pure" charismatic leadership, in which the irrational was the central defining feature. But how was such leadership to accomplish rational, planned transformational change—real, comprehensive, durable change, changes that advanced the great public values? And how was it to be analyzed, evaluated, in real-world terms? Leaders who fill bellies can be tested on the basis of how many bellies filled. How to test leaders defined in terms of the satisfaction of an array of murky psychological needs, of "hungers" of the "mind and spirit"?

"Pure" charismatic leadership also distorts constructive and mutually empowering leader-follower relationships. Followers are portrayed as so loyal or obeisant that, even when measured in the millions, they can have little impact on the leader beyond gratifying his own psychological hungers. The creative leader-follower interaction, in which the leader offers initiatives that followers pick up, amplify, reshape, and direct back onto the leader, is lacking. Just as charismatic leadership fails to empower followers, so leaders are not empowered by subservient followers. Mutual empowerment means exactly that: the empowering of one makes possible the other's empowerment.

At best, charisma is a confusing and undemocratic form of leadership. At worst, it is a type of tyranny. It should be studied, I think, as an exotic or lopsided form of transforming leadership that does not exclude the subjective but integrates it with multiple other factors, which as a whole produce a "completely new orientation" capable of pursuing significant social change. Organization scholars David A. Nadler and Michael L. Tushman argue that the strongest components of charismatic leadership are envisioning, energizing, and enabling. These are even more the functions of transforming leadership, which it achieves not by enslaving followers but by liberating and empowering them.

THE POWER OF VISION

If you're teaching a class in leadership and want to fire up a lively discussion, try posing this old chestnut of a question: "Was Adolf Hitler a leader?" The last time I tried this, in an honors class, a woman student vehemently answered, "YES." Evil though he was, she declared, he mirrored the hopes and hates of the German people, he won elections, and he fulfilled his promises by changing Germany along the lines his followers wanted—so how could he not be called a leader? She had the class all but convinced and almost had me, too. Almost.

It was not, of course, that she was in any way pro-Hitler, who stands as perhaps the most universally detested man in all of human history. The problem is confusion not about Hitler but about the essence of leadership. Is leadership a neutral thing, a mechanical process or power potential available equally to a Hitler and a Gandhi? Or should it be defined as a *good* thing? According to Joanne Ciulla, a leading authority on the ethics of leadership, the "question of what constitutes a good leader lies at the heart of the public debate on leadership."

I see three types of standards or norms as they relate to leadership. Virtue refers to the "old-fashioned" norms of conduct—habits of action— such as chastity, sobriety, cleanliness, honesty in personal relationships, self-control. These normally develop early in life, especially in the home, under, as child psychologist Robert Coles has insisted, exemplary parental leadership. Children learn the rules and sometimes take them quite strictly, turning them back on parents with the cry, "but it's not *fair!*" and so provide a little leadership themselves. Ethics reflect modes of more formal and transactional conduct—integrity, promise keeping, trustworthiness, reciprocity, accountability—supremely expressed in the golden rule. In leadership terms, as leadership scholar Joseph C. Rost has written, ethics are the criteria for "the ways leaders and followers interact as they attempt to influence one another and other people." By transforming *values,* I mean such lofty public principles as order, liberty, equality (including brotherhood and sisterhood), justice, the pursuit of happiness.

Politicians all too often offer vivid examples of the distinctions among virtues, ethics, and public values. Franklin Roosevelt as a young man transgressed the virtue of marital fidelity and later as president violated a cardinal ethical value when he lied to the country about the extent to which the American navy was aiding British ships against Nazi submarines, at a time when the United States was supposed to be neutral. Bill Clinton was roundly criticized for his unvirtuous conduct with a young White House intern. Still, he was found more gravely at fault—and was impeached— for lying about it. In this case the American public seemed to understand the difference between virtue and ethics.

Did FDR's and Clinton's lapses in virtue trump their transforming values? Many say that leaders' failings in virtue and ethics send wrong messages and can even influence people's behavior. Others argue that these messages are superficial and ephemeral, that the real test of presidents' values lies in their degree of success as leaders, in their realization of public values, in the good they did for the country. FDR led in the transformation of American government and society. Could Clinton rightly claim that his own leadership was successful enough—produced changes that benefited the people—to neutralize his failings? We can wait for historians with longer perspectives to deal with that question.

So *was* Hitler a leader, even a transforming leader? Certainly he "transformed" Germany! But by what standards could his rulership be measured? Clearly he would not be described as virtuous or ethical except by Nazi standards. His own "higher" vision was to restore order in the increasingly turbulent Germany of the early 1930s and then create a "Greater Germany" that would dominate Europe if not the world. In fact he left his country in defeat and devastation, so he was a terrible failure measured even by his own standards. If we test him instead by Enlightenment values of liberty and equality, he was a fanatical enemy of both. Nor did Hitler achieve another of what I call transforming values, one that perhaps embodies the others: he failed—utterly—to create for the people of Germany lasting, meaningful opportunities for the pursuit of happiness. My answer, then, to the question I put to my students: Hitler ruled the German people, but he did not lead them.

Transforming leaders define public values that embrace the supreme and enduring principles of a people. These values are the shaping ideas behind constitutions and laws and their interpretation. They are the essence of declarations of independence, revolutionary proclamations, momentous statements by leaders that go to the core meaning of events, that define what is at stake, such as the Gettysburg Address. Such values are not ordinarily part of the daily discourse of the citizenry. But at testing times when people confront the possibilities—and threat—of great change, powerful foundational values are evoked. They are the inspiration and guide to people who pursue and seek to shape change, and they are the standards by which the realization of the highest intentions is measured. Transforming values lie at the heart of transforming leadership, determining whether leadership indeed can be transforming.

Part Two

LEADERS

3

KINGS AND QUEENS, KNIGHTS AND PAWNS

Since ancient times chess has been known as the "royal game." It was a training ground for future rulers, who learned to manipulate the pieces on their little boards. A game of "intellectual combat," as the *Encyclopaedia Britannica* put it a hundred years ago, chess called for imagination and creativity—and for ruthless calculation of the power potential of one's sixteen pieces. Can chess help us understand leadership?

Sometimes when I flounder at the board my fancy soars. I see the chess pieces come alive. The king turns hostile and bitter as the marauding queen ranges up and down the battle lines. A favored bishop is whispering into her ear while a handsome knight contends for her hand, as in *Camelot.* The castles plot to overthrow the crown through a radical endgame, while a sole knight is pursuing a middle game on the board. And the pawns?

Ah, the pawns—the poor, hobbled infantrymen, the proletariat of the chessboard. Unlike the others they cannot move backward and hence they cannot retreat—only hunker down or advance step by step under fire. How do they feel about being sacrificial lambs, cannon fodder? Would they rebel if they could? Then I remember a happy twist in the game, queening. If a pawn makes it across the board to the king's row opposite, the lowly foot soldier can be transformed into a queen and wield her mighty power. So every pawn carries a scepter in its backpack. Still, how many actually get there before being picked off?

To play the game of chess is to calculate and control the levels of quantifiable power. To play "human chess," with all its incalculable and shifting elements, its crosscutting forces of conflict and collaboration, its turbulent sea of variables, is to enter the world of leadership, its theory and practice.

I'm not good at chess—my six-year-old grandson could beat me—but at least I know why I'm not good. As a "pawn pusher," I play pragmatically, piece by piece, move by move, swapping pieces here and attacking there, stumbling along. I think in terms of individual pieces in narrow, localized situations. I'm an incrementalist, not a theorist.

Grandmasters take in the whole board. They consider not only individual pieces but their complex interplay, their changing constraints and potentialities. They play the total game, on the basis of an overall strategy. They comprehend the game's evolving structure, anticipating possibilities, searching out the key variables in the entire multitude of forces. They also recognize the limitations of their appraisal—the X factors, the mysteries and contingencies of the game.

How then should we think about the elusive phenomena of leadership? Like grandmasters, we must attempt to take in the whole board. We must account for the situations and structures that shape human beings, that limit and extend their possibilities, and also for the human capacity to shape and even to transform their lives and the world. We need, in short, a general theory of leadership.

Yet we cannot begin with such a general theory, I fear, because we do not have it—we must construct it. I propose to start with a series of studies of leaders and rulers: queens and engineers, revolutionaries and statesmen, generals and party general secretaries. However diverse and idiosyncratic they may be, we must first see them in their rich human contexts, their gritty, sweaty environments of conflict and power—in tribal Africa, malarial Panama, and off the English coast; in Harvard Yard and Jacobin Paris; in Congress, Parliament, and Politburo. Let us, over the next few chapters, learn what we can from these practitioners—the circumstances that confront them and how they respond, the ideas and values that inspire and guide them, the purposes they pursue, how they use their power, make or evade decisions, plan boldly or blunder along. Are they leaders, transforming leaders, who mobilize and respond to followers and create changes that are real, deep, comprehensive, durable, grounded in values? Or are they instead merely rulers?

Our first look, however, will be at the origins of their power, how it is gained and how societies seek to contain the conflicts that can arise in struggles over the power to rule, conflicts that might otherwise threaten stability and order and even survival.

KINGS OF AFRICA

Who is empowered to rule, and how? For millennia diverse peoples have found this a formidable problem often leading to bloody outcomes. In the grasslands and swamplands of Africa, people had painfully tried out solutions for who succeeds whom in positions of power—processes for succession and legitimization that would foster less violence and more authoritative and beneficent results—and in recent times political anthropologists were able to study them at first hand. They could learn from tribal peoples with long memories and revealing tales. They could also compare African societies with other experiments in political succession far away in place or time. Consider the mid-twentieth-century Siuai on the Solomon Islands in the South Pacific.

The Siuai's polity offered in bald form the essence of leadership everywhere—the interdependent relationship between leaders and followers. An aspiring "big man" began by acquiring wealth in the form of wives. He needed them to grow taro, which in turn he needed to feed his pigs. He needed pigs to serve pork at feasts, because it was with feasts that he drew supporters. By attracting scores, sometimes hundreds, of people he became a big man who could compete with other big men in offering the best feasts. Such competition sometimes escalated to warfare but by and large it offered the Siuai people a measure of stability, except when a big man died. He left no realm, only widows and taro and pigs. There was no successor, until a new big man built a following. The Siuai were a stunning example of personalistic rule, with all its instability and recurring violence.

In southeastern Africa over the past few centuries, Bantu families and clans were often on the move searching for better land for their cattle and crops. Survival depended on solidarity and loyalty, and as the Bantu grew in numbers they needed an ever more unified leadership. Powerful royal clans rose that could unite followers in foraging for cattle. But unity was always precarious in the harsh and dangerous conditions of migratory life, and allegiance flowed to the most dynamic and skillful men. A weak Bantu chief could find himself abandoned. Like a Siuai big man, he had to keep the loyalty of his people. As anthropologist Robbins Burling wrote, "power built up and collapsed rapidly as individuals and groups fought, conquered, migrated, rebelled, and split up."

W as the solution simple patrilinear succession? Perhaps the most common practice of succession in the world was to put sons first. The Baganda, for centuries the strongest tribe in the area that is now Uganda, sought to ensure that only the deceased kings' sons would take over the throne as their *kabaka*. A dead king's brothers were thus barred from the crown. The Bagandans had a patrilinear structure throughout their society, with hereditary heads ruling the fifty or so clans that stretched across the kingdom, as well as the several hundred subclans composed of small family groupings.

On the face of it, the Bagandans achieved stability, but not without horrendous killings, partly because any eligible prince from any of the king's many wives could be chosen by tribal and clan elders, often sparking a ferocious competition that led to the murder not only of princes but also their wives, mothers, and sisters. Suuna II, the twenty-ninth *kabaka*, killed all but a few of the sixty half brothers who might have challenged him. Despite the instability of many successions, however, and submission to British rule for much of the twentieth century, the institutional *kabaka* leadership endured; by the early 1970s, Baganda's king was the thirty-fifth in his line.

If patrilinear succession met such troubles, why not try matrilinear? Other African peoples did. Among the Bemba, a strongly centralized tribe in southeastern Africa, succession could occur only through the female line, that is, only the male offspring of royal women were eligible for the kingship. While women were titled and might have a crucial role in the crowning of sons, they were only begetters, incubators, typically not allowed to hold power themselves. But matrilinearity could sow its own confusions. It was weirdly complex. Claims to the crown could pass through a generation of brothers by one mother, and then on to their cousins by their mother's next senior sister, and then to nephews by *their* sisters, etc. Quarrels broke out over who was senior—the eldest of one generation of sisters' sons, or the eldest son of the eldest sister of the king. Second and even third cousins might enter the succession struggle. The rules had enough ambiguity to legitimate multiple claims. Not surprisingly, few successions were accomplished without a resort to force.

Of course, not only in Africa did predictability, security, and stability prove elusive. In larger realms in Asia or Europe, wars of succession could draw in tens of thousands of soldiers—indeed, entire societies—many of whom would die for outcomes in which they had no evident stake. So most peoples, during most of history, learned one paramount lesson—ideally it would be best to have regimes both properly chosen and stable, but if you have to choose between autocracy and instability, take autocracy. Though a despot may oppress and murder citizens who threaten his power, civil war resulting from succession struggles can ensnare whole societies and cause the deaths of thousands.

Across the Arabian Sea from Africa, India offered more proof of this unhappy lesson. For a hundred and fifty years, until the British deposed the last king in 1818, the Marathas ruled a Hindu kingdom that stretched inland from what is now Bombay. As in much of Africa, succession rules gave sons preference over uncles, elder brothers over younger, natural sons over adopted, and in India the lines of succession were rooted in a rigid class and caste system. As in Africa, too, competition among kinsmen resulted in bloodletting and the fragmentation of royal authority, which only strengthened the people's urgent need for order and stability.

Succession struggles reached not only across space but also far back in time, even into the mythical past. Chroniclers in ancient Greece had watched the savage succession struggles in Persia and other empires, but they had had no need to look abroad. Their own myths and legends carried images of horrible successions—among the Titans and Olympians, in the house of Atreus and of Oedipus. Athenians gradually tamed dynastic rule through the broadening political participation of aristocrats and warriors and, later, small traders and artisans. Eventually an assembly of thousands of citizens governed the city, delegating authority to magistrates for only short terms and with limited powers. Even so, in Athens's golden age democracy was never extended to women, slaves, or the poor.

The Greeks did not act only by trial and error. They learned their lessons from philosophers—from Plato's speculations about the best form of government and the empirical findings of Aristotle in his compilation of city constitutions. And the lessons of the Greeks were not lost on the

Romans, whose republic surpassed even Athens in the sophistication of its representative institutions. As in some relentless tragedy of history, however, as Rome's power waxed, so did these institutions decline into imperial rule, with no authoritative system of succession. The result often was bloody chaos; between the assassination in 192 C.E. of the emperor Commodus and Diocletian's emergence in 284, no fewer than thirty men claimed the imperial purple. All but one or two of them died violently.

On the momentous question of who could—and who could not—succeed to power in these distant and ancient lands, one broad generalization is possible: one-half of the population was almost always excluded from high office, no matter what their kinship or abilities—women. But there were notable exceptions. Even though no Maratha woman could occupy the throne, some ruled in the names of their sons. One, Tara Bai, whose infant son succeeded on the death of his father, took power into her own hands and saved the kingdom from destruction by the Mughals. A famous trio of royal widows even led military expeditions in the late eighteenth century. In the long history of the Marathas, though, rulership by women was intermittent and short-lived.

What can we learn about rulership from these experiences in succession? That power has so vital a role in human societies that determined people will go to great—and sometimes terrible—lengths to win it and hold it. That conflict is natural and even inevitable among power seekers, conflict exploding not only between rulers and subjects but also among kings and queens, monarchs and their children, among siblings, between clans. That societies will act imperatively to build structures and processes that can tame those ambitions while ensuring continuity, stability, and effectiveness. Containing these conflicts through laws and institutions is crucial not only to survival but to the emergence of true leadership, with its dynamic, participatory, *mutually* empowering relation between leaders and followers, leadership that can overcome obstacles to meaningful change and social progress.

ELIZABETH I: RULER OR RULED?

Elizabeth I ruled England from 1558 to 1603. At times unpopular during her long reign, feared and despised by rival monarchs, in posterity she would be remembered not only as "Good Queen Bess" but as a masterful leader who reshaped her country, its institutions and its people. In recent decades Elizabeth's halo has been clouded by revisionist historians digging into records relating both to the life of her court and to the lives of her people and raising questions about her achievements. To frame the question in our terms, was she more a transforming leader, causing permanent changes in English institutions and policies, or more a transactional or traditional ruler who looked first to the survival and expansion of her own power? Was she more the maker of history or a product of it?

During her early years, she nearly became history's victim. Her very life had been in danger from the age of two when her mother, Queen Anne Boleyn, had been accused of adultery by her father, King Henry VIII. Within three weeks, Anne was beheaded on Tower Green. Elizabeth was left a bastard, stripped of her title of princess and barred from the succession. Only when her father decided to improve her attractions to foreign suitors—and potential allies—were her title and place in the line of succession restored.

Even so, it seemed unlikely that she ever *would* become queen. A younger half brother and an older half sister both had precedence. But Edward VI survived his father by only six years, dying of tuberculosis at fifteen in 1553. Mary, imbued with the Catholicism of her royal Spanish mother, came to the throne determined to reverse her father's break with Rome. She married a Catholic prince, Philip, heir to the Spanish throne, and declared Protestantism heresy; hundreds of Protestants were burned at the stake. Elizabeth, despite professions of loyalty, was regarded by the queen as the natural leader of the Protestant resistance, so the princess risked losing not only her claim as next heir, but also her head. Imprisoned in the Tower on suspicion of conspiracy and treason, then exiled to the country, she lived for five years in a limbo of danger until Mary's death in 1558. Elizabeth said she owed her throne—and her survival—to no one but the people, who had remained loyal to her.

A brutal apprenticeship, one historian called it, and the situation that confronted Elizabeth throughout her reign was scarcely less perilous. Reformation and Counter-Reformation had left the country in a state of near civil war. Abroad Elizabeth faced the great Catholic powers of France and Spain, which sought to bend her to their will, if not by diplomacy—or a diplomatic marriage—then by fomenting internal strife and waging war.

Most menacing of all was another female monarch, Mary Stuart, Queen of Scots, who embodied the double danger Elizabeth faced, of war at home and abroad. A cousin of the childless Elizabeth, Mary Stuart held a claim to the English throne. A Catholic, she was a potential rallying point for English "papists." The wife—then widow—of the dauphin of France, she made Scotland the base for foreign interventions in English affairs. Only Mary's penchant for reckless and ill-fated conspiracies and risings, and Elizabeth's swift and harsh responses to them, neutralized this threat. After provoking—and losing—a civil war in Scotland, Mary fled to England in 1565, putting herself at the mercy of Elizabeth, who kept her safely for two decades despite Mary's incessant plotting against her, until she was shown written proof of Mary's assent to a scheme to assassinate her, and the reluctant queen was persuaded to send her Scottish cousin to the block.

Throughout Mary's captivity, as plots proliferated and war with Spain threatened, Elizabeth was hard-pressed by her Protestant councillors and leaders in Parliament and the country to crack down on Catholics. Though herself a moderate reformer inclined to conciliation, the religious divisions at home and abroad created what historian John Guy has characterized as an "inexorable logic" for her: that "Protestants were loyalists and Catholics traitors." Nevertheless she resisted—not always successfully—measures she believed unnecessary and excessive, or that would deepen rather than relax enmities.

In the grave circumstances she and her country faced, her toughness and resolution were inevitably called into question. No one—least of all Elizabeth—was allowed to forget that the monarch was a woman. In the Catholic hotbed of Ireland, the queen's own representative, the lord deputy, burst out that she would not rule him—"God's wounds, this is to serve a base, bastard, pissing kitchen woman!" A laborer prayed for a king on both gender and class grounds: "The Queene was but a woman and ruled by noblemen," he said, "so that poore men cold not gett nothinge." Elizabeth recognized of course the prejudice against women rulers, but declared herself exempt: "I know I have the body of a weak and feeble woman, but I have the heart and stomach of a king." Inevitably, when things went badly in the country, the queen's gender was blamed. Yet Elizabeth herself would make no allowances for "sexly weakness."

Today we measure leaders and their deeds by the full range of high public values: order, liberty, equality, justice—the conditions necessary for the pursuit of happiness. Yet for Elizabeth and for most of her people, it was the first of these—order—that counted above all others. This meant foremost the queen's own survival, because her death, especially in the earlier years of her reign, might have set off civil war. It meant more than this, however, a vision of a stable society with her throne at its apex. Despite her image of a queen with a common touch and her campaignlike "progresses" through cities and countryside by carriage or saddle, Elizabeth was no democrat. Her people were subjects, not citizens, and she was their protector, their sovereign, their ruler, but not their representative. The society she sought was sharply hierarchical, where one and all knew their places, a society of deference and status. Differences— religious, political, economic—were to be submerged in common loyalty to England and to the throne, that "still center, the very presence of which insured the stability of the whole social and moral order."

Stability was to be guarded at the expense of other values, such as liberty and justice, which by that point had developed further in England than elsewhere in Europe. John Stubbs touched a politically inflammatory issue, raising the specter of religious conflict as well as stoking anxieties about succession to an aging and childless monarch, when in 1579 he published a tract denouncing a rumored marriage of the queen to a French Catholic duke. Stubbs, a respectable lawyer with Puritan connections, also struck at Elizabeth's fierce pride of independence and command, writing that she would be mastered by her foreign lord and England "gouerned by him that shal be her gouernor." The queen exploded with anger, banned the work, and saw to it that its author was appropriately punished: his writing hand was chopped off with a cleaver.

How did Elizabeth, along with her throne, survive and then thrive in this cruel and unpredictable environment? She was a worldly woman, alive to the fresh currents of the Renaissance. Given a humanistic education, she was tutored in Sophocles and Plutarch, Cicero and Livy, and learned enough French and Italian to converse with foreign envoys without the need of translators. While not herself given to philosophical speculation, she listened to leading Oxford and Cambridge scholars of the time and made her court, according to the historian Wallace MacCaffrey, into a "centre of intellectual sophistication where the high literary culture of the age could flourish."

But the main secret of Elizabeth's success was in her shrewd judgment, her intellectual grasp of rival leaders, their motivations and power resources, combined with an intuitive understanding of the play of human ambition and rivalry in her own and foreign courts. She best showed her skills in working with her Privy Council over four decades. The councillors, usually not more than a dozen, met twice a week at Greenwich or one of the other courts in the London area. Despite their deep deference to the queen in everyday contacts, the council members were mostly proud and imperious men with their own "constituencies" in Parliament and country. They knew one another well; indeed, most were related to the queen or to one another.

While Elizabeth was not above slapping their faces or throwing a slipper at them, she drank deeply of their political and military experience. She did not completely control appointments to the council, but she learned how to manage it as needed, meeting in advance with councillors singly or in small groups in order to work her will. And they learned how to manage her, sitting through her tirades, postponing decisions until more favorable times, but mainly reasoning with her. Oddly, given the queen's reputation for forthright action, the council often had to press her toward decision, as she had a tendency to vacillate, especially in military matters. Over the years a balance developed between the imperious but wary monarch and a loyal but questioning and prodding council. It was almost a collective leadership.

Toward the end of his penetrating study of Elizabeth, MacCaffrey asked, "What now, in retrospect, can be said about the character and the quality of her rulership?" The beginning of an answer, he wrote, lay in her inheritance of a monarchy with "a tradition of strongly centralized leadership." But her personal inheritance was quite different. She grew up in an era of religious violence and murderous political conflict. Her father had executed her mother as well as another of his wives and dozens of kinsmen and counselors. Elizabeth confronted rival claimants to the throne conspiring against her life, hostile churchmen, rebellious noblemen, and threats from Spain and other countries.

So her supreme goal was to overcome the instability she inherited, and to enthrone her highest value, domestic order, without which no other value was achievable. Rulers' classic means of maintaining order has been to impose iron rule on the populace. Except in aggravated cases, Elizabeth did not take this harsh path. The people she governed already savored the idea that they were secure against arbitrary power in their persons and property. Nor was she by temperament a despot. Her greatest strength lay in her indomitable, single-minded will.

How could that will overcome the seemingly intractable circumstances that faced the queen? Early in her reign, she resolutely pushed through a settlement of religion that satisfied neither Catholics nor Protestant zealots. She intended to convert the Church of England into a national and more secular institution, a great broad stabilizing center that reflected her own relative tolerance and pragmatism and that marginalized extremists. Having accomplished this, she characteristically repelled all proposals for further reform.

Motivated by a deep unease over "the perturbations of the unstable world around her," she used pragmatic tactics to accomplish the small changes that made stability possible and a larger transformation unnecessary, or at least avoidable. Beyond the achievement of stability, she had no desire for change, no broader goals. MacCaffrey concluded that in change she apprehended "a menacing rupture in the social structure," the threat of disorder and, "at the worst, treason and rebellion." Her motto, he noted, was *semper eadem*—always the same.

Elizabeth had the temperament of a survivor, and to achieve the stabilizing changes she sought she used a survivor's careful, transactional strategies, a low-risk pursuit of limited but clear goals. As a survivor herself, she helped her country survive. Yet great transformations lay ahead.

REINING IN THE KNIGHTS

"For God's sake help us," young Princess Tsahai appealed to the "women of the West" in April 1936, as Italian troops with machine guns and mustard gas overran Ethiopia. "Rally your husbands, brothers, sons, and force them to use their massed strength to compel the parliaments and rulers to take action." *All* civilization was threatened by aggression. Humanity had been set "a test. If you fail to help us now, we all shall die." The women of the West did not—could not—respond.

"I, Emperor of Ethiopia, am here to-day to claim that justice that is due to my people, and the assistance promised to it eight months ago by fifty nations who asserted that an act of aggression had been committed in violation of international treaties." So proclaimed Princess Tsahai's father,

Haile Selassie, King of Kings and Conquering Lion of the Tribe of Judah, to the Assembly of the League of Nations in Geneva a few weeks later. "What answer am I to take back to my people?" The answer was acceptance of Italy's aggression.

The failing League was only the most recent, though most ambitious, attempt by visionaries and statesmen to create a structure of international collective leadership with the transformational goal of ending war. And Ethopia became only the forerunner in a dismal sequence of weak nations falling to fascist aggression, only the latest victim in the long history of assaults on the security of defenseless peoples. What could people do when Mongolian horsemen or tribal aggressors or Russian cossacks or rogue knights swept into their lands and homes? They could hide in caves or forests; they could flee to distant parts; they could fight and probably die; or they could submit.

Sometimes a better solution could be found in alliances. Myriad minor kingdoms in the Mediterranean gained safety in the armed might of Rome—not always voluntarily or lastingly. They inherited the allies of Rome, but also its enemies. And siding with the loser in a Roman civil war could be disastrous—such was the fate of Cleopatra. In the Middle Ages the art of finding the right allies required diplomacy of the rarest skills as well as a Machiavellian nose for enclaves of power. Diplomacy, however, usually brought only temporary peace.

Centuries later, from the wreckage of Napoleon Bonaparte's empire, the victors formed the Concert of Europe, which along with the Pax Britannica, protected the security of the Great Powers while they colonized the globe. A huge swaying balance of power kept Europe's dominant nations at peace through the nineteenth century except for "minor" wars like those between Prussia and Austria and between France and Prussia. The system was inertial, dedicated to preserving political and economic elites and managed by leaders far removed from the daily wants and needs of their peoples. Within a few years of Napoleon's fall, Austrian armies suppressed liberal revolution in Naples, as did the French in Spain. British and German capitalists propelled industrial expansion, international trade, ruthless colonial exploitation, and through their navies they dominated much of the commerce of India and China, the most populous societies on earth.

Yet for centuries a very different vision of international leadership had been forming even while the practical statesmen went about their business of readjusting the balance of power.

That vision—of peace enforced by the collective action of European powers—appeared early in the seventeenth century amid one of the most ferocious and destructive conflicts in human history, the Thirty Years' War. A French monk, Emeric Crucé, urged sovereigns to set up in a chosen city meetings of ambassadors to settle disputes; if "anyone should refuse to follow the decision of such an august body," he would be brought "back to the path of reason"—with force if necessary. The Duc de Sully's plan called for nations to unite in a federation and form a pan-European army capable of punishing a renegade sovereign. The Quaker William Penn in 1693–94 proposed a parliament of princes to "establish rules of justice" among nations and enforce compliance with its judgments.

The question of peace excited some of the most creative minds of the eighteenth-century Enlightenment. From his Geneva study, Jean-Jacques Rousseau suggested a contract of nations based on the common interest of princes to "make sure of their true rights," in exchange giving up "those which do not belong to them." Utilitarian economist Jeremy Bentham foresaw a kind of world court that would encourage free trade, disarmament, and colonial emancipation, with defiant states put under the "ban of Europe." Philosopher Immanuel Kant suggested in 1795 that since people were rational and just, governments should be the same, surrendering their "savage lawless freedom" and yielding, as "individual men have done," to "the coercion of public laws."

And so the debate ran on through the next century. The "visionaries" were attacked for being just that. Keeping the peace should be left to practical, experienced statesmen and diplomats versed in the nuances of power. The visionaries asked how "practical" were the statesmen whose balances of power had the tendency of collapsing into wars.

Indeed, the guns of August 1914 shattered remaining illusions about the balance of power as a cure for war. As the casualties soared, statesmen reassessed their strategies of peace. In June 1915, William Howard Taft, recent president of the United States and a Republican, presided over a conference in Independence Hall, Philadelphia, that established the League to Enforce Peace. The title told the story. Encouraged by this act of Republican leadership, President Woodrow Wilson vowed at the league's first national assembly in May 1916 to take leadership in establishing a "universal association of the nations" that would indeed be a league to enforce peace.

Much has been told of Wilson's trip to Europe on the *George Washington* a month after an armistice in November 1918 brought the world war to an end, and of the roaring welcomes in Paris, London, Rome. Still more has been told about the president's statecraft at Versailles in the first months of 1919 as he hammered out a peace treaty and postwar plans with the other Allied leaders, and about his alleged stubbornness and rigidity in dealing both with his fellow heads of state in Paris and with his adversaries back in Washington. What has often been underestimated is the excruciatingly difficult choices that Wilson faced as he pursued his transformational goal—a strong league that could enforce peace through collective action.

Consider one of the lesser-known decisions he had to make in Paris. India, which had suffered heavy losses in the war, came to the conference with high hopes: to achieve the same status as the British dominions and to become a member of the proposed League, both of which would help it achieve its ambition of self-government. But in fact India was still a British colony, and Wilson had to recognize that on League issues New Delhi would vote as London directed. And if India was given a vote, what of other dependent territories? With its dominions and colonies, England might dominate the League—a prospect that would incite xenophobic rage in the United States. The president, though, had to recognize something more important, the aspirations of a quarter of a billion Indians to independence and a place on the global stage. He supported India's admission to the League, knowing that he would have to pay a political price back home.

The central and vital issue in Paris for Wilson was always the League of Nations. It was "a definite guarantee of peace," he said, and would rectify other deficiencies in the settlement. He was fortified by his conviction that he represented the hopes of peoples everywhere, a shining contrast to the cynical statesmen even now bent on playing the old balance-of-power game. But to win the League he had to compromise on other issues—arms limitation, tariff reduction, reparations, "open covenants of peace, openly arrived at."

The president gained his supreme goal in Article 16 of the League's charter, providing that any member that resorted to war in violation of its covenants, "shall *ipso facto* be deemed to have committed an act of war against all other Members of the League." Ultimately, the League's Council would recommend "what effective military, naval or air force the Members of the League shall severally contribute to the armed forces to be used to protect the covenants of the League."

THE PLIGHT OF THE PAWNS

With the Covenant of the League of Nations in hand, Wilson returned to Washington in July 1919 convinced that the American people were behind him. Contrary to the story that he arrogantly presented his League on a take-it-or-leave-it basis, the president followed up a formal presentation to the Senate the day after his return by talking for several weeks with senators individually and in groups, writing private letters to wavering members, and trying to work out compromises with moderate Republicans of the Taft school. But he faced two giant obstacles. One was the constitutional requirement of a two-thirds vote in the Senate for treaty ratification.

The other was Henry Cabot Lodge. The Republican senator from Massachusetts despised Wilson as a lofty moralist, an interventionist, and a Princeton, rather than a Harvard, scholar. Wilson was also a Democrat, and the president had not helped matters by calling on the American people to give his party a congressional majority in the wartime election of 1918. The voters had responded with a Republican Senate, and Lodge was chairman of the Foreign Relations Committee. Now Lodge lobbied and negotiated with his fellow Republicans, knitting together a coalition that could stop the League.

Rarely has history recorded a more dramatic and portentous testing of the dynamic of personal leadership interacting with the stubbornness of situation than in Wilson's clash with Lodge in 1919. Conducting a defensive operation, the Massachusetts senator starred as an astute transactional leader. His was not the simple task of pitting fellow Republican senators against the Democratic president and the League. His colleagues were an independent lot, ranging from the fiercely isolationist William E. Borah of Idaho to moderates who feared a backlash from constituents favoring some kind of effective international policing. Lodge used every weapon the Senate situation allowed, including his committee chairmanship. He employed every tactic of delay, tying up the committee by demanding a two-week, word-by-word reading of the entire 268-page text of the Versailles Treaty. His motivation was strong—he loathed Woodrow Wilson and hated Wilson's internationalism.

And Wilson himself? For months he had to play on Lodge's chessboard. Finally he tried to break free of the Senate stymie by resorting to *his* larger chessboard, the nation's voters who would choose a president in a year's time. For Wilson this would not be another election campaign but a moral evocation that would penetrate to the heart of the American psychology as well as polity. It would be to ask the people not for votes but for affirmation of a new internationalism.

Other politicos had "gone to the country"—it was an old American custom. But no president ever before had gone so directly, and so passionately, to the great masses of people assembled in cities and towns across the United States. Wilson's tour by presidential train in September 1919 became an American epic, a heroic and exhausting campaign that ended in physical collapse and devastating political defeat.

As he spoke Wilson brought audiences alive, but even more he spoke increasingly with a kind of austere desperation, warning that the people might once again pay the cost of war in lives lost and maimed—the great mass of people who were most powerless and most desolate. Nations did not consist of their governments, he asserted, "but consist of their people!" This was a rudimentary idea, he admitted, but most war settlements had been based on national advantage and trade values, not on the wants and needs of people. What had happened to the leaders in Versailles, he told an Ohio crowd, was that "we got messages from our people." The settlement was "in truth a people's treaty. It is the first people's treaty," he proclaimed to a Montana audience. It was, "for the first time in civilized society," a treaty "for the weak and not for the benefit of the strong," he said in Los Angeles. "It is for the benefit of the people who could not have liberty themselves, whose weakness was profitable to the ambitious, whose weakness has been traded on by every Cabinet in Europe." In speech after speech he complained that the weak—the soldiers killed, their widows and orphans—would once again become the pawns of history if another great war was not averted by united nations.

Wilson appeared more impassioned with every stop. "It is a people's treaty, that accomplishes by a great sweep of practical justice the liberation of men who never could have liberated themselves," he told a crowd in Pueblo, Colorado, on September 25, 1919. He looked ill, gray with fatigue. It was that night his physician found him vomiting, his face a grimace, hardly able to catch his breath. His train was immediately rerouted back to Washington.

In the end Lodge's transactional leadership paid off handsomely. He had so loaded down the treaty with reservations that the president himself, from his sickroom, instructed Senate Democrats to vote against it. Wilson's attempted transformational leadership failed, frustrated by a master broker operating within a political system that amplified his powers. The League survived without the United States, but Washington's absence weakened it from the start. At stake was not only collective security but collective leadership and collective sacrifice. When the powerful Americans would not share the burdens of peace enforcement, other nations were less willing to bear heavier ones. So perhaps it was inevitable that in its first great test— Italian aggression against Ethiopia—the League would fail. Drowned in the public uproar about the "deal" that Paris and London struck with Mussolini was the hard fact that France hoped to bargain Italy away from casting its lot with Hitler. The European democracies, eager to avoid war, Frederick L. Schuman wrote, "rejected utterly the Wilsonian contention that 'any war anywhere is everybody's business.'" Ironically the reversion to a "practical" balance-of-power strategy, which marked the end of the League as a credible guarantor of peace, failed in a few years anyway, as Mussolini joined the Axis and Europe went to war. Twenty years after Wilson's campaign soldiers and civilians would once again die by the millions.

Woodrow Wilson had failed in a supreme effort at transformational leadership, a failure that, perversely, helped assure the proliferation of brutal rulerships in a fragmenting Europe.

History tells us that such rulerships are often established by those who ruthlessly exploit disorders and fear. For them, the issue is power: they effectively size up and subvert the material and motivational resources of their foes and look to maximize their own. They calculate two or three moves ahead on the chessboard of conflict, all the while aware that the price of failure is not lost elections but lost heads.

The greatest appeal of rulers is that they will restore and maintain order, safeguard people's security, protect the survival of the state. Those were Hitler's promises to the German people, yet in the end he brought them—and millions of others—death and destruction. Or consider England in the decades after the death of Elizabeth I. In retrospect, the apparent stability her rule achieved masked deep political and religious tensions that a far less capable ruler, Charles I, saw explode into revolution and civil war in the 1640s.

Undermining rulers' guarantees of order and security is that, unlike leaders, they are isolated from the people they rule. However they might have acquired their position and whatever they must do to keep it, the crucial and empowering engagement between leaders and followers, based in leaders' continuing responsiveness to the wants and needs of followers, is absent. This was the central political issue in the English Civil War: Parliament asserted supremacy in the name of the people against a remote and unresponsive king.

The people who are not led but ruled—especially the poor, the vulnerable, those in greatest need—are indeed pawns. In succession battles, for instance, the struggle for power may take place on a small stage that allows them only to watch from afar, or it may burst out into society, embroiling them in unsought conflicts or even civil war. They are spectators or victims, but in neither case are they true participants, real followers of leaders who speak to their needs. They are not citizens but disempowered subjects, in a polity not of leadership but of rulership. The pawns may keep batons in their knapsacks, but they cannot expect to advance very far, and certainly not to become queens.

4

LEADERS AS PLANNERS

If you're like me, this is what happens when you can't find your umbrella. You first dart around to all the obvious places—closet, front door, kitchen— exclaiming peevishly, "Where *could* I have left it?" As the mystery deepens you think of other possibilities—in the car, in the bathroom?—and become a little paranoid. Someone must have "borrowed" it. What you do not do, if you're like me, is sit down and ask why, when, and where you last had the umbrella.

There is a simple reason why you rush around rather than stop and reconstruct. Thinking is difficult, as it calls not only for recall but for patient analysis. It means questioning assumptions and considering alternatives. Have you in fact actually used the umbrella since last winter? Did you leave it at the office because it was not raining when you came home? You have to step back for a moment and see possibilities in a wider view.

Quite the opposite happens when, instead, you desperately rush about. Your horizons narrow as you focus on immediately finding that darn umbrella. You lose possession not only of your umbrella but of your perspective, reacting so obsessively that you become a victim of the situation.

In our day-to-day activities most of our thinking is reactive. It is spurred by immediate needs and demands. It takes things as they are; the problem is to adjust to them, make them workable, acceptable. We adjust as best we can—to low incomes, aches and pains, the neighborhood, bad weather, problems in school or at the workplace. Our thinking is practical, expedient, sometimes shrewd, usually short-run. We cope.

Of a qualitatively different nature is thinking that looks not to cope with things but to alter them. It, too, is in a sense reactive, but it is a considered response to deep and fundamental needs and it seeks solutions—changes—that go to their roots, that are significant and lasting. To think this way is to think transformationally. When you reform an institution, establish an innovative business, foment a revolution, write a book urging change, build an arts complex, you are initiating immediate changes that, as you carry forward your intentions, hold fast to your purpose, may produce a transformation.

All this requires planning, the process of constructing a future sequence of significant actions to bring about the desired change. Planners, like chess grandmasters, must proceed step by step, but with a constant strategic grasp of the interplay of forces on the wide field of action. The pursuit of real change not only involves broadening circles of collective effort but typically sets off counteraction by opponents of change, defenders of the status quo, as well as competitors, rivals, critics, hostile publics. Since planners cannot operate in some cordoned-off enclave of society, every step draws them into a widening arc of external support and obstruction.

Plans go awry, of course, much to the satisfaction of later historians who know that spectacular flameouts and epic disasters attract hosts of readers—witness Wilson's tragic failure with the League of Nations, as well as the doom of Antony and Cleopatra, the charge of the Light Brigade, the sinking of the *Titanic* on its maiden voyage, the American debacle in Vietnam. But planners score successes as well as failures. What do both tell us about the role of leadership in the process of transformational change?

THE WINDS AND WAVES OF WAR

Of all planners the military have both the hardest task and the most at stake. Civilian planners must analyze complex terrain, estimate their own resources, and plan for contingencies of weather, shortages, disease, incompetence. Military planners face all these problems but much more—an enemy with little-known tactical plans and military strength. Hence the confusion and blunders in the fog of war that Tolstoy loved to expose. So we can only look back in awe at the story of the Grand Armada, one of the most ambitiously conceived and meticulously planned yet strategically miscalculated and tactically mishandled military expeditions in history, a venture that almost came off at the cost of over fifteen thousand seamen.

Philip II of Spain planned his diplomatic and military strategy for several years before launching the Armada in the summer of 1588. First he had to secure his backyard—the Mediterranean—against attack by the Ottoman Turks while he concentrated his forces in the north. He negotiated a series of truces with Istanbul. Then he set about isolating England from other European powers. He achieved this by careful diplomacy with the French and the Austrian courts. The pope himself helped mightily in lining up Catholic regimes, though the shrewd Sixtus V made clear that no cash would be forthcoming until the goal was achieved.

That goal was indeed audacious: an assault into the heart of England. The Spanish navy would deliver infantry to a carefully selected target within a few leagues of London. Soon Queen Elizabeth would be captured, or at least sent packing into the hinterland. Catholicism would be restored, Protestantism suppressed, and the execution of Mary, Queen of Scots the year before avenged.

Implacably, month after month, Philip assembled military and economic resources from the Continent. He did not spare his own country; his agents—including a skinny poet named Cervantes—ransacked shops and homes for grain, fodder, and oil, simply appropriating what they needed. Upon all the planning Philip kept an autocratic hand. When he summoned the Duke of Medina Sidonia to captain the Armada, the duke piteously tried to beg off; he was simply not up to the task, which he believed impractical, and was prone to seasickness. But Philip insisted, and of course the king had his way.

Philip consulted, however, as well as commanded. While he had no war cabinet in the modern sense, he conferred and corresponded day after day with aides, diplomats, admirals, generals. After long consideration of alternatives, Philip reached his core strategic decision, and then even the doubts of his top commanders would not shake it. The king's fleet would storm through the English Channel and anchor off Flanders, long held by seasoned land and naval forces commanded by the Duke of Parma. Then, as the Armada screened off the attacking English, Parma's transports would dash across the channel and unload troops on the English coast. Philip warned that the fleet must "sail in the name of God straight" for junction with Parma and not be drawn off to attack the enemy. Ship captains who strayed would be hanged. Still, in the event that Elizabeth's swift, seaworthy ships swarmed out of channel ports to harass the slow-moving fleet, the galleons and galleasses were instructed to protect themselves by cannonading the English, and then exploit their favorite and fearsome tactic, boarding.

Early in May 1588 the vast Armada—130 ships packed with thirty thousand men including eighteen thousand soldiers, thousands of horses and mules, twenty-five hundred siege guns and other ordnance, and many millions of pounds of biscuits, bacon, cheese, beans—headed north to England.

As the Armada, stretching two miles, entered the English Channel, ships were cleared for action. Gun decks were flooded with water a foot deep to prevent fire. Sailors placed vats of vinegar and water to cool the guns. Behind cover the surgeons lighted their braziers and collected turpentine and bandages. Musketeers and harquebusiers assumed their positions. Pilots maneuvered to take the enemy forces from windward and then to heave alongside, poop to prow. Shear-hooks would claw holes in the enemy's protective nets, while armed boarders prepared to vault over the rails and cut down their foes.

Watchers on the Plymouth cliffs sighted the advancing Spanish ships just after dawn on July 30, 1588. They touched off tar-soaked beacons, igniting a chain of watchfires to London. They also touched off panic. England was not ready to stave off a huge battle fleet. English intelligence about Spanish intentions was contradictory or misinterpreted. The critical question for Elizabeth and her advisers was, where would the Spanish land? They could not decide, and so the home forces were scattered in small garrisons along the coasts. Many were untrained; equipment was lacking; and the maps even of coastal areas were inaccurate.

Off Plymouth, Lord Admiral Charles Howard, Sir Francis Drake, and their colleagues faced an immediate dilemma. Their fleet was bottled up in the harbor and sound by an unfavorable wind. Had the Spanish attacked, the war might have ended before it had properly started. But the Spanish command was indecisive, divided over Philip's order to proceed directly to Flanders, and lost its chance literally overnight: in a bold, brilliant improvisation, the English fought their way against a damp wind into open waters, and when the Spanish awoke next morning they found the enemy behind them to windward. Soon the fleets bore down on each other in full battle array. They expected a showdown, but none occurred. Her Majesty's ships cannonaded the enemy with their long guns, but at such a distance that they could not inflict lethal damage. The Spanish tried to close in for boarding but the English were too nimble for them. The real commander in chief was the wind, as each side shifted direction to get to the windward of the other. Medina Sidonia lost two major ships, but to mishaps, not enemy fire.

Day after day the Armada plowed slowly east, fighting off attacks so skillfully that even the English had to credit their discipline and courage. But as the fleet approached Flanders, Medina Sidonia faced a new crisis. The Duke of Parma's fleet with its thousands of soldiers soon was supposed to sally out into the straits and join the Armada for the climactic assault on England. But Parma had not been heard from. Letter after letter, dispatched on the sea by pinnaces or sent overland, went unanswered.

Assailed by ships as fierce as hornets, and in growing numbers, Medina Sidonia sought safe anchorage off Calais, twenty-five miles down the coast from Parma's planned embarkation point at Dunkirk. There he finally heard from the duke. It was catastrophic news: Parma could not bring out his forces—twenty-seven thousand soldiers—for *six days,* and then only with Medina Sidonia's support in beating back a Dutch threat to his defenseless troop transports. Parma simply was not ready to sail.

At this critical moment Howard launched eight fireships against the bunched-up Spanish fleet. Filled with combustibles and with guns that fired automatically when heated, the "hellburners" panicked the Spanish. Ship captains cut their cables and scattered "in a thousand directions." Howard's big ships moved in and hounded the Armada out to sea. A hard southerly wind pushed the battered fleet up the east coast of England, farther and farther from Flanders—and from Parma. Little more than a week after the Armada was first sighted off Plymouth, the expedition was over.

Could the amphibious invasion have succeeded? Parma had assembled troops from all over Europe—even Ireland—to back up his own crack Spanish forces, and from the fertile lands around him he had collected provisions to feed them. He had hundreds of boats, mainly shallow craft that could each carry two hundred men and their equipment onto the beaches. But to embark such an army in good time required the most precise planning as well as the closest coordination with Medina Sidonia. Parma ever after maintained that he had learned of the Armada's arrival in the channel only on August 6, when the fleet had already reached Calais. Those siding with Medina Sidonia in the search for blame pointed to "the delays of the Duke of Parma," who "(whether through malice or carelessness) had failed to carry out his orders."

After thoroughly canvassing possible landing sites in England, Philip and Parma had chosen the area between Dover and Margate near the mouth of the Thames. The first assault would secure a beachhead, from which the attackers could advance along either bank. The Spanish had little doubt that they could brush through scattered English forces and descend swiftly on undefended London.

None of this was to be. As the Armada fled up the North Sea with the Royal Navy in full pursuit, Parma pulled his men off the invasion boats. The Armada rounded the Shetlands to the far north essentially intact but on the voyage south, west of Ireland, the fleet encountered gales and even a hurricane of a ferocity beyond the memory of any sailor present. Great ships were blown onto the reefs and rocks of the Irish coast. Hundreds of Spanish sailors and soldiers were drowned or slaughtered on shore by nervous troops fearing an invasion. The survivors were starved and diseased. Still, almost two-thirds of Medina Sidonia's fleet made it back to Spain.

If Philip had had better luck, *if* the winds had blown differently at critical times, *if* one pinnace had brought a timely message between the two dukes. . . . But nothing fails like failure. Today Philip is remembered as a stubborn man fatefully obsessed with Elizabeth and her England. His indomitability, his absolute focus on the goal, was what most characterized him as a military leader and made the Armada militarily a near success. Even so, Philip's aim went beyond simple invasion of England. He wished to convert the country—indeed, to transform it.

In this he would certainly have failed. Philip imagined that he had "better information and advice" on England "than anyone else," yet, not surprising in a ruler who absolutely dominated his own subjects, he underestimated the determination not only of the queen and her commanders but of the English people. Even before the Armada sailed, the counties had mobilized. "High and low," wrote historian Winston Graham, "rushed to offer their arms to the Queen." A successful landing would have ignited a long guerrilla resistance by men fighting for church, queen, and country. The English would have repelled Spanish rule in the hinterland, just as people two centuries later in little towns called Concord and Princeton threw off the imperial yoke of Elizabeth's successors.

* * *

What is the situation? This is the most commonly asked question in military operations. When a company commander comes back from the front to report to a battalion headquarters, that will be the first question, as it will be when regimental headquarters queries the battalion. Battle planning can be defined as constant groping for an understanding of the situation. In civilian life, too, this will be the first question a fire chief asks of his men, or a surgeon of a nurse. The next question is predictable too: what can be done to maintain or change the situation? Generals must be analysts of causation.

Through all the success and failures of his plans, Philip II held stoutly to his own theory of causation—God's will. And as Defender of the Faith he identified God's will with his own, once writing to a subordinate, "You are engaged in God's service and in mine—which is the same thing."

It was by God's will and his own religious values that Philip justified his purpose of conquering England. An ardent supporter of the Papacy and of the Inquisition—during his reign, an inquisitor later wrote, "the Inquisition experienced great felicity"—Philip's opposition to the Protestant heresy mixed piety with power politics, fanaticism, and war. In the Netherlands, Spain's great trading outpost, he had thousands of restive Protestants executed and their religion proscribed. "No prince," Philip wrote two years before the Armada sailed, "allows to his subjects any other religion than his own." And no prince, in this time of religious upheaval, could combine Philip's determination, aggression, and power in a plan to subject England and its people to his—and God's—will.

Yet though God steeled Philip's motivation, the Lord did not make clear where He left off and humans must take over. This helps explain why Philip left crucial matters to Providence and was himself at times indecisive and at other times inflexible. The weather was a wild card in the king's plans, yet he ordered the Armada off in a season when the prevailing winds were unfavorable to his fleet and with no channel port for haven, trusting that "God will send good weather." Historian Geoffrey Parker noted Philip's "complete confidence that God would make good any deficiencies and errors" in planning or execution. When God did not, though the king prayed for a miracle, and the Armada failed, his faith suffered only briefly. Soon he was planning a new invasion of England: "I shall never fail to stand up for the cause of God."

DREAMERS WITH SHOVELS

Between the second decade of the nineteenth century and the second decade of the twentieth, while Europeans found surcease from the mass killings of world war, some leaders poured their imaginations and energies into a less murderous activity—transforming the earth. They gouged out huge waterways, diverted rivers, constructed big dams, tunneled down into iron and coal seams, erected skyscrapers. New kinds of leaders arose: builders, engineers, promoters, architects. Like military heroes, many had moments of great fame and then steep falls.

Like great generals, too, these leaders were planners. They would not leave things to chance, to the errant winds and waves of fortune. They would dream about their work, then lay it out and get it done, come what may. But like all power wielders, they found that they could not dike off their plans from the people in the political and economic worlds around them.

Of all their enduring works, the most extensive and remarkable were the canals. The salty seas carried most of the world's commerce, but even engineers could not alter the shape of the ocean, only adjust to it by building ports, quays, lighthouses, coaling stations. Internal waterways, however, they *could* make. And of all the canals that were built in that century of relative peace, two above all touched off the soaring imaginations of the great builders, those in Egypt and in Central America. Others might connect this lake with that river, but Suez and Panama would each cut apart continents and unite seas. They would create vast new currents of travel and trade.

Linking the Mediterranean to the Red Sea had been the dream of three millennia. According to Herodotus, Egyptians late in the seventh century B.C.E. began a canal extending east from the Nile, but quit after a hundred thousand workers perished and their king, Necho, was told by an oracle that he was only clearing the path for a barbarian enemy. That enemy came less than a century later with the Persian invasion. "With the power of Persia," Darius boasted in a stone inscription, "I conquered Egypt. I ordered this canal to be dug from the river"—the Nile—to the Red Sea. But Darius quit as well on hearing that the Red Sea was many feet higher than the hinterland and hence Egypt would be flooded by a canal.

The dream seemed to attract strong men who were not quite clear about the lay of the land. Napoleon became inspired with the hope, while his forces occupied Egypt in 1798, that by building the canal he could bring "the free and exclusive possession of the Red Sea to the French Republic." But his surveyors reported mistakenly that the Red Sea at high tide was thirty-two feet higher than the Mediterranean at low tide, and after inspecting ancient, choked-up canal beds the First Consul left his dream in the desert.

Still, the dream refused to die. In 1832 it captured the mind and heart of a young Frenchman in Egypt, Ferdinand de Lesseps. Born in 1805, son of a well-connected diplomat and educated at the Lyceum Napoleon, de Lesseps quickly won attention for brilliant service in consular posts in Egypt—from gaining a close relationship with the ruling viceroy, Mohamed Ali, to risking his life in personally succoring victims of a plague. After a tour in the Netherlands and the ambassadorship in Spain, de Lesseps was sent to Rome in 1849 to handle a matter of urgency. He was unfairly accused of exceeding his instructions and forced to retire. At forty-four he appeared to have no future.

De Lesseps had never forgotten a book he had read on his posting to Alexandria in 1832, when his ship was quarantined in the harbor because of a cholera epidemic. It was the story of Napoleon's exploits in Egypt. What excited the young consul was not Bonaparte's military campaign but his ambition to pierce the Suez isthmus. De Lesseps could not get the idea out of his head. In 1854, the retired diplomat got word that Mohamed Ali's young son, Mohamed Said, whom he had befriended as a child in Cairo, had ascended to power on the death of his father. De Lesseps saw his opportunity at once. Soon he was in Cairo hobnobbing with the new viceroy and filling him with enthusiasm for the grand project.

The obstacles ahead were not in Cairo but in Istanbul and London. Egypt was under the rule of the Turks, who in turn dared not arouse the enmity of the British, and the British insisted on their right to be "consulted." For no great power had a stronger interest in the Suez connection. Her Majesty's Navy and English merchantmen had to sail more than ten thousand miles around the Cape of Good Hope to maintain lifelines with India and the rest of Asia. A canal would reduce the distance by four thousand miles. As usual de Lesseps hurried to the place of decision, London. He lobbied journalists, cabinet ministers, members of Parliament. But he found the government hostile and the press, headed by the *Times,* full of scorn. De Lesseps decided to take his case directly to the people of England. In 1857 he toured the British Isles, appealing to merchants, ship owners, and the public, touting the canal as not merely a commercial venture but a moral one: by uniting East and West, the canal would break down the barriers dividing humankind.

The government was unmoved by the crowds and applause he attracted. The prime minister, Lord Palmerston, dismissed de Lesseps's dream as a "bubble scheme" palmed off on "gullible capitalists." But now de Lesseps resolved to go ahead on his own.

His plans took shape. He would receive from his friend the viceroy a ninety-nine-year concession to cut the canal between the two seas. All nations would be charged the same tolls, and none would receive special advantage. To raise the 200 million francs in capital needed, shares would be sold to the public, with half reserved for non-French investors to maintain the project's "universal character." The governing board would be drawn from a number of interested nations. Thus—and at the heart of de Lesseps's strategy—the canal would be internationally funded and controlled.

In the event, the shareholders were less than "universal." Mohamed Said became the principal investor, while the shares allocated to the United States, England, Austria, and Russia went unsold. Yet, as de Lesseps had hoped, many middle- and working-class Frenchmen subscribed, moved as much by national pride as by the investment opportunity.

During this planning phase de Lesseps came into his own as an extraordinary leader. He had earlier been known for his boyish enthusiasms and infectious charm; now he also was demonstrating steady commitment, endless resourcefulness, and a versatility in seizing opportunities to advance his goal.

He was proving his mettle as a planner, a diplomat, a promoter, and something of a philosopher; what he was not was a hands-on engineer. He knew where talent could be found, though, and he surrounded himself with some of the best engineers in Europe. The diplomatic and financial problems settled at last, on April 5, 1859, at Port Said, the first shovelful of sand was dug up. Once begun, work on the Suez canal moved steadily. The engineers experimented as they went along, particularly in creating and perfecting huge dredging equipment. De Lesseps stayed on the job with them, dealing with daily decisions and crises. It was collective leadership at its best.

What actually built the canal—or at least excavated the first few tens of millions of cubic feet—was the forced labor of twenty thousand fellahin supplied by the Egyptian government. Many died, and many complained that they had not come on their own but were "driven by sticks." After a

British campaign against the forced labor, the canal company began to recruit "free" workmen—French, Italians, and other Europeans, as well as Arabs. Yet the workforce remained largely fellahin, now voluntary laborers and paid fair wages. Intensive mechanization gradually reduced the need for human labor. On August 15, 1869, the two seas were joined.

By the time of the triumphant opening of the canal three months later, de Lesseps had become the most celebrated man in Europe, his fame comparable to that of only Wellington and Nelson of earlier days. The president of France saluted him as "*le Grand Français.*" The French Academy admitted him as one who had "marked out a great battlefield for the future." Doubtless the most delectable tributes for de Lesseps came from the naysayers of old. Even the *Times* of London gracefully apologized, noting that Britain, the canal's greatest opponent, had become its greatest beneficiary.

De Lesseps was in his mid-sixties when the canal was finished, still a man of remarkable vigor. His imagination soared again. Like victorious generals—Caesar or de Lesseps's hero Napoleon—he looked for new conquests, not of empires but of the earth. And what could be more challenging than another dream, another splitting of continents that would link two oceans? Cutting through the Isthmus of Panama, a long-debated enterprise, would create a more direct route between Atlantic and Pacific, eliminating a detour of thousands of miles around Cape Horn.

De Lesseps was not only intoxicated by the success of Suez but fatally wedded to the strategy he used to achieve it. Suez was a canal without locks, and so must be the Central American one, even though Panama was hilly compared to the desert flatness. Suez had been financed mainly through private capital, so must Panama, and de Lesseps wanted middle-class investors to make money from Panama as they eventually had from Suez. And once again he would direct the project, which would be carried out by the best engineers—French engineers. Over and over, when de Lesseps met obstacles in Panama, he would promise to solve them "as we did at Suez."

But once the work began, in February 1881, the obstacles proved insurmountable. De Lesseps's Panama venture proved as colossal a failure as Suez had been a success. Why?

The planners underestimated the excavation needed for a sea-level canal without locks. Landslides and floods slowed the already arduous work of digging through marshy jungles. The French engineers, and many of the workers, were ravaged by yellow fever. Excellent hospitals were built, but what was needed was prevention, and the French did not know yet that mosquitoes caused yellow fever. Sanitation was primitive. Finally de Lesseps agreed to "temporary" locks, cutting down the amount of earth removal, but it was too late.

De Lesseps had to raise more money, but Panama bonds had never sold to his expectations. Desperate, he turned in 1885 to the idea of a lottery loan. This, he reminded the skeptical, was how he had rescued the Suez venture. But a lottery loan needed parliamentary authorization, and this ensnared de Lesseps in the corrupt politics of the Third Republic. Whether or not he was involved directly, money changed hands. Investigations were spurred by a press that now denounced the canal builder as blatantly as it had once lionized him. Some members of parliament were convicted of bribery, but all eyes were on de Lesseps and his son Charles, both of them charged with fraud.

The verdict, on February 9, 1893: guilty of swindling subscribers. De Lesseps and Charles were sentenced to the maximum of five years in prison. By a technicality—the statute of limitations was found to have expired—the sentence was never carried out, but the old man, sick and broken, was spared few other indignities.

Still another indignity, years earlier, might have been the worst of all: in 1875, the British had bought out the Suez shares of Mohamed Said's bankrupt successor and now in effect controlled the canal. The very British who had done so much to obstruct Ferdinand de Lesseps's great venture!

There was much moralizing: "Pride goeth before destruction." But de Lesseps's failure in Panama was less moral than intellectual. He had drawn assumptions from a situation in one part of the world that fatally compromised his work in another. Sometimes nothing fails like success.

THE POWER OF STEAM SHOVELS

Leadership takes many forms—visionary and opportunistic, collective and individual, transforming and transactional. Not often has the complex interplay of these forces been more potent than in the planning and building of the Panama Canal. De Lesseps's tragedy served as the prelude to more episodes in which the actual digging of earth seemed at times to symbolize a wider wielding of power.

The idea of a direct link west to Cathay was almost as old as the vision that led to Suez. Aristotle and Seneca had speculated that the Indies of Asia could be reached by sailing west from Spain. Columbus was searching for that route when he found a new continent. The colonizing Spaniards talked of building a canal until Philip II, with his pipeline to God, was said to have found it contrary to Divine Will to link two oceans that the Creator had made separate. He decreed even discussion of it a capital crime. Madrid settled for a "royal highway"—in fact, a crudely paved jungle trail—over which they carried the silver stolen from the Incas of Peru.

North Americans claimed a special interest in the canal idea. It would provide a water passage to the west coast and the wider Pacific thousands of miles shorter than the voyage around treacherous Cape Horn. And as the fledgling republic began to feel its strength, a canal under American control would represent an assertion of authority against the colonial powers in the hemisphere. President Thomas Jefferson, with his sweeping imagination, probably discussed such a passageway when he met in 1804 with Alexander von Humboldt, the famed naturalist who had journeyed for five years through Spanish America and later became an ardent advocate for a *Nicaragua* canal. The completion of the Erie Canal in 1825, connecting the Great Lakes with the Hudson River across almost four hundred miles, and its stunning impact in opening the Midwest to trade and settlement, further heightened the American appetite for an isthmian canal—and confidence that it could be built. The California gold frenzy ignited in 1848 made it seem imperative.

But every expedition into the hinterland between the Atlantic and the Pacific brought tales of horror—blinding deluges, slime-covered swamps, bottomless muck, bugs, vermin, dysentery. An American navy party of twenty-eight men sent into the jungle in 1854 lost its way soon after it arrived and suffered seven weeks of sickness and starvation before it reached the Pacific. That only seven of the men died was considered a miracle.

Still, there stood that enticingly narrow strip of land separating the great oceans, and the fear that some other nation would grab the isthmus first. Officials in Washington—and American bankers—greeted de Lesseps's private venture coldly. President Rutherford B. Hayes warned that "the policy of this country is a canal under American control," and support grew for a competing canal in Nicaragua. De Lesseps's collapse and then the acquisition in the Spanish-American War of the Philippines renewed American attention to Panama.

Many Americans were much taken by the doctrines of Alfred Thayer Mahan, whose genteelly titled *The Influence of Sea Power upon History* cloaked a potent theory that military and economic power depended largely on control of the oceans—and a blunt assessment of American naval weakness. What better application of the doctrine than control of an isthmian canal? Writing in 1890, Mahan foresaw the "piercing" of the isthmus, "a strategic center of the most vital importance," as a tonic to American isolationism. "Whether they will or no, Americans must now look outward" and assert "a weight of influence proportioned to the extent" of their interests.

But was a canal feasible, after the bitter experience of the French? By the turn of the century American engineers were confident they had the skills and technology necessary for the giant venture. They also had the benefit of a multitude of studies, including those by the French. As for managing the effort, there was the simple assumption that only the United States government could take on the task. It would hire the personnel, buy the machinery, lay out the plans, and own the product.

Then there were the Colombians. They owned the real estate. As early as 1869, the United States had negotiated a Panama canal treaty with Colombia, but the Senate had voted it down. After the flirtation with a Nicaraguan route, the United States came back to Bogotá in earnest, completing negotiations on a new treaty. It was the turn of the Colombian Senate to reject the canal—by unanimous vote in August 1903.

By now a boisterous new element had been added to the parallelogram of forces, President Theodore Roosevelt. Along with a faith in Mahan's big-navy doctrine, Roosevelt brought to the table some Anglo-Saxon prejudices. He simply could not see a "backward" country as an equal in negotiations. By holding up the canal, the "contemptible little creatures in Bogotá" were simply trying to gouge more money out of him.

Teddy Roosevelt could do more than name-call. He discovered he had a wonderful card to play. Ever since Panama's incorporation into Colombia in 1821, separatists had waged campaigns for independence, only to be suppressed. Colombia's rejection of the canal treaty brought new calls to remove the "halter around the neck" of Panama. Here was the opportunity: why not make a deal with the rebels, help Panama win its independence, and sign a canal treaty with *them*? All that was needed was a leader who would take the initiative.

That leader was Roosevelt. Bursting with impatience to bring off a feat that had eluded previous presidents, he saw the canal as above all a strategic project. With the two fleets united, America would be a Pacific as well as an Atlantic power. But TR knew that he could not openly "take

Panama"; isolationist-minded Americans already were uneasy with his brand of "big stick" diplomacy.

So Roosevelt rebuffed the rebels' pleas for direct military assistance but agreed that if they were able to capture Panama City and Colón, the American navy would prevent Colombian reinforcements from landing. Thus encouraged, the rebels seized Panama City and on November 4, 1903, proclaimed the Republic of Panama. Meanwhile the U.S.S. *Nashville* had assumed a station off Colón, and the next day, after a tense standoff, the last Colombian troops left the city.

Three days after the secessionists declared independence, the United States recognized the new republic. Within two weeks Roosevelt had the treaty he wanted, granting the United States not only the right to dig and control a canal, but also near-sovereign possession "in perpetuity" of a canal zone ten miles wide across the isthmus. In return, the United States guaranteed Panama's independence.

Roosevelt was publicly discreet about his central role in the affair. It was only in 1911, three years after he left office, that he took complete credit. The "Panama Canal would not have been started if I had not taken hold of it. . . . Accordingly I took the Isthmus." In fact, of course, TR had not acted alone but with many collaborators—diplomats, lobbyists, rebels, as well as those excellent foils in Bogotá he called "foolish and homicidal corruptionists." And the president, who always had to clothe his actions in a moral frame, needed assurance from his cabinet that he had done the right thing. Shortly after the affair, he asked them whether he had answered the charges against his conduct. "You certainly have, Mr. President," spoke up War Secretary Elihu Root. "You have shown that you were accused of seduction and you have conclusively proved that you were guilty of rape."

With the canal zone secured, and the president impatient for action, the way seemed open for quick mobilization. Instead the Americans got off to a poor start that reminded some of the blunderings of the French. Curiously, for a job that called above all for single and focused direction, a Washington-based commission was appointed of seven members of equal power—and of equal inexperience in administering large construction projects. The first chief engineer was fired; the second quit out of frustration.

But disarray and delay among the project's leaders in Washington were countered by gradually increasing momentum on the ground in Panama. American canal builders approached the challenges there much as the North had beaten down the South in the Civil War—by pouring masses of men, money, and machinery into the breach. The key weapons were ninety-five-ton steam shovels, three times the size of those used by the French. These were ordered by the dozen. It seemed vastly appropriate that the most symbolic photograph from the canal's building was of TR, attired in tropical whites, determinedly sitting at the controls of one of these huge digging machines.

The hero of the construction battle of Panama, though, was a forty-eight-year-old colonel from the Corps of Engineers, George Washington Goethals, the project's third chief engineer, appointed in 1907. Experienced in major harbor and river works, Goethals brought a steely leadership to Panama, seeking and gaining supreme command from Roosevelt. "If at any time you do not agree with his policies," Roosevelt said to the colonel's associates, "do not bother to tell me about it—your disagreement with him will constitute your resignation." Goethals quickly justified Roosevelt's faith in his talents. As an administrator he proved demanding but fair, encouraging everyone on the project to freely air grievances and concerns. He treated workers "like human beings, not like brutes," an associate recalled, and in return they gave him "the best service within their power." As an engineer, Goethals was decisive and bold, dramatically revising the canal's plan and reorganizing the work until it ran like an "endless-chain system of activity in perfect operation."

Another battle was medical, the war against yellow fever. For a time the Americans simply repeated the French experience. Men would sicken and die horribly, sometimes within a week or two of arrival. In 1905 a fear of epidemic among Americans working in the canal zone led almost three-quarters of them to flee for home. The hero of this battle was Dr. William C. Gorgas, the project's chief sanitary officer, who embraced the long-controversial theory that yellow fever, as well as malaria, was caused by mosquitoes.

Gorgas organized a massive fumigation campaign of military efficiency and took it beyond the zone to Panama City and Colón. By 1906, after a year and a half, he had virtually eradicated yellow fever in all of Panama. Malaria, spread by a different mosquito breed, proved more resistant, but Gorgas's aggressive efforts cut its incidence and its death rate.

Even with all this talent, knowledge, and technology, the digging of the Panama Canal proceeded slowly and exacted a terrible toll in lives. Men died from dynamite blasting and heavy machinery as well as from disease. There was an inequality of misery and death as the unskilled construction workers—thousands of West Indian blacks, Chinese, Spaniards, Italians—often toiling in debilitating heat, sickened and died in far greater proportion than skilled workers, most of them white Americans. Working for ten cents an hour, ten hours a day, six days a week, they found their housing and sanitation conditions as miserable as their work site; blacks suffered most of all, living segregated in squalid, regimented barracks.

The building of the Panama Canal was often compared with a battle, appropriately enough. The casualties, the yard-by-yard progress, the disease and the filth, the gap between ranks—all this would be made even more familiar in the war that broke out in Europe on the same day early in August 1914 that the humble cement boat *Cristobal* became the first oceangoing ship to pass through the canal.

Within a decade, five thousand ships a year were sailing the channel, as many as at Suez, fulfilling Mahan's vision of the canal as an interoceanic bridge with transformational impact on American naval power. Soon the United States would consolidate its dominion in the Western Hemisphere and project its influence far into the two great seas. With his imperializing eye, Roosevelt had foreseen much of this, well before he had taken the first step to accomplish it. We must build a canal, he had said, and grasp "the points of vantage which will enable us to have our say in deciding the destiny of the oceans of the east and west."

So it had not seemed appropriate, somehow, that the president who, a year before the *Cristobal* sailed, had pressed a button in Washington to explode a crucial charge of dynamite down in Panama had been Woodrow Wilson, not Theodore Roosevelt. Nor that the first passage of the American Pacific fleet through the locks occurred late in 1919, seven months after TR's death. Its prime mover never saw the completed Panama Canal, or the consequences of his vision. Among all the vagaries of the French and American builders of the link between the seas, not least were the vagaries of leadership.

THE TRANSFORMATION OF HARVARD UNIVERSITY

Early in the nineteenth century Harvard had the distinction of being the oldest American college but was otherwise not so different from struggling rivals like Princeton and Yale. Small, parochial, Unitarian, Harvard

offered dull recitation courses, remote professors, inexperienced classroom teachers, and compulsory chapel. Its main concern, even during
the antislavery struggles, was not the grand issues of the day but how to
maintain discipline among students, some of whom contrived to blow
up a college building.

If you had been one of the overseers searching for a new Harvard
president in the late 1860s, among the last candidates you would have
considered was a diffident, thirty-five-year-old chemistry professor, even
though his name was Charles William Eliot. Though his family had long
been connected with the place and had helped run it, and he had shown
some administrative skill in various jobs around Harvard Yard, there were
other Harvard "names" available, and he had displayed no great distinction or originality as a scholar. Indeed, in 1863, after losing out to another
chemist for a prestigious chair, he had left Harvard for a European tour
and a job at MIT. And with all this he had a distant, even frosty personality, not helped by a birthmark that scarred the right side of his face.

Not a likely candidate! Yet enough overseers saw some kind of promise in Eliot to elect him president by a 16–8 vote in May 1869. Five months
later Eliot inaugurated a presidency that would last forty years and transform Harvard.

Eliot began by raising professors' salaries from $3,000 to $4,000—a
move that enabled him to draw and retain a brilliant faculty over the decades. He then proceeded to reorganize departments, immensely strengthen
professional schools and create new ones for business and education, abolish
compulsory chapel, and—above all—offer students a free choice of courses
in place of the venerable prescribed curriculum. Meanwhile he raised a
lot of money, preached his educational views around the country, and kept
his eye out for talent. He knew the marketplace; when an able young professor came in ostensibly to ask Eliot's advice about attractive offers elsewhere, the president said he had obviously come in to get a pay raise—and
he gave it to him.

Still, all these achievements did not necessarily create a transformed
institution. Other presidents—not only of universities but of huge financial and industrial entities—were expanding and improving their enter-
prises. Yet by the turn of the century Eliot was indisputably the most
admired and emulated university president in America, as well as a national
and world leader in the realm of ideas. Why?

His aspiration to create a great university? All rival presidents had high ambitions for their institutions. His fund-raising ability? Others surpassed Eliot on this score. His self-discipline, manifested by his pledge, in a self-confrontation when he was ten years old, that he would never let his birthmark stand in the way of his goals? But other nineteenth-century leaders, some of them scarred in military service, overcame their disabilities as well.

The explanation for Eliot's transforming leadership lies in an extraordinary combination of clear goals and relevant means, the strong values by which he measured both goals and means, and a broader economic and social environment of change that gave him myriad possibilities for leadership, which he seized.

His major goal for Harvard—and what came to be viewed as his single most important success—was free electives, or open course selection. Student choice was a burning question in Eliot's time (and remains a simmering issue today). The idea of giving freshmen—teenage boys!—the right to pore through course catalogues and concoct their own "menu" was anathema. Didn't the faculty know best? People marveled not only at Eliot's faith in free electives but in his persistent and uncompromising demand that his elective system be extended to all courses, from freshman to senior, from introductory to specialized.

Eliot's absolute conviction on this score was grounded in his supreme value: the liberty of the individual, his right to freedom from intellectual coercion. This faith was common enough in the nineteenth century, almost as common as its violation in fact. Eliot did not compromise or brook exceptions. Freedom, he believed, would bring out the best in the students—their self-determination, maturity, responsibility, sense of discrimination—just as civil liberties could do for all Americans. He extended this doctrine even to the point that most grated on some faculty nerves—student freedom to attend class or not.

This radical individualism plunged Eliot into conflict, but the struggle seemed not to deter him, only to encourage him. He jousted with eminent professors, vocal students, complaining parents, interfering politicians, rival presidents—indeed, presidents in Washington—over not only academic freedom but Harvard's new secularism, its emphasis on professionalism, and the like, and also over his support for political causes such as civil service and the League of Nations. Boston reporters avidly seized on his latest unorthodox pronunciamento. He liked student agitation; a "quiet term," he said, was hardly the acme of success.

But conflict changed *him*, too. His commitment to the first principle in the American pantheon of democratic ideals—liberty—slowly broadened out to include the second, equality. He believed in equality of opportunity, not of condition, but he began to see that real equality of opportunity would call for sweeping changes in American society as well as at Harvard. He insisted that the school be inclusive, admitting Catholics, Jews, blacks, Chinese, even women (to Radcliffe College). W. E. B. Du Bois, one of a small band of African-American students at Harvard and later a brilliant radical critic of American orthodoxies, remembered the place in a kind of golden haze—visiting William James in his home, reading Kant with George Santayana, talking with Josiah Royce. One professor "invited" a southerner who objected to sitting beside Du Bois to leave his classroom.

For all his individualism Eliot came to see, in historian Hugh Hawkins's words, that it was necessary to "embrace collective solutions to social problems." His own leadership was collegial. Despite all the plaudits showered on him as a lone prophet and dissenter, he was dependent on the extraordinary faculty he had gathered at Harvard, on the patronage of wealthy Boston financiers, and, later, on the heightening progressive tone of American life at century's end. He lived long enough, to age ninety, to see that his reforms were not perfect—even his cherished electives had been carried too far—that Harvard sports and clubs, which he had criticized, had escaped unscathed, that he had not done enough to improve the lives of undergraduates in the Yard and outside. Still, his transformation of Harvard largely stood intact, and served as a beacon for other education leaders.

Underlying Eliot's achievements at Harvard was his deeply rooted faith that humanity was "meant for progress" and "in the main improving from the beginning, though weak and wandering." Some such faith in transformational goals—that change is possible, in Ferdinand de Lesseps's phrase, "*pour le bien de l'humanité*"—is a precondition of planning leadership. But their achievement—the difficult, step-by-step advances, the overcoming of obstacles, the constant adjustments to means and ends—cannot be the work of a single person, however "great." De Lesseps's friend the Egyptian viceroy Mohamed Ali had advised him that "when you have something important to do, if there are two of you, you have one too many." Eliot had been closer to the mark when he noted that change was the product not of any individual will but of "combinations of many men working to common ends." Planning leadership is inevitably collective, "combinations" whose leaders move and empower followers, who in turn empower and impel their leaders—become leaders themselves—in the complex, far-reaching dynamic of transforming action.

Part Three

LEADERSHIP

5

THE TRANSFORMATION OF AMERICAN LEADERSHIP

All leadership is collective, but the collectivity varies widely. Monarchs like Elizabeth I and Philip II "ruled down" through hierarchies of advisers and administrators tightly situated in their courts. The rise of popular resistance and reform in the eighteenth century was generated by grassroots and cobblestone leadership that "led up" from the bottom. The collective rulership of monarchies was held together by force and favor. What unified the leaderships rising from below? This was a burning question because most popular risings against royal rule had ended in disarray and defeat.

The answer lay in the intellectual coherence and power of Enlightenment ideas. The *philosophes* often disagreed with one another vehemently, but they drew their ideas from a shared background in classical Greek philosophy, Roman concepts of statecraft, and religious and secular creeds that had simmered through the long years of the Renaissance and Reformation. Notable in the eighteenth century, however, was the dynamic convergence and clash of fundamental ideas, with consensus on the central questions and fierce disputes over the answers.

What is the true nature of man? Is he a rational being? Or is he best understood by his sentiments? Is liberty essentially an end in itself or a means to some greater end? What are such great ends? Progress yes, but what is it, what causes it? Equality yes, but are all men truly equal by birth? What causes differences among them? Are they entitled to equal rights, equal opportunity, equality under the law? Happiness is the supreme goal, but is it a rational and achievable end or an elusive chimera of feeling and unreason?

It is hard, in today's skeptical age, to grasp the explosiveness of such questions for eighteenth-century thinkers. Consider Immanuel Kant. A quiet student, short and pigeon-breasted, as an English scholar described him, Kant labored for years in the university at Königsberg without a professorship or other recognition. But he was teaching ideas that increasingly intoxicated other young scholars, who flocked to his lectures and hailed him as an intellectual messiah. In Scotland David Hume and Adam Smith, in France Rousseau, Voltaire, and other *philosophes* attracted their own coteries.

Still, it was not only from the power of these ideas but their dissemination that creative leadership emerged. It was the era of the extensive use of huge encyclopedias offering the ideas of the *philosophes;* of an upsurge of newspapers, journals, and pamphlets; of a proliferation of books, and of libraries for the "learned" elite, bookstores for the bourgeois, and, for the poor, reading rooms that rented books by the day or hour. Readers varied in class, religion, and politics, but they were as one in their subversion of government censorship as they consumed radical, revolutionary, and even pornographic writings.

The reading public was unified still more, though, by rising dissatisfaction with the holders of entrenched privileges and with the incompetence and brutality of unrepresentative government and unresponsive rulers. Divided though they were politically and personally—Montesquieu disesteemed Voltaire who loathed Rousseau who broke with Diderot—the intellectuals in effect founded a sect that had a unity and a doctrine. The "common denominator," historian Rémy G. Saisselin wrote, "was a cosmopolitan spirit, a certain view of humanity, a desire to reform and in some cases to change the existing order or disorder of society, though not in any radical manner."

This European impulse for change, and the ideas that drove it, was borne across the Atlantic by all the media of the day—and by such travelers as Benjamin Franklin, Thomas Paine, and Thomas Jefferson—and they formed the backbone of an unprecedented collective leadership that transformed the American people.

COLLECTIVE LEADERSHIP ON TRIAL

The Declaration of Independence was the most radical summons to leadership in American political history. Paradoxically this bold, extremist action has long been the most celebrated by patriotic, firecracking Americans. Everyone knows its date, July 4, 1776. Who remembers another crucial date, the adoption of the United States Constitution, which was—let's see, now—June 21, 1788? Or the anniversary of the ratification of our most precious possession, the Bill of Rights, on December 15, 1791? Anniversaries are biased.

If the declaration was a call to leadership, its making was itself a supreme act of collective leadership. Three men drafted it—Thomas Jefferson, Benjamin Franklin, and John Adams—but many others made it possible, even necessary. State conventions had called for independence; newspapers had agitated the issue; the Continental Congress, which had appointed and instructed the drafting committee, held strong ideas of its own, as did each committee member. Franklin and Adams, formidable writers themselves, could not forbear from changing Jefferson's basic draft. Then Congress made further alterations before approving it unanimously. But this collective leadership in turn drew from the diverse works of generations of Western thinkers and practitioners.

As an act of collective *intellectual* leadership, the declaration sprang from decades of philosophical and political controversy in America and Europe. Jefferson and his fellow rebels had not only been schooled in the classics— some of them could quote Greek and Roman thinkers in their ancient languages—but they had been steeped in the new thinking of their own day.

Historian Adrienne Koch and others have demonstrated that these leaders were not mere products of the European Enlightenments; rather, they created an *American* Enlightenment that supplied the overarching principles of the American Revolution. The French Enlightenment, "in all its brilliant achievements and rich profusion of doctrines and dogmas," Koch wrote, "did not cast up the kind of sagacious and flexible leadership that came to the highest places of power in the American Revolution," and after. Under the pressures of conflict with the British, seeking to explain and justify their revolt and to imagine what an *independent* America might become, the rebels fashioned their ideas out of both their learning and their collective experiences as soldiers and lawyers, merchants and farmers, legislators and governors.

He consulted no book or pamphlet in drafting the Declaration of Independence, Jefferson said, but sought only to "place before mankind the common sense of the subject, in terms so plain and firm as to command their assent."

The declaration's long list of grievances against King George made clear what the Americans were against. But what were they for? The answer lay in the second paragraph, in words that had been deeply contemplated and fastidiously composed: "We hold these truths to be self-evident, that all men are created equal, that they are endowed by their Creator with certain unalienable Rights, that among these are Life, Liberty and the pursuit of Happiness. That to secure these rights, Governments are instituted among Men, deriving their just Powers from the consent of the governed. That whenever any Form of Government becomes destructive of these ends, it is the Right of the People to alter or to abolish it, and to institute new Government, laying its foundation on such principles, and organizing its powers in such form, as to them shall seem most likely to effect their Safety and Happiness."

The right to *Life*—what did it mean? Historians have often skipped over it, assuming it meant simply that there must be bare existence before there could be anything else. Beyond that, it referred to the founding rationale of civil society—that people came together for self-preservation, for order and stability under the protection of laws. But "life" needed more than brute physical "Safety" under rulership, and to flesh out the meanings of this right to life was to begin to define the reach and responsibilities of government and leadership, their values and practices in respect to the most fundamental human needs. If the right to life was to be secured, then, what about the means of subsistence—food, shelter, health? How to ensure that all had the opportunity to obtain such means by what Jefferson would later call "the exercise and fruits of their own industry"?

The right to *Liberty*. All agreed that this was the jewel in the crown of "natural" rights. It was at the heart of the colonials' outcry against the tyrant across the sea who had denied them the liberty not only to govern themselves but to oppose lawfully those who ruled them. Outright rebellion therefore was their only recourse to regain the collective liberty of Americans, and the liberty of a self-governing people was to be the founding idea of a new American republic. But what if the tyrant now became the people themselves? How to protect the freedom of individuals—or a minority in society—against a despotic majority wielding governmental powers? And how to restrict such powers without impairing government's ability to achieve the "Safety" for all the people that was the bedrock of liberty? Moreover, where were slaves, women, indentured servants to turn to recover *their* liberties? Hence, while some wanted to protect liberty from government, might others seek to achieve it *through* government?

The pursuit of Happiness—this was the wild card in the deck, seemingly incalculable but potentially the most gripping idea of all. Jefferson did not coin the phrase, and the pursuit of happiness as a source for both individual and social good had been brilliantly and imaginatively explored by the Scottish philosopher Francis Hutcheson. Even so, the words came to life in the context of the Declaration of Independence, teeming with potentiality and ambiguity. What did they mean in revolutionary America? Were they merely a variation on John Locke's natural-rights trinity of life, liberty, and *property*? If not, did they refer to individual happiness, and so emphasize personal autonomy and liberty in pursuit of private ends, or rather to what Hutcheson described as "the general happiness" that was "the supreme end of all political union"? Or did Jefferson, like Hutcheson, see no conflict between these two meanings, finding the pursuits of individual and collective happiness interdependent, and mutually enhancing, and that the "supreme end" of government was the creation of opportunities for both? Yet what government, what leadership, were needed to achieve it?

The declaration, with the bold signature of John Hancock and the names of more than two score other revolutionary leaders, was publicly proclaimed in Philadelphia on July 8, 1776, read before General Washington and his troops in New York the next day, and dispatched posthaste to the most distant towns and hamlets of the thirteen colonies. Americans had been at war for over a year; six more years would pass before the British surrendered at Yorktown, and another two before peace. The war ended in military victory and political turnover. It had not been a social or ideological revolution. Nor had a common foe, burning grievances, and the shared sufferings of war lastingly fused the Americans of the 1780s into one people. Soon the old differences among the newly independent populace—of religion, class, region—returned to the fore. And immigrants began to flood in from Europe, further straining republican ideals of a unified, homogeneous citizenry. The aristocratic Gouverneur Morris of New York wrote optimistically in 1784 that "a national Spirit is the natural Result of national Existence," but his Massachusetts colleague Rufus King feared disintegration and anarchy, suggesting that "it behoves every one to withdraw in season, to effect, if possible, some sort of personal security."

For some Americans the right to pursue happiness soon came to seem a ringing lie. Farm wages dropped sharply in the mid-1780s, while taxes remained high. When the lawmakers in Massachusetts adjourned in 1786 without responding to desperate farmers' pleas for relief from taxes, debt, and foreclosure, armed mobs in the western part of the state stopped the sitting of courts. Several hundred "malcontents" later gathered in Springfield under Captain Daniel Shays and advanced on the arsenal there. After troops called out by the governor cannonaded them, the rebels scattered to the north and the west, where they were captured and killed in the winter of 1787.

It was not much of a rebellion, except in the reaction to it. The rebels of 1776 were appalled by the rebels of 1786.

The collective revolutionary leadership had largely disbanded after Yorktown, its members retreating to private pursuits or to political responsibilities abroad or in the separate states under the Articles of Confederation. But now the lines of communication among them came to life with expressions of anxiety and dismay.

Revolutionary War hero Henry Lee of Virginia wrote to his brother Richard that "the East is in tumult, the dreadful appeal"—revolution—"is too probable." George Washington's wartime aide-de-camp David Humphreys reported to his old commander that "the troubles in Massachusetts still continue. Government is prostrated in the dust." Meanwhile Washington was writing to Henry Lee of his fears that the rebellion gave "melancholy proof" that "mankind when left to themselves are unfit for their own Government." To General Henry Knox, Washington exclaimed that only an Englishman would have predicted such a collapse of the American experiment.

Even the normally level-headed James Madison was carried away. He labeled the rebellion as treasonable, a threat to the security of the states. So he informed Jefferson, now ambassador in Paris. But Jefferson flatly disagreed, though not in his replies to Madison. Instead, to John Adams's wife, Abigail, he wrote, "I like a little rebellion now and then," and later added in a letter to her son-in-law that the "tree of liberty must be refreshed from time to time with the blood of patriots and tyrants. It is it's natural manure."

"THE MOST REMARKABLE WORK"

Was it not surprising that the postwar galaxy of American leadership—men who had fought and won a revolution, survived Valley Forge, put down troop mutinies, negotiated tough settlements with foreigners—should quake and quail in the face of a minor uprising? That they should so quickly despair of the government their own leadership had created to secure the great values expressed in Jefferson's declaration? Washington

and other leaders were suspected of exaggerating the menace in order to rally support for "sinister designs." But their concern was genuine, and it was, at its core, an intellectual and ideological reaction. The 1786 rebels were threatening values that the 1776 rebels held dear—"life, liberty, and property," in the Lockean phrase now invoked repeatedly by Washington and others. Something had happened to "happiness."

Washington as usual minced no words. He had responded to pleas that he attend a constitutional convention, he wrote his friend the Marquis de Lafayette, because it would "determine whether we are to have a Government of respectability under which life, liberty, and property will be secured to us, or are to submit to one which may be the result of chance or the moment, springing perhaps from anarchy and Confusion, and dictated perhaps by some aspiring demagogue who will not consult the interest of his Country so much as his own ambitious views."

Months of collective talk preceded the delegates' arrival in Philadelphia for the convention in the spring of 1787. Much of the debate took place in newspapers, books, taverns, and parlors. Most of it, though, occurred in correspondence among the notables and among lawyers, businessmen, teachers, clergy. It is both the depth and the scope of their thinking that strike us two centuries later.

The writers had time to reflect and reason. Helpful to this thought process—and to the unity that the constitutional reformers wanted—was the civility with which they exchanged ideas, in letters that might run thousands of words and conclude, "wishing you every possible felicity, I have the honor, etc.," or at least, "with great esteem and regard."

Still, civility did not dampen controversy over the decisions facing the proponents of "radical" action, as Madison called it.

Should they junk the existing system—the Articles of Confederation—or modify it? The articles had been adopted during the Revolution, essentially as a league of the states, and made do so long as the states were united over winning the war. After independence was secured, they declined into disunion. At a time when the young republic most needed collective leadership in pursuit of clear and principled goals, the articles offered only conflict and competition between states and irresponsibility and injustices within them, bringing into question, in Madison's scathing review, "the fundamental principle of republican Government, that the majority who rule in such Governments, are the safest guardians both of public Good and of private rights." Congress under the articles had no authority to remedy such "vices."

As historian Jack Rakove wrote, it "could neither coerce the states into doing their duty nor act independently in the event of their default."

If the articles system was abandoned, what should take its place? Among reformers, there was consensus toward a stronger central—national—government, but they debated its form. A few political leaders leaned to a monarchical system, American-style, but not too openly. A true democracy? This meant direct popular rule, and few except perhaps Tom Paine advocated such an extreme solution. A republic, then, with some mix of direct and indirect popular rule? Most reformers favored one or another variation on this.

The correspondence was more than an exchange of ideas—it fostered the reemergence of a national leadership that had successfully waged the independence struggle and then faded with the triumph. The epistolary discussions and debate represented a collective learning experience. People changed their minds as they grappled with tough questions of representation, federalism, executive power, majority rule, and minority rights. And the more they connected the mechanics of change with the goals of change, the more radical became the thought of some leaders about the means. Madison early on had favored gradual reform of the articles and opposed holding a convention. Then, under the impact of the disturbances, he not only supported a general constitutional convention but he wanted it to attack the "vices" he had found within the states because such vices had an "indirect influence on the general malady and must not be overlooked in forming a compleat remedy." Madison now sought a national power with supremacy over the states—in short, a second revolution in American government. Such a transforming goal was in the minds and hopes of not a few of the delegates—George Washington among them—as they met in Philadelphia.

After the "Grand Debate" through correspondence, it was not surprising that delegates arrived in May 1787 with practical ideas to accomplish fundamental changes. Madison had shaped his analyses into an extensive plan—later to be known as the Virginia plan—that above all called for a strong federal government with a new Congress empowered to veto acts of state legislatures. Most delegates would not go that far, but they were determined to find a way to strengthen national authority.

And so, in the long hot summer days in Philadelphia, the delegates shaped, clause by clause, the document that a century later British Prime Minister William Gladstone would deem "the most remarkable work known to me in modern times to have been produced by the human intellect, at a single stroke (so to speak), in its application to political affairs." Gladstone was derided for this blurb, but today, with the perspective of two centuries, we can say he was right. The Constitution is the finest example of political planning, by creative intellectual leadership, in the long history of the West.

This intellectual leadership was, to an astonishing degree, a product of collective thought. Close study of the Philadelphia proceedings suggests that the framers operated at two levels. One was the transactional level: they analyzed problems and alternatives from local, state, regional, and class perspectives, as they competed to shape decisions and broker compromises responsive to the interests they represented.

But the framers were also transforming leaders who rose above horse-trading to focus on *national* needs and a transformational goal: a new and far stronger national government.

Madison's Virginia Plan was the basis for debate, and ultimately the source of the Constitution's core principles and key provisions. But it did not want for alternatives. A "New Jersey Plan" proposed in effect an amended Articles of Confederation still too weak, Madison argued, to remedy the "dreadful class of evils" that "vitiate the political system of the United States." Alexander Hamilton, on the other extreme, proposed so powerful a central government that it would, he implied approvingly, "swallow up the state powers."

Alongside the debate over how much power was to be allocated to a national government were arguments over how that power was to be apportioned, and here delegates drew on their own experiences and their close readings of the failures of past republics. They planned that the new government be stabilized in an intricate system of mutually balancing and checking legislative, judicial, and executive powers. At this level of transformational change, as political scientist Calvin Jillson has noted, the framers acted more on the basis of shared *ideas* than of shared interests.

As transforming leaders, the framers pulled off their intellectual coup because they were working as both theorists and practitioners. Madison, noted one of his fellow delegates, "blends together the profound politician, with the Scholar," but that could have been said about many of the Constitution's drafters. What manner of men were these? Twenty years ago I wisecracked that the framers could be summed up as well-bred, well-fed, well-read, and (financially) well-wed. Today I would add that they were also well-*led*. All leaders themselves, they were led toward a common purpose by Washington and Madison and Hamilton (when he deigned to attend) and a dozen others of the most creative thinkers in the convention hall. But they were also led by others not in the chamber—state and local politicians, editors, teachers, businessmen, religious leaders—who would have much to say when the new Constitution came before state conventions for ratification.

The framers proved to be as skillful in the politics of ratification as they had been in the intellectual processes of drafting. Many if not most newspaper editors were nationalist in attitude. And the Constitution had the active support of the influential big businessmen of the day, if only from their desire to lower state trade barriers. Historian John K. Alexander has compared the Federalists' "selling" the constitutional convention and its work to modern media management. The Anti-Federalists in opposition, diffused in rural areas, localistic in temper, fearful for their individual liberties in a stronger national union, were slower to unite among themselves, but they came to produce, in pamphlets and debate, forceful rebuttals to Federalist claims and reassurances, and to field an impressive team of leaders of the caliber of George Mason, New York Governor George Clinton, Samuel Adams, and the fiery Patrick Henry of Virginia.

The drafting and final adoption of the Constitution was a long and sustained demonstration of leadership—in correspondence, in federal and state conventions, and in the press. It returned to the fore the collective leadership of the Revolution, and also divided it, as many of the rebels of 1776 became rebels anew in 1787, believing that the Articles of Confederation, for all its flaws, better embodied the values of the Revolution than a Constitution that threatened to annihilate not only state governments but the people's liberties and happiness. These Anti-Federalists supplied, at critical times, the conflict that lay behind the creative changes of the founding era. In that respect, however much they disdained the new charter, they were collaborators in the leadership that transformed the American people's hopes and prospects in the late 1780s.

ONE MAN'S LEADERSHIP FOR RIGHTS

Liberty-loving Americans who eagerly scanned the draft Constitution in the fall of 1787—or crowded around a local notable to hear it read in a tavern or parlor—were in for a shock if they expected a reassertion of the values of the Declaration of Independence. Something funny had happened on the way back to Philadelphia ten years later. The framers' draft started off with three fine words: "We the People." But the Preamble seemed to have little in common with the declaration and its evocation of life, liberty and the pursuit of happiness. What would this "more perfect"—and far more powerful—Union be *for*?

Establish Justice. But for whom—owners safeguarding their property? Or for farmers facing foreclosures?

Insure domestic Tranquility. Was this a reaction—or overreaction—to that little rebellion in Massachusetts? So one reader of the draft, Thomas Jefferson, suspected.

Provide for the common defence. Of course, but did this mean that a powerful national standing army would replace state militias?

Promote the general Welfare. Was this a tame substitute for the evocative pursuit of happiness?

Secure the Blessings of Liberty to ourselves and our Posterity. At last! But what were these "blessings"? How were they to be secured? Doubtless this would be spelled out later in the charter, as in the declarations of rights adorning various state constitutions.

That was another shock. Neither at the end nor anywhere else in the Constitution was there a bill of rights enumerating the liberties of the people. Even as Federalist politicians and publicists swung into their campaign to win ratification of the Constitution, a wave of indignation slowly spread up and down the Atlantic seaboard. The absence of a statement of rights became the rallying point for Anti-Federalists. In the many debates over the Constitution's provisions, *lack* of any provision for rights was the most contentious issue for a simple reason—it involved everyone's liberty.

Few were more concerned about it than Thomas Jefferson, waiting impatiently in Paris to hear from James Madison about the convention's work. And few could report as authoritatively as Madison did in a six-thousand-word letter sent six weeks after the convention's close to his fellow Virginian, or as proudly. He not only described the intricacies of the structure he had authored, but he defended them in both theoretical and practical terms. His argument ran closely parallel to the Federalist essays he was writing in public defense of the Constitution at the same time.

Madison's letter took almost two months to reach Paris; Jefferson responded almost immediately. "I like much," he wrote, "the general idea of framing a government which should go on of itself peaceably, without needing continual recurrence to the state legislatures. I like the organization of the government into Legislative, Judiciary and Executive." He listed some more of what he liked. Then—

"I will now add what I do not like. First the omission of a bill of rights providing clearly and without the aid of sophisms for freedom of religion, freedom of the press, protection against standing armies, restrictions against monopolies," habeas corpus, trials by jury. Jefferson waved aside the key Federalist argument that no bill of rights was necessary because the federal government would not even have the power to pass laws infringing liberty. A bill of rights, he argued, was "what the people are entitled to against every government on earth."

Thus the debate began between these two gentleman planters three thousand miles apart. Many weeks passed as Madison's letters made their slow way by packet to Le Havre and then Paris and as Jefferson's replies sailed back to New York. But this gave time for reflection, they agreed. And also for Madison to gather and relay political gossip, news about canal work on the Potomac, tobacco prices, corn crops, and droughts.

The penetrating exchanges between them epitomized the discourse that was firing up Americans. And the two Virginians each corresponded with a host of others, reflecting a debate over the Constitution that became a collective intellectual effort among thousands of people of all classes and regions, leaders and followers alike. The populace could hardly avoid being dragged into the constitution-making process, which called for discussion of the draft in state assemblies, then elections of delegates to state ratifying conventions, then the conventions themselves. For months the country was engaged in an almost continuous dialogue.

Political strategizing flourished at the grass roots, too. Rather than flatly oppose the Constitution, some Anti-Federalists called for a new national convention to consider a bill of rights. This idea was abhorrent to the Federalists, who could imagine a second convention running hog wild and undoing the work of the first. In fact, they feared any kind of delay that might allow Anti-Federalists to build feeling against the Constitution. A solution emerged in January 1788 from the Massachusetts convention in Boston: a Federalist agreement that proposals for amendments could be sent along with ratification. Enough Anti-Federalists bought this pig in a poke to help produce ratification there and in other states.

Even so, in state conventions ratification was a close-run thing. Virginia ratified in June 1788, 89–79, over Patrick Henry's violent opposition, and sent along twenty recommended amendments. New York's vote was even closer, 30–27, despite a virtuoso performance by arch-Federalist Alexander

Hamilton. Of the two last of the thirteen states to approve, North Carolina had to hold a second state convention and Rhode Island did not ratify until May 1790. But by mid-September 1788, a year after the Philadelphia conclave had completed its work, enough states had ratified for the "old" Congress to be able to set a convening date—March 1789—for the new.

When the senators and representatives met, the first order of business was supposed to be action on a bill of rights. But who would lead the legislative effort? None other than James Madison, the same man who in Philadelphia had opposed a bill of rights and then defended its omission to Jefferson and others, arguing that the limited powers and checks and balances of the federal government would protect rights against majority tyranny more effectively than "parchment barriers."

Three things had changed the mind of this "profound politician" and "Scholar." As Jefferson continued to rebut Madison's arguments, Madison the intellectual had to recognize the transcending force of his friend's fixed principles. Madison the political observer, impressed by the fierce conflicts over rights in the state conventions, concluded that "some conciliatory sacrifices" were needed to "extinguish opposition to the system." And above all Madison the political activist wanted to win a seat in the new House of Representatives, and to do so he had to hold the support of people in his central Virginia constituency bent on religious and political liberty. Madison campaigned vigorously—on a platform that "the Constitution ought to be revised" at "the first Congress meeting under it"—and won.

Madison's leadership in pushing a bill of rights—what became the Constitution's first ten amendments—through the first Congress stands as one of the most creative and undercelebrated feats in American history. It was an historic act of transforming leadership at a time when Congress, perhaps weary of the strenuous days of revolution and constitution making, was far more interested in the transactional business of interest-group representation and coalition building. And Madison was handicapped by what historian Leonard Levy called a "colossal error in judgment"—his own earlier opposition to a bill of rights and the lucid arguments he had made against it. But fighting for a bill of rights posed an even grimmer paradox for Madison. At the convention he had supported an arduous process for amending the proposed charter. Now he would have to gain a two-thirds majority in both houses of Congress for a bill of rights, and then help win the assent of three-quarters of the states.

His campaign in Congress for the amendments began in frustration. After sifting through hundreds of rights proposals Madison rose in the

House to offer his package. Repeatedly he was told to stand down, while the representatives debated taxes and tariffs—and their own salaries. Finally, after two weeks, on June 8, Madison got the floor, where he made a profound and eloquent case for a bill of rights, with many arguments he had borrowed from Anti-Federalists. Again the House pushed the business aside. Six weeks later, a select committee was appointed to consider the proposals. At last, in mid-August, the House took up the bill, and Madison found himself navigating a tricky course between Anti-Federalists eager to maximize amendments and resentful Federalists who would reduce them, ideally, to nothing. Decision came on August 24, with approval of seventeen amendments. Then action shifted to the Senate, which deliberated behind closed doors for a week and clipped the House package to twelve amendments. Madison was chief arbiter on the conference committee that reconciled the two versions and he led the House debate on the final measure. In the end, Congress endorsed twelve amendments and submitted them to the states in September 1789. Two amendments— regulating congressional pay and apportionment in the House of Representatives—failed in the states, but after two years a sufficient number of states finally ratified ten amendments to the Constitution.

And so a bill of rights was passed, propelled by a groundswell of support among the populace, by determined Anti-Federalist leaders, and by James Madison. Once he had been convinced of the need for amendments, hearing the deep public concern over the threat to liberty, their most cherished value, Madison took the lead in distilling eternal and transcending principles from hundreds of proposals and—resisted by his Federalist allies, allied with his Anti-Federalist opponents—succeeded in pressing them through Congress. Madison came to be called Father of the Constitution— wrongly so, because that charter of course had multiple parents. But he surely was the Father of the Bill of Rights. And Thomas Jefferson, for his absolutely principled and consistent stands for liberty in correspondence with Madison and others, deserves the title at least of godfather.

"A DEPENDENCE ON THE PEOPLE"

The Federalists had won a constitution, now decked out with the Bill of Rights. Had they won a government? Yes, a federal contrivance as intricately powered and levered and balanced as the clock that had ticked away at the convention in Philadelphia's Independence Hall. Now some of the same men who had built it—Washington, Madison, Hamilton, and others—would have to make it work. But was it workable? Would it make possible leadership that responded to people's needs, that secured and extended great public values?

The Federalists not only had neatly divided power between the states and the new national government; they had not only separated power among the three branches of that government. They had done something even more intellectually creative out of fear that ambitious men in the legislative and executive branches might conspire to overcome their separated powers and combine against the people's liberties. No one has described their solution better than Madison himself, in a passage from *The Federalist*:

> But the great security against a gradual concentration of the several powers in the same department, consists in giving to those who administer each department, the necessary constitutional means, and personal motives, to resist encroachments of the others. . . .
>
> Ambition must be made to counteract ambition. The interest of the man must be connected with the constitutional rights of the place. It may be a reflection on human nature, that such devices should be necessary to control the abuses of government. But what is government itself, but the greatest of all reflections on human nature? If men were angels, no government would be necessary. . . . In framing a government which is to be administered by men over men, the great difficulty lies in this: you must first enable the government to control the governed; and in the next place oblige it to control itself. A dependence on the people is, no doubt, the primary control on the government; but experience has taught mankind the necessity of auxiliary precautions.

Why wouldn't "dependence on the people" be enough, in this grand experiment in republican government? Simply because Madison and many of his fellow delegates did not trust the people any more than they trusted the ambitions of politicians. They did not trust the people to be wise and prudent and moderate. Hence they did not believe in unchecked majority rule, for they had seen how under the Articles of Confederation popular majorities led by demagogues had threatened people's liberties in the states.

Madison demonstrated a remarkable grasp of political psychology in those seven words—"ambition must be made to counteract ambition."

He extended his insight from the struggle for power within government to the clash of interests in society. "If a majority be united by a common interest," he wrote, "the rights of the minority will be insecure." But Madison saw that "society itself will be broken into so many parts, interests and classes of citizens, that the rights of individuals, or of the minority, will be in little danger from interested combinations of the majority." And in the "extended republic" of the United States, the "multiplicity of interests"— and the conflict of ambitions—would be greater, and rampant majorities therefore less likely, than in any single state. So man's fundamental nature—his ambitions and passions—would be the ultimate barrier to curb both tyrants and the tyranny of popular majorities.

This was where Jefferson departed from Madison. Jefferson's idea of human nature was not so dark; he believed in the possibility of a republic of virtue and so foresaw and welcomed majority rule. "After all," he had written Madison from Paris, "it is my principle that the will of the Majority should always prevail."

Many Americans agreed, yet they favored checks on officeholders and popular majorities for a simple reason: they fervently believed in liberty and they fervently believed that government was the main threat to it. Yet there was a huge flaw in this thinking that was bound to roil that consensus sooner or later. Had the framers, in their fear of tyrannical rule, made real leadership impossible? The new Constitution, after all, had been designed to take on national tasks, to provide for the "general Welfare" of the nation by collecting taxes, regulating commerce, coining money, establishing a postal system, promoting science, maintaining an army and navy, and much else.

All very well, but could a weak federal government, its potential leadership apparently checked at every turn, its powers fragmented and dispersed, take on these tasks efficiently? Or further responsibilities as the need arose? Alexander Hamilton, secretary of the treasury in Washington's cabinet and the leading "nationalist" in government, had ambitious economic projects in mind. Jefferson, now secretary of state, who as the apostle of limited government founded on the virtues of the independent yeoman detested Hamilton's plans for a commercialized republic, had repeatedly called for "restriction against monopolies"—but would that not require a relatively strong national government? The most predictable development in the 1790s was not only that leaders would call for government action, but that *people* would, as they developed new wants and needs, new hopes and expectations, and that, as Madison had foreseen, what people wanted and needed, hoped and expected from government *differed*.

Superficially, the 1790s would seem destined to be a decade of order and harmony. The great constitutional issues of the 1780s had been settled with the new charter and its Bill of Rights. The country was relatively prosperous at home and at peace abroad. The magisterial George Washington, the living symbol of the leadership that rises above division, presided over an administration neatly balanced between two factions, Hamiltonian Federalists and Jeffersonian Republicans. Of course they fought over politics and policy but it was expected, according to historian James Roger Sharp, that "a group of elites, who had had considerable experience dealing with one another in previous national bodies, would be able to resolve disagreements in a gentlemanly and trusting way and, even more importantly, would, in line with civic humanist ideas, be able to discern and legislate for the general good."

As it turned out, that decade was one of the most contentious and divisive in American history. In the cabinet, Hamilton and Jefferson soon came to loathe each other personally and politically. Americans split over foreign policy, as most Republicans—notably Jefferson—backed the French Revolution while most Federalists were horrified by its excesses. Exacerbating such political combat was a violently partisan press.

By the mid-1790s the two sides were waging a fierce ideological war. How would ambitious young leaders, still echoing Washington's nonpartisan preachments, deal with such conflict? Once again James Madison displayed his astonishing intellectual flexibility and creativity. In a series of essays in the pro-Republican *National Gazette,* Madison analyzed the role of public opinion, especially the rising partisan feeling. Now he had to recognize the inevitability of political parties divided over fundamental issues of government, while making clear of course that *his* party spoke for the "mass of people" against Federalists who were "more partial to the opulent" interests.

Here were the intellectual seeds of a momentous change in American political theory and practice. But then Madison went even further as he began to expand his thinking about checks on political leaders and popular majorities to include a fundamentally different set of checks— political parties that would serve as "mutual checks on each other." This theoretical shift had crucial implications for Madison's dread of majority rule. Any party that won at the polls would presumably act for that majority in government. This was majority rule. But any extremism would be checked—and respect for minority rights enforced—not only by the blocking and tempering mechanisms built into the federal system, but by the counteracting ambitions of the losing party, which would work to broaden its appeal and become the majority party at the next election. With such additional safeguards in place against abuses of power Madison was able as never before to embrace majority rule.

Was the remarkable anti-party author of the *Federalist* now fully incorporating parties into his constitutional scheme? Not quite. Madison had not relinquished the republican ideal that, whatever other and beneficent divisions existed in society, citizens would be united on great political values, in agreement on what was "to the general interest of the community" and "conducive to the preservation of republican government." When agreement broke down—as in the 1790s—parties would emerge and compete to forge and lead a new consensus. One party would come to embody that new consensus and "ultimately establish its ascendance," while the other faded away.

Madison did not foresee that parties might become a *lasting* addition to his system of checks and balances, that the embryonic parties of the 1790s would not disappear but transform themselves into highly disciplined organizations reflecting the enduring elusiveness of consensus on "the general interest."

He was not alone in his limited understanding. All over America men and women were building parties in practice without fully recognizing what they were doing in theory. Most citizens did not need a grand theory. They were expressing themselves through their grievances, causes, and hopes, and saw themselves inevitably on the side of the angels battling the devils in the other faction. They were choosing local officials who joined hands with others in their own states, and with fellow partisans across the nation, to form tickets or slates of Republicans and Federalists.

We do not know the full story of this proto–party building, since few of the activists kept memoirs or wrote letters. We do gain some sense of the intensity of the political conflict from accounts of several dozen "Democratic-Republican societies" that sprang up to carry on the "principles of the Revolution," to serve as watchdogs over elected officials so that the ordinary citizen might know "whether he is faithfully served or basely betrayed." They were linked to Republicans, and most of the elected officials they targeted were Federalists, so they further embittered the war between the two parties. George Washington, still the icon of national unity whose sympathies were all with the Federalists, inevitably denounced the societies for fanning dissension and partisanship.

In 1796, John Adams succeeded Washington as president, and two years later, at the height of the hysteria over the "Quasi-War" with France, he and Hamilton and the Federalist-controlled Congress unleashed their partisanship by enacting a Sedition Act that made it illegal to bring the president or the Congress into "contempt or disrepute" or to "excite" against them "the hatred of the good people of the United States"—a direct threat to Republican oppositionists and a flagrant violation of the First Amendment. Beaten in the congressional elections that year, the Republicans became desperate for office, the only way to check new Federalist efforts that might suppress *all* opposition.

The galaxy of American leadership had written the anti-party Constitution of 1787 and won the consent of the people; now the *people*, responding to grassroots leaders, were slowly shaping a rival system with parties as the means to press *their* needs and values on the national leadership. Everything depended, as the election year of 1800 neared, on realization of the basic premise of a party system—that the victors in a fair and open election take office and the losers yield it. What if the Federalists—who after all had been brazen enough to curb basic freedoms—lost the presidential election and mobilized the army to keep themselves in power, on the patriotic pretext of saving the republic from its enemies?

PARTIES—THE PEOPLE'S CONSTITUTION

Succession, whether settled by blood or by bloodlines, has confounded almost all rulers—African kings, Roman emperors, European monarchs, Chinese warlords, Latin American *caudillos*. No matter how much they might have groaned under the burden of power, they hated to give it up even to legitimate heirs or trusted colleagues. The "voluntary, peaceful transfer of vast powers from one set of committed leaders" to their adversaries has been called by a scholar "one of the most complex and mysterious phenomena in political life."

Yet at least in a democracy succession would seem simple. One side rules, the other side opposes, the voters decide, the ins are kept in or voted out. But to those called on to quit, it seems anything but natural. To yield power to an opposition that at best would be stupid and incompetent, at worst venal and even treasonable? And on a mere promise that the new leaders would quit office if *they* were defeated? It requires a political leap of faith, a commitment to the democratic process and the judgment of the people, and trust that the other side shares that commitment.

Facing reelection in 1800, Federalist John Adams hardly had such trust in the former comrades who now led the Republicans. He had come to associate opposition with treason, criticism with seditious libel. But even Jefferson and Madison seemed confused about the role of opposition. In response to such legislation as the Sedition Act, they had secretly authored the Kentucky and Virginia Resolutions, declaring that any state could nullify or obstruct a federal law it decided was unconstitutional, and so challenging the core principle of a constitutional order Madison himself had fought to bring into being. Clearly neither he nor Jefferson had fully accepted the democratic idea of a party opposition fighting it out at the next national election. Like the Federalists, they seemed willing to subject the Constitution to partisan warfare.

Intellectual confusion helped foster a rising political turbulence as the 1800 election approached. Enmity was pervasive, and not only between the parties. Adams and Hamilton loyalists despised one another as much as they hated the common Republican enemy. Hamilton called the president vain, vacillating, blundering. Adams castigated the former treasury secretary as "destitute of every moral principle." On the Republican side, backers of Aaron Burr suspected that Virginia Republicans would support the New Yorker for the vice presidency only to get his backing in the North for Jefferson's presidential ambitions, and then would dump him. A cloud of fear and hate hung over the South as a rising of hundreds of Virginia slaves in the summer of 1800 was narrowly averted. Reports that the rebels had planned to kill all whites in Richmond, except for the poor who owned no slaves, terrified the South.

Could a critical national election be held fairly under such conditions? The outcome was in suspense for months as legislatures slowly chose presidential electors. Finally, Jefferson and Burr handily carried the electoral college over Adams and Charles Cotesworth Pinckney, but now a new complication arose. The electoral system had not been designed with parties in mind. Under it, whichever candidate had the most electoral votes became president, the second-place finisher vice president. But because

Jefferson and Burr had run together as a Republican ticket, they tied with 73 electoral votes apiece—and Burr proved reluctant to stand down. The election was thrown into the lame-duck House of Representatives where the Federalists, who still controlled the chamber, pounced on the opportunity to manipulate the deadlock. While Federalists sought for ways to deal their archenemy Jefferson a devastating blow by electing Burr, rumors flew that armed supporters of both parties were planning to march on the new capital at Washington, D.C.

How close the American republic came to foundering will never be certain. The crisis ended when three leaders acted out of character. Moving decisively with other leaders to confirm his election, Jefferson congratulated Burr but indicated again that he expected him to accept second place. Clear in his priority of hatreds, Alexander Hamilton dismayed his Federalist followers by supporting the "contemptible hypocrite" Jefferson over the "most unfit man in the U.S. for the office" as a matter of principle. And Burr himself, the man of "*extreme & irregular* ambition," proved a realist in drawing back from a deal with the Federalists and settling for the vice presidency.

So the young republic passed its first real succession test—a test that would be failed numberless times in other nations over the next two centuries.

The system was still imperfect. The presidential election procedure had to be reformed to prevent a repetition of the Jefferson-Burr deadlock. The Bill of Rights, wounded in the partisan turmoil of its first decade, had to be reaffirmed and made more explicit. The parties were still rudimentary. The suffrage franchise still excluded most of the poor, women, slaves, and many immigrants. Still, the momentum had been created to promote life and liberty, eventually more equality and community, perhaps even happiness.

At least, at the start of a new century, the people had a government. But did the government have a people? Not yet. Not only did most Americans lack the right to vote, but those who had it were entwined in a system of indirect representation that fragmented and obscured their direct power over government. So "the People" were hardly sovereign. Yet the creation of elections, and later of parties, meant that politicians would have to compete with one another to win majorities that could govern. Both winners and losers in electoral contests had incentives to attend the needs and expectations of the people.

Americans were coming to understand that "government by the people" would not depend on consensus except over constitutional arrangements and election procedures. After that, political combat was not only proper but necessary. As historian Robert H. Wiebe has pointed out, parties were integrating American society by dividing it in half. Only by being conflicted could Americans be united, and thereby justify those glorious words, "We the People."

To win independence, to establish a confederacy that at least held the states together, to frame a new Constitution establishing a strong national government, to add a Bill of Rights to limit that government—all this was a remarkable display of transforming leadership and a breakthrough for an *activist* concept of leadership, demonstrating that fundamental and constructive change need not always come slowly, incrementally, but can be achieved through great leaps of thought and action. And then to reverse course, to add a new kind of conflict between parties to the conflict inherent in the Constitution's checks and balances, and above all to overcome the fear of majority rule that had inhibited James Madison and other framers by successfully achieving a transfer of power between parties—this was another extraordinary feat.

Behind the transformation of institutions lay a revolution of values. The 1787 Constitution established a national government strong enough to undergird the order and stability that the young nation desperately needed. The Bill of Rights laid out a charter of liberties that converted vague beliefs in individual liberty into curbs on government that have lasted more than two centuries. The dominant view of happiness as individualistic had to coexist with the conception of social or collective happiness rooted in republican ideals of public virtue and egalitarianism.

Behind the transformation of values lay a vital shift in thought. Pre-Revolutionary thinkers in America reflected the ideas of the moderate Enlightenment savants of Europe. Political scientist Thomas Rochon had discerned in eighteenth-century Europe a "critical community" that united *philosophes* across the continent. American thinkers challenging heavy-handed British rule shifted toward new libertarian and egalitarian ideas under the pressure of the gathering conflict. The leader in this epochal change was Madison, who made that heroic leap from a fear of majority rule to embracing it as a pivotal concept for the triumphant Republican party of 1800.

There was nothing neat or tidy in these intellectual and political changes, but the decisive force behind them was the rise in popular expectations on the part of grassroots and cobblestone activists inspired by the Enlightenment and increasingly insistent that national leadership reflect not bland consensus, as Washington had sought, but conflict between the rival parties of Federalists and Jeffersonians. Nor were the politicians riding these shifts aloof and disinterested leaders of an American Enlightenment; they were men of ambition fueled by conviction.

Despite the confusion that marked the American revolutions, the world had never seen a grander display of collective intellectual and political leadership as men navigated through the treacherous crosscurrents of the era.

6

FRANCE:
TRIALS OF LEADERSHIP

As the tocsin from the church bell rang out on the morning of October 5, 1789, the market women and fishwives of Paris were already gathering. For them the tocsin was a call to action. With shouts of "When will we have bread?" a small procession formed in front of the Church of Sainte-Marguerite. Carrying cudgels and knives, they strode off to the center of Paris. Joined by crowds on the way, they were seven thousand strong by the time they converged on the Hôtel de Ville.

The women were gripped by wants that gave rise to the most powerful of emotions—anger and fear. They were furious over the shortages and the price of bread, which typically made up about three-quarters of their diet; furious over the hoarders and price gougers; furious over government ineptitude and corruption. Above all they were alarmed by rumors that Louis XVI had summoned the crack Flanders regiment to Versailles in preparation for a royalist coup d'état against the National Assembly. Drunken soldiers, it was said, had trampled the tricolor cockade underfoot.

Soon the crowd at the Hôtel de Ville became intoxicated by its own boldness. Now they decided to march to Versailles and confront the king. They set off armed with muskets and pikes and dragging two cannon.

What could cause such audacity? It was not—yet—anger against the Crown. As they marched they sang that they were going for "*le bon papa.*" They wanted to bring their remote king to Paris, close to them. Arriving in Versailles, the thousands of marchers besieged the National Assembly, where they disrupted proceedings with demands for bread. A delegation was chosen to see the king. But the triumphant spirit turned tense when twenty thousand national guardsmen arrived from Paris, commanded by the Marquis de Lafayette. Early the next day a crowd of women and men broke into the palace and climbed the stairs to the royal apartments. Now the crowd was in an ugly temper. A woman shouted that they must "tear out the heart of the *coquine*"—Marie Antoinette—"cut off her head, *fricasser* her liver . . ."

A badly shaken king and queen agreed to return to Paris. When Marie Antoinette appeared alone on a palace balcony at Lafayette's suggestion, the mood of the crowd suddenly changed again and shouts of *"Vive la reine!"* rose up to her. Soon a remarkable procession formed: Lafayette and his guardsmen escorting the royal carriage, followed by ministers and deputies, followed in turn by tens of thousands of women and soldiers escorting a train of wagons packed with flour from the royal bins. Women now sat astride the two cannon, symbols of power.

These "October Days" of 1789 marked a critical turning point in the French Revolution. Louis XVI never returned to Versailles. He and his queen and two children would stay in Paris, "more like prisoners than Princes," it was observed. Since the National Assembly had abjectly followed the king back, even the laws of France might be at the mercy of the Paris mobs. But the symbolic change was also critical. With the king weakened and the assembly still lacking authority, crowds had taken the initiative of leadership in France. Women responding to the most palpable wants and fears had invaded the sacred precincts of power and worked their will.

Yet the image of brave women shepherding a king stirred among many not hopes for social progress, but fear and hatred. The French Revolution's powerful British foe, Edmund Burke, later called the marchers "a band of cruel ruffians and assassins," reeking with blood. The royal family, he said, had been escorted "amidst the horrid yells, and shrilling screams, and frantic dances," and "all the unutterable abominations" of the "vilest of women." Almost a century later, the onetime liberal and historian Hippolyte Taine would describe them as "foul scum"—a rabble "at once anarchical and imperious." Whether portrayed as good or evil, the crowd, which played a critical role at several points in the French Revolution, was seen, in historian George Rudé's term, as a "disembodied abstraction."

"Disembodied" the revolutionary crowds certainly were not. Rather they were *persons*, mainly working people—shopkeepers, working housewives, petty traders, and journeymen such as cobblers, barrel makers, lock-smiths, tailors, wig makers, weavers, cabinet makers. Police records showed that the vast majority were of "fixed abode," contradicting the charge that the crowds were composed of jobless vagrants and petty thieves. Many of these *sans-culottes* were unable to read or write, except their names. Even the literate were hardly students of the Enlightenment. But in wine shops and street gatherings the talk now was of revolution, and who should lead.

CROWN RULE AND CROWD LEADERSHIP

Hardly two years earlier Louis XVI was sitting on a throne that appeared as secure as any in Europe. He had inherited the trappings of his grand-father, Louis XV, great-grandson of Louis XIV, including the magnificent palace and grounds at Versailles that the "Sun King" had created a cen-tury earlier. A goodhearted but rather simple man, Louis XVI wanted to do well by his people, including the poor, if only he could determine what that meant. Indeed, his coronation in 1775 had aroused a burst of hope for new departures. But circumstances and character made him more a pris-oner than a prince, and far removed from his subjects. His Austrian-born queen, Marie Antoinette, intensely unpopular for her foreign birth and rumored depravities, came to indulge in political meddling with such force and intransigence, especially in the revolutionary years, that she was called the only man among the king's counselors. His ministers, given little authority to depart from the orthodoxies the king had also inherited, devoted themselves to intrigue and corruption. Louis XVI reigned but rarely governed, and could not lead.

He presided over an immense system of privilege and purchase. Honors, titles, monopolies, and gratuities were the central instruments of political exchange and order. Not only persons but groups—guilds, the nobility, the church, entire provinces—demanded and received special legal and financial privileges. Titles of nobility had long been for sale; by the 1780s they numbered in the hundreds of thousands. Government jobs were also on the market—some fifty thousand "venal offices." Corruption was institutionalized, and the Crown depended on it for the loyalty and money it brought. The king and queen, along with favored members of their court, served as grand brokers in an elaborate system of political and commercial exchange.

Still, Crown rule had the strength of its weaknesses. So settled and structured was the hierarchy of privilege that no force appeared capable of upsetting it. After all, the monarchy, in its various forms, had lasted hundreds of years, surviving internal upheavals as well as devastating military defeats abroad. In 1787, while Americans were writing a new Constitution, the insular rule of Louis XVI seemed as impervious to transforming change as a mountain.

Yet emerging from the grass roots of Brittany and Burgundy and Provence and dozens of other ancient regions was an astonishing array of Frenchmen who in just one year, 1789, would lead a transformation of Crown rule—and then see their work consumed in the fires of violence and terror. But these men did not initiate the revolution. The spark of leadership came from an unruly combination of mob and aristocracy.

Beginning in the late 1760s, disorder erupted again and again in France over the most fundamental of wants—food. Poor harvests and erratic government policies brought shortages and price spirals and hunger. The wretchedness of the poor contrasted more and more with the unprecedented opulence of the nobility and the haute bourgeoisie, and Versailles readily became the symbol of the extravagance and rapacity of the rich and the detachment of government from the people. The rich had their own grievances, above all about the state of the exchequer. Drained by the costs of the Seven Years War and its aid to Americans fighting the British for independence, Crown rule faced bankruptcy. By 1787 an "Assembly of Notables" was pressuring the king to convene the Estates-General.

The Estates-General? A medieval institution summoned by kings to "consult" in times of crisis, it had never had any authority and had not even met for over a century and a half. But the nobles saw a big opportunity. The Estates-General was composed of the First Estate of the clergy, the Second Estate of the nobility, and the Third Estate representing the commoners. Since traditionally each order had a single vote, a natural alliance of the First and Second Estates could be expected to dominate the Third; but the nobles were outfoxed. In August 1788, the king, a week away from bankruptcy, agreed to convene the Estates-General in the following year. When the formal convocation letters were published in December, however, the Third Estate was granted six hundred representatives to three hundred for each of the other estates. Though the tradition of voting by order and not by head was upheld, the king's surrender to a powerful campaign for double representation was celebrated as an acknowledgment that, in the words of the Comte d'Antraigues, "the Third Estate is the People" and "the People is everything."

So on a May morning in 1789 a thousand men took their seats in a magnificent hall hung with tapestries and adorned with paintings of thirteen centuries of kings. Louis sat on a decorated stage, surrounded by the queen and an entourage of princes and courtiers. The nobles sat on padded benches at the king's left, the clergy on his right, and the commoners at the rear of the hall. Two thousand onlookers jammed the balconies. A crowd estimated in the tens of thousands, including many women, stood expectantly outside.

It hardly looked like a revolutionary assembly. In attitudes and dress the Third Estate reflected the diversity of France, and also its localism. These commoners had no national organization or communication; they hardly knew one another. A youngish group, averaging in their forties, they were important back home as attorneys, judges, local officials, and—far fewer in number—as businessmen, doctors, or professors. Few among them spouted Montesquieu or Rousseau. These were practical men who at the start had little notion of doing more than tinkering with government to make it more efficient and less bureaucratic.

In their meetings apart from the other estates, the deputies for a time wandered lost amid the grandeur of the occasion; they broke into disorder and factions, and they orated, endlessly. Then, by some alchemy of self-transformation, they drew together, established parliamentary procedures, and, in several swift steps, without quite intending to, produced a revolution.

On June 10, after their demand that the Estates meet as a general assembly with voting by head was rejected, the commoners proclaimed that they were prepared to conduct business on their own and brashly invited the other two orders to join them in what they soon decided to call the National Assembly.

On June 20, finding the hall assigned to the Third Estate closed by royal order, the shocked deputies commandeered an indoor tennis court and took an oath that they would never separate until they had established a constitution.

A week later, Louis capitulated. He ordered the other two estates to join the National Assembly, something many of their more liberal delegates had already chosen to do.

After an all-night session on August 4–5, the deputies issued a sweeping decree: "The National Assembly entirely destroys the feudal regime," in one blow abolishing the system of privilege that, in historian William Doyle's words, had been the "fundamental principle of social and institutional life since time immemorial."

On August 26, after a week's debate, the assembly adopted the "Declaration of the Rights of Man and the Citizen," proclaiming the nation itself—not the king—the source of all sovereignty, and the equality of all men in their "natural, imprescriptible, and inalienable rights."

At the same time, the assembly was drafting a new constitution that would place the preponderance of state power in a Legislative Assembly, with the king granted only a limited veto over legislation.

How to explain this torrent of creative action? In part by the unity forged among delegates in their conflicts with the king and the other estates, which deepened their sense that fundamental principles were at stake, that their resoluteness had opened up potentialities for transformational change. The delegates were not *philosophes,* but as they grappled with issues of sovereignty, natural rights, liberty, and equality, they turned almost inevitably to the Enlightenment ideas that were now flowing powerfully across national borders in the West. It was not wholly coincidental that James Madison was pressing a Bill of Rights in the American Congress during this same summer.

Probably the most decisive single force urging the National Assembly toward more and more radical action were the crowds streaming in from Paris. Everywhere that the deputies walked or rode or gathered in Versailles, they met protesters reminding them of their responsibility to the people. Noisy and persistent, the crowds were formidable enough on one occasion to force the release from jail of guardsmen arrested for refusing to fire on mobs during a confrontation at Versailles. Crowds held the threat of riots over both king and assembly. Their crowning feat of leadership was the siege and capture of the Bastille state prison in Paris on July 14—an incident that came to symbolize not only the collapse of royal authority but the dependence of the assembly on the street revolutionaries who had thereby secured its existence. It was a bloody affair: the hundreds of attackers had suffered 150 casualties and killed or wounded scores of defenders.

Yet the draft constitution spoke not of crowds but of citizens, for the revolution was bent on transforming the king's subjects into *citoyens* and *citoyennes.* The change was not simply in form of address but in status. "Membership in the nation, rather than privilege mediated through the monarch," wrote historian Michael P. Fitzsimmons, "became the basis of rights in the polity." There would be only a single estate, united by equality and fraternity. Hopes for the new dispensation were unbounded. When citizens of every rank and age had joined the tumult of the revolutionary week that led to the Bastille's fall, *Révolutions de Paris* reported at the time, it was "the voice of the nation" and the "bonds of blood" that ruled. "The rich graciously welcomed the poor; rank did not exist, all were equals."

But there were ominous undertones in the press tributes to the new citizenship. As paeans to "good citizens"—dutiful and socially useful—proliferated, so there developed a mirror image of "bad citizens," not only aristocrats but any who failed to "truly desire public welfare." One publication threatened to display a "canvas of bad citizens" every Saturday throughout France. Even more ominously, the National Assembly differentiated between "active" and "passive" citizens by establishing a suffrage qualification based on wages that excluded more than half of the potential electorate. Fearful that the poor were, in Fitzsimmons's words, "susceptible to the influence of others with ulterior motives," the assembly effectively excluded them from "the fraternal community of citizens."

All in all, though, the people of Paris had good reason to rejoice when they celebrated their first "Bastille Day"—July 14, 1790—on the ruins of the fortress with a ball, fireworks, and much patriotic oratory. Changing sets of leaders—a new collective leadership—had begun the transformation of France. As celebrants danced on Bastille Day, they assumed that their revolution was over.

THE RULE OF TERROR

Nothing could be more daunting for the student of leadership than fathoming the behavior of the revolutionaries who came to the fore during the French Terror. That men could turn on close comrades and coldly kill them seems almost incomprehensible, though hardly unknown in history. But that zealots out in the country, away from hyperbolic Paris, could drown women and children or cannonade them en masse—their own people, not barbarians at the gate—staggers the rational mind. It is not surprising that historians disagree over the causes of the Terror. The patterned scroll of history seems to curl and crinkle and fold over on itself as one tries to make meaning of such horrors and the rulers who perpetrated them.

As a series of events, the chronicle of revolution has a certain logic. The erratic Louis XVI, virtually imprisoned in Paris and threatened by growing republican feeling, decided in June 1791 to make a dash for freedom. Intercepted at the frontier, the royal family was herded back to Paris in humiliation. Quickly exploiting suspicions that the king had planned to return with an Austrian army to crush the revolution, republicans in the National Assembly demanded the abolition of the monarchy. It was the debate over the king's status, together with threats of invasion from Austria and Prussia to restore Louis to a position "becoming to the rights of sovereigns," that tore the National Assembly's successor under the newly ratified Constitution, the Legislative Assembly, into bitter factions. Enflamed by the outbreak of war with Austria in April 1792, radical dominance grew until, in August 1792, there came a revolution within the revolution, as a crowd of twenty thousand Parisians besieged the royal palace. The monarchy was suspended and soon abolished, and the Legislative Assembly was replaced by the Convention, its members chosen by universal manhood suffrage.

The Convention became the main arena of the Terror, as the radicals divided over Louis's trial and his execution in January 1793, over the foreign threat, over the very meaning of the revolution. Political conflict soon became murderous. First the radical Montagnards secured the trial and the execution of the more moderate Girondins in October 1793, and then they turned on each other. Robespierre's faction joined with the Dantonistes to destroy the Hébertistes, the "ultras," leaders of the *sans-culottes,* and then within two weeks Danton and his followers themselves were borne to the guillotine. Terror became the system of government and spread from Paris throughout the country and to every manner of dissent— from relics of the old nobility to peasant rebels, heroes of 1789, clergy resisting "dechristianization." More than half a million people were arrested and tens of thousands executed.

How could France fall from the "enlightened" Constitution of 1791 into the darkness of the Terror? Some historians point to a fanatical and inhuman effort to implement absolutist ideas, especially those of Jean-Jacques Rousseau, the thinker most often invoked by the radicals. Others attribute the descent to events and exigencies, and the reactions to them by leaders and the people, that at critical junctures produced abrupt turns in the revolution's course.

Perhaps the explanation is simpler. Only the most powerful of forces could produce the vast social convulsion of the French Revolution, and these are found in the aching wants and needs of the French people in the 1780s and early 1790s. For weeks and months on end large sections of the populace simply starved. Noting that half the French wage earner's budget was spent on bread, historian Ferenc Fehér writes: "Only those who have experienced famine know what this means in terms of human existence: ceaseless irascibility and fits of anger as a general reaction to external events, including political ones; short-term scheming, with the constant and exclusive objective of ensuring, and if possible expanding, the next day's food ration; envy as the main sentiment between oneself and one's neighbour; a negative proximity to nature, involving daily use of physical violence and the belief that this is a natural part of social and political life. These conditions shaped the largely dark and cruel world view of the wage-earner and small artisan; they constituted their cosmos."

In the time of the Terror, hunger bred fear, not only about the next day's food but the risk of nighttime theft, or the next day's arrest—and possibly execution—for hoarding. Peasants dreaded brigands who ravaged the countryside. As fear of foreign foes mounted the external threat was linked to the internal—foreigners or royalist émigrés plotting to starve workers and peasants into submission. "The Foreign Plot was a myth," historian R. R. Palmer concluded, but when rulers like Robespierre played on it, they were responding to intense feelings among hungry citizens.

Thus the radical revolutionaries were often led by the wants and fears and hates of those who looked to them for leadership. Who were these would-be followers? They were most notably the *sans-culottes*, the foot soldiers of the radical revolution. Historians have been hard on these "cobblestone leaders." Historian Alfred Cobban found them utterly incoherent, their literature unreadable, and their leaders "completely contemptible." Marxists admired their revolutionary militance but not their indiscipline, individualism, and lack of ideology. Numbering in the tens of thousands, organized loosely in "sections" around a hard core of activists, they were a decisive factor in the radicalization of the revolution, and for a time in 1793–94 even governed Paris. The leading radicals feared to provoke them; when aroused they could mobilize eighty thousand persons to besiege and even invade the Convention and other power centers.

The *sans-culottes* were not a proletariat or even a social class, but a network of journeymen, laborers, small shopkeepers, and traders, and included some men of wealth. Extolling unity and virtue, they exalted the popular will as an expression of both. They were ardent fraternizers, exchanging kisses and calling one another *tu*. They were egalitarian, with a steady hatred of the aristocracy, as reflected in their own simple attire, adorned only by a red cap and tricolor cockade, and their disdain for the silks and jewels of the rich. Above all, they were propelled by a fierce faith in revolutionary progress, even if that involved violence, for, as one carpenter said, "we will have bread only by spilling blood."

The *sans-culottes* were hard on leading radicals who appeared not to share this revolutionary faith, insisting on the right to recall deputies who ignored their constituents' demands. In vain, Robespierre complained that democracy was "not a state in which the people, continuously assembled, directly controls all public affairs." The *sans-culottes* could hardly have disagreed more.

The radical Jacobin core, which included Robespierre, was of a markedly different stripe. The Society of Friends of the Constitution had begun in 1789 as a parliamentary discussion club, composed mainly of Third Estate deputies and liberal nobles who came together to defend the proposed Constitution against both the reactionary aristocracy and rising radicalism. Even their popular name, Jacobins, was innocuous in origin, derived from a convent in Paris where they met for a time. By late 1790 the club had established affiliates throughout the provinces and built a correspondence network. Then Louis XVI's aborted flight in June 1791 split the club between those who continued to support a constitutional monarchy and those who now called for the creation of a republic.

As fear and hatred deepened among the French in the face of continuing threats abroad and turbulence at home, the Jacobin left took over the club, driving out the moderates and bringing it into alliance with the street revolutionaries. By late 1792 the radicals controlled a nationwide membership of more than a hundred thousand activists, maintaining tight discipline and aggressively purging dissidents.

Thus the Jacobins were building a centralized political machine that became more and more remote from the animating ideals of the revolution of 1789. Jacobin ideology "became increasingly narrow," according to Cobban, "with the development of ritual, tests of orthodoxy, purges and public confessions." Was there no role for ideas, for ideology? At the start,

Jacobins had upheld the principles of the Constitution and looked to Roman models of virtue and leadership. By the time of the Terror, Enlightenment ideas had become little more than opportunistic covers for dictatorship and repression.

If any one man epitomized Jacobin radicalism—its dedication and extremism—it was surely Maximilien Robespierre. Raised by relatives in a small northern city after his mother's death and father's disappearance, Robespierre attended school as a charity scholar and studied law at the University of Paris. Elected to the Third Estate, Robespierre maneuvered and harangued his way to prominence in the National Assembly and the Jacobin clubs. He was a master of floor tactics, a champion of the people's right to cheap and plentiful bread, and a tireless orator whose speeches bored his listeners even as they succumbed to their relentless logic. Soon he became, in historian Simon Schama's words, the "manifest leader of the revolutionary left."

Despite Robespierre's professions of identity with the people, he grew almost as remote from them as Louis had been. More and more he was drawn into the internal rivalries among the radicals, consolidating his power as a member of the Committee of Public Safety, established by the Convention in April 1793 and authorized to take extraordinary measures to defend the revolution from its enemies. With his indomitable will, his ability to out-radical the radicals, and his unrelenting hatred and suspicion of opponents, he soon was preaching and practicing judicial terror as the crucial instrument of centralized, autocratic revolutionary rule. A sometime defender of the people's liberty, now Robespierre saw *la liberté* as the government's unconstrained freedom to crush the revolution's enemies wherever he found them.

Once hero to the *sans-culottes,* he was now colliding with them. More than ever the cobblestone leaders were demanding direct democracy and local autonomy, ideas Robespierre scornfully derided. His Committee of Public Safety took the Terror to the *sans-culottes,* executing their "disloyal" leaders and purging dissidents from the sections. The street people had little power to strike back. By the spring of 1794 the revolutionary government had become a lethal king-of-the-hill struggle. Robespierre's success finally brought his downfall. "It's not enough for him to be master," said one survivor, "he has to be God." And when his turn came, his old supporters among the *sans-culottes* were not there to rescue him. Soldiers loyal to the Convention carried him off, racked with pain after a suicide attempt, to the guillotine.

What had gone so terribly wrong? For two years, from 1789 to 1791, the French had conducted an almost exemplary revolution. The monarchical rulers had yielded power, however grudgingly. The leaders of the revolution had not been very revolutionary as they struggled to realize the promise of the Declaration of the Rights of Man and the Citizen and the liberal principles of the proposed Constitution. Monarchists and revolutionaries were delicately if uneasily balanced, leading France toward deep but stabilizing change.

Then extremists took over, as the foolish king's failed escape triggered the most xenophobic elements in Paris and the provinces. A gap opened at the political center that no leadership appeared able to bridge. Instead of the two-sided balance between king and commoners, the new men at the top battled mercilessly for power and survival. No stabilizing force remained. As people's wants and needs mounted, as their hopes and expectations were dashed, as liberty gave way to license, equality to extremism, fraternity to fratricide, a desperate citizenry looked for survival and security—and for a savior.

NAPOLEONIC RULERSHIP

Two hundred years after Napoleon Bonaparte's rise to power, tourists—many of them from Africa and Asia—swarm through the Invalides in Paris to gaze down at his ornate tomb. How is it that this man still fascinates a worldwide audience? Doubtless they know, from books and broadcasts, something about his obscure origins in Corsica, his dazzling military conquests across Europe, his re-creation of himself as emperor, his Elba and Waterloo. His is perhaps the most dramatic modern example of the classic rise and fall of the "heroic" leader.

Legends about Napoleon the man also draw the visitors. However short in physical stature, Napoleon was symbolically larger than life, an imposing man who could intimidate as tellingly, and as calculatingly, as he could charm. His mental acuity, prodigious memory, and capacity for disentangling the most complex situations enormously impressed his rivals as well as his friends. It was said that he could dictate separate letters to four secretaries simultaneously, always picking up a sentence where he had left off.

Many other rulers have possessed such mental gifts. What kind of leadership did Napoleon in fact offer, judged by the criteria of achieving real, intended, comprehensive, and lasting change based on fundamental values? His spectacular military triumphs hardly met this test, for after the disaster of his Russian campaign, he left France open to invasion and mourning the deaths of several hundred thousand young soldiers. As for principles, Alexis de Tocqueville decades later concluded that he was "as great as a man can be without virtue." Curiously, for all his famed military genius, his civil legacy both in France and across Europe far outlived his military achievements.

More than any other historical figure, Napoleon created the model of the intensely personalistic ruler of the administrative state. He out-Caesared Caesar. "I alone am the representative of the people," he shouted at members of his legislature. The British idea of a loyal opposition was anathema to him. He saw any opposition as a personal challenge, and to yield to it was to admit personal weakness. He was no bloodthirsty tyrant— he did not typically use violence to suppress diverse interests. Rather he balanced, immobilized, and marginalized them. He censored the press, regulated the book trade, set limits to the theater, restricted workers' associations, curbed street demonstrations.

If Napoleon lacked principles or virtue, he did have one overwhelming value—order. Nothing, he sensed, was more important to the French people after the turbulence of revolution than stability, and there was nothing he felt more capable of providing. But what kind of order? For the life of the nation, Napoleon would have said. Yet once the Terror had passed, the citizens of France wanted more than survival. Like Americans, they wanted life and liberty and the pursuit of happiness.

Order required the appearance of legitimacy at the top, and here Napoleon was especially creative politically in his use of the plebiscite. Originating in Roman times, this "consultation with the people" had been used to ratify an earlier Jacobin constitution, but Napoleon wedded it to his own ambitions. The 1802 plebiscite asked of voters a simple question: "Should Napoleon Bonaparte be consul for life?" No alternative was offered, nor any indication of what the consul for life would try to achieve. There was no secret ballot; adult males voted by signing their names in the "yes" or "no" column of the public register, thus risking retaliation by the police. The outcome was foreordained: 3.6 million *oui;* 8,272 *non* (brave souls!).

The propaganda battle was as one-sided as the electoral system. The Bonapartists evoked Napoleon's name for national unity, a single voice, patriotic solidarity. "Jacobins, royalists, all were to put aside sterile ideol-

ogy and become simply Frenchmen," wrote historian J. Christopher
Herold, noting that Napoleon told one of his ambassadors: "In France there
is but a single party and a single will."

This "single will" turned out to be ephemeral. Napoleon's much more
lasting and substantial legacy was his Civil Code. Looking back on his
career while in exile on St. Helena, he judged this a greater victory than
any he had won on the battlefield. Not only the revolution's chaos but the
ancient patchwork of French government offended his orderly mind. The
judicial crazy-quilt in particular created huge regional differences in property rights, ancient privileges, inheritance, employment, marriage, and
divorce. Despite its "abolition" of the feudal regime, the revolution had
not fully abolished such remnants as primogeniture or the dowry system.
Now land was freed of remaining feudal obligations, a crucial step in this
largely agricultural economy. In protecting individual property rights,
Napoleon built on the legacy of the early revolution; as in that first phase,
the bourgeoisie gained far more than did the poor.

If the code was more conservative than liberal in its economic impact, it was more patriarchal than egalitarian in its social provisions. The
early revolution had emphasized individual rights, while the code sought
a balance between the family and the individual. A father could block his
child's marriage. While marriage was secularized and dowry rights liberalized, the code drew back from the generous divorce provisions of the
revolution. Bonaparte yielded little to women. They were not allowed to
vote, to be active in politics and public affairs, or to enter into contracts
without their husbands' permission.

Napoleon's Civil Code won wide acceptance, in part because he had
consulted widely in drawing it up. He worked closely with legal experts, one
of whom had served on the Committee of Public Safety and now contrib-
uted to a modest liberalization of the penal code. Despite its mixed principles the code helped spread revolutionary ideas around the world. "It
became an instrument of French conquest," according to historian Martyn
Lyons, that "promised to liberate Europe from clericalism and feudalism."

Napoleon could not consider his regime secure, however, unless
French youth was taught to respect its laws. Having inherited from the
revolution a promising new array of secondary schools that were locally
controlled, he was determined now to unify teaching across the nation. An
1802 law provided for forty-five *lycées* where government-hired instruc-
tors would teach exactly the same syllabus from identical textbooks.

Organized in companies and ranks, the students wore uniforms and were marshaled by drum rolls rather than school bells. Napoleon boasted that he could check his clock at any time of day and know precisely what every pupil in France was studying.

There was a certain grandiosity in all this that contrasted with the results. Many families preferred that their children attend Catholic schools rather than face military discipline at the *lycées*. Napoleon's response was to centralize education even further under the "Imperial University," in effect a state monopoly of all teacher training. Still, a dozen years after the 1802 act, only thirty-six *lycées* existed, with a total of nine thousand students out of a population of 30 million.

Conscription not only provided the vital fuel for Napoleon's military machine, but was regarded by the regime as the highest test of citizenship, "a cornerstone of the new civic order." Millions of young Frenchmen served in the armies that swept across Europe. Yet draft evasion, especially among peasants, became an art form: hiding out, fleeing over the Pyrenees, self-mutilation, marriage (the wedding market boomed). Conscription was regarded as "the most baneful of civic obligations," wrote historian Isser Woloch, the one issue that "produced mass resistance of a sustained, endemic character."

And "conscription" aptly characterized all of Napoleon's new order. In 1789, the king's subjects had become citizens. Now Napoleon reduced them to conscripts in his regimented society. He "led" the French people as a general commands his troops; they were to "follow" him as the ranks obey superiors. The vital—and potentially transformational—interchange between leader and followers was absent. Meaningful political life was extinguished, and Napoleon's rulership, for all the drama of its military adventures, was stagnant, retrogressive, and—as was demonstrated after the emperor's battlefield defeats—hollow at the core.

Napoleon had wanted to be a transforming leader not only in France but across Europe and perhaps the whole world. In his new order of things, he said on St. Helena, there had been a chance of "creating everywhere uniform codes, principles, opinions, feelings, outlooks, and interests. Then, perhaps, with the help of the universal spread of education, it would have been permissible to dream of applying the American Constitution to the great European family."

His invasion of Russia was his way of unifying the "European family." He was urged to liberate the serfs of Russia as he marched eastward, but he rejected this great revolutionary act for narrow military and diplomatic reasons. He led 650,000 soldiers into that war. When he retreated back to Paris an army bulletin detailed the ghastly losses in men and horses. Then it concluded, "The health of His Majesty has never been better."

THE GAULLIST BRAND OF LEADERSHIP

The student of leadership owes a big intellectual debt to the French. For two centuries they have been conducting a series of experiments in moral and practical—and sometimes lethal—leadership and rulership. The monarchy, the revolution, the Terror, the Directory, and Napoleon were followed by the monarchy's restoration, the July monarchy, the Second Republic, the Second Empire of Napoleon III, the Paris Commune, the Third Republic, the Vichy regime, and the Fourth and Fifth Republics. During one decade of teaching French government, I had to explain four shifts in systems to somewhat baffled undergraduates, who believed that if you adopt a constitution you stick with it for centuries, American-style.

Of course the French did not know they were experimenting with leadership. Each time, except for the Third Republic, most doubtless expected that the new system would last. To the researcher, however, French history offers a laboratory for analyzing the interaction of leaders and institutions, values and conflict, in the dynamics of change.

Of all these regimes the Third Republic began with the lowest expectations, lasted the longest—from 1870 to 1940—and emerged as the world's most observed example of multiparty, parliamentary government. It has also been the most condemned—for the hair-trigger coalitions that exploded under the least pressure, for splintering citizens into factions instead of unifying them, for ineffectual executive leadership, and for the resulting instability, drift, compromise, corruption, and cowardice. Ministries rose and fell, premiers came and went in an endless carousel without music. Legislative action was diluted and fitful. Extremists on both left and right thrived in the confusion.

The Third Republic was the consummate example of transactional leadership, in its action and inaction. Its ideal leader was a master broker. In the factional maze of the Chamber of Deputies, it was never enough to deal only with party chiefs, who might or might not speak for the factions and subfactions in their delegations. The dance of the factions and the merry-go-round of ministries may often have seemed entertaining but were rarely edifying. Usually the result was centrist government with a rightward tendency.

Still, the Third Republic survived the Panama Canal disaster and countless other scandals, the Dreyfus affair, the cataclysm of the First World War. Its very flexibility helped gain it longevity. A severe test of leadership would come when the left won an electoral majority in the postwar depression—that is, with Leon Blum's Popular Front government of 1936. A sixty-four-year-old bourgeois politico, and a Jew, Blum as head of the Socialist party formed a left-wing coalition with the Radical Socialists, who were commonly and correctly derided as being neither radical nor socialist. Amid a nationwide rash of sit-down strikes of workers exhilarated by the left's victory, Blum and his cabinet pushed through measures for the forty-hour week and for two weeks' annual holiday with pay. Some armaments firms were nationalized, and even the august Banque de France was brought under limited government control.

The Popular Front would last only a year, aside from a brief recall. Many reasons were advanced for its short life, including its inability to solve the economic crisis, but central to the regime's brevity was the failure of collective leadership that had to bridge the gap between disciplined Communists on the left and the Radicals on the right, with Blum caught in the middle. Pledged to fundamental reform, he was forced by the parliamentary system into political brokerage that sapped the militancy of his coalition.

The fall of the left epitomized the frailties of the Third Republic. For most of its long existence, the price of survival was government that mirrored divisions among the populace rather than responded to people's fundamental wants and needs. Yet what ultimately destroyed the Third Republic was Hitler and the Wehrmacht.

The greatest tribute to the Third Republic might have been its essential replication in the Fourth. Asked in a referendum a year after France's liberation from Nazi rule whether a new constitution should be adopted, 96 percent of respondents answered "yes." But the constitution approved narrowly by a lukewarm electorate in 1946 possessed the core weaknesses of its predecessor. It placed all real power in the National Assembly, making the government accountable to the legislature and thus to no one. Even the old Senate, obstructionist for decades, was resurrected with a new, more delicate name, the Council of the Republic.

What kind of leadership might such a system promote? Much like its predecessor, it would call for "the perfect broker," in political scientist Stanley Hoffmann's words, possessed of "a certain indifference to policy outcomes, resignation to letting events impose decisions which can then be 'sold' as inevitable . . . inexhaustible patience for bargaining with a wide variety of groups, scrupulous observance of the dogma of equality among members of Parliament and of the sacrosanct distance between them and the electorate (that is, no appeal to the people above the heads of the parliamentarians)."

Why did the French restore a political system that had come under almost universal condemnation? Partly it was reaction against the recent, oppressive Vichy regime, partly the feeling that the Third Republic had been crushed by Hitler, not repudiated by the people. Mainly, though, it was the preference of party bosses for a weak government each might have a piece of, over a system offering the potential for leadership that could transcend the multifactional tumult.

Looming over this constitutional struggle—and often part of it—was the imperious figure of Charles de Gaulle. Everything in his character and credo cried out against the disorder and instability of both the Third and Fourth Republics. Born to a Catholic royalist family in Lille, he was imbued with patriotism and piety, values fortified by his Jesuit schooling. He was wounded in World War I at Verdun and left for dead, picked up by the Germans, and put into a prisoner-of-war camp, from which he tried to escape but was recaptured. After the war, as a rising star in the army, he provoked controversy and angered superiors when he urged that France abandon the static defenses of the Maginot Line in favor of greater mobility and mechanization for the army of the future. De Gaulle above all was an independent thinker and actor, demonstrated most notably in his leadership of the Free French resistance during World War II. Though himself a rebel in the military ranks, he brought strong ideas about authority and discipline to the civilian domain.

If the executive power emanated from the legislature, he contended in 1946, the result would be "a confusion of powers which will reduce the Government to a mere conglomeration of delegations. . . . The unity, cohesion and internal discipline of the French Government must be held sacred, if national leadership is not to degenerate rapidly into incompetence and impotence."

With growing alarm, and doubtless a certain elation, de Gaulle watched the Fourth Republic flounder through a series of postwar crises. He feared another convulsion triggered by Communist zealots and far-right extremists. But he also helped produce the problems he had predicted. By organizing the rightist Union of the French People—a new party he denied was a party—he squeezed the centrist leadership in the National Assembly between his own forces and the left, producing ever more immobility.

The denouement came at last in 1958, precipitated by a crisis in the government's long, fruitless struggle to settle the problem of Algerian independence. On May 13, right-wing extremists in the French army seized power in Algiers and called on de Gaulle to lead a "government of Public Safety" in Paris. Two days later, he proclaimed that he was "ready to assume the powers of the Republic," and for two harrowing weeks he allowed the threat of a coup d'état by his army supporters to dangle over France.

A panicked National Assembly turned to the man who with brutal cunning had made himself indispensable, the one man who appeared able to prevent civil war and to avoid national humiliation. On June 1, by a divided assembly vote, de Gaulle was summoned to the premiership with the mandate he had demanded: the authority to restore order and to draft a new constitution.

Prepared in private by a team of young attorneys under de Gaulle's close supervision, the constitution of the Fifth Republic was an authentic Gaullist concoction. Its keystone was the shift of power from parliament to the president, who was to be the nation's "arbiter" and "protector." He would be chosen for a seven-year term by the people, not by parliament; and yet not directly by the people, rather by eighty thousand electors who were mainly local officials. The president had the right to appoint prime ministers, dissolve the National Assembly, and demand that it "reconsider" its legislation. And in the event of crisis, he was authorized to take "whatever measures are required by the circumstances." The new charter was ratified overwhelmingly—by 80 percent of voters—in a September 1958 referendum, and de Gaulle was elected the first president of the Fifth Republic by a similar margin three months later.

Now that de Gaulle had his constitution, what would he do with it? As "guide of France," he claimed the right to "exercise supreme power over the whole range" of the nation's affairs. He dismissed the last vestiges of parliamentary rule with his assertion that "the indivisible authority of the state is entrusted wholly to the president by the people who have elected him."

Yet de Gaulle often governed as though the concentration of powers in the presidency was an end in itself. Heading up an administration that included a host of young *modernes,* he introduced efficiencies and innovations. But the result was a denser bureaucracy staffed by depoliticized technocrats remote from the needs and concerns of the people. In an increasingly affluent society, and in spite of much oratory from the president about a government that acted for all the people, a "poor France"—the title of a work by a Gaullist publicist—remained and even grew, as commercial farming displaced peasants, supermarkets drove shopkeepers out of business, small, local industries struggled to survive in competition with conglomerates, immigrants from former colonies faced discrimination and joblessness, and the aged languished on tiny or nonexistent pensions. In the wake of Gaullist "modernization," the gap between rich and poor, as historian Maurice Agulhon has noted, was extreme.

De Gaulle's great claim to leadership, however, was about order and unity, not the economy. After all the tumult of the 1930s and '40s, and especially after the Algerian settlement, he could say that he had come through on his fundamental promise of security and stability.

Then, early in May 1968, a student protest at the Sorbonne mushroomed into a confrontation between two thousand students and hundreds of police. The rebellion—provoked by overcrowded universities with unresponsive administrations that historian Robert Gildea described as reflecting "in microcosm the authoritarianism, hierarchy, and bureaucracy of the Gaullist state"—set off a "moral and social crisis." As demonstrations spread to Montparnasse and even the Champs Elysées, twenty thousand more students fought the police with Molotov cocktails and paving stones. In one day six hundred were wounded. The university quarter of Paris, littered with burnt-out cars and smashed barricades, looked like a scene of war.

So ineptly did the Gaullists deal with the violence, mixing weakness with repression, that Parisians came to side with the students. Ten days after the first clashes workers called a one-day general strike in solidarity, followed by more walkouts and sit-ins throughout the country. De Gaulle cut short a state visit to Romania and returned to Paris. In a rage, he dismissed the revolt as "student bedwetting" and declared, "Play time is over!" But the crisis spread, to Lyon, Bordeaux, Strasbourg, with several hundred more casualties. De Gaulle's inflexible and paternalistic governing system, political journalist Anthony Hartley wrote, could not bend, so it broke, in the face of social and economic change seeking new political expression.

Everything had slipped through his fingers, de Gaulle admitted later: "I no longer had any hold over my own government." Did he still have any hold over his own people? Early the following year, he decided to appeal to them directly, not through a presidential election, since his second seven-year term would not expire until 1972, but through his favorite device, the plebiscite. He demanded a vote of confidence, yet packaged it in a form his closest advisers considered suicidal. The referendum offered two reforms—strengthening regional government, a popular enough measure, and further limiting the Senate's powers, widely unpopular—and presented them to voters in sixty-eight complex provisions spread over thirty pages. De Gaulle made clear that if the public would not swallow this, he would "depart immediately." And when the referendum failed, he left.

It was grimly ironic that a referendum felled him, for it had been his key to rising above the factional politics he detested. His idea of leadership was intensely personalistic. It assumed a near-mystical identity among leader, followers, and nation—a savior guiding "the great people brought together" to advance the "grandeur" of France. Yet nothing so clearly reflected his essential contempt for the French people as the "absurd" 1969 referendum. Like Napoleon, de Gaulle would be their shepherd, protecting them from the wolves, but only so long as they followed him like sheep.

De Gaulle spoke glowingly of France's grandeur, but what did that mean for France's people? One could not fail to be struck, wrote Stanley Hoffmann, by the "ideological emptiness of Gaullism." The power and prestige of the state—de Gaulle's vision of France's "exalted and exceptional destiny"—were not enough, especially when its government appeared indifferent to or uncomprehending of the real wants and expectations of its people, when its president gave the impression of loving France far more than he loved the French.

France's promiscuous creation and demolition of regime after regime offers not only glimpses of the agonies of leadership but also lessons in an old and still central question—how to allot power on the one hand to kings and dictators, presidents and premiers, and, on the other, to the people, the citizens, the voters. During the French Revolution, the masses were empowered through bold declarations of rights and grants of electoral power that were both intoxicating and disappointing, putting the vote in the hands of burghers and peasants who had little experience of the complexity of democratic procedures.

At the heart of French experiments in government lay derangements in the interaction of would-be leaders and potential followers. Between the obtuseness of Louis XVI and of Charles de Gaulle to the needs and the power of the people were two hundred years of largely failed encounters between the French and those who attempted to lead them. Now the power of the people was given full vent, as would-be leaders whipped up enthusiasm or fear; and now they shrank back from it, sought to suppress it, or to tame it with the cheap and false "democracy" of plebiscites. The complexities and fragmentation of parliamentary regimes on the one hand insulated politicians from the demands of popular majorities, while on the other hand their need to stitch intricate coalitions of minor parties meant that their power to govern was sapped at the least turn of public opinion.

One trial the French did not make, at least never for long: the mutual empowerment of leaders and followers, that *together* they might transform France and its people, on the basis of *liberté, égalité, fraternité.*

7

LEADERSHIP AS CONFLICT

During the early years of this century an angry teenager was laboring on the family farm in China's Hunan province. He hated the work, and hated his father too, in part for making him toil through the endless hours. At sixteen, defying his parents, he left home for school in Changsha, where he read Western classics and Chinese tales of heroism. Then he traveled to Beijing, in 1918, to gain some kind of work at the university. His name was Mao Tse-tung.

Beijing University did not assuage Mao's anger, only focused it. A lowly library assistant, he shared a room with eight Hunan students. He had no status; when he summoned up the courage to ask a question of Hu Shih, the world-famous philosopher did not deign to answer him. Drinking in the ideas of left-wing professors and students, Mao joined Marxist study groups and soon was engulfed in the revolutionary fervor of the university. He was now—in 1920—a committed Marxist excited by the triumph of the Bolsheviks in Russia.

As a Marxist he studied the foundations of conflict in history, in capitalist society, between the elite that monopolized power and the often impotent toiling masses. In 1927 Mao returned from revolutionary activities in Canton to the Hunan countryside and observed the "peasant movement" there. He was excited by a newfound militance. In a very short time, he wrote, "in China's central, southern, and northern provinces, several hundred million peasants will rise like a tornado or tempest, a force so extraordinarily swift and violent that no power, however great, could resist it." Revolutionary comrades had three alternatives: to march at their head, leading them; to follow in the rear, criticizing them; or "to face them as opponents." He knew where he belonged.

The issue was the leadership of conflict. Working in a library, Mao had had access to both the classic and the contemporary treatises on the subject. Dramatic conflict had been staples of the Greek and Elizabethan stage, of fiery religious tracts over the centuries, of the most stirring novels such as Tolstoy's *War and Peace*. Psychologists were studying conflicts between and especially within individuals. Philosophers reflected on the dialectic of ideas, anthropologists and sociologists on the function of conflict in maintaining social stability or in propelling social change, political scientists on the ongoing combat of political leaders and political parties.

Was there any absolutely central and universal kind of conflict that transcended, or at least cut across, all the other types? Marxists thought so—the economic conflict that divided humankind into two social classes and therefore two sets of political antagonists. All other forms of conflict—religious, cultural, ethnic, even psychological—could be explained by the fundamental socioeconomic divisions. Most Marxists, like Marx himself, recognized conflict as inevitable and necessary, a positive if difficult force for social change and progress. But once the proletariat came into power and a classless society emerged, all would, in theory, be harmonious. Conflict would evaporate.

There was nothing more utopian in the communist vision than the idea that human beings would no longer have cause to differ, to oppose one another, individually or in groups. Mao himself did not believe it; even in communist society, "not everybody will be perfect" and sources of conflict would remain. When in 1949 he at last seized power in China, so it proved, as his regime waged unending war on waves of "bad people" whose "thinking is relatively incorrect." Mao continued to maintain that "Marxism develops through struggle" and "does not fear criticism," and a hundred flowers might be allowed briefly to bloom, as they were in 1957, but the lines of permissible dissent were drawn narrowly and subject to dizzyingly abrupt shifts. The Hundred Flowers campaign was swiftly followed by the imprisonment or removal to far rural places of hundreds of thousands of those who had dared speak up. In fact, Mao persistently manipulated conflict to cut down rivals, frustrate the emergence of formed opposition, push forward often-catastrophic policies against resistance within the Communist party and in society. Amid the vast sea of turmoil he created and exploited, through disasters of crash industrialization and a long, violent ideological purification campaign, until the very end of his life, Mao's power remained buoyant, at appalling cost to the nation he ruled.

In China's unstable, personalistic dictatorship, opposition never was legitimized or represented as more than imperfections to be overcome. Yet a functioning democracy not only acknowledges that conflicts without end are woven into the fabric of human society and accommodates them but attempts to turn them to vital and progressive purpose. Antagonistic groups, or classes, oppose one another, accept defeat, and return to fight again for their values or interests in another election on another day. The test of a democracy is the acceptance of majority rule *and* minority rights. The majority's right to govern is matched and validated by the minority's right to oppose and struggle to replace it.

The great engines of conflict in democratic societies are the opposing political parties and their leaderships. The party battles we remember—Pitt's Tories against Fox's Whigs, Disraeli's Conservatives against Gladstone's Liberals, Lincoln's Republicans against Douglas's Democrats, Hoover's Republicans against Franklin Roosevelt's Democrats—resonate because they involved questions closely affecting the lives and hopes of millions of people. Political conflict that sharply poses alternatives related to the nation's values mobilizes citizens and opens possibilities of decision and change. When party leaderships offer voters keenly defined choices, the victory of the winning party constitutes both a mandate for change and a course of action for governing.

In the real political life of democracy, alas, such matters are rarely so simple and clear.

HIS MAJESTY'S OPPOSITION

A young English Tory, Henry St. John (later Lord Bolingbroke), learned about leadership from the very beginning of his extraordinary career. Elected to the House of Commons in 1701 at the age of twenty-two, he immediately assumed leadership of the Tory backbenchers, became minister of war in Her Majesty's government within four years, and a secretary of state following that. His progress benefited from the eighteenth-century willingness to distinguish—at least where aristocrats were concerned—

public leadership from private virtue. A notorious womanizer, he mistreated his first wife, drank heavily, and was not above advising a fellow rake that he had heard of a "certain housemaid that is very handsome: if she can be got ready against your arrival, she shall serve for your first meal."

Bolingbroke's conception of leadership was strictly elitist. He saw society as inevitably hierarchical, directed by men of superior birth who provided order and stability by safeguarding the landed gentry, the backbone of the nation. He had only disdain for those he led in Parliament, once likening them to sheep who will "stand sullen and be run over, till they hear the bell-wether, and then they follow without knowing very well where."

Yet Bolingbroke, whose own brash independence and contrariness seemed made for opposition, learned of its perils in 1714 when he and other Tory ministers were dismissed by the new king, George I, for opposing the Hanoverian succession; one, Lord Oxford, was thrown into the Tower, there to languish for two years. Fearing similar treatment, Bolingbroke fled to France. When it was safe to return he picked up his political career with a pardon, a second wife, and a brief return to influence, then remained in opposition for the rest of his political life to the powerful ministry of Robert Walpole.

Bolingbroke became a theorist of political opposition but his ideas reflected the vast confusion and uneasiness in England about the right to oppose. After a century of domestic and foreign wars, religious strife, and succession struggles, people were more interested in stability and tranquillity than in the ability of defeated leaders to challenge winners. Still, individual and factional opposition had existed in various forms for centuries. What it had lacked was a theory to legitimize it.

Slowly, unwittingly, the English took faltering steps toward the institutionalization of opposition in the political process. The first step was tolerance of criticism of the king's government, though not on untouchable matters like succession—hence Bolingbroke's flight to France.

Next was the emergence of a *formed* opposition, when opposing politicians came to attack the government not only as individuals but in organized groups. This was a fearsome step, because such groups, led by aggressive politicians, might be used not "to watch over the political rights of the people," James MacPherson, a Member of Parliament, worried in a 1779 pamphlet, but as "an engine of private ambition and personal interest" against the "defense of our country." But what politician was free of interest and ambition?

No one wrote more feelingly about the role of the opposition than Bolingbroke, partly because he had suffered so long in that role. Of course his views tended to shift depending on whether he was in office or not. But in his later years, he argued that opposition should be based on "great principles" of patriotism, not selfish motives. This pious thought revealed Bolingbroke's actual opposition to opposition. He imagined an opposition—his Tories, perhaps—that was a band of patriots standing against a corrupt and tyrannical government. This opposition would "last and grow" until, joining hands with a wise king, it came to power and led men "from acting with a party-spirit, to act with a national spirit." The "true image of a free people, governed by a Patriot King," Bolingbroke declared, "is that of a patriarchical family . . . animated by one common spirit." It was ideas like this, so persuasive to a people weary of conflict, that made it hard for the English to think their way through to a democratic frame that embraced both those who governed and those who opposed.

Still, they kept thinking and experimenting. A momentous step was acceptance of the idea of *parties*—one in power, the other out; one holding office, the other seeking it—and here Bolingbroke drew back. The only legitimate party was one that represented the whole nation. But this left him and his supporters in a hopelessly unrealistic position, claiming for themselves a monopoly on political virtue, while imputing to their opponents a monopoly on corruption.

Of course, Bolingbroke was hardly thinking dispassionately. He and his Tory colleagues were practical men looking for political gain. Indeed, as the eighteenth century wore on, British politics retrogressed into intense factionalism, abetted by the fierce partisanship of Hanoverian kings and their heirs. Central was the individual leadership of powerful personages, most of them aristocrats, rather than the collective leadership of the amorphous parties. The Marquis of Rockingham, for instance, led his Whigs in jousts year after year with William Pitt and his Tories.

During the 1760s and '70s, the American struggle for independence and other divisive issues sharpened the focus on the role of party and party opposition. Though the debates were bitter, supporters of the American rebels against the king were not prosecuted or generally regarded as traitors. This growing acceptance of party opposition was reflected in an anonymous 1768 letter to the Duke of Grafton. Reprinted as a pamphlet, it was judged by the British historian J. A. W. Gunn as "one of the great documents in the history of political parties," for it explained the virtues of a two-party system without any apparent party bias or reservation. "An able united opposition in parliament," the author wrote, "will always have the effect of rouzing the activity, and fixing the attention of government; of perplexing bad measures and purifying good ones."

But it would take a person with extensive experience in parliamentary politics combined with a fine grasp of the moral aspects of political structure to see the crucial importance of parties for governmental leadership. That person was Edmund Burke. Born on New Year's Day, 1729, in Dublin, of a Protestant father and a Catholic mother, Burke grew up in a comfortable middle-class family and was sent to good public schools and to Trinity College. Law studies at Middle Temple in London led to fruitful contacts with leading parliamentarians, notably Rockingham and other Whigs, and, in 1765, election to the House of Commons. Burke was immediately involved in the factional battles over policies toward America, India, and Ireland. He learned that in factions people could acquire "a narrow, bigoted, and proscriptive spirit," sinking the "general good" in "partial interest." Yet he also concluded that "when bad men combine, the good must associate; else they will fall, one by one."

This need for "honorable connexion" in politics brought forth from Burke a panegyric to political parties. In "Thoughts on the Cause of the Present Discontents" in 1770, he presented what became the classic definition of party—"a body of men united, for promoting by their joint endeavors the national interest, upon some particular principle in which they are all agreed." And if the party in power had certain roles and responsibilities, so did the opposition. A party out of office should oppose not in a factional spirit but for the sake of good government. Strong party competition would make for strong leadership.

At the heart of party leadership, Burke insisted, lay moral values. The party itself must be formed and led on the basis of the most elevated principles—above all, liberty, of which parties were both the guardians and the beneficiaries. A well-considered and ordered set of principles was the strongest basis for party unity.

How was it that this Irish "outsider"—as some Tories dubbed him—should present the most powerful case yet for political parties, and by extension party leadership? In part it was because he indeed had come from the outside and could analyze British politics with some perspective and detachment, and in part because he was an accomplished moral philosopher, as his later writings would brilliantly attest. But even more it was because he was able to capitalize not only on the thinking of earlier generations but on the sentiments of his own British public. A working politician paying close attention to the concerns of his constituents, and an avid reader of tracts and sermons and press articles, Burke divined the mounting feeling of people who wanted a more just and representative system of government.

Burke died in 1797, as the gripping party battles between the Tory forces of William Pitt the Younger and the Whiggish followers of Charles James Fox were at a pitch, an extraordinary clash of principles, interests, and temperaments that at its worst confirmed every dread of party conflict, but that at its best vindicated Burke's hopes of a "generous contention for power" based on "manly and honorable maxims."

Pitt was in the saddle as prime minister almost continuously from 1783 until his death in 1806, while Fox led the opposition much of that time, often in utter frustration. Fox was a charismatic figure, and much of his strength lay in personal relationships cultivated in private houses and London clubs. Attentive to his followers' concerns, he built a national network of Whig clubs, "the first broad party association of a more than temporary or local character." But no amount of party solidarity or brilliance in parliamentary repartee empowered him and his close colleague Charles Grey to unseat Pitt.

The problem was partly the continuing undefined role of the opposition. Even more, Fox's sympathy for the French Revolution became political poison when the Jacobins came to power and the French threatened to spread their revolution across the Continent. English fears mounted to the point that the old linkage of opposition with betrayal of king and country was revived. The Foxites escaped the repression of "radicals" that followed, but their ability to perform the central task of an opposition— to seriously challenge the party in power—was reduced to almost nothing. Even a dramatic "secession" from Parliament in 1797 in protest of Pitt's dominance, which left him with no organized opposition for four years, failed to rouse the public against one-party rule.

It would take another decade following Waterloo for the long, frustrated Whig opposition finally to pay off—and demonstrate the crucial role a combative and persistent opposition could play in spurring principled change—as Grey and other leaders planned a controversial democratization of the electoral system, culminating in the Reform Act of 1832. And it would be more decades before the British constructed a full-fledged party system, organized and disciplined, with an opposition party given the unquestioned legitimacy and institutional resources needed to challenge the incumbents. But the British would get there, step by step.

IRREPRESSIBLE CONFLICT?

In 1840, the recently formed American Whig party nominated for president William Henry Harrison, a hero of the War of 1812. The old general was hardly a matinee idol, but the Whigs took care of that. They put on a rollicking campaign with barrels of cider, coonskins, effigies, floats, catchy slogans ("Tippecanoe and Tyler too!"), and newspaper ads. When a Democratic newspaper suggested that Harrison would quit the race for a $2,000 pension and a barrel of cider, the Whigs seized on the remark as an insult to the man of the people, a simple son of the frontier. So it became a coonskin campaign.

Hijinks worked; Harrison beat Democratic incumbent Martin Van Buren soundly. Ever since, historians have derided the 1840 contest as an orgy of personal abuse and policy irrelevancy, and so it was. But it was something else too—the shattering of one-party rule and the re-creation of a competitive two-party system, demonstrating that the "outs" could defeat a strongly entrenched presidential party. With the two parties organized in every state, the election produced a new high in voting turnout.

The first test of an aspiring democracy is the acceptance, by the politicians in power, of an organized opposition. Americans had met this test in 1800 when the Adams Federalists had yielded the presidency to the Jeffersonian Republicans. A second test lies in the *nature* of party conflict. Do the parties confront one another on central issues reflecting the people's fundamental needs? Do they offer *moral* leadership, grounded in the great public values?

The Democrats and the Whigs, as they alternated in power through the 1840s and 1850s, not only failed the second of these tests. They precipitated the most catastrophic failure of leadership in American history.

The deadly course of politics in those two decades—the long road to civil war—was unimaginably complex. It was a struggle of parties but also of factions, regions, ideologies, and interests, raised to an unbearable heat by the awful issue of slavery. We can make some sense of it by viewing it from the vantage of the headquarters of the Whigs and Democrats, as they stumbled through the messy terrain under enormous pressures.

Both parties had the weakness of their strengths. Both were *national* parties, in a nation growing increasingly divided over slavery. With their

Jeffersonian and Jacksonian inheritance, the Democrats retained voting strength across the country and proved it in 1844 by winning the presidency back from the Whigs. Their electoral base lay in the South, where slaveholders ruled the party. But even this Democratic bastion was not free of divisions, especially between slaveholders and poor whites. The Democrats also were strong in some northern states, but a faction that came to be called the "Barnburners" opposed slavery's extension beyond the South and threatened to bolt the party rather than yield to southern domination. The unity of the Democrats would hold only so long as slavery remained the subject "upon which by common consent no party issue had been made."

The national Whig party, divided since its beginnings in the early 1830s, had no smaller stake in tamping down conflict over slavery. Southern Whigs were devoted to "states' rights" and particularly opposed federal interference in the "rights" of slave owners. In the North, the party was split between "Cotton Whigs," conservatives who opposed slavery but sought to subordinate it to economic issues on the national agenda, and "Conscience Whigs," leaders in the antislavery cause alarmed by the hold of the "Slave Power" over the federal government. To maintain unity, the Whig party bosses, like the Democrats, tried to play down the slavery issue and keep it out of politics. So both parties wrestled over comfortable old issues like foreign policy, tariffs, immigration, and railroad expansion rather than the incendiary question of African Americans in chains.

What Whigs and Democrats specialized in was brokerage among section and interest-group demands—in short, transactional leadership. The men rising to the top were expert negotiators and bargainers in the mold of Whig senators like Kentucky's Henry Clay and Daniel Webster of Massachusetts, or Democrats like Stephen A. Douglas of Illinois. The brokers had their work cut out for them, as year after year the question of whether new states were to be admitted to the Union as "free" or "slave" kept roiling the slavery issue, pushing it to the fore. Meanwhile the party seesaw continued, as the Whigs regained the presidency in 1848.

How long could peace through brokerage last? The answer turned in large part on compromises along the lines of fissure within each party. At their zenith, the brokers brought off what seemed their greatest feat: the Compromise of 1850. An omnibus bill introduced by Clay was ground through Congress's brokerage mill to produce a few carefully balanced agreements: the admission of California as a free state and of other states with or without slavery, according to their own decision; the strengthening of the Fugitive Slave Act; and the abolition of the slave trade in the nation's capital, though slavery itself was not outlawed there.

Limited as it was, the Compromise of 1850 seemed a fitting climax to a decade of horse-trading in Washington. It attempted to give some partial satisfaction to every faction in each party, and now, as a northern Whig said, it was time for "every man" to "set himself to suppress the further political agitation of this whole subject." But it was too late. Instead of pacifying the hostile sides, the settlement aroused fury north and south. Southerners, angered by the concessions made to abolitionists, talked openly of secession. Conscience Whigs were appalled by the prospect of slavery's spread into new states on "the voluntary principle," and saw that it portended perpetual domination by the "Slave Power." They began an exodus from the Whig party—and the search for an alternative home.

"It is an irrepressible conflict," lamented Senator William H. Seward of New York, "between opposing and enduring forces, and it means that the United States must and will, sooner or later, become entirely a slave-holding nation, or entirely a free-labor nation."

It was precisely the "irrepressibility" of conflict over slavery that both Democrats and Whigs had sought for so long to deny. At stake, they believed, was the survival of their parties, and of the nation. When the issue could no longer be subordinated to others, or regarded as merely local or sectional, party leaders invoked the "higher law" of national unity. But what was to be the price of such unity? As historian William R. Brock has noted, "the compromisers sacrificed older values when they appealed to patriotism."

The Compromise of 1850 marked the moral bankruptcy of a two-party system in which the leading figures of neither side dared to *oppose*, in the name of such "older values" as liberty, equality, and justice, the enslavement of human beings. The Whigs suffered most. By 1854, the party had begun to disintegrate as Conscience Whigs, along with many northern Democrats, fled to a new party that began to form that summer. This new party promised to present a true opposition to the status quo of slavery, its founders vowing to "put our action upon the moral ground." The "active, life-giving principle" of the Republican party, as one of its leaders, Abraham Lincoln, himself a former Whig, declared, was "hatred to the institution of Slavery; hatred to it in all its aspects, moral, social, and political."

* * *

Sometimes principled leadership pays off in a most practical way—election results. In 1860 the Republican party, competing in only its second presidential election, with Abraham Lincoln as its candidate, won a smashing victory in a four-way race against Stephen Douglas's Democrats, a southern proslavery party, and the nearly moribund Whigs.

As the party that had been born in opposition to slavery and then led the war to save the Union, the Republicans had claim to be the "principled" party, with a grip on the presidency that they relinquished only briefly over the next seventy years. The Democrats, with roots still in the defeated South, failed to mount an effective opposition to what came to be called the Grand Old Party.

It would take a mighty blow to unseat the Republicans, who governed imperturbably—if not always according to any recognizable "principles"—through decades of tremendous change in American society. That blow came with the Great Depression and the young Democratic governor of New York who crushed President Herbert Hoover in 1932. Over the next four years, the Republicans put up as feeble and erratic opposition to Franklin Roosevelt and the New Deal as the Democrats had earlier to the GOP.

In 1936 FDR's coalition of old and new Democrats, of labor and business, farmers and consumers, of blacks and southern segregationists, of liberal intellectuals and urban masses, brought the president and congressional Democrats a sensational sweep. Yet Roosevelt saw the challenge in the unwieldiness of the winning coalition. He feared that "without any organized opposition" from the much-reduced ranks of congressional Republicans, he would face "shifting blocks" of resistance from within his own party, mainly among southern conservatives who, in his first term, had backed the New Deal grudgingly. The Depression and the New Deal had only begun the transformation of the Democrats into the liberalized party that for years Roosevelt had been calling for, capable of providing the "continuous liberal government" he sought; it would be up to him to complete the revolution.

Much as the president had feared, the huge Democratic majority in the new Congress splintered, with southern conservatives often joining Republicans in opposition to his policies. Partly this was due to Roosevelt's bold effort to pack the Supreme Court with liberal justices in 1937, a maneuver that angered many in both parties. Above all, though, the southern conservatives were increasingly determined to resist the escalating power of a northern liberal president within the party they had dominated for generations. As an example of his threat, they pointed to FDR's leading part in the abolition of the rule at Democratic national conventions that presidential nominees needed support of two-thirds of the delegates, a rule that had long given the South a near veto over nominations.

Now, in 1938, Roosevelt embarked on a courageous and controversial trial of transforming leadership. Even though FDR did not relish face-to-face combat, especially with veteran Democrats who had given some support to New Deal measures, he would invade the conservative bastion of the South in person to intervene in Democratic party primaries with calls for the nomination of liberal or moderate Democrats. And he largely failed. Partly this was due to his lack of a long-term and comprehensive strategy of mobilizing popular support behind a transformation of the Democratic party; the purge was hastily and inadequately organized by an inexperienced "elimination committee." Even more, he could not overcome the bulwarks set up in southern states that kept blacks and poor whites away from the polls. Thus FDR had not achieved a crucial step to change—the reorganization of conflict.

Frustrated in the purge, weakened by a conservative backlash, Roosevelt continued to struggle for ways to transform his party. He had long reached out beyond Democratic borders to win support from independents and liberal and moderate Republicans. At times he even indicated he would desert the Democratic party if it became a conservative party. In 1940 he tried to put a firmly liberal stamp on the party by insisting on the nomination for the vice presidency of longtime progressive Henry Wallace. And though he played down partisanship during World War II, he pursued liberal objectives in economic and social legislation and called stirringly for an "Economic Bill of Rights."

But in the end, though he had created one of the broadest, most successful electoral coalitions in American history, FDR did not have what he most sought—a *principled* party "willing to stand up and fight night and day . . . to meet actual needs." A happy warrior in political and ideological conflict, Roosevelt also appreciated the role of principled party strife in achieving progress, giving voters a "definite choice of direction" at times of crisis and change. And he knew from history that, without a strong party strongly committed to them, New Deal gains might "evaporate into thin air under the next Administration." The Democratic party of the 1930s came to be dominated by liberals, but its base remained in the old South, where it still ruled nearly without opposition. FDR worried that, without forceful liberal leadership, that conservative base would make Democrats and Republicans "merely Tweedledum and Tweedledee," and elections "meaningless when the two major parties have no differences other than their labels."

Yet though the ideals of the president's New Deal leadership lastingly transformed the field of ideological conflict in American politics, he ultimately failed to create a principled Democratic party. Neither Roosevelt nor his Democratic successors could resolve the irrepressible conflict within the party between northern liberals and southern conservatives. After decades of rising tension, that conflict culminated not in civil war but with the secession of southerners and their transfiguration into Republicans. A new "Solid South" took shape and came to dominate the Republican party, creating new lines of conflict within and between the parties.

THE RUSSIAN OPPOSITIONISTS

The oldest method of dealing with political opposition is to extinguish it by imprisoning or exiling critics, or by simply killing them. Joseph Stalin was unique in the colossal scope of his murders, rooting out not only real or imagined foes but their cadres and followers and families.

Stalin ruled a people that for centuries had demanded of their rulers one thing above all: security. For centuries Russia's tsars had fought to protect and extend their huge lands, lacking natural barriers and exposed to invasion from all sides. To preserve internal order people were treated as subjects—serfs—not citizens. Opposition was treason. Social change and individual initiative were threats to order.

The German defeat of the Russian armies in the First World War proved again the cost of weakness and disorder. Tsarist rule collapsed and power passed first through the hands of moderate revolutionaries, then to Lenin and the Bolsheviks. Civil war and social chaos led to "war communism" and the fierce repression of internal opposition. Lenin had envisaged a transition to fundamental social change that might take as long as two generations. But within a few years of the revolution he was dead. His successor was Stalin, who ruled for almost three decades with a calculated policy of brutal terror and mass indoctrination that had, it was thought in the West, reduced the Soviet people to utter submission.

After centuries of suppression under the icy crust of rule by tsars and commissars, had the Russian people retained enough autonomy and vitality to express themselves politically? The answer came in the mid-1980s as a new, reformist Communist party general secretary, Mikhail Gorbachev, loosened party controls and the Russian people sprang to life like spring flowers. First independent recreational clubs and youthful rock bands appeared, then cultural and historical and ecological groups, and soon thousands of cooperative societies, until by the end of 1987 there were at least thirty thousand unofficial grassroots associations. Like Lenin and Stalin, Gorbachev needed active followers to carry out his plans for *perestroika*—economic and political revitalization—but his approach called "for a new kind of mass mobilization, stimulated, as before, by policies initiated from above," according to sociologist Victoria E. Bonnell, "but sustained over the long term by institutional structures permitting autonomous political and social action and a broad sphere for political discourse."

A harsher test of democratization would be official toleration of overtly political groups. Informal clubs were one thing, collective organizations that could easily become an opposition were something else. Some of the new political organizations emerged from the gradual splintering of the Communist party itself, while others burst up from the grass roots. Complicating the rise of organized political activity was a widespread suspicion of anything that might be called "party," reflecting both experiences of Stalinist party control and longer memories of the divisions and disorders of parties that had helped bring the Bolsheviks to power. Still, parties, or proto-parties, blossomed. Early and notable were the Democratic Union, "the first outright opposition party," and Memorial, established not only to expose crimes of the Stalin era but to ensure by pursuing "complete democratization" that they would not be repeated.

After decades of subjection to one centralized body it was only natural that Russians would tend toward political pluralism. But it was more than a tendency—it was an orgy, a frenzy of party formation. Organizations ranged from nationalist and religious groups on the right, to a Peasant party in the center, to Social Democrats on the left—perhaps in all more than a hundred. Few drew more than two or three thousand members. Many were little more than debating societies, luxuriating in the newborn freedoms of thought and discussion, and paying scant attention to recruitment and participation.

The organizations that emerged by 1990, according to historian Judith Devlin, "were either parties of the intelligentsia—which relied mainly on intellectual debate to draw support and which remained very small and weak—or parties of politicians formed in a discredited political culture, which they were unable to jettison in its entirety. In neither case were the party leaders entirely aware of how to mobilize support in a modern democracy and, after the initial euphoria, the new parties led a tenuous existence, insecurely anchored in the country's political life and in public opinion."

It was amid this heady but fractious milieu that Gorbachev sought to maintain his control of the direction and pace of change. "Timid, creeping reforms," he acknowledged, were not enough.

"*Perestroika* has already awakened our people," Gorbachev told the editors of *Time* magazine after five years in power. "They've changed. We have a different society now. We will never slip backward." The process would go both slowly and fast, and there would be some "zigzags" along the way. But, he said, "we will certainly keep moving ahead." *Time* anointed him "Man of the Decade." Yet the heroic reformer of the 1980s soon became the forgotten man of the 1990s. What had happened?

Gorbachev led the revolution from above, against the angry resistance of party hard-liners. Yet, as a would-be transforming leader, he was unable effectively to mobilize the "initiative and creativity" below, of a huge, discontented, but largely passive populace, concerned mainly with the hardships of daily life. Meanwhile, an engaged, increasingly aggressive minority not only supported his reforms but wanted to move much faster toward deeper democratization. Gorbachev recognized the value of conflict in driving reform, but, long unwilling to relinquish the Communist party's primacy, he sought to limit the field of conflict to the "socialist pluralism of opinions," fought within the confines of a party-state monopoly of power. "With hindsight," concluded political scientists Carol Barner-Barry and Cynthia A. Hody, "Gorbachev began a revolution from above that gradually turned into a revolution from below. Those who launched it and were attempting to guide it lost control of the forces they had released."

In evaluating the efforts toward change of Gorbachev and his reformist party colleagues, one must note the horrendous difficulties they faced: an old order that was disintegrating but determined to cling to power; a vital but incoherent and divided democratic opposition; and the nation's inexperience in democratic or pluralistic politics. Added to these were the continuing economic crisis that had provoked the reform effort as well as the rapid dismantling of the Soviet empire. Under such circumstances, Gorbachev performed well. A new political order emerged without the terrible violence that has accompanied other revolutionary transitions.

But was Gorbachev more "eventful" or "event-making," in Sidney Hook's formulation? Certainly his years in power were eventful, and he was at the center of radical changes. The test of event-*making* leadership, though, turns on his causal role in those changes, the overcoming of obstacles to achieve an intended and well-articulated goal. In short, was Gorbachev a transforming leader? Or might he be better seen as a transactional leader, adept at mediating and brokering among diverse forces, yet ultimately overtaken by events and outcomes far beyond his intending?

A decade after his fall, Gorbachev stands as the crucial initiator of change, breaking open a decrepit but still monolithic political system. But the opposition he invited in the name of reform gathered a momentum and an intensity he had never foreseen. He was beset by the teeming complexities of a new and yet unformed politics, for which his training in the rigid and hierarchical state-party bureaucracies had done little to prepare him. He was faced with new ideas, new networks of association and rivalry, dispersed and shifting loyalties and ambitions, multitudinous sources of challenge, conflict, and threat. In the end, these forces, which he could neither dominate nor yield to, denied him the crucial role of leadership—not only to initiate change but, collectively, with mobilized followers, to help channel it through to an intended goal. By the time he surrendered power in 1991 he had few supporters. He was despised both by party hard-liners and by many democrats, and widely dismissed as a transitional figure.

If the Gorbachev transition was largely without violence, neither was it orderly. It had the character, finally, of collapse. The opposition he had called forth and then resisted was never able to gain maturity or coherence within the declining system. Liberated after decades of repression, the oppositionists found themselves required to fill a growing ideological and political vacuum. As the Communist party disintegrated, so did hopes for the creation of a mass, disciplined, democratic party to oppose it. And after the deluge, the opposition remained much as it had begun: a fragmented collection of debaters and demagogues, of liberal intellectuals and technocrats and old Communists. There were many would-be leaders, never able to form a collective democratic leadership but acting instead like little bosses, each with his own claque, squabbling among themselves over policy, precedence, and power.

A self-described "people's tsar" who governed through a corrupt court of cronies and "oligarchs," Russia's first elected president, Boris Yeltsin, stood aloof from the efforts of his ostensible allies, the democrats, to combine their factions into a single coherent party. Even the creation of a *governing* party seemed beyond Russia's reach in the 1990s. As dozens of ephemeral parties competed in elections, the Communists, with their habits of organizational discipline, regularly made the strongest showings. Yet they, too, floundered, alternately colluding with Yeltsin and declaring themselves a "responsible and irreconcilable" opposition.

Even in developed, stable democracies, where winning and holding power is arduous enough, sustaining a coherent opposition is still more daunting. Politicians whose party wins an election have every reason to stick together—to put through their promised program, to share the spoils of office, to hang together so as not to hang separately, as Benjamin Franklin put it. The losing party lacks these unifying forces. Blame for defeat is bandied about, opportunists look elsewhere for opportunities, factions break away, some now to support the winning party.

What opposition leaders then shall oppose? Interest groups will emerge to press their various causes. A free press will encourage individual critics to speak out in newspapers and journals. Clergy will preach from their pulpits, actors from their stages, poets in rhymed couplets. None of this usually suffices. The only threat to the governing party lies in the next election. Step by step, opposition leaders work out coalitions of the disinherited and the disenchanted.

Most of this coalition building requires transactional leadership. What happens when a moral issue arises that leaders cannot duck? Slavery in America posed such an issue. For twenty years the Democrats and the Whigs tried to duck it, culminating in the compromises of 1850.

The absence of real oppositional conflict on the issue reflected a broader failure of two-party politics when the two parties are, as they typically have been in the United States, massive coalitions of diverse and often conflicting interests. Success for such parties means the suppression of deep-cutting issues. Brokerage thrives as conflict is muted. Yet the emergence in the 1850s of the Republicans in opposition to slavery, and the liberalization, albeit incomplete, of the Democratic party after Republican failures to respond to people's dire wants during the devastation of the Great Depression of the 1930s, show the transformational power of principled conflict when people seek real solutions through the reassertion of submerged values.

Part Four

PEOPLE

8

THE ANATOMY
OF MOTIVATION

If most biographies of leaders offer more questions than answers about leadership, at least the questions may help pave the way toward a general theory of leadership. My own study of Franklin D. Roosevelt illustrated the possibilities and limitations of such investigations. FDR's presidency provided insights into the social and political forces both undergirding and thwarting leadership at the very highest level. His adventurous leadership raised questions that led me into unexpected paths—especially into the lives of the *people* of the 1930s, the poor and the jobless as well as the beneficiaries of the New Deal—yielding invaluable clues to the wants and needs, the motivations and aspirations of those who might become followers of responsive leaders.

Part of the poverty of the poor is the paucity of records of their lives. Impoverished people rarely send protests to the editor, have the opportunity to speak freely or candidly to candidates or pollsters, or give money to politicians. But one political act some do perform, aside from voting— they write letters to the president or first lady, as the only persons they "see" on the national stage. In recent years I have read hundreds of these letters at the Roosevelt Library in Hyde Park, New York.

Many are heart-wrenching. I remember particularly a letter to Eleanor Roosevelt from a woman whose husband was acutely ill and whose son was jobless. She asked the First Lady for a loan and enclosed her wedding and engagement rings as surety.

Such desperation I had expected, but what surprised me was the uniformity of these letters over time. I had assumed that the "Hoover Depression" letters of 1930–32 written to Governor Roosevelt would reflect the most dire wants, and that the letters of 1933–39 would mirror the economic improvement and hopefulness we associate with President Roosevelt's New Deal. But the correspondence files belied this assumption. The letters of the mid- and late-1930s cried out a desperation rivaling that of the earlier years, as though their authors felt their voices still were not being heard. They were sometimes more hopeful, to be sure, but the hope seemed only to deepen the later disenchantment welling out of the city streets and grass roots.

What I found in such letters was sheer want burdening people, going unmet, the kind FDR later responded to in his famous call for "freedom from want." The president had also called for "freedom from fear," and I found I was tapping a whole substratum of fear that seemed linked to want.

Roosevelt recognized that the New Deal had not realized its early promises with his January 1937 admission that one-third of the nation remained "ill-housed, ill-clad, ill-nourished . . ." It was a frank confession of failure on the part of a president who had been in office for four years. A little later, he warned his fellow Democrats:

"If we do not have the courage to lead the American people where they want to go, someone else will."

SHEER WANT

Where does leadership begin? Where change begins. Where does change begin? In my view, with the burgeoning in humans of powerful physical and psychological wants. Leadership is so intertwined with fundamental change, and change with the dynamics of wants and needs, as to make rather arbitrary any locating of origins in what is really a seamless web. I begin with the power of wants because I know of no global change more massive and persistent than the birth every day of tens of thousands of babies starting off on their own lives with imperious demands and immediately transforming the family environments around them.

Raising four children forced me to think about managing, or at least redirecting, their surging wants. At first we parents were subject to their unrelenting demands for food and warmth. Then, as they grew, we sought to regulate their diet, sleep, speech, clothes—they preferred to go barefoot. And to regulate their social life. "But we *want* to stay out late," they would cry. "But you don't *need* to," we would reply. "But it's not *fair*," they'd say.

I was a bit slow in recognizing the implications for leadership of what we were doing. We were legitimizing some of their wants as genuine needs and vetoing others. In defining their needs we were assuming a leadership role in the hope that they would follow us, which of course they often didn't. Wants and needs were inseparable—needs grew out of wants—but the two were different. The distinction became crucial to my own thinking about leadership. In puzzling out that difference I turned, like a typical academic, to received wisdom on the subject.

Liberal thinkers of the Enlightenment viewed the proliferation of wants with approval, or at least complacency. David Hume, distinguishing humans from animals because of the former's insatiable wants, saw man as endowed with abilities proportionate to those wants. Jeremy Bentham held that every person sought to maximize his pleasure and each fulfilled want created fresh ones, which became new pivots of action. John Stuart Mill, distinguishing between crude wants and more elevated ones, held that the satisfaction of material wants should lead to the cultivation of intellectual and moral wants.

All saw limits, perceiving that the pursuit of wants without restraint might threaten the social order, and found moral danger in undisciplined acquisitiveness that would cripple the development of higher human qualities. Still, these and other philosophers hailed the expansion of wants as the social and economic horizons broadened in the eighteenth and early nineteenth centuries.

It was this explosion of wants that, a century later, alarmed Mohandas Gandhi in India. He saw rampant wants as the force driving industrialization in the West, as well as the resulting concentrations of power and wealth amid pervasive exploitation and inequality. The "unrestricted individualism" of the West, he wrote, was the "law of the beast of the jungle." The only remedy lay in people transforming themselves. The satisfaction of wants "must meet at a certain point a dead stop," and each must do his share of "bread labour" rather than exploit others. Few in the West were tempted—intellectually, or in practice—by the asceticism of the East.

How then to comprehend the "jungle" of wants of nearly six billion people? Abraham Maslow saw the possibility of order where others saw only disorder. A psychologist at Brooklyn College, Maslow in the early

1940s shaped a theory of the rank-ordering of wants and needs into a kind of hierarchy. Most analysts of wants had written of their denial and the resulting social violence. Maslow was more interested in the *satisfaction* of wants and the resulting changes in people's motivations and behavior as they move higher in his hierarchy. (Maslow usually used the term *needs* rather than *wants.*)

At the bottom of Maslow's hierarchy lie the inborn physical and biological wants for subsistence noted above. Once these begin to be met, a new urgent want—for security—becomes the dominant motive. Then humans develop wants for affection and belongingness, realized in home and neighborhood, in local associations, in workplaces. These activities in turn lead to the emergence of self-esteem as primary motive, and beyond that, the pursuit of self-development, with the need for self-actualization at the pinnacle of Maslow's hierarchy.

Maslow did not have the impact on political and social studies that some felt he deserved. An early exception was the work of political scientist James C. Davies, who emphasized the political implications of the hierarchy. Davies began with physiological wants, as Maslow did, suggesting that anyone who doubted their most basic quality should simply stop breathing for a minute or go without food for a few days. Davies also agreed with Maslow on the higher stages in the hierarchy—wants for the "social-affectionate," or just plain love, and for self-esteem and self-actualization. Davies, though, saw the want for security—for "order, predictability, dependability of the environment"—as not just another stage in the hierarchy but at the core of the process, as the crucial means of making attainment of all other wants possible.

I was struck by this emphasis on security because I wanted to build a leadership hierarchy out of these priority lists. I had found in historical studies an overwhelming want for political and social security. Millions of people—in Europe, Asia, Africa, Latin America—felt such a desperate imperative for sheer survival that they were led to embrace dictatorships that promised to deal with marauding bands of killers and other anarchic behavior. So my own hierarchy began with *order,* which supplied the foundation for wants and needs, hopes and expectations, that political leaders must satisfy.

What appealed to me most, though, was the potential link between Maslow's drive for self-actualization and the motivation for leadership. The qualities that motivate and characterize self-actualization—creativity, the capacity for growth and learning, flexibility, openness, and what psychologist Robert White called "effectance," skills in dealing with others or with the environment—are near to those of leadership. A crucial distinction is that while Maslow describes self-actualizing persons as self-contained, autonomous, dependent on "their own potentialities and latent resources," leadership self-actualization is pursued through a process of *mutual* actualization with others, motivated, in the words of political theorists Agnes Heller and Ferenc Fehér, by commitment "to a value or a purpose that stands higher than the person."

When I wrote my book *Leadership* in 1978, I described this process as one of "leading by being led." The leader's self-actualizing qualities are turned outward. He empathetically comprehends the wants of followers and responds to them as legitimate needs, articulating them as values. He helps followers transform them into hopes and aspirations, and then into more purposeful expectations, and finally into demands. Leaders, I hypothesized, rise one step ahead of followers in this political hierarchy, but continued progress depends on their ability to stay closely attuned to the evolving wants, needs, and expectations of followers—in short, to learn from and be led by followers. And it requires a commitment to a process in which leaders and followers *together* pursue self-actualization. Their wants for belongingness, for esteem, are recognized and satisfied, efficacy is enhanced, and the potential for self-fulfillment—"to become everything that one is capable of becoming," as Maslow put it—is activated. What leaders and followers become, above all, are active agents for change, capable of self-determination, of transforming their "contingency into destiny."

Maslow's concepts struck me as the most promising I had encountered in leadership studies, most of all because they offered an illuminating explanation of human change that could be linked closely to leadership. I had my own hopes and expectations—that psychologists and other scholars interested in leadership and impressed by Maslow would improve his ideas, and go further than I had in laying the basis for a full-blown explanation of the first and fundamental processes in the long chain of leadership. Aside from some modest testing and tinkering, however, this did not happen. Perhaps this was due to inadequacies in the concepts or to the challenges of verification, given the highly complex questions that would arise. More likely, I have concluded, follow-up failed because Maslow did not adequately recognize some fundamental assumptions that gravely influenced his ideas.

What assumptions? In political terms, that liberal democracy was the universal model of government, that protection of individual rights was the main, perhaps the only, test of that democracy, that most changes were brought about by individual ambition and striving, that the analytical spotlight should concentrate on the developing wants and needs of individuals.

Maslow's theory of actualization exemplified this ideology of individualism. It was *self*-actualization. Internal physical and psychological forces in persons propelled them to rise to the next higher stage in the hierarchy of needs. But what about the external, social forces—family, school, workplace—that also shaped the developing individual? And could the idea of *mutual* self-actualization—the transforming impact people have on one another—serve as the crucial dynamic in a leadership process that would advance great social, public values, above all the collective pursuit of happiness?

REAL NEED

For a short time during our children's development we as parents played an almost exclusive role in satisfying some of their growing wants, recognizing some of them as needs, and denying others. Gradually we had to yield our privileged position as the children went to school, made friends, learned about the world beyond the neighborhood, as they chose their own movies or television programs, eventually demonstrated for political causes and candidates we deplored.

Wants develop as children grow. They become more diverse, more complex, though no less compelling. As children are exposed to broadening circles of influence, the legitimation of wants as needs falls increasingly to teachers, peers, clergy, media, employers, government, and ultimately to society. Needs are social, and the conflicts over their legitimacy, their meaning, their extent, their satisfaction, take political form. More than anything else, wants and needs motivate leaders and followers to struggle for social change. They are the powerhouses of leadership.

Typically the conversion of wants into needs is a lifetime experience, because humans are never free of emerging wants that seek sanction as needs, or of social forces that regulate the process. Nor, it seems, of philosophers ready to define the wants that society ought to acknowledge as needs. The liberal-individualist tradition set fewer roadblocks and signposts to the legitimation of wants as needs because its very credo validated the right of humans to break through restrictions if necessary to realize their hopes and ambitions. But an alternative approach that cast a skeptical eye on the extent of human needs has an even older intellectual patrimony going back to the Stoics and Epicureans. Let us start with a more modern thinker, Jean-Jacques Rousseau.

The Geneva philosopher boldly confronted the crucial question: what are the human wants that ought to be recognized and satisfied? In contrast to the liberal focus on individual autonomy, Rousseau emphasized the social or communal nature of needs. He saw humans developing from an early primitive state with few, largely physiological wants, to a civilized society characterized by a plenitude of new needs. But here was the rub. The crass materialism of the mercantile society Rousseau saw growing around him in the mid-eighteenth century convinced him that most of these needs were artificial, unconnected to true wants, the products of a society that had made the proliferation and possession of *objects* its highest value. It was, he wrote, "the fewness of his needs" that made "a man really good," while the "multiplicity of needs" bred the "hateful and angry passions" that "spring from selfishness" and made reasoned and moral choice among needs impossible.

All this was intellectual fuel for a philosopher-activist of the next century, Karl Marx. In Marx's materialist theory of history, wants and needs powered the mechanisms of class struggle and social change. As primitive subsistence wants were satisfied, new needs emerged and in turn generated new forms of production and new class structures.

Yet Marx offered more than historical generalizations. He looked at nineteenth-century European life hard in the face and, like Rousseau, asked the fundamental question: what do human beings really need? As political scientist Patricia Springborg has noted, Marx distinguished "between 'fixed needs,' those found in all social formations whose form merely changes, and artificial needs, those which are entirely the product of a specific mode of production." Marx did not share Rousseau's disdain for materialism, but he saw capitalism as a machine for the production of distorted and debased needs, from the hypersophisticated needs of the rich to the "bestial barbarisation" of needs in the poor, an inequality of needs that reflected and reinforced the artificial inequalities in capitalist society and degraded all relationships among human beings.

Under capitalism, Marx wrote, every product was "a bait with which to seduce away the other's very being, his money; every real and possible need is a weakness which will lead the fly to the glue-pot," an "opportunity to approach one's neighbour under the guise of the utmost amiability and to say to him: Dear friend, I give you what you need but you know the *conditio sine qua non;* you know the ink in which you have to sign yourself over to me; in providing for your pleasure, I fleece you."

Still, Marx, unlike Rousseau, had a spacious view of *real* human wants. While his abiding concern was with industrial workers and their economic conditions, he saw them not as stick figures but as people with a wealth of real wants beyond the material—cultural, aesthetic, political, and even romantic. The satisfaction of material wants was the basic condition of human existence, but "the *rich* human being is simultaneously the human being *in need of* a totality of human manifestations of life—the man in whom his own realization exists as an inner necessity, as *need.*"

Both scholarship and political argument over true and false needs continued largely within the materialist parameters set by Marx for over half a century after the revolutionary philosopher's death in 1883, with even liberals and conservatives accepting those terms. But some scholars were dubious about the whole enterprise of distinguishing false from true needs. Could anyone besides the person experiencing the want that was the need's basis make such a judgment?—a question that brought the debate back a bit to the old liberal individualist position.

While the subjectivity of wants might make it difficult to distinguish conclusively between natural and artificial needs, the conflict over needs and the distribution of resources that satisfy them is fundamentally political. Rousseau and Marx, after all, were not only philosophers but advocates and activists whose analyses of needs were in the service of calls for transformational change, and the debate between individualist and social approaches to needs—and their implications for government—has a long history in Western politics. Increasingly, needs analysis is gaining force on a world scale, with the recognition that, as political scientists Roger A. Coate and Jerel A. Rosati concluded, the "deprivation of human needs has been a major source of social and political change around the globe."

Nothing offers so clear—and urgent—a challenge to leadership, nothing tests it so decisively, as human wants and needs. Leadership has its origins in the responsiveness of leaders to followers' wants, and in followers' responsiveness to leaders' articulation of needs, empowering both leaders and followers in the struggle for change.

Leaders express wants and needs most forcefully in the language of *values*. Wants-as-values both motivate and guide leaders and followers as they seek change and also serve as measures and authentications of outcomes. Though values embody wants, the two concepts are not interchangeable. While the satisfaction of many wants is to some extent at least quantifiable, how to judge the realization of such values as liberty? What if the pursuit of individual liberty threatens such real needs as the social stability that protects both individuals and the people as a whole? And what if the reigning values are framed and controlled by narrow elements in a society—say, an economic or military elite—reflecting their own interests rather than the real human wants of all the people?

Some of these questions assume an almost limitless potential for wants to be fulfilled. But in most societies wants are remorseless and resources are limited. Even recognized human needs, expressed in the loftiest values, wrote political scientist John W. Burton, "can be achieved or satisfied only to the extent that conditions allow: if not so satisfied they are required to be suppressed by self-control, by acceptance of law and custom and by moral obligation."

These conditional restraints reflect the larger struggle inherent in the competition of needs, described by Coate, Rosati, and David J. Carroll as the "conflicts between the institutional values and structures of society on the one hand, and human needs at the level of the individual on the other hand." As the arguments of philosophers attest, such conflicts will never disappear. They reflect the duality and tension in human beings between their individual and social natures. Leadership stands at the crossroads, broadening individual aspirations to embrace social change and building a society that responds to human wants, needs, and values.

EMPOWERING MOTIVES

Now we come to the intellectual dilemma that poses both crucial implications and complications for the analysis of change and leadership. The wants and needs of people—surging, soaring, tumultuous wants and needs—are the most powerful forces on earth. Humankind has to some degree learned to cope with hurricanes and floods, with wildly rampant wars and violence, with atomic and nuclear power. We humans have not learned how to control our day-to-day behavior and misbehavior in the face of mounting wants, hopes, and demands, because we have not learned how to analyze the turbulent processes involved.

The mystery centers on the real nature of motivational forces, how they move people, how they expand and change, and how leaders might summon, direct, and shape them for the protection and even benefit of people. Under close scrutiny, motives can appear opaque, convoluted, even incomprehensible—the psyche's equivalent to Tolstoy's ungraspably infinitesimal causes in history—but hopes for understanding them ran high by the mid-twentieth century. Freud and his followers had elaborated a theory of three drives—sexuality, aggression, ego—that they claimed determined much of human behavior, with particular emphasis on the pathologies that rose from the conflict among drives, or between them and the demands of society. A behaviorist tradition, pioneered by psychologists Edward L. Thorndike and later Clark Hull, dismissed mental states as unknowable and found the motivational key in a mechanistic stimulus-response process that could be objectively observed and measured. Behaviorists began with survival wants such as hunger and pain avoidance and, experimenting with starved kittens, thirsting chickens, and rats in electrified mazes, they concluded that motivation was the drive to reduce tensions induced by the stimulation of wants. Higher wants, more complex behaviors, learned drives all proceeded from the primary survival wants.

Most motivational theories were hierarchical, often based in stages of development. In 1950, psychoanalyst Erik Erikson offered a model of motivation that was for a time enormously influential. He described a sequence of conflicts that defined the life cycle—from the balance of trust and mistrust in infancy, to issues of identity and role confusion in adolescence, to, in old age, the tension between ego integrity and despair. Development depended on the resolution of each conflict as it appeared, optimally with the positive qualities achieving a favorable ratio over the negative. But for all its novelistic richness, Erikson's framework was too fixed in its stages and too intricately deterministic in its dynamics to account for human motivation across the broad range of experience, and particularly the complex processes of leadership. For that we turn again to the work of Abraham Maslow.

Few other motivational theories matched Maslow's in boldness and intellectual creativity. His theory had the virtues of clarity, economy, and flexibility, without sacrifice of comprehensiveness. Like the behaviorists,

Maslow began with survival wants, yet he saw the higher wants as more than the mere compounding of these lower-order motivations. People were *qualitatively* transformed as they proceeded up the hierarchy of wants, and this motivation for continual betterment was at the heart of Maslow's idea of human nature. Unlike the Freudians, Maslow was above all an optimist. Not only did he describe ultimate human potential in the most generous terms of self-actualization, he held that people were powerfully motivated to achieve that potential. A theorist of leadership found in Maslow's ideas an account of progressive change grounded squarely in the motivations of leaders and followers alike.

Yet the question remained: how generalizable—how universal—was Maslow's theory, or any other comprehensive developmental theory of motivation? Maslow was taken to task for his bias toward individualism, and other motivational schools were similarly criticized for parochialism, notably psychoanalysis with its origins in fin de siècle Vienna. There was little dispute that motivational forces—especially the higher needs—would experience enormous variations in diverse cultures. Was there no way to bring them into a single framework that would overcome the apparent Western bias in motivational theory?

The complexity of this task led scholars to put aside concepts of densely structured stages of motivation and development in favor of simpler levels of analysis involving loose clusters of inward-directed wants and motives centered on the "self," such as self-realization, self-determination, self-esteem.

This new approach demanded a more precise analysis of motives and their dynamics than had Maslow's broad and structured categories. In the analysis of change and leadership, motives of individuals are want-driven, situation-specific, goal-oriented. Innate wants encounter external forces that can promote or obstruct their satisfaction. The translation into *action* toward satisfying wants depends on the strength of motives, which in turn is influenced by the power of wants; on the expected probability of success in reaching intended goals; on the extent of resisting forces and the potential intensity of conflict. The desired end is a *change* by which wants are satisfied.

A vital element in this process is power—or perceived power—understood motivationally as the individual's control of both self and other. The effort to create change—the assertion of power—is directed both inward to the self, toward self-determination, self-esteem, and so on, and outward to the environment, including power over "fate" or intransigent institutions or irreconcilable oppositions.

Here perhaps is a missing link between inward- and outward-directed motivations, between "self" and situation in individual and collective processes of change: the capacity to produce a final result or effect. In a word, it is *efficacy*. "People strive to exercise control over events that affect their lives," psychologist Albert Bandura wrote in 1995. "By exerting influence in spheres over which they can command some control, they are better able to realize desired futures and to forestall undesired ones. . . . Inability to exert influence over things that adversely affect one's life breeds apprehension, apathy, or despair. The capability to produce valued outcomes and to prevent undesired ones, therefore, provides powerful incentives for the development and exercise of personal control."

Nothing strengthens the motivational power of efficacy like success. Persons with a high feeling of efficacy have great confidence in their ability to make changes, to remain committed to goals, to overcome difficulties and failures, to exercise control. Those with little conviction that they have the capacity to master their fate characteristically lack the motivation to try.

While psychologists of the self, especially Bandura, discussed the social or collective aspects of efficacy, the striking qualities of their analyses were *self*-knowledge, *self*-regulation, *self*-development, *self*-directed change. "An understanding of motivation and its connection to an individual's specifications requires an investigation of the self-relevant cognitive instigators of goal-directed behavior," according to researcher Nancy Cantor and her colleagues. Hence the primacy of the interest in individuals' personally significant goals, motives, hopes, and fears.

By isolating a single crucial and "universal" factor—the workings of the self—the self-concept approach strengthens the generalizability of motivational analysis. But its explanation of the contents and goals of behaviors that enhance the self-concept tends to circularity: they are whatever enhances an individual's self-concept.

To return again to the level of basic wants, the self-concept is at stake in their pursuit, but the self also is motivated by something *substantial*— the want of food, shelter, relief from pain—and any evaluation of outcomes must include not only the impact on the self-concept but also, and inseparably, the success or failure in achieving these wants, which means an actual change in the environment or situation. The "higher" wants, too—for security, love, belongingness, even self-actualization—bring real, quali-tative changes in the world when they are satisfied. And in leadership pro-cesses, the motivations of leaders and followers extend to both selves and purposes. Transforming change transforms people *and* their situations.

Yet leadership is a collective process, whose dynamic is more than the simple sum of individual motivations and efficacies. Writ large, moti-vation and efficacy are a function of political and social power, and hence have to be analyzed in collective terms. Writ larger, motivation and effi-cacy are the power of leadership that produces significant change.

The more we probe into the origins of leadership, the more we dis-cover the complex matrix among expanding wants and needs and the two-sided dynamics of motivation. The process is "vertical" as individuals are motivated to higher and higher levels of want and hope and ambition and demand. There is an equally important "horizontal" dimension as these spiraling motives of individuals interact, creating integrated structures of collective motivation.

What sets this intricate mobile of empowered motives into motion is the spark of creativity.

9

CREATIVE LEADERSHIP

The highest form of efficacy is creativity. This is both a most dramatic and a most puzzling human phenomenon. What causes it? We tend to seek answers in the lives and frustrations of geniuses. Albert Einstein is a classic case. Thrust into a harshly regimented school as a youth in Munich, he was so confounded by the formidable examinations that he turned away from an early interest in science. After months of distress he moved to Zurich with the hope of enrolling in the Polytechnic Institute there, only to fail the entrance examination. Later the brilliant physicist remained obscure until his radical theory of the nature of light received conclusive verification fourteen years after its publication.

This fate was nothing new in science. René Descartes set aside a treatise advancing a Copernican theory of planetary motion when he learned that Galileo had been condemned for his Copernicanism by the Vatican. Evariste Galois's pioneering work in modern algebra was shunned by the French Academy of Sciences, and he was killed in a duel at age twenty-one, before he had the opportunity to develop the revolutionary implications of his insights. Isaac Newton so feared rejection that he withheld many of his groundbreaking treatises from publication for decades, some even until his death.

Every creative artist and writer has had his or her own dining-out story of rejection and failure. Dostoyevsky complained of the "hellish agony" of writing a commissioned novel. Fretting about people who interrupted his work, Charles Dickens talked about the "penalties" of writing books. Even success had its sting. The Nobel Prize, T. S. Eliot worried after winning it in 1948, was "a ticket to one's funeral. No one has ever done anything after he got it." Good reviews seemed only to paralyze the novelist Thomas Wolfe. For ambitious poets Anne Sexton and Sylvia Plath, it was the impact of multiple constraints—from money problems, broken relationships, and depression to a male-dominated literary tradition.

Still, these and many other creative people produced transforming work. Why? Perhaps because institutional constraints under some circumstances develop into institutional supports in others. Einstein later enrolled in a Swiss "remedial" school that encouraged creative thought and student initiative. The harassed Dickens benefited from a burgeoning publishing industry and an avid and growing readership. The Nobel secured Eliot's leadership of the cultural establishment—a literary example of the revolutionary come to power—while Sexton and Plath became founding figures of a new countertradition.

Even more mysterious than the impact of institutions on creative individuals—and for our purposes, more important—is the reverse impact of creative persons on society. At its simplest, creative leadership begins when a person imagines a state of affairs not presently existing. This initial creative insight or spark is elaborated into a broader vision of change, possible ways of accomplishing it are conceived, and—in a fateful act of leadership—the vision is communicated to others. Because most ideas of significant change make some persons followers and others opponents, conflict arises. It is such conflicts that supply powerful motivation for transforming leadership and followership, fusing them into a dynamic force in pursuit of change.

Still, the indispensable spark is supplied by the imagination. Few have expressed this idea, and its moral possibilities, more eloquently than Robert F. Kennedy, borrowing from George Bernard Shaw: "Some people see things as they are and say: why? I dream things that never were and say: why not?"

LIBERATING IDEAS

No one is more arresting than the person who breaks through his confining environment, seizes opportunities, overcomes all obstacles, and changes how the rest of us perceive, think, and act. Consider the man who ranks as perhaps the supreme creative artist in the history of the West, Leonardo da Vinci. Though his ideas and accomplishments have been celebrated for five hundred years, they still astound. His great works of art—drawings and such paintings as *Mona Lisa* and *The Last Supper*—draw armies of visitors. But it is the sheer profusion and variety of all his work that is so dazzling.

Although no musician, Leonardo devised instruments and theatricals that were "the wonders of the courts of Milan and France," according to biographer Alessandro Vezzosi. Although not a professional soldier, he planned elaborate defensive fortifications and even sketched a crude submarine. Although not trained in architecture, he designed villas, arcades, churches, and citadels. He dreamed up a bridge 1,250 feet long to span Constantinople's Golden Horn. He made sketches of clocks, looms, "wind machines." Enamored of flight, he studied the action of birds to conceive a flying machine that flapped its wings. While he indulged in such fantasies as perpetual motion, his engineering plans alone would have made him famous.

One might assume that the artist, engrossed in such a myriad of projects, would have little chance or inclination to step back and glimpse the "larger picture." On the contrary, Leonardo thirsted for unity and synthesis. In map drawings he sought to combine the best knowledge of terrain with cosmology and the highest principles of aesthetics. He sought the underlying order in all he did, in ways of thinking about human anatomy, optics, mathematics, and about the ubiquity of change in nature that reflected his own mind's restlessness. He came nearest to achieving his dream of unity in sublime paintings that, art historian James Ackerman wrote, fused "empirical observation, mathematical order, and imagination," and even rose to the level of a natural philosophy in oils.

How to explain Leonardo's inexhaustible and prodigious creativity? He was born in a most artistically fertile region during the Renaissance in the fifteenth century. He grew up in a large, cosmopolitan, and nurturing family. He was mentored by leading teachers and artists of the day, most notably the painter and sculptor Andrea del Verrocchio. Throughout his life he mingled not only with artists but also with businessmen and statesmen; he offered military ideas to Cesare Borgia and perhaps even collaborated with Machiavelli.

Does all this throw much light on the origin of Leonardo's creativity? Many of his contemporaries shared similar backgrounds and advantages. If we can only speculate about the influence of his social milieu on Leonardo, however, we can grasp more surely his impact on the artistic and social world around him. "Leonardo's art," in art historian Andrew Butterfield's words, "is magical, superhuman, paradigmatic. Wherever he went—Florence, Milan, Rome, France—he changed the course of painting. By the middle of the sixteenth century, he was already regarded as a figure of epochal importance, a father of the High Renaissance" and without him, "the subsequent path of European painting would be inconceivable."

He was more than a change agent; he was a cultural revolutionary, a leader in the artistic and intellectual transformation sweeping Italy.

Leonardo's inventiveness and insight—and later Charles Darwin's conceptual breakthrough with the theory of evolution—testify to the huge role of creative leadership in producing artistic and scientific change. Mohandas Gandhi showed how creative leadership can produce real political and social change—within limits.

Both Gandhi's leadership and political strategy were forged in the racial cauldron of South Africa, where the young Brahmin had come from India in 1893 to practice law. In August 1906 the authorities decreed that all Indians, Arabs, and Turks must register with the government. Gandhi, who had for years been organizing the Indian community, called a mass meeting to protest the humiliation of fingerprinting and body checks. He first termed defiance of the new law "passive resistance," but disliked the phrase because it suggested a weapon of the weak. The "meaning of the struggle," he decided, was better expressed by a word he coined, *satyagraha*—the power "born of Truth and Love or non-violence." Gandhi's idea was to conquer hatred by love. He compared satyagraha to a "banyan tree with innumerable branches," including civil disobedience. Gandhi's invention of the concept of satyagraha was the distinctive act of his creative leadership, and it was to be the distinctive weapon of his protest leadership.

If satyagraha was the weapon, *swaraj* was the supreme goal. Swaraj literally meant self-rule, and in Gandhi's reformulation of the concept, it stood above all for freedom, both political and spiritual. While he accepted Western liberties of thought and speech, true freedom meant "disciplined rule from within." Swaraj fused independence from racial or colonial oppression with *inward* liberation, a transformation of both society and self; indeed, the "swaraj of a people," he said, was the "sum total" of the swaraj of individuals.

Like so many other resisters and revolutionaries, Gandhi deepened his ideas about moral ends and political means while practicing swaraj in a Pretoria prison, where he was jailed for civil disobedience. There he read Tolstoy, Emerson, and Thoreau, as well as the *Bhagavad-Gita* and the Bible.

Gandhi's leadership would meet its crucial test when he returned to India in 1915. He faced the enormous task of mobilizing millions of people divided by caste, religion, region, living in tens of thousands of villages. He confronted not only the British Raj but ideological rivals who were also appealing to the masses. The most notable of these was Communist leader M. N. Roy, a former terrorist who was calling for revolution in India and had only contempt for satyagraha and swaraj, which, he argued, would not empower the suffering people but emasculate them.

How could Gandhi lead the people of India when he had built his reputation in South Africa? For a year he analyzed his homeland's political and social problems. He knew that he would need to go beyond the call for independence from British rule, to offer a program to abolish untouchability, improve health in the cities and villages, advance the status of women. But he wanted people to look inward as well as outward, in the spirit of swaraj. For a real awakening, he said, their struggle must be personal as well as political.

Speechifying, he decided, would not be enough; it must be backed up by direct action. Suddenly an opportunity opened when indigo share-croppers in the northwest corner of Bihar asked him to look into their grievances with planters. Ignoring threats by the authorities to jail him, Gandhi drew up a long indictment of the planters and gained a good settlement for workers, then remained to launch a broad social reform program, building schools, improving medical care and sanitation, encouraging village industries. His successes in Bihar strengthened his claim to have found the path to freedom and dignity for suffering Indians. Continuing his nationwide mobilization campaign throughout the 1920s, he searched for the dramatic act that would spark Indian liberation.

Opportunity came again in 1930 when, after much deliberation, Gandhi resolved on a long march to the coast to gather salt from the shore in defiance of the government's monopoly on its collection. For decades, the British had not only monopolized this "greatest necessity of life" (after air and water), but had also levied a salt tax that especially burdened "the starving millions, the sick, the maimed and the utterly helpless." Salt was a powerful, inclusive symbol for a satyagraha campaign against British injustice, yet as the time approached many of his supporters in India and England warned him that the campaign was too risky, and that he probably would be imprisoned. But Gandhi kept steadily to his plans, convinced that the government would not act if his followers heeded his insistence on disciplined nonviolence. Then, for twenty-four days, across two hundred miles, Gandhi led his following, which grew as he went to thousands of women, children, and men. He closely regulated the "purity" of the march and brilliantly orchestrated press and newsreel coverage that made the campaign a worldwide sensation. His arrival at the sea was greeted with jubilation—except among Raj officials left sputtering with frustration.

The salt satyagraha was a colossal success, mobilizing millions of Indians behind Gandhi's leadership. The march had dramatized the political tactic of nonviolent direct action that would be emulated by many moral leaders and protesters around the world, not the least Martin Luther King, Jr.

Though nearly twenty more years of struggle would follow the salt march, the British never regained their balance, alternately negotiating with Gandhi and imprisoning him, until in 1947 Britain's Labour government acknowledged the inevitable: Indian independence. Yet freedom brought its own catastrophe. In their hasty withdrawal, the British divided the colony into two nations, Hindu-dominated India and Muslim-dominated Pakistan, and the partition caused tens of thousands of deaths in sectarian warfare and millions of refugees. Gandhi continued to preach satyagraha and swaraj and—having developed fasting, or the threat of it, into a fine political tactic—vowed to fast until "sanity returns to Calcutta." His fast brought Calcuttan Hindu and Muslim leaders quickly together to promise that "we shall never allow communal strife in the city." A fast in Delhi a few months later, in January 1948, was equally successful in bringing peace there. Gandhi's steadfast belief in nonviolence in the face of such intense and bloody conflict as India experienced after partition made all the more shocking his assassination that same month by a fanatical Hindu.

Many view Gandhi as the greatest moral leader of the twentieth century as well as a brilliant tactician, and both these qualities flowed from his extraordinary political creativity. The new thinking that led to satyagraha and swaraj had its deepest roots in his own experiences, especially his encounters with racist power in South Africa, which appeared to him to reflect both a moral and a political crisis. And his creative leadership, as it evolved there and in India, proved both deeply principled and shrewd strategically.

Identifying Indian independence with the need for inward independence of the individual, Gandhi sought to teach and transform people who in turn would join him in the collective, national struggle; and the strength of his cause, which ultimately trumped the vast material—but feeble moral—resources of the British, was in his followers' unshakable inner discipline and devotion to Gandhi's transforming concept of nonviolent direct action.

THE SPRINGS OF CREATIVITY

The lives of extraordinarily creative persons do not in themselves explain the complex processes of change and leadership. But they raise the right questions. Where does genius originate? Is creativity above all an individual or a social phenomenon? What is its relationship to its cultural context? And most important, what is its relationship to everyday change and to transforming leadership?

Is it not remarkable that for millennia the finest creative minds have been struggling to answer such questions—genius trying to understand genius? Early on people thought that all creative ideas or acts came from the gods. For the Greeks, the Muses were intermediaries, bringing a divine spark into the human mind. But Aristotle argued that creative insights had their origin in the mind itself, in its powers of association and combination. Speculation on creativity's sources advanced little until the Romantic era and its fascination with individual genius and the mysteries of imagination. Soon a new science claimed to have found the key: the propensity for creativity lay in the genes.

Biology continued to spin off theories of creativity during the twentieth century. Some biologists have held that it is generated from "the inherent creativeness of life," impelled by similar needs and purposes. All nature, wrote Yale botanist Edmund W. Sinnott, is "anticonservative, original, creative"; it "brings forth biological novelties—new forms, types, and patterns hitherto unknown on earth and (still more important) holding promise of greater changes yet to come"; and in the human brain, with its "unthinkable complexity," the "possibilities of new mental patterns are almost infinite."

Yet where was the link between fundamental evolutionary forces and the resulting creative process of the mind? Apart from innate drives, how can we understand "the richness and variety of mental life"? What role did environmental factors play? One further step toward comprehensive ex-planation was taken in the 1990s by scholars advancing—hold tight—a "biopsychosocial" approach. "Biological elements range from the role our genes play in our development to adult health issues," psychologists John S. Dacey and Kathleen H. Lennon explained. "Psychological elements include all aspects of cognitive and personality development. Social ele-ments involve such influences as family, school, peers, and culture." Was biopsychosocialism the wave of the future?

Most analysts of creativity today agree that genius is indeed a prod-uct of interacting forces—the biological and psychological, or "internal," and the social psychological and sociological, or "external." The crucial and intimidating question is which of these variables are on the whole more dominant.

In early explanations, the emphasis was on individual creativity pro-duced by some inner quality. This individualist approach looked, first of all, to heredity. Typical is the investigation of families that produce gen-erations of people of high achievement. In America, this has led to elabo-rate studies of such political dynasties as the Adamses, the Roosevelts, and the Kennedys. But the studies stumbled on the difficulty of sorting out the contribution of genetic inheritance, compared with the inheritance of fam-ily wealth, power, connections, traditions, and expectations.

Aiding and abetting the individualistic approach were the famous psy-choanalysts of the early twentieth century, who tied creativity to dysfunc-tion and were themselves often the subject of studies of greatness. Sigmund Freud supposed that the creative imagination was an escape from reality driven by "excessively powerful instinctual needs" and unsatisfied desires "to win honour, power, wealth, fame and the love of women." Otto Rank, a student of Freud, argued that creativity was raw self-assertion, a rejection of dumb conformity and neurotic dependence. By contrast, Alfred Adler developed the concept of a "creative self," with the individual as "the artist of his own personality," compensating for feelings of inferiority and inad-equacy by practicing an "active constructive," socially useful style of life.

Abraham Maslow placed creativity at the core of psychic and spiri-tual health, crucial to the fulfillment of human potential. His ideal of self-actualization presupposed a well-developed ability to adapt creatively to change and to improvise with confidence and courage in the face of unex-pected challenges—crucial attributes of leadership. Maslow believed that creativeness was a "fundamental characteristic of common human nature—

a potentiality given to all human beings at birth," but that most lost it as they became "enculturated," inhibited by pressures to conform.

In an era of expanding capitalism, Horatio Alger, Jr., exemplified the individualist ethos in such writings as *Pluck Makes Luck*. Never mind that luck makes pluck, too—the luck, for instance, of being born into a wealthy and influential family. Indeed the emphasis on the feats of aspirants to fame and success became part of an ideology of individualism that left creativity under a political and academic cloud, viewed as elitist in outcome if not intention.

The criticism was telling. It rested on the commonsense view that creativity was not identical with genius. It welled up among the people— the tinkerer in the basement or out in the garage, the inventor "fooling around" after hours in a shop, the kids producing a backyard play, the "dabblers" in music and writing and art. But this "leveling" of creativity would shift the inquiry away from exceptional individuals to the social conditions that made for an inventive and resourceful *people* willing to challenge established ideas and practices.

The central implication of individual creativity lies not in its origin, interesting and challenging as the explanations are. It lies in the impact of creativity back *on* society. The primary importance of an individualist approach to creativity, in short, may be in its contributions to a better understanding of the role of creative leadership in the collective process of transformational social change.

GOLDEN AGES

Scholars of creativity have long noted that civilizations have had their "golden ages," an outpouring of innovations in literature, science, art, political statesmanship that seemed to emerge simultaneously from nowhere. Athens's Periclean Age is the paradigmatic example, leading the Roman scholar Velleius Paterculus to observe that creativity, fostered by emulation, flourished in short stretches of time. Ancient Sumerian and Chinese cultures experienced golden ages, as did Rome in the time of Cicero and Augustus, Mughal India in the sixteenth and seventeenth centuries, and Italy during the Renaissance.

Even more extraordinary was the global reach of some of these creative epochs. Consider the six decades from the 1770s to the 1830s. In that time, as we have seen, Americans conducted a revolution, fashioned a new political system, passed a Bill of Rights, and established a democratized party system. The caliber of American leadership of the founding era has never been equaled, or even approached, in the following two centuries. Meanwhile, the French launched a revolution that overthrew the monarchy, passed through a dizzying series of phases and leaderships, and ended in the establishment of a new empire under Napoleon. And Britain began to develop a modern system of political parties, took first steps toward democracy with the Reform Bill of 1832, and, in addition, incubated poets of dazzling artistry and even political influence. Towering German poets, philosophers, and composers defined the spirit of Romanticism. In that era, the creators in politics, the arts, the sciences, and the social sciences acted as an international collective leadership, as their ideas and influence radiated into other parts of the world.

What causes such eruptions of creativity? Perhaps when we try to account for cultures that engender creativity, the emphasis ought to be on the word *culture*—the cross-fertilization in a given place and time of individuals and their turns of mind and ambitions, of developments in education and knowledge techniques, of new ideas or the gropings toward new ideas. Even more important is the interaction of creative people, and the opportunities for interaction—within and among families, at schools and in workplaces, in political and scientific and artistic groups and professional associations, and across entire societies. There are leaders and there are followers, and there are followers who become leaders. Newton wrote that, if he had seen farther, it was "by standing on the sholders of Giants." In epochs of collective creative ferment, the uplift is mutual.

At such times, wrote William James, the whole community started "vibrating." "Blow must follow blow so fast that no cooling can occur in the intervals. Then the mass of the nation grows incandescent, and may continue to glow by pure inertia long after the originators of its internal movement have passed away." Leadership interactions reach a catalytic pitch that generates a momentum of its own, producing such transformations as paradigm shifts in science or innovative movements in the arts or revolutionary reconceptualizations of social and political problems—new ways of looking, thinking, understanding.

Such communities mix collegiality and collaboration with competition and combat. Conflict is crucial to creativity, as when new insights are tested and refined in the struggle to dislodge habitual patterns of thought.

The status quo, the old guard—in politics and society, as well as in the arts, sciences, social sciences—will fight to maintain its dominance, forcing reformers and revolutionaries to marshal all the resources of their creativity, to deepen and extend and sharpen the new thinking. Through these exchanges and conflicts, they learn to act like leaders.

If the old "nature versus nurture" issue can be decided mainly in favor of nurture, the early lives of great leaders need all the more scrutiny. This field of study consists more of impressions and anecdotes than of solid empirical data. Many are the stories of geniuses who were raised in supportive households, finding both intellectual stimulation and parental discipline at home. In some cases, though, parents were more demanding than supportive, and even tyrannical. Yet stress and estrangement seem able to produce, or at least not suppress, creativity. One study found that "75 percent of a group of 400 eminent historical figures had been troubled—by broken homes, rejecting, overpossessive, estranged or dominating parents" and that 85 percent of 400 noted people of the twentieth century—novelists, playwrights, artists, scientists—had come from markedly troubled homes. Other studies suggested that parents of creative scientists had shown their children relatively little warmth or affection. It was an old story. Johannes Kepler pictured his father as "vicious, inflexible, quarrelsome, and doomed to a bad end." And a new one: "Hatred of one parent or another," wrote Gore Vidal of a fellow novelist with the "bad luck" of having come from a happy family, "can make an Ivan the Terrible or a Hemingway," but the protective love of two devoted parents "can absolutely destroy an artist."

If early home life is a poor predictor of creativity, could formal education serve as a better guide? This would assume there *was* an education—Thomas Edison and Michael Faraday both left school at about the age of fourteen, and some geniuses never attended school at all but were taught at home.

"Schools suppress creativity," Dacey and Lennon assert bluntly, a conclusion that brings a teacher up short. They contend that after children have attended school for a while, "most become more cautious and less innovative." Teachers simply lack the time or skill or patience or desire, or the freedom within the formal environment of the classroom, to encourage students to experiment or create.

What can schools do to encourage creativity? They must begin by harnessing the potential of teachers as transforming leaders in the classroom. Empowering teachers with the proper training, resources, and encouragement would give them the opportunity to give their students the opportunity to think and to act creatively. Creative leaders, in short, would foster creative students. These students would go on to their own mentoring roles.

British physicists Ernest Rutherford and J. J. Thompson between them trained seventeen Nobel laureates, who in turn trained many more scientists. Of course the laureates could be dismissed as mere role models. But what models!

Times of revolutionary change create new cultures of creativity, where leaders become followers of the turning tide, and followers become leaders. The Bolshevik seizure of power ushered in a brief "golden age" of theater when great directors like Vsevolod Meyerhold created brilliant and innovative productions and plays were staged in village halls, prison chapels, factories—even Red Square, where the celebration of the Bolshevik Revolution's ninth anniversary in 1926 became a theater without walls, a "drama of remembrance" and "prophecy of the future." As the great watching crowds along the parade route dissolved, wrote Hallie Flanagan, an American observer, "spectators become actors and march along with their comrades." Attending a lover's quarrel that turned into a slugfest at Moscow's Revolutionary Theatre, Flanagan imagined that any of the audience of enraptured workers might "leap upon the stage and take a part. It is their theatre," speaking to their lives, their hopes, needs, and fears, the drama "forged from a belief which audience and actor shared." Within a decade, such transforming theater, always vulnerable, had succumbed to Stalinist orthodoxy and repression.

Across the Atlantic, hundreds of theaters had succumbed to a capitalist depression. When Franklin Roosevelt established the Works Progress Administration in 1935, he chose as its head Harry Hopkins, who knew that actors, too, needed work. He created the Federal Theatre Project under the same Hallie Flanagan, an innovative director and teacher at Vassar College. Soon she was enlisting thousands of demoralized and dispersed show people in a national effort "equal to the gigantic task of bringing to people across America" theater that was "free, adult, uncensored." To celebrate the teeming diversity of the land, she sponsored everything from classical and modern drama to vaudeville, religious pageants, children's theater, and even circuses.

Flanagan believed that drama could "influence human thought and lead to human action" and fiercely defended its right—even obligation—to give "apoplexy" to the powerful, though she insisted that the FTP not become a tool for any political party. But the FTP ran into congressional opponents who feared that its performances might "radicalize" their constituents. And with good reason. *Triple-A Plowed Under,* playing to packed and enthusiastic houses, depicted farmers and consumers uniting against the middlemen who fleeced them both. *One-Third of a Nation,* echoing FDR's striking evocation in 1937 of those Americans who were "ill-housed, ill-clad, ill-nourished," touched off a cry of moral indignation against slumlords and helped bring passage of a new housing law, exhibiting just the sort of transforming political power the FTP's conservative foes feared.

In 1965, when Luis Valdez, a son of migrant workers and a theater activist, learned of Cesar Chavez's campaign to unionize farm workers in the vineyards of Delano, California, he began to imagine the possibilities of theater as a consciousness-raising tool. With Chavez's support, Valdez searched through the picket lines to assemble his troupe. Gathering them at the United Farm Workers office, he tried to explain what political theater was about but sensed he was not getting through. Then he scribbled *huelguista* (striker) and *esquirol* (scab) on sheets of paper and hung them around the necks of two workers. Everyone knew that story. An improvisation began, and the *Teatro Campesino* was born.

Valdez and his group had a specific message: "Join the union." Their skits, loaded with slapstick and metaphor, entertained as well as enlightened. Audiences trusted the actors as members of their own community and were receptive, said Valdez, to their calls for transformation, not only "the mass struggle of La Raza in the fields and barrios" but "in the very corazón of our people."

Augusto Boal, Brazilian director and activist, had an even broader vision of the theater's transformational potential for liberating the oppressed. Boal was convinced that dictatorship could be challenged by new theatrical tools, and in the 1960s, when Brazil suffered two military coups, he began to develop his "Theatre of the Oppressed." Defining oppression as a power dynamic based on monologue rather than dialogue, his goal was to inject a second voice—the voice of the people—that would open the system to question and challenge.

At one performance of an agitprop play in northern Brazil, peasants became so aroused by the action that they wanted Boal and his troupe to lead them in overthrowing the government. Boal had to explain that he was an actor and the weapons only props. But the incident gave him the idea for a theater in which participants enacted their own stories, investigated the root of a problem, and acted to solve it according to principles of social justice. As scenes unfolded, audience members were invited to stop or redirect the action if they had a solution to offer, thus rehearsing for real social change.

Imprisoned and exiled in 1971, Boal refined and extended his technique in Argentina and France. Fifteen years later, he was asked back to Brazil to work with the impoverished. In 1992 he was elected to the legislature on a mandate that proposed democratization of the political process through theater. After three decades of making "political theatre," he was now making "theatre as politics," with the possibility of "creating and transforming laws." And instead of people going to the theater to escape their problems, theater was coming to them, liberating their minds and empowering them to make change.

Boal shaped his ideas on a powerful intellectual forge. He identified two perspectives in popular theater. One—the perspective of the bosses—sought to demonstrate that the present system was "the best of all possible worlds" in which "the masters have gained possession of the land, the means of production, while the workers work with God's consent."

Opposed to this was the "transformation-oriented perspective of the people," which, Boal wrote, "reveals a world in permanent transformation," showing that "men enslaved by work, by habits and traditions, can change their situation." Performed before workers at union meetings or in the streets, transformational theater could address urgent problems of the moment—explaining, enlightening, enlisting—or it might deal with broader, timeless human problems of justice and freedom "in a concrete and sensory manner" that would "reach the consciousness of the masses." Nothing, Boal emphasized, could be excluded from the democratic space where the "desire for change" was stimulated and experienced. "All human life is relevant to the people."

THE TRANSFORMING VISION

On the face of it, nothing is more mysterious than the sources of creative ideas, unless it is the linkage between those ideas and the process of leadership. In that process, creativity appears as a response to frustrated wants and needs. But if frustration is the spur, its resolution takes many forms. The potential for creativity may be crushed from the start because of despotic parents, powerful pressures for conformity and harmony, religious or ideological fervor that bars independent thinking. Or creative thinking may be nurtured among sympathetic friends and colleagues who, however, weaken or flatten out its force and novelty, whether because of constraints on their own vision or in order to win wider acceptance of new ideas.

Creativity also breaks through restraints, most transformationally, perhaps, in those bursts of inspiration so contrary to conventional thinking that they seem to come from nowhere. Such innovative uncommon sense transcends routine problem solving to address the deep human needs and crises from which it emerges.

Crisis is the prime source of transforming creativity, as when familiar meanings become exhausted or debased or inadequate to account for severe changes or threats of change. Or meanings may have become the preserve of a subgroup or elite who wield them to exclude alternatives that might challenge their dominance. In conditions of what political scientist Peter C. Sederberg has called "explanatory collapse," real, growing wants are ignored or delegitimated, defined out of existence. Values such as liberty and equality are proclaimed while people are neither free nor equal. Forms of justice cloak arbitrary power. Creative leadership in the American Revolution, for example, was spurred by the yawning divide between the professed values of the ruling British—representation in government, say—and their actual treatment of the colonials.

Transformational creativity can flourish amid such tensions. Innovative political theorists, wrote political scientist Sheldon Wolin, were motivated "by a profound belief that the world had become deranged," affording "an opportunity for a theory to reorder" it. Conventional restraints are loosened as new explanations are sought. The unthinkable becomes thinkable, perhaps even imperative.

Sensitivity to deep conflict between accepted meanings and actualities—and frustration at the inability to reconcile the two—is creativity's precondition. Cognitive dissonance, as social psychologist Leon Festinger found, is a "motivating state" for change. It produces a powerful need to reduce or to eliminate doubt, perplexity, contradiction, incongruity, and other conceptual conflicts through a search for new explanations. Or, as the Czech playwright and, later, president Václav Havel described his struggles as a dissident against a regime of topsy-turvy values, "The deeper the experience of an absence of meaning—in other words, of absurdity— the more energetically meaning is sought."

As the creative mind breaks down the "institutionalization of hypocrisy," sociologist Kenneth Keniston wrote in a study of the American New Left and hippies, "the universal gap between principle and practice appears in all of its nakedness." This recognition is only a beginning. Creative leadership is more than a critique. The "decomposition" of old meanings opens "new spaces and new prospects for action" where the creative mind can roam to find fresh and vital answers to basic questions amid complexity, conflict, and change. The creative insight is, in short, transforming. It might raise a fundamental challenge to an existing paradigm or system, calling for its overthrow and replacement, or it might call for a deep restructuring, or the inclusion of significant excluded elements, or perhaps a revitalization, a new birth of "founding principles."

So the spark of creative leadership is both destructive and constructive, through a process that analysts of collective action call "framing work." The frame refers to a value-laden "condensation" of the meanings and assumptions that underlie our sense both of society and of our own place in it. A frame is what we take for granted as we interpret the way things are, as though it were God-given or natural or at least beyond our own making— until we are given strong reason to question it. Creative leadership, then, "re-frames" meanings to close the gap between ideas and actualities.

Creative leadership re-frames values above all, as the highest-order and most potentially transformational "condensations" of our sense of the world and ourselves. Its critique of the gap between wants or values and actualities involves moral judgment, while its remedy—its vision of what might be—is grounded in the fulfillment of a moral purpose, in bringing values to life, and its achievement is measured, finally, by the same standards it has used to condemn the old regime: fulfillment of the principles it professes.

Re-framing means the transformation of values. Thomas Rochon has outlined three ways of values-change: "value conversion," where the "new valuations" of what is important, just, or legitimate "contradict and replace the old"; "value connection," meaning the creation of a "conceptual link between phenomena previously thought to be unconnected"; and "value creation," as with the emergence of "conservation" as a new value during Theodore Roosevelt's presidency. Social movement scholar Sidney Tarrow points out that new meanings are not "fabricated out of whole cloth," but blend "inherited and invented fibers" to create a new frame. But all transforming values, new or old, are deeply and freshly dyed in fundamental human wants.

The *philosophes* of the Enlightenment gave new meaning to "equality," at once condemning the institutional inequalities of the ancien régime and opening vast new possibilities for change. The French revolutionaries elevated "fraternity" to the status of a supreme value, thus transforming the meaning of community and nation. "Happiness" apart, perhaps, the American revolutionaries did not innovate values so much as they revitalized those that were their inheritance, infusing with fresh power the transforming civic values the British had tarnished and overturned.

For creativity to become leadership, however, conceptual transformation is not enough. As scientists must go beyond "revolutions on paper" and put their ideas to the test in a struggle to win acceptance by their peers, all the more so must creative leadership. Leadership is a social phenomenon, and leaders are "intimately tied to other people and the effects of their actions on them." According to Wolin, the groundbreaking political theorists were motivated by "the ideal of an order subject to human control and one that could be transfigured through a combination of thought and action." They intended "not simply to alter the way men look at the world, but to alter the world." Plato, Machiavelli, Hobbes, Marx—all considered their new ideas to be guides to healing their sick societies. They meant to *lead*.

So the ultimate test of creative leadership lies not only in having a new idea but in bringing it to life, accomplishing the real-world change it promises. To do so, the would-be leader must reach out to others for help. But would-be followers will respond only if the new frame articulated by creative leadership speaks directly to them, to their underlying wants, discontents, and hopes. They, too, as Sederberg noted, must "experience something of an explanatory collapse." They, too, must know the "aha!" moment of realization, grasp the urgency of the need for change, see its possibility, and envision its direction. They are transformed in a way closely parallel to the earlier experience of the emergent leader. But transforming leadership mobilizes only those who are, if latently, ready to be mobilized, and then only if the frame is true to their wants.

The "truth" of a transforming frame is in its potency, its ability to strike a deep chord. A resonant frame can liberate a person from the isolation of frustrated, unacknowledged wants, into the realm of new and shared meanings, to become a "reflective participant" in what creativity scholar Robert Paul Weiner described as a collective effort to shape and reshape those meanings "as they grow and change through the interaction of the participants and in the crucible of theory and praxis."

At their best, creative thought and action engender, for leaders and followers together, the conviction that the reality of their situation is not, in the words of the great Brazilian educator and theorist of liberation Paulo Freire, "a closed world from which there is no exit," but "a limiting situation which they can transform," a mobilizing and empowering faith in the collaborative struggle for real change.

10

THE LEADER-FOLLOWER
PARADOX

Nothing carries more cosmic weight—nor more earthly ambiguity—than invoking "the People." The words "We the People" begin the American Constitution. The Declaration of Independence proclaims that "whenever any Form of Government becomes destructive" of "certain unalienable Rights," it is "the Right of the People to alter or to abolish it." Abraham Lincoln asked that government of, by, and for the people not perish from the earth. In courtrooms, prosecutors charge suspects in the name of "the people."

But we all know the hard truth. There is no set entity called the people. Nations' inhabitants are divided by gender, age, class, locality, income, education, cultural outlook, national origin, religion, ideology. The latent causes of faction are "sown in the nature of man," James Madison wrote in *Federalist* No. 10. Parties and factions dance together in their variations of the Virginia reel, meeting and separating in changing formations. Conflict among peoples is not only accepted as inevitable but viewed as essential to the process of change.

Students of leadership have their own way of analyzing concord and conflict. They divide people into leaders and followers. On leaders we have a mountain of evidence—biographies, memoirs, letters, archival sources—"thousands of books," as Garry Wills wrote, but "none on followership. I have heard college presidents tell their students that schools are meant to train leaders. I have never heard anyone profess to train followers. The ideal seems to be a world in which everyone is a leader—but who would be left for them to be leading?" So let's look at followers.

FOLLOWERS AS LEADERS

The relationship seems so simple at first glance: leaders lead, followers follow. Leaders dream the dream, take the initiative, connect with followers, start the action. Followers hear the call, share the dream, respond to the initiative. But on further reflection problems arise.

Does the potential follower even *hear* the leader? Nothing is more common in politics than the unheeded voice. This is true in business as well. New products are invented, touted, and fall flat. Washing machines are promoted in a developing country, but overworked women might still prefer to wash their clothes with neighbors down at the river. Businessmen conduct surveys, politicians run election polls, but the minds of potential followers can remain mysterious, hence business bankruptcies and failed candidacies. Something must happen to spark people, transform them into followers. Yet the triggering act—a speech or manifesto or demonstration—is influenced by some estimate of the followers' likely response. Even at the very first stage of the leader-follower relation—even before they join together—followers may lead and leaders follow.

A further complication is that people play different roles in different contexts. The business tycoon may meekly follow her husband's decisions about house and home, the quiet bureaucrat may turn into a dynamo in a street protest, the politician may be a transforming leader in oratory but submit to transactional leadership in negotiations. Even where rigid hierarchies exist—as in the military, with the private following the sergeant who follows the lieutenant and so on up to the general—the relationships may be reversed in the heat of battle.

All this poses the Burns Paradox—a designation that would be immodest but for its being not a solution or formula but a problem. If leadership and followership are so intertwined and fluid, how do we distinguish conceptually between leaders and followers? With which do we even start? It seems natural to start with the leader. For three decades, though, the psychologist E. P. Hollander had been urging heightened focus on followers, on the dependence of leaders on followers' perceptions and expectations and potentials. "All initiatives need not come from the leader," he noted. "Followers also have the potential for making significant contributions to successful leadership," and in turn, "leaders are called upon to be responsive also as followers." Political scientist Charles C. Euchner pointed to "the need for enlightened and engaged followers as well as leaders." Passive followers, he added, "make leadership difficult"—impossible, I would suggest.

The resolution of the paradox lies initially, I believe, in the distinction between persons with unrealized wants, unexpressed attitudes, and underlying predispositions, on the one hand, and, on the other, persons with strong motivations to initiate an action relevant to those with such wants. The key distinctive role of leadership at the outset is that leaders take the initiative. They address their creative insights to potential followers, seize their attention, spark further interaction. The first act is decisive because it breaks up a static situation and establishes a relationship. It is, in every sense, a *creative* act.

Is this the only role, the unique role, of the leader—simply that of initiator? It depends on the situation. If an orator ignites a mob that then takes over the streets, and if a rebellion follows that leads to a revolution and the creation of a new regime, it is the followers who have taken over, but without the speaker nothing might have happened, even though he could not have predicted or controlled—or perhaps even desired—the series of actions that followed. New leadership may emerge, perhaps from among the followers, better suited to the demands of the changing situation and the developing expectations of followers. Yet as Hollander contends, the role of the followers—their picking up the cues of leaders, the quality of their response, their continued pressure on leaders—remains crucial at every stage of the change process. Leaders may become merely enhancers in the continuing evolution of followers.

Some may wonder why so much is made of just where leadership and followership begin and end. But this question lies at the heart of the core issue—the relationship of leadership and followership not only to each other but to social change and historical causation. Franklin D. Roosevelt's first term illustrates the importance and complexity of this linkage.

The 1930s witnessed a momentous change of national leadership in the United States from Hoover Republicans to Roosevelt Democrats. What caused this? Was it the normal seesaw of politics after twelve Republican years? The emergence of an unusually skillful leader or collective leadership? The Depression that gripped America? Or the culmination of deep-running social and economic changes?

Historians usually begin the story of the New Deal with Franklin Roosevelt's emergency actions of the first "Hundred Days" of his presidency in 1933. But who put FDR into the White House so that he could take this leadership? Almost 23 million voters who rejected Hoover's warning that "the grass will grow in streets of a hundred cities" if the Democrats should win. They also gave the Democrats majority control of both houses of Congress. This transition was not ordained by fate. Almost 16 million voters stuck with Hoover. But millions of others broke with old party loyalties to follow Roosevelt.

The new president's rapid-fire initiatives during the "Hundred Days" from March to June 1933 presented FDR as a bold man of action but obscured the reality that his proposals to Congress were a mixed bag of liberal, conservative, and emergency laws that would not break the country out of mass unemployment and deprivation.

The New Deal set off a tidal wave of hope and expectation, a surge of followership, that turned sour as recovery faltered. The first to experience the effect of the "honeymoon," and the first to feel let down, was organized, unorganized, and disorganized labor. The National Industrial Recovery Act with its Section 7(a) provision for the right to organize gave tremendous impetus to industrial unions, as labor leaders exploited the federal government's new backing of unionization. "President Roosevelt wants *you* to join the union," proclaimed posters that United Mine Workers leader John L. Lewis plastered across coal country.

Lewis, with his shock of hair, pugnacious face, and growling oratory, symbolized labor at its most militant, never hesitating to pit his leadership against the president's. Yet he and other union chiefs were in turn followers of workers who took leadership on their own and spearheaded a rash of strikes across the country: shipyard mechanics in New Jersey, streetcar men in Milwaukee, copper miners in Butte, fruit pickers in California, grocery clerks, journalists, lumberjacks, teamsters. Soon the demands of the burgeoning labor unions on employers and the government were far outrunning FDR's leadership agenda.

Protest was building on the farms as well as in the factories. The passage of the Agricultural Adjustment Act, designed to restore farmers' earning power by cutting production, raised their hopes more than their income. Discontent in the farm states boosted the ambitions of such pro-gressive leaders as Senator Robert La Follette, Jr., in Wisconsin, who broke away from the GOP and began a skittish relationship with the president. Minnesota Farm-Laborites followed their separate ways from Minnesota Democrats. Nationally, the radical Farmers' Union denounced "scarcity economics" and pointed out that "what we have overproduction of is empty stomachs and bare backs."

Everywhere, it seemed, new grassroots leaders were rising in the land, stimulated by the New Deal yet often turning against it to build their own followings. None could rival an ungainly trio, as diverse in their agendas as they were united in their growing hatred of the president: Huey P. Long, Father Charles Coughlin, and Dr. Francis Townsend.

Exploiting massive poverty and discontent, Huey Long had become the political boss of Louisiana. As a senator, the Kingfish was winning national attention through his potshots at stuffed shirts, his antics in res-taurants, but above all his simple platform, Share Our Wealth. On this issue he was in deadly earnest. Having supported FDR at the 1932 Demo-cratic convention, he drew on that political debt to arrange meetings with the president that strengthened Long's standing as a national leader—and potential rival to Roosevelt. He freely offered FDR advice, but he wouldn't be "working fer him," he insisted. "I ain't goin' to."

Nothing could better demonstrate Long's mass appeal than the re-sponse to his talks on the NBC radio network. "After an average broad-cast," according to historian Alan Brinkley, "Long would receive up to 60,000 letters through the network and more than that through his own Senate office." Sixteen thousand people turned out in Philadelphia to hear him denounce FDR; when faculty opposition at the University of South Carolina thwarted a speech there, Long simply moved to the grounds of the statehouse and spoke to thousands.

Even more phenomenal was the response to Coughlin's radio pro-gram. A Catholic priest in Depression-racked Detroit, he had begun as an ardent supporter of the president—"Roosevelt or Ruin!"—but when FDR spurned his advice on banking and monetary policy, Coughlin became an equally ardent—and quite formidable—foe. With a rich speaking voice that could hit every register, access to a CBS network that could reach a radio audience of 40 million, and a demagogic message dripping with hatred for "plutocrats," communists, and Roosevelt, Coughlin sometimes received a million letters a week, many with cash or a postal money order enclosed. When Coughlin set off on speaking tours, police had to be ready to cope with blocked traffic and thousands of followers desperately trying to get into packed halls.

The third member of the trio stood in sharp contrast. Dr. Townsend was a gaunt, white-haired California physician who, almost destitute himself, had been appalled by the sight of elderly persons rummaging in garbage cans near his Long Beach home. He conceived the Townsend Old Age Revolving Pension Plan, which would provide everyone over sixty with a sizable monthly pension, on the delicious condition that they quickly spend it, to give the economy a boost. A host of Townsend Clubs emerged in California and quickly spread eastward. By 1935 there were nearly half a million dues-paying Townsendites, capable of unleashing a torrent of mail on Washington.

By 1935 all three protesters realized that speaking tours and mailing lists were not enough; they must organize nationally. There was even talk of their movements merging into a single mighty political organization. While the leaders hardly knew one another and had different agendas, on the broadest values they were united: fairness, justice, sharing the wealth.

LEADERS AS FOLLOWERS

In late winter 1935 Roosevelt's leadership appeared to be waning, pundits agreed. "Once more," according to the magisterial columnist Walter Lippmann, "we have come to a period of discouragement after a few months of buoyant hope." In his State of the Union address in January 1935, FDR had called for "a genuine period of good feeling, sustained by a sense of purposeful progress," but the state of the nation was not good. Millions were still unemployed despite the flurry of New Deal initiatives. It was the sixth year of the Depression. And now the president faced potent rivals for leadership in Long and Coughlin and the rest.

Roosevelt was puzzled. He had tried to steer a middle way, between right and left, to assist business recovery while providing billions of dollars for relief of the poor and the jobless. He had helped boost his party's numbers in Congress in 1934, defying the old rule that presidents' parties lose seats in midterm elections, but now Congress was moving further left than he wished to go. After his early flirtation with conservatives, they too were turning against him. Attacks from "populists" like Long were intensifying. Worse, they were organizing against him at the grass roots and in the city streets.

Alarmed friends urged the president to reassert the bold leadership of his first days in office. Otherwise, they warned him, Long could do to him what Theodore Roosevelt had done to President Taft in 1912, divide the party and cost him reelection in 1936. A White House aide returned from the West with reports that the Townsend movement was vigorous and fast-moving. A Woodrow Wilson biographer urged FDR to keep before the country a high moral purpose.

The president did not agree. Public psychology, he replied to the biographer, "cannot, because of human weakness, be attuned for long periods of time to a constant repetition of the highest note in the scale." Wilson, he granted, had stirred profound moral convictions, while Theodore Roosevelt's skill had been in arousing people to passionate and brief enthusiasm over specific problems. Neither president had accomplished both.

He had another thought, FDR went on, relating to "continuous leadership." People "tire of seeing the same name day after day in the important headlines of the newspapers, and the same voice night after night over the radio. For example, if since last November I had tried to keep up the pace of 1933 and 1934, the inevitable histrionics of the new actors"—including Long and Coughlin—"would have turned the eyes of the audience away from the main drama itself!" He would again stimulate "united American action," he added, but at the right time.

Certainly the president did not ignore his political foes. The Democratic National Committee conducted a secret poll in the spring of 1935 and found that the Kingfish might win 6 million votes in the coming presidential election, perhaps giving him the balance of power. Coughlin scored a remarkable number of "write-ins" in the same poll. Roosevelt was more mystified than alarmed, facing a strange opposition, noisy, extremist, personalistic.

He must act, he realized, but when and how? First he tried a sortie in transactional leadership. The White House made a deal with Mississippi's notoriously demagogic senator Theodore Bilbo, in an effort to check Long's influence in the South. Besides conducting investigations of Coughlin's finances and radio network, the White House tried to mobilize Catholic leaders against him and followed with hope the church hierarchy's quiet campaign to have the unruly priest dispatched to Rome to head the American College there. All to no avail.

What could break Roosevelt out of his impasse? A hard blow came from a surprising power center—the Supreme Court of the United States. On May 27, 1935, the High Court in a unanimous vote invalidated the National Industrial Recovery Act, mainly for wielding power beyond the scope of federal authority. A few days later, in a carefully managed press conference, the president quoted from messages he had stacked on his desk—"pathetic appeals," as he called them, from jobless workers, desperate farmers, failing businessmen. While Eleanor Roosevelt sat by, FDR excoriated the Supreme Court's decision for thwarting national action and collective leadership. It represented, he said, a "horse-and-buggy" idea of the Constitution—three words that fit neatly into huge headlines.

Roosevelt had become expert in exhibiting outraged indignation, but now he really meant it. He was used to dealing with Republican or conservative opposition. And almost always he had bested his opponents by appealing to the voters. But now he faced conservatism with a bite; there was no appeal from a High Court decision.

The president had every expectation that the Supreme Court would continue to strike down New Deal policies and initiatives, at a time when the protesters were organizing to defeat Roosevelt at the polls, so he was caught in a political vise. Since FDR was a complex and many-layered man, his motives at certain junctures still remain unclear. Did he assume leadership of a renewed New Deal from outrage over the judicial veto, or his concern for people who would be left unprotected, or his fear of political tumult and even electoral defeat? Perhaps all three of these. What we do know is that, between June and September 1935, he took a series of creative legislative and administrative acts surpassing in terms of political impact and social change even the Hundred Days of 1933. Long ago I labeled this transformational episode the "Second Hundred Days."

The list of achievements still looks impressive: the original Social Security Act; the National Labor Relations (Wagner) Act; a holding company bill aimed at curbing the power of giant utility holding companies; a "wealth tax" that steeply graduated taxes on higher incomes; the creation of a huge Works Progress Administration with a $5 billion budget. At the time, and since, critics on the left scoffed that much of this legislation was inadequate or mainly symbolic, but these laws were *enacted* and their impact could be and would be broadened and deepened as the years passed, under the presidencies of Truman, Kennedy, and Johnson—a collective leadership over time.

*   *   *

Roosevelt offered bold and creative leadership, but how would the people react? The neopopulists were still laying their own plans to seize leadership in 1936. What they needed was a man who could transcend the petty conflicts among them and make followers of the millions of Americans who apparently had turned away from FDR's leadership. By late summer 1935 that man appeared to be Huey Long. But in September, Long was shot to death in Baton Rouge—just outside the House chamber where he had been bulldozing the members—by a young physician. Immediately Long's slavish and demagogic deputy, Gerald L. K. Smith, sprang forward to seize control of the Share Our Wealth movement.

Long's death barely slowed the neopopulists' momentum. Local organizations were recruiting members and planning get-out-the-vote drives. The Coughlin, Townsend, and Long/Smith forces were still the political heavyweights, but other protesters were active in 1936. Town and city and country erupted in activity. Communists and socialists vied for recruits in working-class sectors. Lewis's industrial unions conducted independent political operations. Radical farm leaders campaigned through the prairie states and the West. Ominously, scores of crackpot groups mushroomed, even proto-fascist organizations at a time when Hitler and Mussolini were seeking to export their ideologies.

Combined, these militants and their supporters might have numbered 10 million. But who could combine them? Only a leadership capable of organizing a political party that could recruit, nominate, and elect candidates. The disparate Coughlin, Townsend, and Long/Smith forces came together long enough to fashion such a vehicle, which they named the Union party, but the leaders were too rivalrous to agree on one of them as the presidential candidate. So in the summer of 1936 they chose a neutral and colorless North Dakota congressman, William Lemke, who had fought single-mindedly for bills to protect farmers against foreclosures. The new party patched together a platform but they were most united on a single plank: beat Roosevelt.

The object of all this attention pretended to ignore his adversaries, but, in fact, as always Roosevelt was following their every move. When a new poll in July 1936 showed that FDR's support among voters had reached a new low of 50 percent, advisers again urged immediate action, but the president stuck to his usual schedule, including vacation trips. All the while, he was quietly putting together his own election coalition of progressives, laborites, blacks, southern populists, impoverished farmers, and women, as well as the more traditional ingredients of the Democratic party.

With his fine sense of political timing Roosevelt waited until the end of September before he launched his formal campaign. Gone now was the caution and compromise; he was in full battle array. Nothing captured the power of his "crusade" more than the climactic speech he gave to a frenzied Madison Square Garden audience. "Government by organized *money*," he declaimed, "is just as dangerous as Government by organized *mob*." Never before in "all our history," he went on, "have these forces been so united against one candidate as they stand today. They are unanimous in their *hate* for *me—and I welcome their hatred* . . ."

A few days later the people voted. The turnout of 78 percent was remarkably high. The results: the Communist candidate Earl Browder, 80,171 votes; the Socialist Norman Thomas, 187,833; the Union party's Lemke, 892,267; the GOP's Alf Landon, 16,684,231; the Democracy's Roosevelt, 27,757,333.

In the end, the neopopulists with their Union party captured just 2 percent of those voting.

How did Roosevelt fend off this most serious threat to his political leadership? One answer is luck, notably the assassination of Long. He was the one national neopopulist leader who might have mobilized and spearheaded the opposition forces, held the attention of press and public, and seized a decisive balance of power in the electoral college.

Another explanation of Roosevelt's vanquishment of the neopopulists is almost as simple—FDR was the better politician with more resources. He had long before mastered political wiles. By 1936 he was exploiting all the potentialities of his office, including an enormously expanded press and propaganda operation. Roosevelt himself, reporters said, had "the news sense of a managing editor." His "fireside chats" he had fashioned into a political work of art. His weekly mail averaged in the tens of thousands and, since he had it analyzed, served as a guide to public opinion.

An even more crucial resource was Roosevelt's support from the Democratic party. Parties have deteriorated so much in the past half century that memories of real party organization are dimmed. In the 1930s, both major parties were still formidable vote-getting machines across the country. The new Union party, neopopulist clubs, and other local organizations lacked the infrastructure and skills of precinct and ward and county chairmen to actually deliver voters to the polls. In the battle of parties, the Democrats simply overwhelmed the Union party.

Still, none of this had seemed sufficient as Roosevelt faced the neo-populist uprising a year before the election. There must have been some-thing more, and there was—the Second New Deal. The neopopulists could talk about leadership, the president could *act*, and he did, with policies that responded to the real and throbbing needs of the American people and to their rising demands and expectations. FDR moved, wrote political sci-entist Mario Einaudi, "with imagination and with the skill of a 'creative artist' among the tangle of conflicting and confusing views and interests." In the very process of developing his programs, Roosevelt reached out early to build a following. The Social Security Act was shaped long before its passage by Congress in 1935, with FDR soliciting support not only from the interests involved—doctors, hospitals, social workers, nurses, insur-ance companies, labor, industry—but from "just about everybody," as one participant said, "who had ever written anything" on the subject.

Many of the neopopulists had begun as followers of the New Deal. As the Great Depression continued, they had broken with Roosevelt and become leaders themselves, finding a following among those frustrated and hurt by the failures of the early "experiments" to bring relief, real and last-ing change. With the Second New Deal, FDR turned to follow his erst-while followers. Leading from the presidency, he heeded the dispossessed and disadvantaged, bidding for their support with a broad and deep program that addressed their needs, taking back the followings of the neopopulists, reclaiming them as his own.

What can we learn about leadership and followership from this most mas-terful politician of the twentieth century?

We see again the power of *situation.* Even in 1932, during the most dire economic crisis in the nation's history, FDR had to placate the tradi-tionally conservative constituencies in the old Democracy. Hence his campaign proclaimed its support for economy in government, a balanced budget, a sound currency, along with new economic and social reforms. In effect, he was offering transactional leadership that would mediate among the Democratic blocs. A few years later, after he had mobilized an army of followers, he offered transforming leadership. He had organized a New Deal coalition, but some of his followers who had been empowered by his policies—notably in union labor—were leaders themselves with strength enough to put pressure back on him.

FDR proved that situations were not intractable, that they could yield to the power of *agency*. His brilliant leadership was decisive in remolding his constituencies and realigning his followers. He not merely followed public opinion—he came to dominate it by recognizing the dire wants of the population, legitimating them in speech after speech as proper demands on government, and responding to economic and social needs in the transforming legislation of 1935.

Roosevelt also demonstrated the critical importance of *innovation*. His torrent of proposals during the Hundred Days of 1933 dazzled the country. Some of them were new, some old but dressed up as new, and overall they lacked ideological coherence, but he presented them with such skill and éclat that he captured a momentum he would refresh in 1935, in the Second Hundred Days, with creative policies aimed at millions of new or lapsed followers. Most of his proposals became permanent federal legislation supported by large constituencies.

Looking back today, we have some perspective on the complexity of the leader-follower interaction during the New Deal. It was not a simple struggle with Roosevelt mobilizing followers first against the GOP and then against the neopopulists. Each side encompassed shifting sets of leaders and followers interacting with one another through stages of aroused and frustrated expectations, of mobilization and alienation, protest and support.

These reflections on the Roosevelt leadership—the interaction of situation and agency, the role of creative innovation, the complexity of the leader-follower relationship in government and politics—raise a central question: is the leader and follower dichotomy too simplistic? Is the essential process much more multidimensional? I hypothesize a more complex differentiation:

The *inheritors* of an existing system or structure are natural defenders of the status quo: the Hoover Republicans.

The *innovators* or *initiators* bring creative insights, new ideas and approaches, into proposals for change that affect the existing system, suggest the means of realizing such change, and emerge as an alternative leadership: Roosevelt and the New Dealers.

The *opposers* reject the proposed change of the innovators and seek to mobilize along another course that may or may not be in conflict with the status quo: the neopopulists.

The *partners* respond to and mobilize behind innovators and opposers: Democratic and neopopulist constituencies.

The *coalition builders* seek to create coalitions among initiators and among opposers: FDR's grand electoral coalition of 1936.

The *splitters* lead factions breaking away from the original formations: southern anti–New Deal Democrats; liberal Republicans.

The *passives* may support the status quo by doing nothing, needing strong incentives from leaders before they become active: nonvoters activated in 1936.

The *isolates* may share the wants and needs of the others but are alienated from political structures and shun the entire process. In times of acute change or crisis, they become short-term and tenuous followers prone to extremism.

Could this formulation serve as a step toward solving the paradox of leaders who are followers and followers who are leaders?

FROM ENGAGEMENT TO EMPOWERMENT

In accepting the Democratic presidential nomination in 1936 on a dark Philadelphia night before a tumultuous throng, Roosevelt had sounded forth: "I accept the commission you have tendered me. I join with you. I am enlisted for the duration of the war."

Roosevelt's "join with you" summed up in three words a vast economic, social, and political process that linked him with tens of millions of Americans—and they with him. It was an epic *engagement* between president and people.

Could this engagement be generalized to explain the interactions of complex sets of leaders and followers and, even more, to explain the behavior of people who accept the terms of engagement offered by would-be leaders? By contrast, what would an unengaged—unengaging—leader look like?

I was pondering such questions, especially the last, when a relevant situation unraveled before my eyes. For some years I had been associated with a small university that had selected a new president from outside. At the start he had seemed almost the stereotypical model of the successful leader—articulate, communicative, personable. He met with the faculty regularly and reported to them. He addressed students on the expected occasions. He observed all the formal procedures. But as the years passed something seemed lacking, especially in his relationship with the faculty. He talked to the teachers but failed to talk *with* them, or truly to listen *to* them. There was a disconnect. Eventually they turned against him, and he resigned. In effect, the faculty and the president had disempowered each other.

The president doubtless believed that he was skillfully leading, perhaps even that he had engaged with faculty and students, but the denouement indicated that he was not truly leading at all. He had set out no vision for the future, mobilized no faculty or students behind a program, produced no significant change.

Yet engagements between leaders and followers typically are only a little less superficial. They do not alter the relationship. The basic balance of power is rarely fundamentally or permanently changed.

Nothing better illustrates the one-sided nature of the typical engagement than the approach taken by many leadership scholars and practitioners in describing its first steps. The initiating party is pictured as approaching a likely partner, with the implication that the initiator comes with a clear assumption as to the other's wants and needs. Rarely do we hear about the *partner's* assumptions about the *initiator's* wants and needs. This is natural, perhaps inevitable, but it establishes a power imbalance at the very start of the engagement.

What is lacking in such failed engagements is the crucial moral and practical function of empowerment.

Empowering leaders not only take the initiative in engaging with followers, as all leaders must do. They also engage creatively, in a fashion that recognizes, and responds to, the material wants of potential followers *and* their psychological wants for self-determination and self-development.

We have earlier noted the motivating power of what sociologist Viktor Gecas has summarized as "high self-efficacy and perceptions of system unresponsiveness and high outcome expectations." Leadership empowers followers by intensifying these motivations: nurturing self-efficacy and collective efficacy, fusing "self" and substantive motivations, framing needs, grievances, aspirations, conflicts, and goals in terms of values. As the leadership and ethics scholar Joanne Ciulla puts it, true empowerment gives people "the confidence, competence, freedom, and resources to act on their own judgments" and "entails a distinct set of moral understandings and commitments between leaders and followers."

What transformational leaders do, sociologist Boas Shamir and his colleagues have found, is to raise "the intrinsic value of effort and goals by linking them to valued aspects of the followers' self-concept, thus harnessing the motivational forces of self-expression, self-consistency, specific mission-related self-efficacy, generalized self-esteem and self-worth." Or in leadership scholar Jane M. Howell's terms, "socialized leaders" recognize followers' needs, respect their autonomy, and engage them, while "personalized leaders" dominate followers and ignore their needs except when necessary to advance their own ambitions.

But Ciulla also warns of "bogus empowerment," when leaders ignore "the moral commitments of empowerment," instead using the forms and language of empowerment to exploit followers more efficiently. Some leaders might lack the "moral courage" to alter "the power relationship that they have with their followers." And when people "are told that they are being empowered, but they know they are not," the "failure to deliver" breeds deep cynicism about leadership and the collapse of followership.

Political scientist Richard Couto examined the differences among community-based organizations engaged in the hard leadership task of forging coalitions of grassroots factions. He contrasted "psycho-political" empowerment that boosts people's self-esteem and mastery of their own lives, and promotes democratic participation in actions for a common benefit, with "psycho-symbolic empowerment" that may gratify people's self-esteem but leaves them otherwise as they were—politically powerless and unmotivated to change their circumstances.

Most of the studies of empowering leadership assume that empowerment is one-directional. But if leaders as initiators evoke positive motives like self-efficacy from followers, why should not followers satisfy the self-directed motives of the leader, such as wanting to be heard, to have his ideas accepted, his leadership acknowledged? After all, leaders, too—perhaps more than followers—need to be empowered, in order to achieve common purposes.

With such a dynamic and mutually empowering interaction between leader and follower, a crucial change occurs. The process is so complex and multidimensional, so fluid and transforming, that persons initially labeled "leaders" or "followers" come to succeed each other, merge with each other, substitute for each other. Leader and follower roles become ephemeral, transient, and even indistinct.

This view of empowerment does not diminish the role of leadership itself but rather enhances it. Leadership electrifies the system as followers become leaders and vice versa. Nothing could better illustrate this process on a historic level than FDR's initially engaging followers, yielding some ground to neopopulists, themselves erstwhile followers who took leadership on their own, then, with the Second New Deal, empowering followers by recognizing their needs, speaking and acting creatively on their behalf, and finally becoming empowered himself by voters in 1936. People and president empowered one another; all were leaders and all were followers.

The Burns Paradox ultimately disappears if, instead of identifying individual actors simply as leaders or simply as followers, we see the whole process as a *system* in which the function of leadership is palpable and central but the actors move in and out of leader and follower roles. At this crucial point we are no longer seeing individual leaders; rather we see *leadership* as the basic process of social change, of causation in a community, an organization, a nation—perhaps even the globe.

To see leaders and followers as mutual parts of an ever-reconstituting system might imply that the organizing force is mutuality or even harmony. In fact what activates and fires this system is conflict.

11

CONFLICT: THE ARMING OF LEADERSHIP

The relation of conflict to leadership is rich in paradox. The most arresting rulers in world history have not been the supreme peacemakers but the warriors. Wars propelled Alexander, Caesar, Hannibal, Philip II, Napoleon, Churchill, and de Gaulle to world fame; warmongering plunged Hitler, Mussolini, and Japanese military chieftains into blackest notoriety. Cromwell, Washington, Robespierre, Lenin, and Mao established their places in history through violent revolution.

Four of the "great" or "near great" American presidents—Lincoln, Wilson, Franklin Roosevelt, Truman—confirmed their leadership in the crucible of war; Theodore Roosevelt lacked a war as president but bolstered his leadership with his earlier exploits in Cuba during the Spanish-American War and the bellicose rhetoric that accompanied both his diplomacy and progressive reforms. Meanwhile, Lyndon Johnson's failure to "win" in Vietnam in the end destroyed his leadership capacities to fight for a Great Society at home.

If the fratricide of millions of soldiers over the centuries—often in leaderless confusion—creates "great leaders," is it not paradoxical that we hardly remember the "great peacemakers" even though the world's dominant religions have all preached peace and reconciliation? In fact, these creeds also have preached, or simply accepted, conflict, especially in defending—or extending—the citadel of faith. The Hindu *Bhagavad-Gita* teaches that the spiritual fulfillment of the warrior class came on the battlefields of righteousness. In Islam, Allah ordained *jihad* against the infidel, the warriors to be richly rewarded. In Judaism, the Lord is described as "a man of war," and while Christ enjoined men to "do good to them that hate you," he also warned that he had come "not to send peace, but a sword" and foresaw grimly the conflict his message of love and forgiveness would inspire: "the brother shall deliver up the brother to death, and the father the child: and the children shall rise up against their parents . . ."

There is one other paradox: analysis of conflict—especially non-violent conflict—may be the key to opening up crucial dimensions of leadership.

THE CONFLICT OVER CONFLICT

When people cry for peace but honor warriors, is it any wonder that the foremost thinkers about conflict and consensus have battled for centuries with one another about the true meaning and application of these phenomena? Philosophers and social scientists have long been divided over two questions: first, the degree to which humans in general, and certain societies in particular, are characterized more by conflict behavior than by consensus; and second, the extent to which conflict, and not consensus, is the crucial source of leadership that achieves intended, comprehensive, and lasting change.

The first question has occupied thinkers since ancient times. The early Greek philosopher Heraclitus believed conflict was inextricably woven into the structure of the universe, and two hundred years later the Chinese philosopher Han Fei Tzu, writing in the third century B.C.E., considered war the arbiter of men and nations. Plato and Aristotle both defined humans as political and social animals, given by nature to consensus and cooperation. Even so, Plato saw his Greek society endangered by "the madness of the multitude" that threatened the "very small remnant" of "champions of justice." Harmony would prevail only in an ideal *polis* ruled by that "small remnant" and only with the identification by citizens of their interests with the interests of all. Aristotle similarly found only the elite truly capable of consensus and leadership. "They wish," he said, "for what is morally right." But the "inferior classes" aimed only "to grab something selfishly" so that "faction is their normal condition." Plato and Aristotle were founders of the great conservative tradition that would develop in the West, a tradition that would have little place for deviants, rebels, revolutionaries, or other sources of social conflict.

Other noted thinkers differed significantly among themselves in their appraisal of the balance of conflict and consensus in people and societies. St. Augustine saw humans as inherently conflict-ridden with fierce drives to control others and to gain material goods and sexual satisfaction. The City of Man was full of strife and despair. Nearly a millennium later, Thomas Aquinas followed Aristotle in holding that humans were naturally consensual but also naturally unequal in their rational appreciation of the common good. Yet Aquinas believed optimistically that as men's reasoning powers expanded, conflict would diminish. Both Hobbes and Machiavelli were pessimists about human nature, but saw the virtues of conflict. In Hobbes, conflict bred by natural selfishness became motivation to consensus: for self-protection from war where "every man is enemy to every man," men would "agree amongst themselves" to form civil society, with absolute order imposed by an absolute sovereign. Machiavelli studied how leaders might exploit and manipulate society's pervasive conflicts to create a stable and prosperous state.

In the past two centuries the debate over the social role of conflict has largely passed from the minds of philosophical giants into the hands of academic theorists. By the late eighteenth century, economists and biologists found new ways of conflict at the heart of human nature and social change. Thomas Malthus expected the struggle for existence to accelerate as human population increased. Adam Smith centered his theory of economic progress in the competitive pursuit of self-interest. Charles Darwin defined evolution as an eternal battle for survival and growth, and scientists traced the evolutionary roots of human conflict to its existence among all vertebrates, most recognizably primates. In early human evolution, it was supposed, social power fell into the hands of the aggressive, and conflict over power defined the structure of the social order.

Sociologists came to dominate the study of conflict in human societies, at first emphasizing its creative role in change. The Austro-Hungarian social analyst Ludwig Gumplowicz saw group conflict driving social and cultural evolution, while the Italian sociologist Vilfredo Pareto argued that all history was an interminable struggle for supremacy among elites punctuated by "sudden spurts" of revolutionary violence, as a new elite displaced the old.

For a time, sociology in the United States reflected and extended the European focus on conflict as the motor of social change. That sociologist-in-disguise, James Madison, pinioned his idea of liberal progress on the checks and balances of a constitution responding to the countless factions in the new republic. Closely following British philosopher Herbert Spencer, William Graham Sumner based his theory of progress on the Darwinist "competition of life"—the "rivalry, antagonism, and mutual displacement" produced by the efforts of each person "to carry on the struggle for existence for himself." Lester Ward assumed a "perpetual and vigorous struggle" among antagonistic "social forces" that resulted "in a march forward to greater social efficiency and higher civilization."

By the late nineteenth century, most American social analysts were also social reformers, and they saw conflict against the established order as necessary to their hopes for change. Early in the next century, however, sociology began to discover equilibrium and adjustment as the keys to understanding society, at least the American brand. *Order* became the dominant, if not always acknowledged, value in assessing societies. These analysts did not ignore conflict and change but saw them as either absorbed into a larger continuity or as marks of dysfunction and breakdown. Their model was of an essentially orderly, structured, and self-perpetuating system.

No one articulated the consensus approach to society more confidently than Talcott Parsons, the Harvard sociologist. In his closely argued *The Structure of Social Action,* and later in *The Social System* and other works, he scrutinized in exquisite detail the great balancing forces that conserved the equilibrium of a nation or a community, and how "deviant tendencies"—sources of conflict—could be "counteracted" and the system restored to "the old equilibrium state." He did not ignore disruption and dysfunction—he simply deprecated and marginalized them. Parsons helped foster a generation of sociologists and others that placed a distinctly establishmentarian emphasis on consensus and stability, amounting to a vindication of the status quo; some of these scholars produced studies that glorified the corporations that subsidized them and decried disruptive attacks—especially by uncooperative labor unions—on smooth-running enterprise.

* * *

It would have been surprising indeed if the consensus paradigm itself had not produced conflict, in the form of a new generation of conflict theorists. Columbia University sociologist C. Wright Mills, extending the Marxist tradition, saw the years after World War II as an era not of equilibrium and stasis but of "terrorized masses and excited mobs, crowds and movements"—the driving forces of social change. Mills charged that, with its "magical elimination of conflict" and its "wondrous achievement of harmony," the Parsons school could give no systematic account of "how history itself occurs, of its mechanics and processes."

Mills was a vivid controversialist, and in the conflict-ridden 1960s he gained a large following among those who saw equilibrium theory as a defense of privilege and oppression, hollow values, and social stagnation—as the ultimate redoubt of the "power elite."

Parsons's most formidable adversary, though, was another sociologist, Ralf Dahrendorf. The German scholar took a strong line, proposing that "all that is creativity, innovation, and development in the life of the individual, his group, and his society is due, to no small extent, to the operation of conflicts between group and group, individual and individual, emotion and emotion within one individual." Social change was ubiquitous; no society was immune to disintegration and transformation; and far from consensual and self-adjusting, every society was "based on the coercion of some of its members by others."

Dahrendorf was most effective on the attack, in his trenchant critique of Parsons as the leader and symbol of the consensus school. He concentrated on the Harvard scholar's apparent discomfort with "deviants," whom Dahrendorf jibingly characterized as disturbers of the "peace of utopia," threats to the "neatness" of theory, even as scapegoats, "villainous outsiders" introduced "to 'account' for unwanted realities"—and in every case to be dealt with through the mechanisms of social control.

This rejection of the "abnormal" reflected the conservatism and complacency of the Parsons school. With their closed "world of certainty," Dahrendorf warned, many sociologists had "lost the simple impulse of curiosity, the desire to resolve riddles of experience, the concern with problems." It was the exclusion of conflict that was abnormal, and it carried a heavy price, for social conflict was the "great creative force" that carried along change.

Change. This was Dahrendorf's ultimate point. But what kind of change? In terms of what kinds of human needs or moral values? And what were the implications for the study of leadership? These questions centered in the conflict-consensus argument but went far beyond it.

THE LEADERSHIP OF CONFLICT

Never mind the scholars. Most people don't believe in conflict; some of them only practice it. Harmony, compromise, consensus are good. Conflict, discord, dissension are bad. This attitude is understandable especially for Americans, given their century and a half of violent conflict. Americans invented, or at least brought to a pitch, mass killing in their civil war, with the development of more lethal small arms, scorched-earth tactics, and merciless demands for unconditional surrender. The rest of humanity picked up these advances. The twentieth century's total number of dead in world wars, holocausts, civil strife, and sheer wanton slaughter: at least 30 million soldiers, 170 million civilians.

Nonviolent conflict is not a mere variant of the other kind. It is its opposite, potentially a powerful force for vitalizing democracy, invigorating leadership, and—paradoxically—for fostering social integration and stability.

Conflict begins in the never-ending struggle among individuals and groups for greater shares of scarce resources, that is, for satisfying material wants. If and when these wants are recognized and satisfied, powerful new social and psychological wants arise, including drives for status and power. These, too, are scarce commodities in a competitive world; hence the willingness of some to turn to force of arms when they cannot realize their aims through peaceful economic and political action.

Why emphasize nonviolent as opposed to violent means to achieve human needs? Not because force is less crucial, but because it diverts analysis into a turbulent world of physical power, unpredictable military events, and chance happenings that can make understanding the process even more daunting. Nonviolent conflict is complicated enough.

How, then, do we draw a continuing pattern of behavior from the infinite number of motivations and actions in nonviolent conflict? By examining the people involved and their mobilization by leadership to satisfy their wants and needs. Such leadership may act for those who already possess power and privilege and wish to retain them but also may work for those who don't and wish to gain them.

Since in most democracies the poor have historically outnumbered the rich, one might assume that the impoverished would simply outvote the affluent. That has been the dream of left-wing egalitarian leaders since the unpropertied gained suffrage. But material wants do not wholly dominate motives except perhaps those of the desperately poor. As people begin to fulfill their most basic economic needs, a multitude of other motives come into play and interplay, influenced by gender, national origin, religion, geography, age, along with more "irrational" ones such as race or xenophobia.

All this closely affects the mobilization of conflict by would-be leaders. It would simplify things—at least our effort to study conflict—if such leaders could appeal to a people mostly divided, say, between conservatives and radicals, or under-forty and over-forty, or even women and men. But this could never be.

Some social scientists claimed to have discovered such simplicity in what they depicted as "mass society," characterized by a profound social void where people lacked attachments to the local community or to occupational or interest groups, and so would be "readily available for direct mobilization by elites." In other words, easy prey for demagogues, fanatics, extremists.

Could such a society really exist? "Mass society" theorists used the Weimar Republic as their laboratory, finding there an unstructured society and an alienated, rootless, normless people, which "caused" Hitler's rise to power. Yet a closer look at Germany in the Weimar period disclosed the opposite. The country was a thick network of political, social, and economic organizations. A small town in Hanover carried by the Nazis in the 1932 elections had dozens of athletic clubs, religious and charitable organizations, veterans' and patriotic societies, trade unions and professional associations, aside from myriad singing and drinking groups. The town's clubs and societies, wrote historian William Sheridan Allen, "cemented individual citizens together." Still, most of them favored Hitlerism.

Typically, aspirant leaders in pluralistic democracies, even less-developed societies, must reach out to diverse and complex electorates. They must not only mobilize a host of formal and informal groups, class and even caste members, and the like, but they must deal with established leaderships in these entities. Moreover, presumed leaders may actually be followers, and presumed followers the leaders, setting up a dynamic and complex structure of interactional leaderships.

It is the structure of interacting and *conflicting* leaderships that provides stability and unity to a democratic society. It might appear that these qualities would be better nourished in a consensual society. In fact, consensus in a free society may reflect passivity and alienation, masking potentials for volatility and change. The closest Americans have come to this phenomenon in the twentieth century was in the old South, where an all-embracing Democratic party acted for white economic elites and ignored the interests and welfare of huge numbers of poor whites as well as blacks.

The transformation of this repressive consensus into creative conflict came when Martin Luther King, Jr., and hundreds of other black leaders rose out of the churches, ghettos, and fields of the South to challenge white supremacy. Wielding the strategy of nonviolence, black ministers, housewives, students, and hosts of leaders and followers conducted protest meetings, demonstrations, boycotts, sit-ins, marches. Their sustained, determined nonviolence provoked arrests by the thousands—notably of King himself—as well as beatings, shootings, and bombings. After a long struggle the protesters won key victories in southern communities as well as passage of the 1964 and 1965 civil and voting rights acts.

At first glance the costs of conflict might seem to argue for maintaining the relative calm that had pervaded the South prior to the protests. But that calm cloaked a spreading black outrage that some day—in a country that boasted of its freedom, justice, and equality—would erupt in demands for change and actions to achieve it. As it was, the climactic though incomplete victory of African Americans would permanently transform the basis of conflict in the South, culminating in new leadership structures and a new balance of power between blacks and whites. Real conflict had replaced the false harmony of black-white relationships in the South.

In a continent that for centuries had witnessed desperate peasant revolts and merciless repression, Peru was a prime example of the power of nonviolent conflict when adroitly and tenaciously led. Reform could be pursued only by challenging economic elites and the military in a way that did not invite suppression and a long-term setback to progress. A leader, Elías Tácunan, arose who tirelessly preached land reform, education, and political organization.

Beginning in the 1930s, Tácunan organized in his native village and slowly moved outward across the sierra, persuading peasants that real change by nonviolent means was possible and teaching them the political tools to achieve it. Imprisonment by the military only spurred him to heightened efforts. While some peasants turned to violence, Tácunan patiently concentrated on organizing his grassroots campaign. In 1963, his voter registration drive helped elect a reformist president, Fernando Belaúnde Terry, who became an ally. But in 1967, just as he was organizing an historic national convention of peasants, Tácunan, "strong man of 500 villages," died suddenly of a heart attack.

The Peruvian experience was a reminder of the leadership necessary to persuade thousands of long-suffering peasants, many of them illiterate, to believe in democratic processes and pursue nonviolence while threatened by the military on the right and tempted by more radical, violence-prone organizations of the left. But if the risk of failure was high, the prize was the continuation of reform—despite setbacks, including Belaúnde's overthrow in a coup—long after Tácunan's death.

In another hemisphere Britain and Portugal offered contrasting experiments in nonviolent reform. It was a lovely irony that after World War II the British party system, with its strongly conflictual political rivalries, could come to a clear-cut decision to dismantle the British empire. A socialist Labour party, after besting Winston Churchill's Conservatives in the general election of 1945, boldly took highly controversial steps to grant independence to India and other colonies. Labour's strategy was to bequeath to former colonies democratic institutions and procedures that would pit strong governmental leadership against effective and secure "loyal" oppositions in nonviolent political and electoral joustings. This strategy worked in many cases, if sometimes tenuously, as in the new India, but failed in others, such as Nigeria, which was racked for decades by civil war rather than rational conflict, in large part because of the enormous cultural diversity within Nigeria.

Portugal in its African colonies had offered none of Britain's concessions to the native peoples. Long dominated by authoritarian rulers, the Portuguese were hardly role models for the handling of conflict. Rather than preparing an orderly decolonization with arrangements for self-government that would sustain nonviolent battles between the "ins" and the "outs" in African terms, the Portuguese in Angola and Mozambique held on through years of bitter rebellion, pursuing "a nebulous cultural policy through which Africans would become civilized and assimilated to a European way of life and way of thinking," in sociologist Anthony Oberschall's words. No wonder that after Portugal finally abandoned its "empire" in the 1970s, its former colonies experienced decades of violent conflict. A rational alternation in power of rival leaderships proved impossible.

THE POWER OF LEADERSHIP

If you have raised children—or closely watched parents doing so—you have probably glimpsed the interplay between leadership and power. In my case, helping to bring up four teenagers in the 1960s, I proposed to exercise parental authority and at the same time to serve as the children's mentor, teacher, inspirer—yes, their leader. What actually happened sometimes reminded me of the old comic strip "Bringing Up Father."

I assumed that I would have both the legal authority and the physical strength to rule this little imperium. Alas, I had miscalculated the power situation. It was not that they were openly disobedient; I could deal with that. They appeared, though, to live in a world of their own special wants, their own hopes and expectations, their own friends and allies. They even made up their own secret language, in which they discoursed fluently with one another in the backseat of the car.

Still, I wanted to be their leader, not their ruler or power broker. I hoped to raise them, along with myself, to higher levels of aspiration, to share with them mutual goals. But their motives seemed to elude me, especially in that rebellious decade. Then a remarkable thing happened—the more I reached out to them, the more I came to share some of their attitudes, whether about American militarism or about how much television they would watch (we negotiated a TV constitution).

Extend this family interaction to a political situation. A ruler may have coercive power over his subjects. They may lack the physical resources to match his, but may have the psychological power—the motives—to rise in opposition. Motives indeed are power, in many cases perhaps the greatest "power of the weak," and strongest when based in deep human wants. They are resources in conflict, particularly when they unite numbers of similarly motivated people, when they are transformed into collective motivations; and when acted upon, they breed new resources. "Power," wrote Hannah Arendt, "corresponds to the human ability not just to act but to act in concert." Protests, marches, boycotts, strikes, speeches and declarations, and other forms of direct action, disruption, noncooperation, "withdrawals of consent"—all build solidarity, collective efficacy. All empower motives.

Implicit in such actions is an appeal to the ruler's own motives—for stability or self-preservation, to maintain the legitimacy of his rule or even his self-image as a just ruler. And he may in turn appeal to his subjects' motives for conciliation—by recognizing their claims and seeking their assent to his actions. In effect, he acknowledges not only the limits of coercion but that, in Kenneth E. Boulding's words, "power is a gift to the powerful by those over whom the power may be exercised, who recognize the power as legitimate." The more that the interplay of motives, rather than brute physical power, dominates the relationship, the more the ruler is acting as a leader and the subjects are acting as empowered followers, as citizens.

The diverse power relationships between "wielders" and "targets," rulers and subjects, leaders and followers, describe a parallelogram of dynamic forces: each has motivations, each has physical resources, whether guns or gold or merely their own bodies. Philosophers of old had grasped the essence of the matter. No one, declared Epictetus, a Greek Stoic philosopher in Rome, "is afraid of Caesar himself, but he is afraid of death, exile, loss of property, prison, disfranchisement. Nor does anyone love Caesar himself, unless in some way Caesar is a person of great merit; but we love wealth, a tribuneship, a praetorship, a consulship. When we love and hate and fear these things, *it needs must be that those who control them are masters over us.*" Sixteen centuries later Pascal put it more pithily: power comes from "the possession of things that men covet." In 1960 Bernard Bass converted these concepts into a formula: the "opportunity to dispense potential rewards gives A power over B, but only if B seeks such rewards; only if what A can dispense is rewarding or punishing to B. . . . If B is hungry and A has food, A has power over B. If B is satiated and A has food," A has no power over B.

This abstract model returns us squarely to the roots of motivation in the barest physiological imperatives for food or shelter or release from pain, and we remember that ultimately there is nothing on earth richer in power and transformational potential than human wants and needs.

*   *   *

While most "normal" power relationships are based on the critical inter-play between motivation and resources, sometimes the balance is so lop-sided as to establish a different, nearly personalized distortion. At one extreme is the power wielder so in thrall to self-esteem needs or other drives as to resort to psychological or physical coercion. We all know the types, much glorified or demonized by Hollywood—the hard-driving CEO or politico capable, at least in the short run, of overwhelming any person or obstacle that stands in her way, or the charismatic leader who preys on people's weaknesses.

At the other extreme is the follower so lacking in self-confidence or self-esteem as to throw himself into the vortex of the power wielder. The most familiar example is the man or woman helplessly in love with an-other who does not reciprocate those feelings. Perhaps without even in-tending it, the object of adoration controls the lover's thoughts, emotions, hopes, even hour-to-hour actions. Still, similar submission and control can develop on a calculated, and even mass, basis, as in the suicidal devotion to Jim Jones of his followers.

The bonds of love also suggest the broader phenomenon of wield-ing power through *inaction*. Power can be exercised by doing nothing, by not deciding, perhaps even by not deciding not to decide, or by the tacit rejection of threatening issues from the agenda. Thus incumbent power wielders are in effect left in control. Or consider the case of Russian gen-eral Mikhail Kutuzov, whose repeated retreats in 1812, despite enormous pressures from tsar and staff to stand and fight, drew the French invader deeper and deeper into the cold embrace of the Russian heartland. After a bloody draw at Borodino, Kutuzov yielded Moscow to Napoleon and waited until fears of "General Winter" drove the French out. Then he blocked their line of retreat and pounced, destroying the French army without fighting another major battle.

Another subtlety of power returns us to the wants and needs that under-lie motivation. If power wielders can shape power recipients' motives through political propaganda or commercial advertising, and thus dominate their very thoughts and desires, then the equilibrium between leaders and followers in the interplay of power is lost—power wielders control both the physical resources and the motivation. This may be malign, as in the creation of false needs, or perhaps benign, as when A persuades B to act in B's real interests even when B does not know what those are.

* * *

These complex concepts of power and leadership enrich our understanding. Yet they are no substitute for the analysis of the two fundamental sources of power, motive linked to resource. Epictetus had it just right: people followed Caesar not from love of Caesar but because they loved the resources he controlled—wealth and titles—and so made him "master over us." But there are people who *don't* want the things that their queens or dictators or presidents control. They might prefer peace over war, bread over circuses, freedom from want over rank individualism, leadership over rule.

Gandhi's independence campaign against the British empire, the civil rights movement against white oppression in the American South, the "people power" rising against Philippine dictator Ferdinand Marcos, the defeat of apartheid in South Africa, the breakdown of totalitarian regimes in eastern Europe—all prove the power of motivation as a resource against entrenched, "formal" power with its superior material resources and presumptive legitimacy. That such efforts fail as often as they succeed—and most success stories have a long train of failures before the ultimate triumph—testifies to the inertial strength of incumbency buttressed by force, but also to power's elusive nature, the uncertain fluidity of the parallelogram of resources in the crux of human motivation and the situations confronting it.

The challenge of mobilizing and harnessing insurgent motivations and pitting them against established power—of transforming the situation—falls on leadership. Only leadership can overcome the abuses of leadership, wrote sociologists Michel Crozier and Erhard Friedberg, only power can fight power, by developing new collective capacities and new relations of power. Lacking the resources of Caesar, insurgent leadership motivates followers with "symbolic and intangible inducements," addressing their grievances, appealing to transformational values, and offering prospects of deep change. The most potent appeal to their wants and motivations is moral. Gandhi, Martin Luther King, Jr., Nelson Mandela, Andrei Sakharov, Václav Havel—all were moral leaders, transforming their societies with the mobilizing power of values.

They were also masters—and victims—of conflict.

Part Five

TRANSFORMATION

12

THE POWER OF VALUES

When the historian Edward Gibbon expressed curiosity "by what means the Christian faith obtained so remarkable a victory over the established religions of the earth," his answers included "the convincing evidence of the doctrine itself" and "the intolerant zeal of the Christians." We might suggest a third cause: extraordinary leadership in the cause of the faith.

First was the rise of Christianity out of searing conflict. When early Christians vied with Jews, pagans, and Roman authority, one of the great weapons of their "zeal" was borrowing from the very adversaries they sought to overcome. Christianity grew out of Judaism and, in parting, took a good deal along with it—above all the idea of one God. From the pagans who persecuted them, Christians borrowed the earthy ways and beliefs of country folk and the concepts and methods of philosophers. Thus early Christianity was broadened and deepened by the dynamics of conflict in ways that would steel it against constant challenges in the centuries ahead.

Christianity's triumph in the West was also marked by unparalleled leadership at all levels. In the early centuries, power rested in its far-flung bishops. As local or provincial heads of the Church, bishops were arbiters, administrators, lay judges, as well as builders of cathedrals, basilicas, roads, and fortifications. They presided over arrays of leaders and followers— priests and monks and nuns as well as missionaries, local influentials, and common parishioners. Even when later the bishop of Rome came to bestride the Christian world as pope, his fellow bishops served as the crucial linkage between the parishes and the Vatican.

Such leadership would have been unavailing and ephemeral without the potent doctrine that invigorated and empowered it. That creed had many dimensions but it was rooted in the needs of people for ritual and mystery, for moral principles and day-to-day commandments, for earthly hope and final salvation. Most important perhaps was the Christian belief in the equality of all before God. The medieval Church sold indulgences to the rich, but it also ministered to the poor. For St. Augustine, according to historian Peter Brown, each Christian was "equally—and totally—dependent on the grace of God. For him, the doctrine of election was a source of comfort to the humble, and a stern warning to the proud."

During its first millennium Christianity confronted a rival creed and cause it could not vanquish, Islam. As powerful as the fierce warriors of the *jihad* was the assault on the most sacred of Christian values, Christ's divinity as the son of God. In the holy Koran, the founders of Islam charged that "Jesus, the son of Mary, was only God's messenger.... It is not for God to take a son." Their challenge spread through the eastern and southern Mediterranean world before it was contained. In the end, Christian armies and ideas kept their grip on the European heartland, but Islam dominated huge populations and areas across Asia and Africa, and planted a great mosque on top of the Temple Mount in Jerusalem, Judaism's holiest site.

In its second millennium, the rise of Protestantism produced the gravest crisis Christianity had known—a civil war within the faith. The battles, among the most violent and costliest in human history, raged among huge and fanatical armies of believers. Just as Christianity had in its founding days, the Protestant Reformation borrowed heavily in moral values and sacred principles from the brethren it was leaving. These commonalities of faith both gave the Reformation's attack on Catholic "corruption" added bite and wider appeal and also made possible later moves toward ecumenism. In the twentieth century the fury of secular ideologies—creeds like fascism and communism—overshadowed for a time the old religious conflict. As much as Christianity and Islam, the new creeds were global in scope, and they were murderous beyond any of the wars of religion. Yet they, too, testified to the homicidal power of true believers captured and caged by the values they proclaimed.

WHAT VALUES FOR LEADERS?

Given the ferocity of conflicts in the mid-twentieth century, only arrant optimists might have hoped that some kind of global pact on human rights could be won. Yet in the years after World War II, even as a new "cold war" divided the planet, political leaders fashioned an accord of astonishing boldness and vision, called the Universal Declaration of Human Rights.

This declaration was the culmination of centuries-old aspirations for some kind of world agreement that would not only define and proclaim the universal rights of all human beings but also pursue and enforce such rights. Advocates of the "Rights of Man" had won notable advances from the English Bill of Rights of 1689 to the American Declaration of Independence and Bill of Rights, the French Declaration of the Rights of Man and of the Citizen, and the campaigns for the rights of women and racial and ethnic minorities that followed over the next two centuries. Still, these were national or local struggles, not global in scope.

Could the victors of World War II frame a declaration that would speak for *all* the nations? In 1941, even before the United States entered the war, Franklin D. Roosevelt had proclaimed that the aim of peace should be to secure for all people the Four Freedoms—of speech and religion, from want and fear. This was followed up by the Anglo-American Atlantic Charter. Roosevelt was ever mindful that the war had come on the failure of Woodrow Wilson's League of Nations to restrain the sweep of fascist aggression not only against states but against political, ethnic, and religious minorities under their domination. Now, as he contemplated the creation of a new international peacekeeping body, FDR might have been struck by his predecessor's prescient linkage of human rights violations and war. "Nothing," Wilson had warned at Versailles in 1919, "is more likely to disturb the peace of the world than the treatment which might in certain circumstances be meted out to minorities." A successor to the League must squarely state not only what it stood against—aggression and war—but also what it stood *for*. And so, late in 1944, as the Allied armies smashed their way into the Nazi homeland, American delegates to a United Nations organizational conference overcame British and Soviet objections to including the need for human rights in the charter of the United Nations. Later the UN established a Commission on Human Rights, which set to work on a separate universal declaration of rights.

"Universal"—the idea was intoxicating but seemingly utopian. How could a declaration with wide enough scope to include the war's winners and losers, communist and democratic nations, empires and their colonies, industrialized and developing countries also have teeth sharp enough to bite deeply into attitudes across such a diversity of cultures and conditions? And what did *human* rights mean? This question led to political and intellectual conflict, but as a starting point, there was considerable agreement, however hazy, that human rights were based in human wants—on those things necessary, in political scientist Jack Donnelly's words, for a "life of dignity, for a life *worthy* of a human being, a life that cannot be enjoyed without these rights."

The obvious problem was the enormous variety of acknowledged needs—social, cultural, economic, legal, political. Could even the most skillful leadership knit together a declaration that responded to them all?

Stabbing into the very heart of this question was an intellectual and political challenge from the communist nations. Reflecting Karl Marx's contempt for individual civil and political rights as a cloak for capitalistic exploitation, the Soviet Union argued that the declaration should enshrine economic and social rights at its very apex. The American position, as one United States official admitted, was to emphasize individual rights by making the world charter a "carbon copy" of the American Declaration of Independence and Bill of Rights.

To distill an international consensus out of these and other conflicting priorities clearly demanded leadership that was politically practical yet dedicated to achieving a truly global and visionary declaration. Almost miraculously, such leadership appeared in the American representative to the Human Rights Commission, an elderly, plainly dressed woman who often came to the sessions in New York by subway. Eleanor Roosevelt was a leader of immense prestige, patrician charm, endless patience, and great transactional skills. She led the drafting committee through tense, emotional debates, defending the American position yet seeking to conciliate the Soviets—as well as expressing her own principled recognition of the interdependence of wants—when she declared that "no personal liberty would exist without economic security and independence. Men in need were not free men." Though the Russians responded stonily, in the end Eleanor Roosevelt coaxed a potentially transforming agreement out of the bickering delegates. No wonder that the General Assembly of the United Nations gave her a standing ovation, followed by its unanimous vote for the draft in December 1948.

To read the Universal Declaration more than half a century later, at the start of a new millennium, is to be struck again by its power—its scope, inclusiveness, explicitness, and absoluteness. Thus "everyone has the right to life, liberty and the security of person" and "no one shall be held in slavery or servitude." And in the battle between democratic and communist conceptions of the priority of rights, civil and political rights were given precedence in the text over the socioeconomic rights necessary for "an existence worthy of human dignity," such as rights to food and shelter, medical care, education, and work.

The human rights proclaimed in the Universal Declaration were not merely a wish list of pieties to be displayed and soon forgotten. They represented people's rightful claims on society and polity. Few celebrants were naive enough to expect quick and heavy impact on the actual behavior of political leaders. Some leaders signed on with little intention of observing the declaration, or soon backslid on provisions they claimed threatened their "national sovereignty" or proved otherwise inconvenient. But there the declaration stood, proclaimed throughout the world as a standard against which the behavior of rulers could be measured from year to year and decade to decade.

In the broader view the charter would serve even more as a statement of global, public *values* with a potentially profound impact on the climate of expectations through which nations moved. It was a moral and philosophical document as well as a political one, setting out transforming ends toward which people might aspire.

Values, in the dictionary definition, are general concepts of "what is right, worthwhile or desirable; principles or standards." They serve as "criteria for selection in action," according to the *International Encyclopedia of the Social Sciences,* as "criteria for judgment, preference, and choice." And *public* values are the most powerful of principles because they represent the most broadly relevant, deeply felt, longest lasting, morally grounded commitments humankind can make. They are actually or potentially powerful causal forces. Public values such as liberty, justice, equality, happiness that have endured, flourished, and evolved over centuries, that are based in human wants and needs, that dominate people's hopes and fears and expectations, that deeply influence their social and political attitudes and shape much of their day-to-day behavior—ultimately such values have a huge causal effect. Virtually all the public values expressed in the Universal Declaration are both the cause and effect of generations of people with large stakes who have struggled to define and apply them.

The strengths of even the most potent values are enormously enhanced if they are part of a cultural value *system,* described by anthropologist Ethel M. Albert as "a summative construct in which the diverse value sets of individuals and groups are related as complementary elements of a single system." In such a system, values not only exist side by side but intertwine and interact, immensely strengthening their collective impact. Order and liberty are different—even adversarial—public values but they fortify each other: order needs liberty to hold off oppression; liberty needs the order of a secure environment to thrive.

Despite its rather prosaic laying out of human rights, the Universal Declaration is itself a striking articulation of a complete system of public values. The declaration casts its net widely enough to include a diversity of values that reflect the wants and needs of people around the globe.

To see the Declaration of Human Rights as a system of public values is to define such values as the embodiment of meanings and policies that have direct and extensive impact on people, because based in fundamental human wants. These values are the supreme measures of the importance, quality, and impact of leadership. All leadership, wrote social philosopher Al Gini, "is value laden. And all leadership, whether good or bad, is moral leadership at the descriptive if not the normative level." Joanne Ciulla, the noted ethicist, sees ethics, broadly defined, as lying at the heart of leadership. Yet can we leave the crucial question there? Some contend that the content or results of leadership cannot be tested because, in Joseph C. Rost's words, there is no consensus as to the "higher moral ground" leaders can stand on. A century ago this argument could have carried some weight. Not today. Representatives of the nations of the earth have agreed on a set of values, of the most extensive and concrete nature, values that speak directly to leadership and its purpose—that declaration again.

All this does not mean that the declaration sits on such high ground that nations will agree on its interpretation and application. On the contrary, it offers a set of values on which people and parties are bound to *disagree.* But that conflict, that debate, will be conducted within a broad value system, so the issue will not be the values themselves but their interpretation and implementation, which, as Eleanor Roosevelt had told the Human Rights Commission in 1948, "would necessarily vary from one country to another and such variations should be considered not only inevitable but salutary." Fortuitously, as I write, a radio bulletin comes in that the Chinese cannot agree to a human rights agenda for an international conference because the West, with its emphasis on civil liberties, fails to acknowledge the needs of the Chinese people for "food and shelter." So the debate goes on, but in the context of a world community pledged to the Universal Declaration.

Is leadership as a concept, then, *inevitably* values-based? Leadership scholar Ronald Heifetz furnished the best answer: "We cannot continue to have it both ways. We may like to use the word *leadership* as if it were value-free, particularly in an age of science and mathematics, so that we can describe far-ranging phenomena and people with consistency. Yet when we do so, we ignore the other half of ourselves that in the next breath speaks of leadership as something we desperately need more of. We cannot talk about a crisis in leadership and then say leadership is value-free. . . . We have to take sides." Or as my old Harvard professor Carl Friedrich liked to tell his students and later wrote: "To differentiate the leadership of a Luther from the leadership of a Hitler is crucial for a political science that is to 'make sense'; if a political science is incapable of that, it is pseudo-science, because the knowledge it imparts is corrupting and not guiding."

TRANSFORMING VALUES

As waves of change engulfed people in more recent eras, it was hard for some to imagine what life was like in the relatively unchanging societies of old. Yet stasis and continuity had been the norms of people's lives for many centuries. They lived under all-embracing rulerships, dominated by a troika of hereditary kingships and established religions backed up by military power. Not that opposition and conflict were lacking. Dynastic ambitions, church-state rivalries, military plots, rabble-rousing heretics, ferocious peasant revolts ceaselessly threatened the feudal systems. But for century after century, in East and West, absolutism prevailed.

Why did impoverished peasants and suppressed townspeople fail to crack this edifice of power? Mainly because the rulers provided one indispensable value in times of external threat and internal turbulence: personal, familial, and community *security.* This was the moral foundation of a value system that underpinned huge and rigid political and religious hierarchies. Free speech, the rule of law, voting, dissent—these were beyond the ken of people imprisoned in a world dominated by religious creeds and authoritarian rule. The idea of opposition, even a "loyal" one, was anathema. Occasional dissenters of unimaginable courage and conviction were imprisoned, tortured, killed. Ensconced and implacable, rulers ruled.

Rarely has an established rulership demonstrated its authority more convincingly than the papacy at Avignon—or more paradoxically, for these were pontiffs in exile. Early in the fourteenth century, Rome had fallen into such tumult that the papacy took refuge in southern France. There, decade after decade, the popes yearned to return to the Eternal City but continued to fear for their security there. Thus over the years they converted the Bishop's Palace in Avignon into a massive religious and governmental fortification. Seven popes ruled on the banks of the Rhône until the brilliant diplomacy of Gregory XI made safe return to Rome possible in 1377.

Historians have wondered how papal rulers could decamp to a foreign city and pick up the reins of power there, during a century dominated by rival monarchies and rapacious principalities. The answer lay in the initiatives the Avignon popes took in boosting their financial resources (ostensibly to raise money for a final and triumphant Crusade), widening their control over thousands of ecclesiastical appointments, and conducting diplomacy on equal terms with kings. Bringing their moral authority wherever they resided, the popes based their constructive rulership firmly on their Christian values and on the principle that "the successor of St. Peter was the leader of the world."

It would take an extraordinary combination of ideological, psychological, political, and moral force to bring down the medieval power structures. The assault was slow and uneven. The French revolted against their monarchy late in the eighteenth century, the Americans earlier against a British king, the Russians well over a century later. The British kept their Crown even as political processes began to be democratized. But the decline of the kingly and ecclesiastical rulers, along with the assault on their ideologies by a host of eighteenth-century thinkers and politicians, led to a new Western leadership based on a revolutionary set of values.

"We the People of the United States," proclaimed a constitution in 1787 that set the "Blessings of Liberty" as its climactic value. The French Declaration of the Rights of Man two years later laid out "inalienable rights" of "liberty, property, security, and resistance to oppression." And two years after that, the Americans amended their Constitution to declare that "Congress shall make no law respecting an establishment of religion, or prohibiting the free exercise thereof; or abridging the freedom of speech, or of the press; or the right of the people peaceably to assemble, and to petition the government for a redress of grievances."

British politicians were not so keen on formal declarations. Instead, poets spoke for Englishmen. William Wordsworth hailed

> ... *the People having a strong hand*
> *In making their own Laws, whence better days*
> *To all mankind.*

And Shelley, in 1819, condemned "rulers who neither see, nor feel, nor know, / But leech-like to their fainting country cling," and urged the people to assert their freedom—

> *Rise like Lions after slumber*
> *In unvanquishable number—*
> *Shake your chains to earth like dew*
> *Which in sleep had fallen on you—*
> *Ye are many—they are few.*

*　　*　　*

As these intoxicating ideas fermented in the late eighteenth century, and as social and economic changes created new and vital linkages among people, broader roles for leadership were slowly unlocked as well. The old rulerships were engulfed in peaceful or violent change from within; some fell, if only temporarily, under the onslaught of Napoleonic armies and others. As ancient monarchies lost their footing, however, their one great value—security, or stability—was lost, too. Rapid change was the new order, as new men rose to power throughout the interstices of transformed political systems.

It was a time of contrasts. Much would be left unchanged, especially in the countryside. The man with the hoe and the woman with the scythe would continue to labor, as they do even unto this day. But there was a rising sense of personal efficacy as people gained opportunities to make their way free of the old state and church restraints. Human wants could now be expressed more openly. Needs could be recognized. Hopes and expectations could be indulged, at the risk of frustration and disappointment, as potentials for real change opened up even for the humble.

Since political activity was still sharply curbed in many countries, and the right to vote, where it was recognized, was limited to the propertied elite, the primary transformational dynamic lay in leaders reshaping followers' values and being spurred by their responses.

Was there any pattern in this early burgeoning of secular leaders preaching values? These were indeed initial efforts to shape and transform major ideas into an array of values that would provide the basis for collective political action, oppositional values that challenged the authority of the status quo. "The world out there" was simplified and condensed into concepts and experiences, hopes and grievances, that reframed conventional meanings and amounted to a call for transformational change. Initiatives were seized by political entrepreneurs who exploited injustices, thereby arousing both support and opposition and in turn stimulating political conflict over ideas. An early example of this process was the French Revolution and its impact inside and outside of France.

To an extraordinary degree European thinkers of that era were analyzing people's motivational forces. Some were thinking globally, at a time when they knew all too little about far-off cultures. A few were seeking general theories of wants and motivation and perception that would underlie the values of diverse peoples. Anthony Oberschall noted in the writings of eighteenth-century moral philosophers frequent references to the cultures of "Egyptians, Persians, Chinese, Turks, Arabs, Thais, American Indians— as well as to the deaf, dumb, and blind, wild boys found in the forest, orangutans and other apes, and the social animals such as ants and bees."

Were apes a bit of a reach? We now know that apes, like humans, have leadership and followership relationships, but we have little evidence that they share the values professed by Western moral philosophers!

The rise of more open, pluralistic societies both broadened and complicated the role of values-based leadership. In a democracy the deep and broad array of local groups poses a dilemma and an opportunity. Most of these groups are tiny leadership-followership entities. National leaders who want to mobilize people in the grass roots and in the streets naturally seek to attract support from local groups that offer them quick and direct access to active citizens and voters. But how to pursue the broadest and most fundamental public values while trying to satisfy parochial, "special-interest" concerns?

The only solution for would-be national leaders in democracies is to attempt to mobilize people behind values that powerfully express the wants and needs, hopes and expectations of large numbers of people. It is in the interactions and likely conflict between general values and more local interests that the opportunity for mobilization appears. In most democracies national leaders—liberals and radicals, conservatives and reactionaries—will compete over the proper interpretation and ordering of the supreme values of security, liberty, equality, justice, and community. To succeed, they will attempt to frame these values so as to bring the broadest range of local concerns within their embrace. In turn, as grassroots leaders already close to their constituents become more engaged with national leaders, their local interests are re-framed by the wider, deeper sphere of values. In the process, their followers are extended beyond narrow self-interests toward a broader view of the common good.

Such analysis relates mainly to developed democracies. Even in a theocratic state like today's Iran, however, one can see the makings of a pluralistic and decentralized leadership structure that responds to national issues. In early 2000, reformist candidates for parliament in the religious city of Qum mobilized modest grassroots efforts, represented by simple campaign offices with one phone, storefronts with posters, talk-filled shops, a "women's brigade." Doubtless the city contained myriad other local groups waiting to "come out" against hard-line theocratic government. If a structure for democratic leadership developed in Iran, these local leadership potentials would be energized and empowered, creating the conditions for a nationwide conflict over values that might transform the country and its people.

EMPOWERING VALUES

Leaders embrace values; values grip leaders. The stronger the value systems, the more strongly leaders can be empowered and the more deeply leaders can empower followers. The transformational dynamic that mutually empowers leaders and followers involves, as we have seen, wants and needs, motivation and creativity, conflict and power. But at its heart lie values.

Can we build a model, stripped down to essentials and beginning with a relatively static situation, of the role of values in the rise and fall of leadership seeking to achieve real, intended, comprehensive, and lasting change?

1. The relatively stable status quo begins to be undermined by change—for instance, population growth and migration, economic innovations or decline, altered social relations—and people develop new material and psychological wants. The failure of the inheritors of the established order to address such significant social changes effectively, to acknowledge and act on these new wants, produces fissures and dissonances that generate creative thinking about needs and values.

2. Activists—would-be leaders—take the initiative by recognizing people's new wants as legitimate needs and articulating them as values.

3. Activists compete with one another for the support of followers. To gain the broadest support, they frame grievances and promises of specific change in terms of values.

4. Activists seek to organize and lead groups, movements, and parties. Followers become arrayed in larger and larger aggregations, supporting general values as well as specific policies.

5. Activists gain leadership positions by responding to followers' wants and needs adequately, and followers will demand more. If leaders respond inadequately to heightened expectations and demands, followers will seek changes in the leadership.

6. Activists who gain office, and hence become leaders with constituencies, discover the limitations of formal power. They must not only gauge the needs and hopes of their followers, expressed as broad and compelling values, but they must have the skill to mobilize resources to satisfy them.

7. Value systems splinter under the pressure of heightened expectations and demands. Followers themselves become leaders throughout the society and act as both consolidating and divisive forces.

8. In a democracy, the crucial issue becomes the power and legitimacy of an opposition capable of taking over office, redefining values to better address people's needs, and governing. If such a transfer fails, conflict degenerates into multiple warring groups, the rise of extremists, a breakdown of the relationship between leaders and followers, and the collapse of the value system.

In this kind of scenario, values play a central role in binding would-be leaders and followers, broadening moral frames of reference, and serving variously as a needed unifying and dividing force.

Values strengthen the whole fabric of leadership by helping to sustain the mobilization and deepen the empowerment of followers during competition and conflict.

Values strengthen leaders' capacity to reach out to wider audiences and to gain support for broader arrays of values and for value systems, and ultimately empower leaders by constituting a foundation for governing.

Addressing fundamental questions of human nature, values help to clarify the relations between individualism and collectivism, self-interest and altruism, liberty and equality—issues at the heart of political conflict—and in the process establish a leadership agenda for action.

In sum, values are power resources for a leadership that would transform society for the fuller realization of the highest moral purposes.

Of all these functions, the mobilizing and kindling power of transforming values is the most essential and durable factor in leadership. Addressing the needs and hopes of millions of people, leaders seek to transcend everyday brokerage and bargaining in order to rally followers behind those values. Once that engagement is made, leaders and the people they mobilize can empower one another more and more as long as people's material needs and visionary hopes are met—and as long as the power holders are challenged by a loyal opposition that will keep them honest. Values by themselves are mere words, or symbols, until backed by empowerment, but the same values, sharpened by ideological conflict in a democracy, empower those who know how to lead.

Above all, values—operationalized, claimed as rights, empowering leaders and followers—are weapons. Not mere decorations on monuments or flourishes in statesmen's speeches, the great public values of the Enlightenment, woven into people's aspirations and expectations, are the weapons of a transforming leadership that would enhance their security and liberty, and so expand their opportunities to pursue happiness.

The clues to the mystery of leadership lie in a potent equation: embattled values grounded in real wants, invigorated by conflict, empower leaders and activated followers to fashion deep and comprehensive change in the lives of people. The acid test of this empowerment is whether the change is lasting or whether it is temporary and even reversible. Deep and durable change, guided and measured by values, is the ultimate purpose of transforming leadership, and constitutes both its practical impact and its moral justification.

And *that* is the power of values.

13

THE PEOPLE, YES?

Our search has been for an explanation of the *human* role in change, of leadership conceived as a dynamic, fluid system of leaders and followers that has deep causal impact. We want to understand not only what has been but what might be. A theory, after all, draws upon the past, but is valued for its capacity to describe the future, for its powers of forecast. Yet a theory of leadership will never be precise in its predictions because its raw material is the most enigmatic of phenomena—human wants and other motivations, human beliefs and intentions and actions. We can indicate the principles and patterns of the leadership process, point out its origins and ends, mark out its stages, suggest its variations and also its universality— how it might work in an Indian village or a Wall Street brokerage, a revolutionary movement or a house of parliament. We can hope to provide a common frame, a basis for continuing investigations. What we cannot do is to give a final answer, to extinguish all the perplexities and paradoxes inherent in this most fateful of human actions.

Because the theory of leadership is bound so closely to its practice, because it is a prescriptive as much as an analytical endeavor, the stakes for understanding leadership's crucial role in change—in transforming change, change that is intended, comprehensive, durable, and grounded in values—could scarcely be higher.

The pursuit of happiness must be our touchstone. As means and end, it embodies the other transforming values—order, liberty, equality, justice, community. It encompasses the highest potentialities for transformation both in people's situations and in themselves. And it epitomizes, as perhaps no other phrase, what it is that many in this world—the millions, billions—most profoundly lack: the opportunity to shape and direct the quality and meaning of their own lives. For them—the people—leadership is the X factor, potentially the indispensable discipline.

THE X FACTOR

What happens when large collectivities of people, driven by urgent needs and fervent hopes, demand and pursue far-reaching change? In particular, why and how do people transform their economic or social systems and in the process transform themselves? Over the centuries, there have been many single-cause explanations: economic, religious, social, intellectual, psychological, or some other motivation.

In the past hundred years such explanations have fallen into considerable disrepute. Theories of incrementalism or of chaos or of contingency have come to the fore, replacing the old "grand theories" of change. Instead of exploring "ultimate" sources of alteration or transformation, scholars have often settled for "secondary" explanations of specific forces with causal impact, as varied as population growth, migration, public opinion, education, disease, or poverty. In recent decades, however, the most widely studied approach to human change has been at the intersection of *agency* and *structure*.

Structure typically meant large systems: governmental, corporate, religious, legal, educational, as well as society or culture in the broadest sense. Agency consisted of people: actors, activists, dissidents, organizers within or outside the structures, variously cooperating with or challenging the "system." In the twentieth century sharp disputes broke out among scholars over the meaning and explanatory value of agency and structure, as well as the causes, nature, and extent of the interaction between them. In general sociologists concentrated on structure, psychologists on agency. But not always.

In the 1960s the functional emphasis that lay at the heart of the structural approach to causation was attacked by no less than a president of the American Sociological Association, George C. Homans. Functionalists, he charged, ignored or played down the causal role of people with needs, values, and other motivations. People were put into boxes or roles that denied their humanity. The functionalist "theory of action," said Homans, "appeared to have no actors and mighty little action," because it "separated the personality system from the social system and proposed to deal with the latter alone." He pleaded: "Let us get men back in, and let us put some blood in them."

If we are to put men—and women—back in, we must scrap the simple agency-structure dichotomy and recognize that structures and social systems are composed of human beings who may complain, rebel, quit, organize, even take over leadership. In short, structures are not giant machines lumbering across the countryside but collections of *people*, organized perhaps in some "system," or multiple systems, but still people, and thus malleable, susceptible to the ultimate agency of human leadership.

In place of a simple dichotomy we need analyses that are more subtle and probing, and that are as universal as we can make them. Perhaps such an approach might be found by examining the leadership of large but specific transformations.

The relative stability of the late nineteenth century masked the origins of just such a transformation. Monarchies ruled, more or less securely, in Germany, Austria-Hungary, Russia, and Spain. Imperial rule had survived in China, despite uprisings and military defeats, and in Japan, despite some constitutional reforms. Colonies in Asia, Africa, and South America lay under the pervasive rule of the European powers. The leaders of the French and American republics were, for the most part, moderates or conservatives. Nearly everywhere, the inheritors ruled.

This global calm was soon to be shattered by vigorous reform movements protesting the disruptions and impoverishment caused by economic expansion, and thereafter by World War I. The Great Depression of the 1930s, leaving hundreds of millions around the globe in fear and want, prompted similar movements as well as radical rethinking about people's deep-seated wants and needs that had been ignored or suppressed. Social philosophers and political theorists, probing the basic sources of inequality, pondered the intellectual failures to anticipate the debacles.

In 1931, amid deepening world depression, British economist Richard H. Tawney wrote an arresting work, *Equality*, in which he pictured privation in Britain not as an aberration, or the product of laws of history or inexorable structures—"uncontrollable forces"—but as a result of the human choices that reflected the ruling "values, preferences, interests, and ideals" of British society. Inequality was *made,* Tawney insisted, built into the organization and distribution of social opportunities and powers— property, status, education, law—and reinforced by "the restriction of the sources from which leadership is derived." Inequality was, in short, a human *creation,* "a national institution."

The social pyramid in Britain and other capitalist economies was perpetuated through a hierarchy not only of wealth but of opportunity, a near monolith of life chances and deprivations. Pious rhetoric about "equality of opportunity" meant little when "the capacities of some are stunted by their social environment, while those of others are favoured or pampered by it." In reality, the poor were offered "equal opportunities of being trampled to death." Tawney saw greater tendencies toward equality in America but, he noted wryly, "a right to the pursuit of happiness is not identical with the right to attain it."

If human beings made poverty, could they make *well-being?* If cumulative differences and deprivations were written into people's lives, could cumulative *equalities* be written into them by firm human leadership? Liberals and reformers had one solution: economic and social planning. Planning would address their main criticism of the received order—its chaos and disarray, its casual and reckless decisions that blighted millions of lives.

To ideological radicals, planning sounded like a technocratic middle way and hence a moral cop-out. To them, poverty was the result of the elite's monopoly on power and resources. But in its full potential, planning was a radical solution. It would reroute the channels of power, transform oppressive structures, give firm and rational direction to comprehensive and intended change grounded in values such as individual opportunity and social justice. The crucial factor was leadership that would conceive and initiate such planning and bring it to fruition.

Socialists could boast of intellectual antecedents stretching back to the Enlightenment for their own answer to deeply rooted inequalities, but planning theory could also claim a distinguished intellectual pedigree. The French philosopher Count Henri de Saint-Simon first fashioned a full-blown theory of social planning early in the nineteenth century, contending that with a "scientific" approach to society, his ultimate value, social harmony, could be achieved. Disorderly and combative in his own life, Saint-Simon was nonetheless a prophet of order and consensus.

Saint-Simon and his followers, including Auguste Comte, turned to mathematics and "social physics" for their science of planning. While they delightfully called on poets and artists to participate in a "Chamber of *Invention*," leadership of this planning parliament would be entrusted to civil engineers, who would have two hundred of the three hundred seats. It was the engineers who would plan the irrigation, land clearing, road building, and canal digging that would make "the whole of France" into a "superb park in the English style." Meanwhile, at "feasts of *expectation*," orators would motivate people to eager participation "by making them aware of how greatly their lot will be improved when they have put these plans into execution." Though Saint-Simon's utopian plans were never put into execution, they anticipated the better-founded engineering feats of the Suez and Panama canals decades later.

Meanwhile, the practical politicians of the nineteenth century paid little heed to visionaries who called for deep transformations of existing structures with comprehensive, countrywide planning. It was grimly ironic that only in two world wars—especially the second—were national economies, governments, and people mobilized on a centralized and systematic basis. Thus was planning developed to its highest degree of effectiveness in destroying millions of the enemy. The crisis of the old order in the Great Depression might have forced national planning onto the New Dealers, but while some of Franklin Roosevelt's advisers advocated it, the president was too experimental and "pragmatic" to offer a unified economic and political program. One thing he did propose was the most ambitious *regional* development plan that the world had ever seen—the Tennessee Valley Authority project. This grand experiment illustrated both the potential and the limitations of leadership seeking to transform—in this case, a whole region.

The broad aim was the creative development of a valley, many of whose 3 million people were profoundly isolated and in desperate want even by Depression standards. A study of four thousand valley families found that their income was far less than they needed to provide even their "relatively simple wants"—under a hundred dollars a year. Illiteracy and mortality rates were stupefying. The TVA's plan was to bring relief and new opportunity to these people within an integrated diversity of purposes: to harness the Tennessee River, generate and distribute electric power, foster rural rejuvenation by expanding jobs, recreation, and community planning on a vast scale.

The idea of physically and socially transforming a valley that wound through hills and mountains for hundreds of miles across several states provoked fiery political opposition. And to have a government do this—the *federal* government—only stoked the wrath of those opposed. Conservatives labeled it socialistic if not communistic, an attack on private property and enterprise. Southern politicians feared intrusions into state authority and even a veiled effort to help blacks. Barons of the United States Senate inveighed against a project that would be accountable, they protested, neither to the voters nor to the market.

The plan for a three-member board of directors sharpened the question of the TVA's own leadership. FDR designated as chairman Arthur E. Morgan, a visionary who might have warmed Saint-Simon's heart. Seeking a balance, the president added a pragmatic "social engineer" and lawyer in David Lilienthal, as well as Harcourt Morgan, a university president dedicated to grassroots democracy.

Arthur Morgan was impatient with politicians "he felt cared for only short-term, selfish benefits," wrote historian Erwin Hargrove. He sought deep reform—even social and economic transformation—that turned on what Hargrove called "the moral transformation of individuals." Arthur Morgan wanted to anchor the project in small communities whose people would work together for the common good. As chairman, too, while seeking consensus through the exchange of ideas, he insisted he would never "make vital concessions of moral principle."

Lilienthal was Arthur Morgan's near total opposite. A Harvard Law School graduate, he viewed himself as a combination of hard-boiled realist and social reformer. Grasping that the TVA was a political as well as a physical entity, he campaigned relentlessly in Washington and across the region for this pioneering approach to planning. Differences between Arthur Morgan and Lilienthal finally rose to such a pitch that the president summoned the two men to a White House hearing and, when the chairman failed to offer evidence to support charges he had made against his fellow directors, dismissed him for "contumacious" behavior.

How could the agency survive such internal and external conflict? Quietly, behind all the headlines, the TVA, mainly under Lilienthal's leadership, went about the business of taming the Tennessee River, building great dams for power, and instilling the kinds of local self-help programs and initiatives that all three board members favored. For his part, Lilienthal did not flee from the internal battle. Unlike Arthur Morgan, he "saw politics and conflict as not only inevitable but desirable," according to Hargrove. Under Lilienthal's militant leadership the TVA carried the battle to private power interests and congressional opponents. Despite continued opposition—including the Republicans' nomination of the TVA's main private utility foe, Wendell Willkie, to challenge FDR for the presidency in 1940, and, later, the hostility of conservative Republican presidencies—the project met the test of sheer durability, though no doubt at the expense of some of its more far-reaching aspirations.

In the end, the acid test of the TVA lay not in its dams and power grids but in its impact on the people in the valley. Some of course no longer lived there; they had been removed before their homes were flooded out. Blacks had suffered discrimination in employment on the project; planners dared not touch the political third rail of racial relations, and the region was mainly left behind in the fierce civil rights struggles of the 1960s. In the long run, though, most of the valley's people gained immensely from the project, with more abundant and better jobs, housing, and educational opportunities, more efficient agriculture, flood control, and plentiful and cheap electricity. They gained also in morale—the efficacy that rising opportunity fosters.

While the TVA might have fallen short of Arthur Morgan's dream "to reconstruct the total pattern of people's living," as Arthur Schlesinger, Jr., put it, the project nevertheless gave them "a wider opportunity to shape and fulfill their own lives." By breaking down the structures of poverty and isolation that had immobilized them, the TVA made the valley's people agents of change—leaders—in their own lives. And it had been bold, persistent, creative leadership—in the White House and the planning offices, among engineers and local leaders, mobilizing support, marshaling resources, facing up to conflict—that brought change to the valley and its people. By all these criteria, the TVA was a transformational project, enabling large numbers of valley people to pursue happiness. Yet despite the potential the TVA had shown, it failed to serve as a model for regional planning. When Roosevelt asked for more such authorities, Congress granted him not one.

Case studies of attempts at transformation in complex situations illustrate the role of leadership in the causal processes of change even when the planned alterations may not be completely realized. To generalize about leadership in this kind of change we may return to our leadership typology, where we come to the nub of leadership as a causal force—as the crucial link between intention and outcome.

Interaction begins when the innovator rallies support to carry out the change he intends. Innovators have a triple burden: they must break with the inheritors among whom they may have been numbered; they must mobilize followers by appealing to their wants and hopes and other motivations; they must adapt their intentions to those of would-be followers without sacrificing their essential goal.

Conflict powers and fructifies the interaction: conflict between innovator and inheritor, possibly between innovator and followers, and definitely between innovator and opposer. The "rebellion" against the inheritor sets off a series of confrontations that will energize the whole process of change. Conflict in turn may liberate even the passives from their misunderstanding that they have no stake. Thus people in remote hollows, far from the centers of political power, were drawn into conflict over the TVA.

A more recent example of the leadership dynamic in a transformational process was the Solidarity movement in Poland. The first rebellious innovators were put down in 1981 by martial law wielded by the Communist authorities, but the tenacious leadership, with a shipyard electrician, Lech Walesa, at the fore, aroused public opinion and mobilized more followers. Passives became actives, followers became leaders, workers and writers became revolutionaries. Demanding liberty, democracy, and justice as well as economic restructuring, the movement worked effectively with the Polish Catholic hierarchy and other restive elements to rob the inheritors of any shred of moral legitimacy, revealing that their defense of the totalitarian status quo relied on sheer force. Eight years after its suppression, Solidarity triumphed.

There is nothing rigid or determined in such transformational processes. Neither the established order nor the challenging forces are monoliths, impermeable structures. They can be as subject to variation and flux, as rigid or yielding, as frail or robust as the human beings that compose them. The progress toward change is itself constantly changing, adapting, renewing itself, exhibiting both continuity and flexibility. Great plans must be loose at the joints, in fact a process of planning and *re*planning. It was the decision of President Clinton's health care planners in 1993–94 to spring on the country a highly detailed plan, a kind of airtight social blueprint, that helped ensure its defeat.

Where is leadership as a causal force? Almost everywhere. At every stage, there will be the need for creative responses to changes in conditions, in the shape of the conflict, in the composition and relative power of established and challenging forces—there will be the need, that is, for leadership. At every stage, there will be the need to hold true to original intentions and valued outcomes—that is, for leadership. The leader-follower relation can become unstable; the dynamic of mutual empowerment may even bring the "creative destruction" of old leaders. Yet leadership itself must persist in its transformational task—its central causal purpose—of turning all such continuities and contingencies to the aim of achieving real change. Leadership is the X factor.

"LIFE, LIBERTY, AND ..."

"Life." The main task of inheritors is to safeguard their inheritance, the status quo. To do so they invoke the single most powerful value dominating peoples, especially in times of unrest and violence, the value of *order*, which in turn embraces those of survival, security—the very life of a nation, the very lives of people. Failing this supreme value, inheritors contend, no other value, no matter how humanistic, is possible.

The issue is stability. "When a society is in homeostatic equilibrium," according to the political scientist Chalmers Johnson, "it is continuously receiving stimuli from its members and from the outside that cause it to make adjustments in its division of labor and its structure of values." Thus the inheritors' world is not a static one, but neither is it transformational. Peter the Great could offer Russia bold innovations, just as the imperial Romans provided bread and circuses for the masses, but all served to consolidate the status quo.

Innovations for a time may help maintain stability, but "adjustments" or incremental change cannot forever cope with—much less overcome—disruptions that tear at society from without or within. Whatever the source of such disruptions, the ultimate cause of instability—and transforming potential—is the same: the failure of the inheritors to meet the basic needs of the people, for security, for adequate food, shelter, work, for freedom, opportunity, social justice. Indeed, incremental change that goes partway to satisfying people's needs, or promises to, can raise expectations that themselves become a destabilizing force. As Alexis de Tocqueville contended in the nineteenth century and James C. Davies in the twentieth, revolutions have often occurred after long periods of at least some political, social, or economic progress, when expectations have grown, as have fears that gains will be reversed. Tocqueville argued that "the most perilous moment for a bad government is one when it seeks to mend its ways," noting that a grievance "patiently endured so long as it seemed beyond redress . . . comes to appear intolerable once the possibility of removing it crosses men's minds."

Still, feelings of deprivation and of frustrated expectations are often in themselves inadequate to produce political action. People can react in a variety of ways—including stubborn adherence to the established order—to similar economic and social stimuli. The leadership of a society's "have-nots" might seek to equalize the distribution of income, but great disparities in wealth alone have rarely generated leadership that could produce a successful revolution in that cause. The most impoverished people of all, the peasants, have often turned out to be the least dependable allies of revolution. How then does it cross people's minds, in Tocqueville's phrase, that their situation is intolerable? What changes in those minds cause men and women to seize the "liberty" to act against an established order with its increasingly threadbare promise of "life"? How do they become followers of transforming leadership, or leaders themselves, in the pursuit of deep change?

Just how central a role intellectual leadership plays as a catalyst of social change has long been disputed, especially by those who would emphasize structural variables or impersonal forces—the "realities" they say determine and limit human beings and their potentialities. They often ignore, however, the towering factor that intellectuals help to define those "realities." It is their interpretation of the state of things and its causes, of the injustice, inequality, poverty, and discrimination they see around them that, in their manifestos, tracts, speeches, their plays, songs, and art, can decisively influence people's perceptions of their society, the quality of their lives, the possibilities for change.

Intellectual leaders sometimes emerge from the very heart of the establishment they attack, inheritors spurning the inheritance; often they rise out of marginal groups and share the wants of their followers. Their leadership begins in a potent vision of what is and what might be, and grows in their ability to convey that vision to people in need of it. They speak to people of the conflict between their actual conditions and the professed values of the establishment, and they offer remedies. But this "pedagogy" is far from one-sided. As followers take from leaders, so leaders take from followers, in what Paulo Freire described as a mutually transforming relationship. As he wrote of the oppressed, "Who can better understand the necessity of liberation?" Leadership brings to consciousness and makes articulate what people already know.

The French *philosophes* of the eighteenth century offer the classic example of the power of intellectual leadership. Through their writings, they propounded the central doctrines of enlightenment, that neither human nature nor the social order is God-given or fixed, and that human beings could comprehend and improve their world. In short, the *philosophes* and their ideas were agents of empowerment.

Long ago we lost for good that array of compelling thinkers, and today we innovate and dispense ideas in different ways. But the values of the Enlightenment retain their transforming potential, and they underpin the thought and work of what Thomas Rochon identified as the modern successors to the *philosophes,* the "critical communities" that in challenging old ways of thinking and offering alternatives produce the "conceptual groundwork" for the broad movements that create social change.

Creative leadership sparks an evolution in followers toward committed, empowered participation in the struggle for meaningful change. With that participation can come an inner, personal transformation comparable to the changes activists seek in the world.

Leadership—the relations between leaders and followers and among followers—has at its affective core efficacy and self-efficacy, individual and collective, the feelings of deep self-confidence, hope and expectation that goals can be attained and problems solved through individual or collective leadership. The sources of efficacy are not well known and in any event vary widely. Even so, a person with strong motivations and values—a Gandhi or Thatcher or Mandela—usually has the efficacy to practice leadership despite endless obstacles and opposers, doing so usually on the shoulders of increasingly efficacious supporters. Thus individual efficacy both strengthens and draws strength from collective efficacy, in a virtuous circle.

Collective efficacy benefits from another virtuous circle, according to Albert Bandura. The higher the efficacy, the greater the participation;

the greater the participation, the larger the potential for success; and the larger the potential for success, the higher the efficacy. Mutual aid and obligations, comradeship, shared values and goals—all enhance and are enhanced by collective efficacy.

Efficacy applies especially to the wide political arena. As Bandura noted, "Shaping the social future through genuine institutional change is a long, tortuous process.... The formidable challenge is to build and mobilize a community-wide sense of efficacy in people who have come to regard many of the aversive aspects of their lives as beyond their control." Building collective efficacy from the grass roots up—as people convert self-interests into common purposes, as activists learn to challenge the power structures around them, as leaders give heart to followers by showing how obstacles are surmountable, as community leadership links up with collective action at broader, even national and global levels—is crucial to achieving leadership for far-reaching social change, and the promise of happiness.

Efficacious leadership, whether individual or collective, can still be fragile and ephemeral in the face of brutal realities.

In 1947 an idealistic young minister, David Burgess, traveled to Rock Hill, South Carolina, to lead an effort to organize a Textile Workers union local. He mounted a collective effort to lift the workers out of decades of long hours and low wages in stifling mills. He soon encountered the naked power of the mill executives who owned the workers' houses, controlled the police, and knew the arts of bigotry.

"Who are the men who lead this union?" the mill owner demanded in a letter to the workers. "I will name some of the chief officers: Baldanzi, Rieve, Chupka, Genis, Jabor, Knapk and Rosenberg. Where do these people come from and where do they live? Are their backgrounds, upbringings, viewpoints, beliefs and principles anything like yours and mine? ... Have they ever given a penny to your church?" The unionists lost the election. Burgess, a graduate of Union Theological Seminary, was appalled by local pastors' support of the company. In the end the defeat was total and devastating, as frustrated workers fell into recrimination against one another and further divided the community.

Another example, from southeastern Kentucky: For decades in an Appalachian community, people had protested the pollution of Yellow

Creek by waste from a tannery. They said they could not fish, boat, swim, or even wade. But these were individual complaints—just "fussin'," they admitted—and had no effect. Finally, in 1980, three married couples, meeting clandestinely in a picnic area, agreed to lead a collective effort that, through face-to-face meetings and phone banks, would eventually expand to several hundred protesters. Women took the lead in organizing meetings, contacting lawyers, reaching outside the community for support.

In 1987 the Yellow Creek activists filed a $31 million class-action suit against their city government. Two years later the suit was settled out of court with a consent decree signed by the federal Environmental Protection Agency, the city, the tannery, and other parties. Celebration was short-lived. The city appealed to the EPA to weaken the decree; the EPA yielded. Sorely disappointed, the Yellow Creek protesters refused to sign the document.

Still the effort to create change, even if it fails in its immediate goals, sometimes can bring the transformation of those involved. In the 1980s, the Morristown plant of General Electric in eastern Tennessee employed several hundred people, mainly women, in skilled jobs at decent wages. Unexpectedly, in 1988, a new management team took over and put through changes that many workers opposed. A union organizing drive failed to enlist more than a quarter of the workforce. A week after the union was voted down, General Electric suddenly closed the plant, laid off around two hundred employees, and sent the whole job thirty miles away to subcontractors who hired part-time and temporary workers at lower wages without benefits or job security.

The first reaction of the workers was of utter helplessness. Rallying, they organized CATS—Citizens Against Temporary Services—and took collective action on several fronts: they sued GE for sex discrimination; lobbied the state economic development agency to block the company's move; and sponsored a bill in the state legislature against the long-term use of "temps." All these efforts failed. Remarkably, the CATS members were undaunted; on the contrary, with the help of organizers from the famed Highlander Research and Education Center, the "school" for the civil rights activists of the 1960s, they became more militant than ever and broader in their goals and leadership skills.

The workers never regained their jobs at GE but, through their collective struggle, which began as a job action and became much more, they were politicized, creating "democratic citizens and political actors out of individuals," in labor scholar Eve S. Weinbaum's analysis.

In the early 1970s, two sociologists who interviewed six thousand men in six developing countries found that they possessed essentially the same qualities that defined a man as politically "modern" in developed countries. "He is an informed participant citizen; he has a marked sense of personal efficacy ... reflected in his belief that, either alone or in concert with others, he may take actions which can affect the course of his life and that of his community." This globalization of efficacy, political scientist James Rosenau concluded in 1990, would lead to a search by people everywhere for "new outlets" where "the individual's micro actions can have macro consequences."

In short, around the world, people of participation and efficacy, liberating themselves, seeking change.

Creativity, conflict, empowerment, efficacy—these and other causal elements make leadership the single most vital force in struggles for real, intended, durable, comprehensive change. Still, if leadership is not a neutral, mechanical process but the transforming human moral factor in converting values into outcomes, leadership must then be held accountable for the progress—or the lack of it—that has been achieved. The change it fosters must be measured by the realization of values, above all happiness.

"... THE PURSUIT OF HAPPINESS"

That phrase echoing through history—"Life, Liberty and the pursuit of Happiness"—is a remarkable distillation of the supreme values of the Western world, values that have reverberated around the globe. The trinity draws its stirring, event-making power from the interdependence of these values. Life—order, security, "safety" in eighteenth century terms—without liberty can diminish the potentials of human lives, even to the extent of being life-denying. Liberty without order can turn to license, even anarchy and violence. The fullest meaning of these values becomes manifest in their mutuality, each secured—fulfilled—through the power of the other.

And the pursuit of happiness? This was not a glib phrase struck off to put a fine gloss on the Declaration of Independence. It, too, is closely bound to the other values, reflecting the most profound and complex thought of the West, stretching back to the Greeks—who agreed with Socrates that "all of us desire happiness" but disagreed sharply and creatively over what that meant—and culminating in the Enlightenment.

No one explored the ideal of happiness more tellingly in the eighteenth century than the genteel Scottish philosopher Francis Hutcheson. A leader in the intellectual ferment of Glasgow and Edinburgh, Hutcheson was eager to take on the imposing philosophical luminaries to the south, most notably Thomas Hobbes. To Hobbes's view of human nature as inherently selfish and aggressive, Hutcheson responded that people are basically virtuous and benevolent. We are led, he said, "by *our moral Sense of Virtue*" to choose among actions on the basis of the "degrees of happiness expected to proceed from the action." Therefore, he argued, "*that Action is best*, which procures the *greatest Happiness* for the *greatest Numbers*; and *that*, worst, which in *like manner*, occasions *Misery*." The Scot believed that the individual pursuit of happiness promoted the general welfare, the happiness of the entire society. And the best social system, in turn, secured the "sacred" and "inalienable" rights to life and liberty that enabled human beings to pursue happiness. He meant *all* human beings, on equal terms; no one in any station of life was to be "excluded from the enjoyment of the supreme good" of happiness.

When Thomas Jefferson came to draft the Declaration of Independence he had long been steeped in the work of Hutcheson and other moral philosophers of the Enlightenment. The American Continental Congress in its 1774 declaration of rights had adopted the common formulation of the day, the Lockean trinity of life, liberty, and *property*. Two years later, though, Jefferson substituted happiness for property. This was not because he denigrated property; he was a substantial owner of land and slaves. Rather he believed that the ends of government soared beyond defense of an absolute right to mere possessions. Those ends called even for the redistribution of uncultivated lands to the poor, so that all men would satisfy "our natural wants." Like Hutcheson, he believed that the purpose— the moral obligation—of society was to guarantee to all persons the conditions for pursuing happiness, and that these individual pursuits would contribute to the welfare of all mankind.

*　*　*

If the happiness of humanity is the first law of societies, if, as Jefferson maintained, "the greatest degree of happiness possible" for "the general mass" of people is the "only orthodox object of government," then the world of the third millennium stands in gross violation. Despite the enormous expansion of potential material satisfactions, several billion people subsist today in social subjection and dire want so deep and pervasive that the affluent among us cannot comprehend it. Our own occasional bouts of ravaging hunger or thirst give us only a passing taste of what those billions suffer on a daily basis throughout their lives. But comprehend that misery we must if we wish to examine how leadership might be employed *with* the poor and the weak in confronting poverty and subjection.

Could we accept Jefferson's advice to his traveling friends and visit the poor, inquiring into the "happiness of the people," or follow a young Eleanor Roosevelt as her cousin Franklin had, accompanying her to New York's decrepit tenements and meeting people he hadn't known "lived like that"? Like most middle-class Americans I was largely insulated against awareness of all that misery. Growing up in a farm town during the Great Depression, I saw some evidence of it in the lunch boxes of children in my grammar school. Trudging through villages in the western Pacific during World War II, I saw endless abandoned hovels, and evidence everywhere of bleak existence. Ironically, though, I finally penetrated into the life of the poor less by experience than by reading books, most unforgettably a 1961 work by the social anthropologist Oscar Lewis about a family living not in a mountain or jungle village but in the heart of Mexico City. The family of Jésus Sánchez consisted of a fifty-year-old man and a score of dependents in three households, all of whom he supported on earnings of less than a few dollars a day. Lewis focused on four of Jésus's children, all in their twenties and three of them—plus grandchildren—crowded into a one-room slum tenement cut off by high cement walls from the teeming city all around.

Their stories, Lewis wrote, revealed a "world of violence and death, of suffering and deprivation, of infidelity and broken homes, of delinquency, corruption, and police brutality, and of the cruelty of the poor to the poor." There was another side—of a little gaiety and family feeling, passages of love and intimacy—but fifty years after the Mexican revolution the Sánchez family had little in prospect except an unending struggle for bare survival, generation after generation of stasis. Averaging less than five years of schooling, the children of Sánchez had no real hope of decent jobs. They existed day-to-day, with no planning ahead.

What struck me most was the sheer impenetrability of their lives. Nothing—government, business, school, church—seemed to connect with them. This profound isolation from the main currents of society, I believe, as much as material privation, defines the world's poor, most of whom are worse off even than the Sánchez family members were. Can *anything* reach them? Only the kind of leadership that would enter into their lives, not to preach to them or placate them but to *connect* with them on their terms, as the initial action in helping them realize their human potential.

This is a large claim, based on the proposition that transforming leadership begins on people's terms, driven by their wants and needs, and must culminate in expanding opportunities for happiness.

EPILOGUE
GLOBAL POVERTY: PUTTING
LEADERSHIP TO WORK

If "ideas are weapons," as my mentor insisted, then theory must be in the vanguard. Cutting-edge ideas about leadership must face the test of applicability to real life. Yet they must also pass the test of ethics and values, because in the end ideas will be effective as weapons only if they are productive of happiness.

Much of the leadership theory in earlier chapters is readily applicable to political and economic situations we face today. No leader can truly lead if he cannot respond to the wants of followers, if she fails to elevate and empower them. No leader can truly lead if lacking in the ability to produce intended change through creative innovation. No leader can lead without seeing that conflict is not only inevitable but often desirable; as Warren Bennis wrote, exemplary corporate leaders not only accept dissent—they encourage and reward it. And leaders cannot be effective in the long run if they are simply power holders—rulers—and fail to see the moral and ethical implications of their work.

Still, the tests of applicability are even harder for transforming leadership, particularly when this biggest, boldest kind of leadership confronts the largest, most intractable problem facing humanity in the twenty-first century: the basic wants of the world's poor.

Data on global poverty are bruited about so offhandedly that we almost take them for granted, like casualties from distant earthquakes or typhoons. But the numbers remain staggeringly horrific. The world's poor are usually estimated at perhaps a third of all humanity, around 2 billion people—human beings who at best exist on two dollars a day. The ratio of the poor to total population varies enormously, from 40 percent in India and 78 percent in Bangladesh to 5 percent in Korea and 25 percent in Indonesia, while the United States "experiences the highest level of inequality" among the developed nations. Overall, half the world's total income goes to 10 percent of the world's population, and it has been estimated that in 1998, the world's two hundred richest people had more wealth than the combined annual incomes of the world's poorest 41 percent, about 2.3 billion people.

The ill-being of the poor takes as many forms as the well-being of the rich. Many are desperately insecure, feeling fearful and vulnerable, hence helpless and powerless—uncertain of life itself. Some suffer endlessly from pain, exhaustion, severe discomfort, or mental health problems such as anxiety and depression. Many simply lack decent housing or adequate clothing, or any shelter at all. In some places, drugs and crime pose the greatest threat. To all these problems, women and children are especially vulnerable.

The most dire and common want of the poor is hunger. The children "sometimes just get sick for no reason," says an Ecuadorian woman. "Sometimes it's because of lack of food. We are poor. We have no money to buy or to feed ourselves. Now, everything is so expensive that we can only buy pasta, salt, and oil. Some days we have nothing to eat but *chichita*"—fermented manioc root—"because there is no money."

The wants of the poor not only pile up, they interlock, in the most vicious of vicious circles. Undernourished people develop health problems that make working difficult, which results in low income and still greater hunger. Poor women living in isolated communities cannot bind together to meet collective needs, or to press the powerful in state and market institutions for their satisfaction, deepening their exclusion and vulnerability. Poor children needing education cannot walk the long distances to schools—if schools exist—and thus perpetuate their family's cycle of poverty. Poor men failing to find jobs become open to the stigma of the community, further lowering their self-esteem and self-efficacy. All these vicious circles spiral into a web of want, isolation, impotence.

How to break out of this thickly intertwined net of poverty? How even to penetrate it? For centuries philosophers and philanthropists, politicians and pundits have advanced solutions for the eradication of mass-scale want and hopelessness. They have proposed shining utopias, religious rededication, huge aid programs, massive migrations, far-reaching development plans. Fiery revolutions around the world raised people's hopes; some realized them for a time and to a degree, but mass poverty persisted. The industrial revolutions of the eighteenth and nineteenth centuries in the West gave employment to millions, often accompanied by abysmally low wages and grinding toil. In the twentieth century, social welfare programs in Britain and other industrial nations alleviated many hardships while putting whole communities "on the dole," often creating an enduring underclass, effectively requiring the poor to trade real opportunity for basic sustenance, pursuits of happiness for meager "life." Franklin D. Roosevelt's New Deal left "one-third of a nation" behind, ill-housed, ill-clad, ill-nourished.

At the dawn of the third millennium, after a century of stupendous economic productivity in the developed world, the billions of the world's poor are still here and probably increasing. What now?

In 2001, shortly before Christmas, Britain's chancellor of the exchequer, Gordon Brown, proposed a $50 billion annual program to improve education and health for the world's poorest people. Brown aimed his message mainly at the administration of President George W. Bush, in light of the dismaying fact that the world's richest nation spent one-tenth of 1 percent of its gross national product on foreign aid, considerably less than other industrialized countries. Brown's proposal would constitute the biggest development effort since the Marshall Plan, whose $13 billion of aid to European recovery after World War II would be the equivalent of around $88 billion five decades later.

Could such a program work? Only if directed by a *leadership* strategy that scrapped failed strategies of the past and offered a new way of approaching the problem lying at the very root of most of the world's other problems.

The central strategic failure of past approaches rose from the assumption that money and technology were the essential and even total keys to overcoming poverty. Developmental aid has had relatively little global impact despite decades of effort and innovation, not only because the money was never nearly sufficient but because outside aid alone—filtered through, and often diverted by, numerous aid agencies and financial institutions with their own agendas and bureaucracies, national and local governments with *their* own agendas and bureaucracies, trickling down eventually in some form or other to some of the poor—could not shatter the vicious circle of intertwined poverties. By the 1990s these failures had bred "aid fatigue," marked by a decline of almost half in "official" aid as a ratio of donor gross national product, as well as by an increasingly fervent but altogether unproven faith in the magic of globalized free markets to improve the lives of even the poorest of the poor.

At the heart of the money strategy's failure was a void, a missing link, an absent X factor and catalyst: leadership. Lacking real engagement among the various institutions and interests involved in aid, from distant donors to local officials, and, most critically, between them and the disempowered, voiceless poor themselves, there could be little if any real chance for the drastic local transformations that, multiplied across the world, were needed to break the back of global poverty.

A leadership strategy first of all would take a hard-boiled view of the misconceptions of the poor's would-be helpers, even those with claims of being "close to the problem." "Closeness" alone does not provide solutions that have evaded both "experts" and victims for centuries. Instead, a leadership strategy would recognize the daunting variety of poverty's burdens by learning to understand how *they,* the poor, see them. A leadership strategy would provide a host of listeners who would *hear* the voices of the poor.

If there is any weapon the poor do possess—a weapon that must come into play at the start of a transformational antipoverty program—it is their ability to express their grievances, their wants, their deprivations. Listen to:

A young Bulgarian woman: "Winters are worst. Summers we can work in the field," but in winters "there's nothing to keep us warm"—no firewood or adequate clothing or shoes, and no money for school.

An Indian mother of seven in Andhra Pradesh: "I have been overstrained with the number of deliveries I have made, which has made me too weak to work."

A Vietnamese woman: "Poor people cannot improve their status because they live day by day, and if they get sick then they are in trouble because they have to borrow money and pay interest."

An Ethiopian man: "Poverty snatched away my wife from me. When she got sick, I tried my best to cure her with tebel"—holy water—"and woukabi"—spirits—"for these were the only things a poor person could afford. However, God took her away. My son too was killed by malaria. Now I am alone."

These were among the tens of thousands of "voices of the poor" captured in a remarkable project organized by the Poverty Group at the World Bank and carried out by teams of researchers in scores of developing countries in the late 1990s. What they did was to listen to the voices of the poor, eliciting "rich descriptions of poor people's realities" and illuminating the leadership failures of aid programs with pervasive "stories of humiliation, intimidation, and fear of the very systems designed to provide assistance." Here is the first step in any strategy of leadership—to *listen.*

Still, the fact that the poor can powerfully express their wants does not mean that they know how to go about satisfying them. They cannot, intellectually, lift themselves by their own bootstraps because they have no bootstraps. This is where strategic leadership comes in as the vital link between wants and available or potential resources, as the vital empowering agent of the dispossessed. For it is leadership, listening closely to the wants of the poor and recognizing them as actionable *needs,* that can marshal and direct resources, both material and psychological, and answer them directly.

Two experiences in India—a traditional "top-down" effort compared with a local *leadership* approach—underscore the distinction between the two strategies.

In the 1950s, estimates that India's population of 400 million would double in thirty years touched off alarms. Pressed by Western governments and international agencies, India became the first nation in the world to adopt a broad program of population control. After early efforts to teach people the rhythm method and to use condoms, diaphragms, and jellies made little progress in reducing the birthrate, in 1961 a new plan set in motion an aggressive reeducation campaign to change the attitudes of the "masses" toward family planning—and toward their own families. Happiness, people were relentlessly told, is a small family.

Yet birthrates remained stubbornly high. Why? Planners in New Delhi, urbanized, Westernized, filled with the self-evident urgency of the population crisis, obsessed with statistics, were blind to the wants and values of the people—especially the rural poor—whose attitudes and behaviors they sought to change. They did not see that in the villages of India, large families were not the cause of poverty but its *consequence.* Among the impoverished, the family was the "basic unit of work" and children were regarded as working assets, not liabilities. From the point of view of villagers, family planning meant "voluntarily reducing the family labor force." They were puzzled—or angered—that uncomprehending outsiders would ask them to sacrifice vital interests for a program that did not respond to any real need of theirs.

To the planners, the "masses" were "uneducated, ignorant, traditional and custom bound." In 1966, the public education campaign a failure, the Family Planning department in New Delhi adopted a sterilization program devised by Western experts, handing down ambitious "targets." To fulfill them—and keep their jobs—state and local family planning workers resorted to endless subterfuges: sterilizing women who were already beyond child-bearing years; operating on the same person twice; offering people bribes to accept sterilization. On paper, results were impressive, but in this game of numbers there was no corresponding drop in the birthrate.

In 1976 Prime Minister Indira Gandhi announced that the time had come for "drastic" steps. The sterilization program turned to coercion. To meet ever higher targets, "police and other officials descended on villages and urban slums where they rounded up every man they could catch, in-cluding those with no teeth and barely able to walk." Some villages that failed to meet quotas were denied irrigated water. Elsewhere children were barred from school until one of their parents was sterilized. The overall target was achieved, and even exceeded—8 million sterilizations were performed in nine months—but the public anger over her brutal methods brought down Gandhi's government. And the campaign had no effect on India's overall birthrate. "Family planning" had reached a dead end, anath-ema to political leaders and the people alike.

If top-down—or "power-over"—leadership from New Delhi so resound-ingly failed to stabilize population in Indian villages, could empowering leadership at the grass roots do better? Could leadership develop from *within* a rural community to meet the social and health needs that led to overpopulation? The remarkable case of the Comprehensive Rural Health Project illustrates what is possible when leadership is informed by the wants and values of those it serves.

In 1970, a husband-and-wife team of doctors, Rajanikant and Mabelle Arole, returned to India from medical studies abroad. Their discontent with what they found—top-down, doctor-centered, and costly medical services that kept the poor away—led the two doctors to Jamhked, a village in

Maharashtra state, where they hoped to promote "people-based" health care. From discussions with villagers, they came to realize that doctors were not only hard to find, but also not really necessary to perform most services. In close collaboration with local people, they developed the Village Health Workers program.

Middle-aged women were chosen from each of eight villages. Mostly illiterate but experienced in childbearing and trusted by their community, these women were trained together in nutrition, herbal remedies, prenatal care, and delivery. To overcome the many caste and religious differences among them, they took turns cooking meals and all slept together under a specially made blanket. In the ensuing years, the impact of the Village Health Workers on public health was profound, from helping to eradicate cholera and malnutrition to encouraging immunization and hygiene. Moreover, they shared their knowledge, enabling other women to take charge of their own families' health care and other villages to develop their own programs. Over twenty years, the birthrate dropped by more than half.

The Aroles, convinced of the potential of the Village Health Workers as change agents, encouraged them to organize village women to attack social ills. They first targeted alcoholism and abusiveness among village men, banding together in groups to lock out husbands who wasted the family income on drink and then beat their wives—a revolutionary act in a culture so deeply imbued with the idea of women's submissiveness. Meetings with local officials to air their concerns encouraged the women to become, in Mabelle Arole's words, "bold and confident and to understand their own worth in a free democratic society." And they began to help one another start small businesses—selling dried fish or bangles or handwoven baskets—and so augment both their income and their standing in the family. This, too, was remarkable, since women's status in India was traditionally dependent solely on childbearing.

The Aroles not only led the way in transforming the life choices of rural women, but they also demonstrated how gifted leaders at the grass roots can empower people by mobilizing local leaders.

A serious campaign against global poverty would spread the Aroles' kind of local leadership around the world. It would recruit from many countries thousands of activists willing to travel and work in remote places. They would constitute a new kind of world army, men and women—call them freedom leaders—who would live close to the poor, hear and understand their wants and needs, and mobilize local leadership capable of marshaling resources of food, shelter, medical care, transport, and jobs that would meet concrete situations. The freedom leaders would learn much from worthy models—both international, such as the Peace Corps, the World Hunger Program, Doctors Without Borders; and indigenous, including Sri Lanka's community-development group, the Sarvodaya Shramadana Movement, the Instituto de Promocíon Económico-Social, which nurtured grassroots organizations in Uruguay, and the Association of Community Organizations for Reform Now (ACORN), working to empower poor neighborhoods in the United States—but the freedom leadership project would be vastly expanded in order to operate in thousands of communities, and for long periods of time.

The obstacles would be predictable—governments that would reject the "intruders" from the start, or throw them out; villagers so suspicious and fearful that they would resist the efforts of activists; wars, revolutions, civil strife, famines, epidemics, and other disasters. To operate globally, the program would cost at least $100 billion a year (one-twentieth of the United States' annual budget). For these and other reasons change would not come quickly; indeed, large results could not be expected for many years, perhaps for decades. Hence the global program would call for unparalleled commitment and determination over the long run.

Utopian?—no. Practical?—yes, because the core strategy would be simple and realistic: partnerships between local followers and leaders from outside, partnerships that would embody listening, mentoring, doing, and a ceaseless effort to raise people to their highest potential. It must be clear to all participants that the essence of the strategy would not be perpetual outside intervention but *the recruitment of fresh cadres of local leaders eventually to supplant the freedom leaders.*

Endless puzzles and difficult choices would inevitably arise in the everyday work of freedom leaders, to be dealt with in the light of specific situations. One predictable issue would be the use of market resources and incentives along with public ones in day-to-day planning, especially with respect to matters involving such governmental infrastructures as exist—health, housing, nutrition, transport, water, sanitation. The balancing of public and private domains should be addressed on the basis not of ideology but of local needs, concerns, and potentialities.

The plan's broader outline also poses many questions. How would it be financed? By all nations, though mainly the richest. How would the freedom leaders be recruited? From volunteers around the world, people with practical skills but above all with the energy and determination to offer leadership in what might be daunting circumstances. Under what sponsorship? The United Nations, which would give the freedom leaders legitimacy and credibility. Would they be paid? Yes, this is not a philanthropic project. How would freedom leaders deal with local violence, civil war, religious strife, tribal killing? By withdrawing; their jobs would not include fighting or hiding. How would leadership cadres relate to existing regimes? As peaceful rivals, goads, alternative agenda setters, but above all as aids and abettors to the progress and well-being of a nation and its people. By what values and other standards should the freedom leaders be tested? By those laid out explicitly in the Universal Declaration of Human Rights. What would serve as the broader, transformational goal of the local projects? To mobilize grassroots support for developing, sustaining, and energizing democratic governments, which are demonstrably more conducive than authoritarian rulerships to people's life satisfactions, their pursuits of happiness.

The ultimate attainment of happiness is a cherished dream, but as a goal of transforming leadership we must view it more as a process, a pursuit. The impoverished or suppressed person lives in stasis with meager hopes or expectations but with acutely felt wants. A leader addresses these wants with challenges to things as they are, with solutions and the ways and means to achieve change, and if this initiative hits powerfully and directly it will motivate the person in need to action. The leader may be only a family member or a concerned friend, a local cop or a social worker, a freedom leader, and the change at first only a small step up. But lives begin to be transformed.

The psychological process may be as critical as the material. A leader not only speaks to immediate wants but elevates people by vesting in them a sense of possibility, a belief that changes can be made and that they can make them. Opportunity beckons where none had appeared before, and once seized upon opens another opportunity, and another. So a pursuit of happiness—happiness as more than a chimera, more than pleasing sensations or gratifications, but as something substantial, something essentially "good"—begins. This pursuit will take many forms, amid confusion and uncertainties and setbacks, but one factor is consistent: *the needs are defined and their satisfaction sought on the needing person's terms.*

The crucial factor in this dynamic comes into play at the outset— the building of efficacy. The wanting person initially suffers not only material but also psychological and spiritual deprivation, feelings of inadequacy, hopelessness, and powerlessness. Nothing seems to work, and nothing can be done about it. But as possibilities appear and are realized, feelings of efficacy are nourished. A sense of empowerment fuels the pursuit of happiness. The "desire for self-fulfillment" is activated, which Abraham Maslow described as people's need to develop "to the full stature of which they are capable." As individuals draw together into action to achieve their needs, their collective efficacy unites them into a transforming force that may surpass the causal role of the original leadership. In this way *people* make change and eventually make history.

All this is change from the ground up. In the broadest terms, transforming change flows not from the work of the "great man" who single-handedly makes history, but from the collective achievement of a "great people." While leadership is necessary at every stage, beginning with the first spark that awakens people's hopes, its vital role is to create and expand the opportunities that empower people to pursue happiness for themselves.

Lao-tzu wrote in the *Tao te Ching*—

> *Bearing yet not possessing*
> *Working yet not taking credit*
> *Leading yet not dominating*
> *This is the Primal Virtue.*

NOTES

PROLOGUE
EMPOWERING HAPPINESS

1 *"happiness of the people"*: Jefferson, "Hints to Americans Travelling in Europe" (1788), in Jefferson, *Papers,* Julian P. Boyd, ed. (Princeton University Press, 1950–), vol. 13, pp. 264–75, quoted at p. 269.
2 *"pursuing happiness"*: Hutcheson, *A Short Introduction to Moral Philosophy,* in Hutcheson, *Collected Works* (Georg Olms Verlag, 1990), vol. 4, p. 4.
2 *Locke on happiness:* see Roy Porter, *The Creation of the Modern World: The Untold Story of the British Enlightenment* (W. W. Norton, 2000), pp. 263–64.

1 THE MYSTERIES OF LEADERSHIP

seshmi, shemsu, seshem-t: see E. A. Wallis Budge, *An Egyptian Hieroglyphic Dictionary* (John Murray, 1920), vol. 2, pp. 699, 742, 699, respectively.
7 *"reform of the State"*: Plato, *Republic,* in Plato, *Dialogues,* Benjamin Jowett, trans. (Random House, 1937), vol. 1, quoted at pp. 736, 737 (Book 5.473).
7 *"every political society"*: Aristotle, *Politics,* in Aristotle, *Basic Works,* Richard McKeon, ed. (Random House, 1941), quoted at p. 1296 (Book 7, ch. 14).

Cleopatra's Nose

Bernard M. Bass, *Bass & Stogdill's Handbook of Leadership,* 3rd ed. (Free Press, 1990), esp. chs. 4–5.
Emory S. Bogardus, *Leaders and Leadership* (D. Appleton-Century, 1934).

Thomas Carlyle, *On Heroes, Hero-Worship, & the Heroic in History,* Michael K. Goldberg et al., eds. (University of California Press, 1993).

Lewis J. Edinger, "Political Science and Political Biography: Reflections on the Study of Leadership," *Journal of Politics,* vol. 26, nos. 2–3 (May and August 1964), pp. 423–39, 648–76.

Alvin W. Gouldner, "Introduction," in Gouldner, ed., *Studies in Leadership: Leadership and Democratic Action* (Harper & Brothers, 1950), pp. 3–49.

Sidney Hook, *The Hero in History: A Study in Limitation and Possibility* (John Day, 1943).

William James, "Great Men and Their Environment," in James, The Will to Believe, *and Other Essays in Popular Philosophy,* Frederick H. Burkhardt et al., eds. (Harvard University Press, 1979), pp. 163–89.

William James, "The Importance of Individuals," in *ibid.,* pp. 190–95.

Maurice Mandelbaum, *Purpose and Necessity in Social Theory* (Johns Hopkins University Press, 1987), ch. 2, and passim.

J. A. Ponsioen, *The Analysis of Social Change Reconsidered: A Sociological Study* (Mouton, 1962), esp. ch. 4.

Philip Rosenberg, *The Seventh Hero: Thomas Carlyle and the Theory of Radical Activism* (Harvard University Press, 1974).

Donald D. Searing, "Models and Images of Man and Society in Leadership Theory," *Journal of Politics,* vol. 31, no. 1 (February 1969), pp. 3–31.

Eric Selbin, "Revolution in the Real World: Bringing Agency Back In," in John Foran, ed., *Theorizing Revolutions* (Routledge, 1997), pp. 123–36.

Piotr Sztompka, *Society in Action: The Theory of Social Becoming* (University of Chicago Press, 1991), part 1.

8 "*Cleopatra's nose*": Blaise Pascal, *Pensées, and the Provincial Letters,* W. F. Trotter and Thomas M'Crie, trans. (Modern Library, 1941), p. 59 (162).

8 "*her actual beauty*": Plutarch, "Antony," in Plutarch, *The Lives of the Noble Grecians and Romans,* John Dryden and Arthur Hugh Clough, trans. (Modern Library, 1932), quoted at p. 1119.

10 "*leader is characterized*": Bass, p. 87.

11 "*Universal History*": Carlyle, p. 3.

11 "*actions influenced*": Hook, p. 154.

Slaves of History

Isaiah Berlin, *The Hedgehog and the Fox: An Essay on Tolstoy's View of History* (Simon and Schuster, 1953).

Steven Best, *The Politics of Historical Vision: Marx, Foucault, Habermas* (Guilford Press, 1995), esp. ch. 1.

G. A. Cohen, *Karl Marx's Theory of History: A Defence* (Princeton University Press, 1978).

Karl Federn, *The Materialist Conception of History* (1939; reprinted by Greenwood Press, 1971).

Helmut Fleischer, *Marxism and History,* Eric Mosbacher, trans. (Harper & Row, 1973).

Alvin W. Gouldner, "Introduction," in Gouldner, ed., *Studies in Leadership: Leadership and Democratic Action* (Harper & Brothers, 1950), pp. 3–49.

John E. Grumley, *History and Totality: Radical Historicism from Hegel to Foucault* (Routledge, 1989), esp. chs. 1–2.

Mike Hawkins, *Social Darwinism in European and American Thought, 1860–1945: Nature as Model and Nature as Threat* (Cambridge University Press, 1997), esp. ch. 4.

G. W. F. Hegel, *The Philosophy of History*, J. Sibree, trans. (Dover, 1956).

Sidney Hook, *The Hero in History: A Study in Limitation and Possibility* (John Day, 1943).

Maurice Mandelbaum, *Purpose and Necessity in Social Theory* (Johns Hopkins University Press, 1987).

Karl Marx, *Political Writings: The Revolutions of 1848*, David Fernbach, ed. (Random House, 1974).

Richard W. Miller, *Analyzing Marx: Morality, Power and History* (Princeton University Press, 1984).

William Fielding Ogburn, "The Great Man versus Social Forces," *Social Forces*, vol. 5, no. 2 (December 1926), pp. 225–31.

J. A. Ponsioen, *The Analysis of Social Change Reconsidered: A Sociological Study* (Mouton, 1962).

Melvin Rader, *Marx's Interpretation of History* (Oxford University Press, 1979).

Donald D. Searing, "Models and Images of Man and Society in Leadership Theory," *Journal of Politics*, vol. 31, no. 1 (February 1969), pp. 3–31.

Herbert Spencer, "Progress: Its Law and Cause," in Spencer, *Illustrations of Universal Progress* (D. Appleton, 1880), pp. 1–60.

Herbert Spencer, *The Study of Sociology* (D. Appleton, 1874).

Svetozar Stojanović, "The Ethical Potential of Marx's Thought," in Tom Bottomore, ed., *Modern Interpretations of Marx* (Basil Blackwell, 1981), pp. 170–87.

Alan Swingewood, *A Short History of Sociological Thought* (St. Martin's Press, 1984), esp. part 1.

Piotr Sztompka, *Society in Action: The Theory of Social Becoming* (University of Chicago Press, 1991), esp. ch. 3.

Burleigh Taylor Wilkins, *Hegel's Philosophy of History* (Cornell University Press, 1974).

13 "*no consciousness*": Hegel, p. 30.

13 "*long series*": Spencer, *Study of Sociology*, pp. 34–35.

13 "*undeserving poor*": Spencer, *The Man versus the State* (Williams & Norgate, 1902), p. 18.

14 "*millions of Christian men*": Tolstoy, *War and Peace*, Louise and Alymer Maude, trans., and George Gibian, ed. (W. W. Norton, 1966), p. 668.

14 "*history's slave*": ibid., p. 670.

What Leadership Analysis Can Do

15 "*proletarians have nothing to lose*": Marx and Frederick Engels, "Manifesto of the Communist Party," in Marx, *Political Writings: The Revolutions of 1848*, David Fernbach, ed. (Random House, 1974), pp. 67–98, quoted at p. 98.

15 "*change evolves*": Swingewood, *A Short History of Sociological Thought* (St. Martin's Press, 1984), pp. 93–94, 93, respectively.

15 "*Men make their own history*": Marx, "The Eighteenth Brumaire of Louis Bonaparte," in Marx and Engels, *Selected Works* (International Publishers, 1968), pp. 97–180, quoted at p. 97.

2 SEARCHING FOR THE X FACTOR

The Quest for Causality

Peter J. Bowler, *Evolution: The History of an Idea* (University of California Press, 1984).

Janet Browne, *Charles Darwin*, 2 vols. (Alfred A. Knopf, 1995–2002).

J. W. Burrow, *Evolution and Society: A Study in Victorian Social Theory* (Cambridge University Press, 1966).

I. Bernard Cohen, *Revolution in Science* (Belknap Press, 1985), esp. chs. 2, 19.

Charles Darwin, *Autobiography, 1809–1882,* Nora Barlow, ed. (Collins, 1958).

Mike Hawkins, *Social Darwinism in European and American Thought, 1860–1945: Nature as Model and Nature as Threat* (Cambridge University Press, 1997).

Paul Heyer, *Nature, Human Nature, and Society: Marx, Darwin, Biology, and the Human Sciences* (Greenwood Press, 1982).

M. J. S. Hodge, "Origins and Species Before and After Darwin," in R. C. Olby et al., eds., *Companion to the History of Modern Science* (Routledge, 1990), pp. 374–95.

David L. Hull, comp., *Darwin and His Critics* (Harvard University Press, 1973).

Maurice Mandelbaum, *History, Man, & Reason: A Study in Nineteenth-Century Thought* (Johns Hopkins University Press, 1971).

Maurice Mandelbaum, *Purpose and Necessity in Social Theory* (Johns Hopkins University Press, 1987).

Anthony O'Hear, *Beyond Evolution: Human Nature and the Limits of Evolutionary Explanation* (Clarendon Press, 1997).

Roy Porter, *The Creation of the Modern World: The Untold Story of the British Enlightenment* (W. W. Norton, 2000).

Stephen K. Sanderson, *Social Evolutionism* (Basil Blackwell, 1990).

Alan Swingewood, *A Short History of Sociological Thought* (St. Martin's Press, 1984), esp. part 1.

Morton G. White, *Foundations of Historical Knowledge* (Harper & Row, 1965).

18 "*World of civil society*": Vico, *The New Science,* Thomas Goddard Bergin and Max Harold Fisch, trans. (Cornell University Press, 1948), p. 85 (sect. 331).

18 "*first, and greatest sociologist*": Swingewood, p. 13.

18 "*not ruled by fortune*": Montesquieu, *Considerations on the Causes of the Grandeur and Decadence of the Romans,* Jehu Baker, trans. (D. Appleton, 1901), p. 378.

19 "*mutual dependence of man*": Hume, quoted in Swingewood, p. 19.

19 *"from a cautious observation"*: David Hume, *A Treatise of Human Nature,* David Fate Norton and Mary J. Norton, eds. (Oxford University Press, 2000), p. 6.
19 *"neither the action"*: Darwin, p. 119.
20 *"new way to make sense"*: Dennett, *Darwin's Dangerous Idea: Evolution and the Meanings of Life* (Simon & Schuster, 1995), p. 25.
20 *"caused a greater upheaval"*: Mayr, "The Nature of the Darwinian Revolution," *Science,* vol. 176, no. 4038 (June 2, 1972), pp. 981–89, quoted at p. 987.
21 *"vast, mysterious"*: White, p. 213.

What Is Transforming Leadership?

Bruce J. Avolio and Bernard M. Bass, "Transformational Leadership, Charisma, and Beyond," in James G. Hunt et al., eds., *Emerging Leadership Vistas* (Lexington Books, 1988), pp. 28–49.

Bernard M. Bass, *Bass & Stogdill's Handbook of Leadership,* 3rd ed. (Free Press, 1990).

Bernard M. Bass, "Does the Transactional-Transformational Leadership Paradigm Transcend Organizational and National Boundaries?," *American Psychologist,* vol. 52, no. 2 (February 1997), pp. 130–39.

Bernard M. Bass, *Leadership and Performance Beyond Expectations* (Free Press, 1985).

Bernard M. Bass, "A Seminal Shift: The Impact of James Burns' *Leadership*," *Leadership Quarterly,* vol. 4, nos. 3–4 (1993), pp. 375–77.

Bernard M. Bass, "Theory of Transformational Leadership Redux," *Leadership Quarterly,* vol. 6, no. 4 (Winter 1995), pp. 463–78.

Bernard M. Bass, *Transformational Leadership: Industry, Military, and Educational Impact* (Lawrence Erlbaum Associates, 1998).

Bernard M. Bass and Bruce J. Avolio, "Transformational Leadership: A Response to Critiques," in Martin M. Chemers and Roya Ayman, eds., *Leadership Theory and Research* (Academic Press, 1993), pp. 49–80.

Bernard M. Bass, Bruce J. Avolio, and Laurie Goodheim, "Biography and the Assessment of Transformational Leadership at the World-Class Level," *Journal of Management,* vol. 13, no. 1 (1987), pp. 7–19.

James MacGregor Burns, *Leadership* (Harper & Row, 1978).

James MacGregor Burns, *Roosevelt: The Lion and the Fox* (Harcourt, Brace, 1956).

James MacGregor Burns, *Roosevelt: The Soldier of Freedom* (Harcourt Brace Jovanovich, 1970).

"Charismatic and Transformational Leadership: Taking Stock of the Present and Future" (special issues), *Leadership Quarterly,* vol. 10, nos. 2–3 (Summer and Fall 1999).

Jay A. Conger et al., eds., *Charismatic Leadership: The Elusive Factor in Organizational Effectiveness* (Jossey-Bass, 1988).

Richard A. Couto, "The Transformation of Transforming Leadership," in J. Thomas Wren, ed., *The Leader's Companion* (Free Press, 1995), pp. 102–107.

Robert J. House, "A 1976 Theory of Charismatic Leadership," in James G. Hunt and Lars L. Larson, eds., *Leadership: The Cutting Edge* (Southern Illinois University Press, 1977), pp. 189–207.

Robert J. House and Boas Shamir, "Toward the Integration of Transformational, Charismatic, and Visionary Theories," in Chemers and Ayman, pp. 81–107.

Robert J. House, James Woycke, and Eugene M. Fodor, "Charismatic and Noncharismatic Leaders: Differences in Behavior and Effectiveness," in Conger et al., pp. 98–121.

James G. Hunt, "Transformational/Charismatic Leadership's Transformation of the Field: An Historical Essay," *Leadership Quarterly,* vol. 10, no. 2 (Summer 1999), pp. 129–44.

Nancy C. Roberts, "Transforming Leadership: A Process of Collective Action," *Human Relations,* vol. 38, no. 11 (1985), pp. 1023–46.

Arthur Schweitzer, *The Age of Charisma* (Nelson-Hall, 1984).

Max Weber, *The Theory of Social and Economic Organization,* A. M. Henderson and Talcott Parsons, trans. (Oxford University Press, 1947), esp. part 3.

Ann Ruth Willner, *The Spellbinders: Charismatic Political Leadership* (Yale University Press, 1984).

J. C. Wofford and Vicki L. Goodwin, "A Cognitive Interpretation of Transactional and Transformational Leadership Theories," *Leadership Quarterly,* vol. 5, no. 2 (Summer 1994), pp. 161–86.

Francis J. Yammarino, "Transforming Leadership Studies: Bernard Bass' *Leadership and Performance Beyond Expectations," Leadership Quarterly,* vol. 4, nos. 3–4 (1993), pp. 379–82.

Francis J. Yammarino, William D. Spangler, and Bernard M. Bass, "Transformational Leadership and Performance: A Longitudinal Investigation," *Leadership Quarterly,* vol. 4, no. 1 (Spring 1993), pp. 81–102.

Gary Yukl, "An Evaluation of Conceptual Weaknesses in Transformational and Charismatic Leadership Theories," *Leadership Quarterly,* vol. 10, no. 2 (Summer 1999), pp. 285–305.

22 "*mothers and fathers*": Campaign Address, October 30, 1940, in Roosevelt, *Public Papers and Addresses,* Samuel I. Rosenman, comp. (Random House, 1938–50), vol. 9, pp. 514–24, quoted at p. 517.

22 "*The country needs*": Address at Oglethorpe University, May 22, 1932, in *ibid.,* vol. 1, pp. 639–47, quoted at p. 646.

23 "*Economic Bill of Rights*": see Annual Message to the Congress, January 6, 1941, in *ibid.,* vol. 9, pp. 663–72, esp. pp. 671–72; and Message to the Congress on the State of the Union, January 11, 1944, in *ibid.,* vol. 13, pp. 32–42, esp. p. 41.

23 *Dr. Win-the-War:* see Press Conference, December 28, 1943, in *ibid.,* vol. 12, pp. 569–75, esp. p. 571.

23 "*continuous liberal government*": Radio Address on Electing Liberals to Public Office, November 4, 1938, in *ibid.,* vol. 7, pp. 584–93, quoted at p. 585.

24 "*first order of change*": Bass, *Leadership and Performance,* p. 4.

26 "*sense of 'meaningfulness'*": Bass, *Transformational Leadership,* p. 175.

26 "*greatest revolutionary force*": Weber, pp. 363, 359, 358, respectively.

26 "*devotion, awe*": Willner, p. 7.

26 *"fervent loyalty"*: Tucker, *Politics as Leadership,* rev. ed. (University of Missouri Press, 1995), p. 94.

26 *"charisma hungry"*: quoted in Bass, *Leadership and Performance,* p. 38.

27 *Nadler and Tushman on charismatic leadership:* Nadler and Tushman, "Beyond the Charismatic Leader," in Wren, pp. 108–13, esp. pp. 109–10.

The Power of Vision

27 *Was Hitler a leader?*: see my Foreword to Joanne Ciulla, ed., *Ethics, the Heart of Leadership* (Quorum Books, 1998), p. ix, from whose language I have borrowed.

28 *"question of what constitutes"*: Ciulla, "Leadership Ethics: Mapping the Territory," in *ibid.,* pp. 3–25, quoted at p. 13.

28 *Coles on parental leadership:* see Coles, *The Moral Intelligence of Children* (Random House, 1997).

28 *"ways leaders and followers"*: Rost, *Leadership for the Twenty-First Century* (Praeger, 1991), p. 153.

3 KINGS AND QUEENS, KNIGHTS AND PAWNS

W. Norwood Potter, "Chess," in *Encyclopaedia Britannica,* 9th ed. (R. S. Peale, 1890).

Kings of Africa

Robbins Burling, *The Passage of Power: Studies in Political Succession* (Academic Press, 1974).

M. Fortes and E. E. Evans-Pritchard, eds., *African Political Systems* (Oxford University Press, 1940).

Max Gluckman, *Order and Rebellion in Tribal Africa* (Free Press of Glencoe, 1963).

Rene Lemarchand, ed., *African Kingships in Perspective* (Frank Cass, 1977).

Lucy Mair, *African Kingdoms* (Oxford University Press, 1977), esp. ch. 9.

Lucy Mair, *Primitive Government: A Study of Traditional Political Systems in Eastern Africa,* rev. ed. (Indiana University Press, 1977).

Douglas L. Oliver, *A Solomon Island Society: Kinship and Leadership among the Siuai of Bougainville* (Harvard University Press, 1955).

36 *"power built up"*: Burling, p. 19.

Elizabeth I: Ruler or Ruled?

Robert Ashton, *Reformation and Revolution, 1558–1660* (Granada, 1984).

Susan Bassnett, *Elizabeth I: A Feminist Perspective* (Berg, 1988).

Susan Doran, *Elizabeth I and Religion, 1558–1603* (Routledge, 1994).

Susan Doran, *Monarchy and Matrimony: The Courtships of Elizabeth I* (Routledge, 1996).

John Guy, *Tudor England* (Oxford University Press, 1988).

Christopher Haigh, *Elizabeth I* (Longman, 1988).

Christopher Haigh, ed., *The Reign of Elizabeth I* (University of Georgia Press, 1985).

William P. Haugaard, *Elizabeth and the English Reformation: The Struggle for a Stable Settlement of Religion* (Cambridge University Press, 1968).

Carole Levin, *"The Heart and Stomach of a King": Elizabeth I and the Politics of Sex and Power* (University of Pennsylvania Press, 1994).

Wallace T. MacCaffrey, *Elizabeth I* (Edward Arnold, 1993).

Wallace T. MacCaffrey, *Elizabeth I: War and Politics, 1588–1603* (Princeton University Press, 1992).

Wallace T. MacCaffrey, *Queen Elizabeth and the Making of Policy, 1572–1588* (Princeton University Press, 1981).

Wallace T. MacCaffrey, *The Shaping of the Elizabethan Regime: Elizabethan Politics, 1558–72* (Jonathan Cape, 1969).

Alison Plowden, *The Young Elizabeth*, rev. ed. (Sutton Publishing, 1999).

David Starkey, *Elizabeth: The Struggle for the Throne* (HarperCollins, 2001).

Julia M. Walker, ed., *Dissing Elizabeth: Negative Representations of Gloriana* (Duke University Press, 1998).

39 *Elizabeth's brutal apprenticeship:* see MacCaffrey, *Elizabeth I* (1993), p. 28.

40 *"inexorable logic"*: Guy, p. 277.

40 *"God's wounds"*: quoted in Haigh, *Elizabeth I* (1988), p. 9.

40 *"Queene was but a woman"*: quoted in Carole Levin, *"We Shall Never Have a Merry World While the Queene Lyveth:* Gender, Monarchy, and the Power of Seditious Words," in Walker, pp. 77–95, John Feltwell quoted at pp. 77–78.

40 *"I know I have the body"*: quoted in Bassnett, pp. 73–74.

40 *"sexly weakness"*: *ibid.*, p. 128.

41 *"still center"*: MacCaffrey, *Elizabeth I: War and Politics* (1992), p. 542.

41 *"gouerned by him"*: Ilona Bell, *"Souereaigne Lord of Lordly Lady of this Land:* Elizabeth, Stubbs, and the *Gaping Gulf,"* in Walker, pp. 99–117, quoted at p. 108.

41 *"centre of intellectual sophistication"*: MacCaffrey, *Elizabeth I* (1993), p. 7.

42 *MacCaffrey on Elizabeth's "rulership":* MacCaffrey, *Elizabeth I: War and Politics* (1992), p. 539.

43 *"perturbations of the unstable world"*: *ibid.*, p. 542.

43 semper eadem: *ibid.*, p. 541.

Reining in the Knights

Lloyd E. Ambrosius, *Woodrow Wilson and the American Diplomatic Tradition: The Treaty Fight in Perspective* (Cambridge University Press, 1987).

Ruhl J. Bartlett, *The League to Enforce Peace* (University of North Carolina Press, 1944).

Paul Birdsall, *Versailles Twenty Years After* (Reynal & Hitchcock, 1941).

James Bohman and Matthias Lutz-Bachmann, eds., *Perpetual Peace: Essays on Kant's Cosmopolitan Ideal* (MIT Press, 1997).

Edward Buehrig, *Woodrow Wilson and the Balance of Power* (Indiana University Press, 1955).

James MacGregor Burns, *The Workshop of Democracy* (Alfred A. Knopf, 1985), chs. 12–13.

Charles Chatfield and Ruzanna Ilukhina, eds., *Peace/Mir: An Anthology of Historic Alternatives to War* (Syracuse University Press, 1994).

Denna Frank Fleming, *The United States and the League of Nations, 1918–1920* (G. P. Putnam's Sons, 1932).

F. H. Hinsley, *Power and the Pursuit of Peace* (Cambridge University Press, 1963).

Immanuel Kant, *Political Writings,* Hans Reiss, ed., H. B. Nisbet, trans. (Cambridge University Press, 1970).

Joel Larus, ed., *From Collective Security to Preventive Diplomacy* (John Wiley & Sons, 1965).

Gerard J. Mangone, *A Short History of International Organization* (McGraw-Hill, 1954), chs. 1–5.

F. S. Northedge, *The League of Nations: Its Life and Times, 1920–1946* (Holmes & Meier, 1986).

Robert E. Osgood, "Woodrow Wilson, Collective Security, and the Lessons of History," in Earl Latham, ed., *The Philosophy and Policies of Woodrow Wilson* (University of Chicago Press, 1958), pp. 187–98.

Grace G. Roosevelt, *Reading Rousseau in the Nuclear Age* (Temple University Press, 1990).

Frederick L. Schuman, *The Commonwealth of Man: An Inquiry into Power Politics and World Government* (Alfred A. Knopf, 1952).

Raymond J. Sontag, *A Broken World, 1919–1939* (Harper & Row, 1971).

D. N. Verma, *India and the League of Nations* (Bharati Bhawan, 1968).

F. P. Walters, *A History of the League of Nations,* 2 vols. (Oxford University Press, 1952).

Arthur Walworth, *Wilson and His Peacemakers: American Diplomacy at the Paris Peace Conference, 1919* (W. W. Norton, 1986).

William C. Widenor, *Henry Cabot Lodge and the Search for an American Foreign Policy* (University of California Press, 1980), esp. chs. 6–7.

43 *"For God's sake"*: quoted in Schuman, p. 356.

43 *"I, Emperor of Ethiopia"*: Address of Haile Selassie before Assembly, June 30, 1936, reprinted in Larus, pp. 136–43, quoted at pp. 136, 143.

45 *"anyone should refuse"*: Crucé, *The New Cyneas* (1623), excerpted in Chatfield and Ilukhina, pp. 67–68, quoted at p. 67.

45 *"establish rules"*: Penn, *An Essay towards the Present and Future Peace of Europe,* excerpted in *ibid.,* pp. 68–70, quoted at p. 69.

45 *"make sure"*: Rousseau, *A Project of Perpetual Peace* (1761), excerpted in *ibid.,* pp. 70–74, quoted at p. 74.

45 *"ban of Europe"*: quoted in Schuman, p. 349.

45 *"savage lawless freedom"*: Kant, *Perpetual Peace: A Philosophical Essay* (1795), excerpted in Chatfield and Ilukhina, pp. 75–77, quoted at p. 77.

45 *"universal association"*: An Address in Washington to the League to Enforce Peace, May 27, 1916, in Wilson, *Papers,* Arthur S. Link, ed. (Princeton University Press, 1966–94), vol. 37, pp. 113–16, quoted at p. 116.

46 *"definite guarantee"*: An Address to the Third Plenary Session of the Peace Conference, February 14, 1919, in *ibid.,* vol. 55, pp. 164–78, quoted at p. 175.

46 *"open covenants"*: An Address to a Joint Session of Congress, January 8, 1918, in *ibid.,* vol. 45, pp. 534–39, quoted at p. 536.

46 *Article 16:* reprinted in Northedge, pp. 317–27, quoted at p. 323.

The Plight of the Pawns

Lloyd E. Ambrosius, *Woodrow Wilson and the American Diplomatic Tradition: The Treaty Fight in Perspective* (Cambridge University Press, 1987).

H. C. F. Bell, *Woodrow Wilson and the People* (Doubleday, Doran, 1945), esp. chs. 17–18.

James MacGregor Burns, *The Workshop of Democracy* (Alfred A. Knopf, 1985), ch. 13.

John Milton Cooper, Jr., *Breaking the Heart of the World: Woodrow Wilson and the Fight for the League of Nations* (Cambridge University Press, 2001).

Robert Eden, "The Rhetorical Presidency and the Eclipse of Executive Power: Woodrow Wilson's *Constitutional Government in the United States,"* *Polity,* vol. 18, no. 3 (Spring 1996), pp. 357–78.

Denna Frank Fleming, *The United States and the League of Nations, 1918–1920* (G. P. Putnam's Sons, 1932).

Thomas J. Knock, *To End All Wars: Woodrow Wilson and the Quest for a New World Order* (Oxford University Press, 1992).

Warren F. Kuehl, *Seeking World Order: The United States and International Organization to 1920* (Vanderbilt University Press, 1969).

Henry Cabot Lodge, *The Senate and the League of Nations* (Charles Scribner's Sons, 1925).

Herbert F. Margulies, *The Mild Reservationists and the League of Nations Controversy in the Senate* (University of Missouri Press, 1989).

Jan Willem Schulte Nordholt, *Woodrow Wilson: A Life for World Peace,* Herbert H. Rowen, trans. (University of California Press, 1991).

Frederick L. Schuman, *The Commonwealth of Man: An Inquiry into Power Politics and World Government* (Alfred A. Knopf, 1952).

Ralph Stone, *The Irreconcilables: The Fight Against the League of Nations* (University Press of Kentucky, 1970).

Ralph Stone, ed., *Wilson and the League of Nations: Why America's Rejection?* (Holt, Rinehart and Winston, 1967).

William C. Widenor, *Henry Cabot Lodge and the Search for an American Foreign Policy* (University of California Press, 1980), esp. ch. 8.

Woodrow Wilson, *Papers,* Arthur S. Link, ed. (Princeton University Press, 1966–94), vol. 63.

48 *"consist of their people"*: An Address to the Columbus Chamber of Commerce, September 4, 1919, in Wilson, *Papers,* vol. 63, pp. 7–18, quoted at p. 15.

48 *"we got messages"*: *ibid.,* p. 17.

48 *"in truth a people's treaty"*: An Address in the Billings Auditorium, September 11, 1919, in *ibid.*, vol. 63, pp. 170–80, quoted at p. 171.

48 *"for the first time"*: An After-Dinner Speech in Los Angeles, September 20, 1919, in *ibid.*, vol. 63, pp. 400–407, quoted at p. 403.

48 *"It is a people's treaty"*: An Address in the City Auditorium, September 25, 1919, in *ibid.*, vol. 63, pp. 500–13, quoted at p. 502.

49 *"rejected utterly"*: Schuman, p. 362.

4 LEADERS AS PLANNERS

The Winds and Waves of War

Felipe Fernández-Armesto, *The Spanish Armada: The Experience of War in 1588* (Oxford University Press, 1988).

Winston Graham, *The Spanish Armadas* (Doubleday, 1972).

Henry Kamen, *Philip of Spain* (Yale University Press, 1997).

Colin Martin and Geoffrey Parker, *The Spanish Armada* (Hamish Hamilton, 1988).

Garrett Mattingly, *The Armada* (Houghton Mifflin, 1959).

Geoffrey Parker, *The Grand Strategy of Philip II* (Yale University Press, 1998).

M. J. Rodriguez-Salgado and Simon Adams, eds., *England, Spain and the Gran Armada, 1585–1604* (Barnes & Noble Books, 1990).

Stephen Usherwood, ed., *The Great Enterprise: The History of the Spanish Armada* (Folio Society, 1978).

53 *"sail in the name of God"*: quoted in Parker, p. 196.

55 *"in a thousand directions"*: quoted in Fernández-Armesto, p. 188.

56 *"delays of the Duke"*: Florentine ambassador to Madrid, quoted in Parker, p. 230.

56 *"(whether through malice)"*: Spanish ambassador in Turin, quoted in *ibid.*

56 *"better information"*: *ibid.*, p. 151.

56 *"High and low"*: Graham, p. 83.

57 *"You are engaged"*: quoted in Parker, p. 75.

57 *"experienced great felicity"*: quoted in Kamen, p. 236.

57 *"No prince"*: *ibid.*, p. 267.

57 *"God will send"*: quoted in Parker, p. 106.

57 *"complete confidence"*: *ibid.*, p. 108.

57 *"I shall never fail"*: quoted in *ibid.*, p. 271.

Dreamers with Shovels

Charles Beatty, *De Lesseps of Suez* (Harper & Brothers, 1956).

Gerstle Mack, *The Land Divided: A History of the Panama Canal and Other Isthmian Canal Projects* (Alfred A. Knopf, 1944), esp. part 3.

John Marlowe, *The Making of the Suez Canal* (Cresset Press, 1964).

David McCullough, *The Path Between the Seas: The Creation of the Panama Canal, 1870–1914* (Simon and Schuster, 1977), part 1.

John Pudney, *Suez: De Lesseps' Canal* (Praeger, 1968).

André Siegfried, *Suez and Panama*, H. H. and Doris Hemming, trans. (Harcourt, Brace, 1940).

58 *"With the power of Persia"*: quoted in Pudney, p. 3.

59 *"free and exclusive possession"*: ibid., p. 4.

60 *"bubble scheme"*: quoted in Siegfried, p. 68.

60 *"universal character"*: quoted in Pudney, p. 76.

60 *"driven by sticks"*: ibid., p. 103.

61 "le Grand Français": León Gambetta, cited in Beatty, p. 282.

61 *"marked out"*: Ernest Renan, quoted in Siegfried, p. 23.

61 *"as we did at Suez"*: ibid., p. 259.

The Power of Steam Shovels

Richard H. Collin, *Theodore Roosevelt's Caribbean: The Panama Canal, the Monroe Doctrine, and the Latin American Context* (Louisiana State University Press, 1990), esp. part 2.

Miles P. DuVal, Jr., *Cadiz to Cathay: The Story of the Long Diplomatic Struggle for the Panama Canal* (1940; reprinted by Greenwood Press, 1968).

Willis Fletcher Johnson, *Four Centuries of the Panama Canal* (Henry Holt, 1906).

Gerstle Mack, *The Land Divided: A History of the Panama Canal and Other Isthmian Canal Projects* (Alfred A. Knopf, 1944), esp. part 4.

A. T. Mahan, *The Influence of Sea Power upon History, 1660–1783* (Little, Brown, 1944).

John Major, *Prize Possession: The United States and the Panama Canal, 1903–1979* (Cambridge University Press, 1993).

David McCullough, *The Path Between the Seas: The Creation of the Panama Canal, 1870–1914* (Simon and Schuster, 1977).

André Siegfried, *Suez and Panama*, H. H. and Doris Hemming, trans. (Harcourt, Brace, 1940).

63 *"policy of this country"*: quoted in DuVal, p. 80.

64 *"strategic center"*: Mahan, "The United States Looking Outward," *Atlantic Monthly*, vol. 66, no. 12 (December 1890), pp. 816–24, quoted at pp. 819, 822.

64 *"contemptible little creatures"*: quoted in Mack, p. 448.

64 *"halter around the neck"*: E. A. Morales, quoted in DuVal, p. 273.

65 *"in perpetuity"*: Hay-Bunau-Varilla Treaty, November 18, 1903, reprinted in *ibid.*, pp. 476–86, quoted at p. 477 (Article 2).

65 *"Panama Canal would not have been"*: quoted in *ibid.*, p. 438.

65 *"foolish and homicidal corruptionists"*: letter to John Hay, September 15, 1903, in Roosevelt, *Letters,* Elting E. Morison, ed. (Harvard University Press, 1951–54), vol. 3, p. 599.

65 *"You certainly have"*: quoted in McCullough, p. 383.

66 *"If at any time"*: *ibid.,* p. 511.

66 *"like human beings"*: Joseph Bucklin Bishop, quoted in *ibid.,* p. 538.

66 *"endless-chain system"*: *ibid.,* p. 543.

67 *Canal traffic: ibid.,* p. 611.

67 *Mahan on canal as bridge:* A. T. Mahan, *Naval Strategy* (Little, Brown, 1919), p. 102.

67 *"points of vantage"*: quoted in McCullough, p. 254.

The Transformation of Harvard University

Hugh Hawkins, *Between Harvard and America: The Educational Leadership of Charles W. Eliot* (Oxford University Press, 1972).

Henry James, *Charles W. Eliot: President of Harvard University, 1869–1909,* 2 vols. (Houghton Mifflin, 1930).

Seymour Martin Lipset, "Political Controversies at Harvard, 1636 to 1974," in Lipset and David Riesman, *Education and Politics at Harvard* (McGraw-Hill, 1975), pp. 3–278, esp. pp. 47–131.

Frederick Rudolph, *The American College and University* (1962; reprinted by University of Georgia Press, 1990), esp. ch. 14.

70 *"quiet term"*: quoted in Lipset, p. 95.

70 *"embrace collective solutions"*: Hawkins, p. 298.

70 *"meant for progress"*: quoted in *ibid.,* p. 144.

70 "pour le bien": quoted in David McCullough, *The Path Between the Seas: The Creation of the Panama Canal, 1870–1914* (Simon and Schuster, 1977), p. 54.

71 *"when you have something important"*: *ibid.,* p. 51.

71 *"combinations of many men"*: quoted in Hawkins, p. 150.

5 THE TRANSFORMATION OF AMERICAN LEADERSHIP

Roger Chartier, *The Cultural Origins of the French Revolution,* Lydia G. Cochrane, trans. (Duke University Press, 1991).

Robert Darnton, *The Literary Underground of the Old Regime* (Harvard University Press, 1982).

John Lough, *An Introduction to Eighteenth Century France* (David McKay, 1960), esp. ch. 8.

Harry C. Payne, *The Philosophes and the People* (Yale University Press, 1976).

Roy Porter, *The Creation of the Modern World: The Untold Story of the British Enlightenment* (W. W. Norton, 2000), ch. 4, and passim.

Thomas R. Rochon, *Culture Moves: Ideas, Activism, and Changing Values* (Princeton University Press, 1998).

John W. Yolton et al., eds., *The Blackwell Companion to the Enlightenment* (Blackwell, 1991).

   76 "*common denominator*": Saisselin, "*Philosophes*," in Yolton et al., pp. 395–97, quoted at p. 396.

Collective Leadership on Trial

Bernard Bailyn, *The Ideological Origins of the American Revolution* (Belknap Press, 1967).

James MacGregor Burns, *The Vineyard of Liberty* (Alfred A. Knopf, 1982), ch. 1.

James MacGregor Burns and Stewart Burns, *A People's Charter: The Pursuit of Rights in America* (Alfred A. Knopf, 1991), ch. 2.

Henry Steele Commager, *The Empire of Reason* (Anchor/Doubleday, 1977).

David Brion Davis, *Revolutions: Reflections on American Equality and Foreign Liberations* (Harvard University Press, 1990).

Edward Dumbauld, *The Declaration of Independence, and What It Means Today* (University of Oklahoma Press, 1950).

Jack P. Greene, ed., *The American Revolution: Its Character and Limits* (New York University Press, 1987).

Jack P. Greene and J. R. Pole, eds., *The Blackwell Encyclopedia of the American Revolution* (Blackwell, 1991).

Allen Jayne, *Jefferson's Declaration of Independence: Origins, Philosophy and Theology* (University Press of Kentucky, 1998).

Michael Kammen, *A Season of Youth: The American Revolution and the Historical Imagination* (Alfred A. Knopf, 1978).

Nicholas N. Kittrie, *The War Against Authority: From the Crisis of Legitimacy to a New Social Contract* (Johns Hopkins University Press, 1995), esp. ch. 3.

Adrienne Koch, ed., *The American Enlightenment: The Shaping of the American Experiment and a Free Society* (George Braziller, 1965).

Pauline Maier, *American Scripture: Making the Declaration of Independence* (Alfred A. Knopf, 1997).

Pauline Maier, *The Old Revolutionaries: Political Lives in the Age of Samuel Adams* (Alfred A. Knopf, 1980).

Henry F. May, *The Enlightenment in America* (Oxford University Press, 1976).

Thomas L. Pangle, *The Spirit of Modern Republicanism: The Moral Vision of the American Founders and the Philosophy of Locke* (University of Chicago Press, 1988).

Jack N. Rakove, *The Beginnings of National Politics: An Interpretive History of the Continental Congress* (Alfred A. Knopf, 1979).

John Phillip Reid, *The Concept of Liberty in the Age of the American Revolution* (University of Chicago Press, 1988).

Carl J. Richard, *The Founders and the Classics: Greece, Rome, and the American Enlightenment* (Harvard University Press, 1994).

M. N. S. Sellers, *The Sacred Fire of Liberty: Republicanism, Liberalism and the Law* (New York University Press, 1998).

Harry M. Ward, *The War for Independence and the Transformation of American Society* (UCL Press, 1999).

Garry Wills, *Inventing America: Jefferson's Declaration of Independence* (Doubleday, 1978).

Gordon S. Wood, *The Radicalism of the American Revolution* (Alfred A. Knopf, 1992).

77 *"all its brilliant achievements"*: Koch, p. 39.

77 *"place before mankind"*: letter to Henry Lee, May 8, 1825, in Jefferson, *Works,* H. A. Washington, ed. (Townsend MacCoun, 1884), vol. 7, p. 407; see also letter to Madison, August 30, 1823, in James Morton Smith, ed., *The Republic of Letters: The Correspondence between Thomas Jefferson and James Madison, 1776–1826* (W. W. Norton, 1995), vol. 3, pp. 1875–77.

78 *"exercise and fruits"*: letter to Isaac H. Tiffany, August 26, 1816, in Jefferson, *Works,* vol. 7, pp. 31–32, quoted at p. 32.

79 *"general happiness"*: Hutcheson, *A System of Moral Philosophy* (1755), in Hutcheson, *Collected Works* (Georg Olms Verlag, 1990), vol. 6, p. 226.

79 *"a national Spirit"*: letter to John Jay, January 10, 1784, in Jay, *Unpublished Papers,* Richard B. Morris, ed. (Harper & Row, 1975–80), vol. 2, pp. 674–75, quoted at p. 675.

79 *"behoves every one"*: letter to Elbridge Gerry, April 30, 1786, in Paul H. Smith, ed., *Letters of Delegates to Congress, 1774–1789* (Library of Congress, 1976–2000), vol. 23, pp. 252–53, quoted at p. 253.

80 *"East is in tumult"*: letter of November 11, 1786, in *ibid.,* vol. 24, pp. 24–26, quoted at p. 25.

80 *"troubles in Massachusetts"*: letter of November 1, 1786, in Jared Sparks, ed., *Correspondence of the American Revolution; Being Letters of Eminent Men to George Washington* (Little, Brown, 1853), vol. 4, pp. 147–49, quoted at p. 148.

80 *"melancholy proof"*: letter of October 31, 1786, in Washington, *Writings,* John C. Fitzpatrick, ed. (U.S. Government Printing Office, 1931–44), vol. 29, pp. 33–35, quoted at pp. 33–34.

80 *Washington to Knox:* letter of December 26, 1786, in *ibid.,* vol. 29, pp. 121–25, quoted at p. 122.

80 *Madison on Shays's rebellion:* see letter of March 19, 1787, in Smith, *Republic of Letters,* vol. 1, pp. 469–74, esp. p. 473; and letter to George Washington, March 18, 1787, in Smith, *Letters of Delegates,* vol. 24, pp. 148–50, esp. p. 149.

80 *"I like a little rebellion"*: letter of February 22, 1787, in Jefferson, *Papers,* Julian P. Boyd et al., eds. (Princeton University Press, 1950–   ), vol. 11, pp. 174–75, quoted at p. 174.

80 *"tree of liberty"*: letter to William Stephens Smith, November 13, 1787, in *ibid.,* vol. 12, pp. 355–57, quoted at p. 356.

"The Most Remarkable Work"

John K. Alexander, *The Selling of the Constitutional Convention: A History of News Coverage* (Madison House, 1990).

Lance Banning, "The Problem of Power: Parties, Aristocracy, and Democracy in Revolutionary Thought," in Jack P. Greene, ed., *The American Revolution: Its Character and Limits* (New York University Press, 1987), pp. 104–23.

Lance Banning, *The Sacred Fire of Liberty: James Madison and the Founding of the Federal Republic* (Cornell University Press, 1995).

Richard Beeman et al., eds., *Beyond Confederation: Origins of the Constitution and American National Identity* (University of North Carolina Press, 1987).

James MacGregor Burns, *The Vineyard of Liberty* (Alfred A. Knopf, 1982), ch. 1.

James MacGregor Burns and Stewart Burns, *A People's Charter: The Pursuit of Rights in America* (Alfred A. Knopf, 1991), ch. 2.

Saul Cornell, *The Other Founders: Anti-Federalism and the Dissenting Tradition in America, 1788–1828* (University of North Carolina Press, 1999).

Calvin C. Jillson, *Constitution Making: Conflict and Consensus in the Federal Convention of 1787* (Agathon Press, 1988).

Jan Lewis, "Happiness," in Jack P. Greene and J. R. Pole, eds., *The Blackwell Encyclopedia of the American Revolution* (Blackwell, 1991), pp. 641–47.

Cathy D. Matson and Peter S. Onuf, *A Union of Interests: Political and Economic Thought in Revolutionary America* (University Press of Kansas, 1990).

Jack N. Rakove, "From One Agenda to Another: The Condition of American Federalism, 1783–1787," in Greene, *American Revolution*, pp. 80–103.

Jack N. Rakove, *Original Meanings: Politics and Ideas in the Making of the Constitution* (Alfred A. Knopf, 1996).

James H. Read, *Power Versus Liberty: Madison, Hamilton, Wilson, and Jefferson* (University Press of Virginia, 2000).

Ronald Schultz, *The Republic of Labor: Philadelphia Artisans and the Politics of Class, 1720–1830* (Oxford University Press, 1993), ch. 3.

James Morton Smith, ed., *The Republic of Letters: The Correspondence between Thomas Jefferson and James Madison, 1776–1826* (W. W. Norton, 1995), vol. 1.

Paul H. Smith, ed., *Letters of Delegates to Congress, 1774–1789* (Library of Congress, 1976–2000), vol. 24.

Jared Sparks, ed., *Correspondence of the American Revolution; Being Letters of Eminent Men to George Washington* (Little, Brown, 1853), vol. 4.

Charles Warren, *The Making of the Constitution* (Little, Brown, 1937).

George Washington, *Writings,* John C. Fitzpatrick, ed. (U.S. Government Printing Office, 1931–44), vols. 28, 29.

Garry Wills, *Inventing America: Jefferson's Declaration of Independence* (Doubleday, 1978), esp. pp. 240–55.

81 *"determine whether we are to have"*: letter of June 6, 1787, in Washington, *Writings,* vol. 29, pp. 229–30.

81 *Madison on need for "radical" action:* see letter to George Washington, April 16, 1787, in Smith, *Letters of Delegates,* vol. 24, pp. 228–32, esp. p. 228.

81 *"fundamental principle"*: Madison, "Vices of the Political system of the U. States,"

April 1787, in Madison, *Papers,* Robert A. Rutland et al., eds. (University Press of Virginia, 1962–   ), vol. 9, pp. 348–58, quoted at p. 354.

82 "*could neither coerce*": Rakove, "From One Agenda to Another," p. 84.

82 "*indirect influence*": Madison, "Vices," p. 353.

82 "*most remarkable work*": quoted in Burns, *Vineyard,* p. 32.

83 "*dreadful class*": Arthur Taylor Prescott, ed., *Drafting the Federal Constitution* (Louisiana State University Press, 1941), p. 83.

83 "*swallow up*": *ibid.,* p. 72.

83 *Jillson on framers' two levels of work:* see Jillson, esp. pp. ix–xiii.

83 "*blends together*": William Pierce, "Character Sketches of Delegates to the Constitutional Convention," in Jane Butzner, ed., *Constitutional Chaff* (Columbia University Press, 1941), pp. 158–71 (Appendix C), quoted at p. 165.

83 *Framers as well-bred, well-fed:* Burns, *Vineyard,* p. 33.

One Man's Leadership for Rights

Lance Banning, *The Sacred Fire of Liberty: James Madison and the Founding of the Federal Republic* (Cornell University Press, 1995).

Herman Belz et al., eds., *To Form a More Perfect Union: The Critical Ideas of the Constitution* (University Press of Virginia, 1992).

Steven R. Boyd, *The Politics of Opposition: Antifederalists and the Acceptance of the Constitution* (KTO Press, 1979).

James MacGregor Burns, *The Vineyard of Liberty* (Alfred A. Knopf, 1982), esp. ch. 2.

James MacGregor Burns and Stewart Burns, *A People's Charter: The Pursuit of Rights in America* (Alfred A. Knopf, 1991), ch. 2.

Edward Dumbauld, *The Bill of Rights, and What It Means Today* (University of Oklahoma Press, 1957).

Pauline Maier, *The Old Revolutionaries: Political Lives in the Age of Samuel Adams* (Alfred A. Knopf, 1980), esp. ch. 6.

David N. Mayer, *The Constitutional Thought of Thomas Jefferson* (University Press of Virginia, 1994).

Jack N. Rakove, *Original Meanings: Politics and Ideas in the Making of the Constitution* (Alfred A. Knopf, 1996).

Robert A. Rutland, *The Birth of the Bill of Rights, 1776–1791* (University of North Carolina Press, 1955).

Bernard Schwartz, *The Great Rights of Mankind: A History of the American Bill of Rights* (Oxford University Press, 1977).

James Morton Smith, ed., *The Republic of Letters: The Correspondence between Thomas Jefferson and James Madison, 1776–1826* (W. W. Norton, 1995), vol. 1.

Herbert J. Storing, ed., *The Complete Anti-Federalist,* 7 vols. (University of Chicago Press, 1981).

Helen E. Veit et al., eds., *Creating the Bill of Rights* (Johns Hopkins University Press, 1991).

85 *Madison letter to Jefferson on new Constitution:* letter of October 24 and November 1, 1787, in Smith, *Republic of Letters,* vol. 1, pp. 495–507.

85 "*I like much*": letter of December 20, 1787, in *ibid.,* vol. 1, pp. 511–15, quoted at pp. 512, 513.

87 "*parchment barriers*": letter to Jefferson, October 17, 1788, in Madison, *Papers,* Robert A. Rutland et al., eds. (University Press of Virginia, 1962–   ), vol. 11, pp. 295–300, quoted at p. 297.

87 "*some conciliatory sacrifices*": letter to Jefferson, March 29, 1789, in *ibid.,* vol. 12, pp. 37–39, quoted at p. 38.

87 "*ought to be revised*": letter to George Eve, January 2, 1789, in *ibid.,* vol. 11, pp. 404–405, quoted at p. 405.

87 "*colossal error*": Leonard W. Levy, *Constitutional Opinions: Aspects of the Bill of Rights* (Oxford University Press, 1986), p. 113.

"A Dependence on the People"

Joyce Appleby, *Capitalism and a New Social Order: The Republican Vision of the 1790s* (New York University Press, 1984).

Lance Banning, "The Problem of Power: Parties, Aristocracy, and Democracy in Revolutionary Thought," in Jack P. Greene, ed., *The American Revolution: Its Character and Limits* (New York University Press, 1987), pp. 104–23.

Ruth H. Bloch, *Visionary Republic: Millennial Themes in American Thought, 1756–1800* (Cambridge University Press, 1985), esp. ch. 7.

Richard Buel, Jr., *Securing the Revolution: Ideology in American Politics, 1789–1815* (Cornell University Press, 1972).

James MacGregor Burns and Stewart Burns, *A People's Charter: The Pursuit of Rights in America* (Alfred A. Knopf, 1991), ch. 2.

Saul Cornell, *The Other Founders: Anti-Federalism and the Dissenting Tradition in America, 1788–1828* (University of North Carolina Press, 1999), parts 2–3.

Stanley Elkins and Eric McKitrick, *The Age of Federalism* (Oxford University Press, 1993).

Richard Hofstadter, *The Idea of a Party System: The Rise of Legitimate Opposition in the United States, 1780–1840* (University of California Press, 1969).

Ralph Ketcham, *Presidents Above Party: The First American Presidency, 1789–1829* (University of North Carolina Press, 1984), esp. chs. 5–6.

Michael Lienesch, "Thomas Jefferson and the American Democratic Experience: The Origins of the Partisan Press, Popular Political Parties, and Public Opinion," in Peter S. Onuf, ed., *Jeffersonian Legacies* (University Press of Virginia, 1993), pp. 316–39.

David N. Mayer, *The Constitutional Thought of Thomas Jefferson* (University Press of Virginia, 1994).

Roy F. Nichols, *The Invention of the American Political Parties* (Macmillan, 1967).

James Roger Sharp, *American Politics in the Early Republic: The New Nation in Crisis* (Yale University Press, 1993).

James Morton Smith, ed., *The Republic of Letters: The Correspondence between Thomas Jefferson and James Madison, 1776–1826* (W. W. Norton, 1995), vol. 2.

Donald H. Stewart, *The Opposition Press of the Federalist Period* (SUNY Press, 1969).

Steven Watts, *The Republic Reborn: War and the Making of Liberal America, 1790–1820* (Johns Hopkins University Press, 1987).

Robert H. Wiebe, *The Opening of American Society* (Alfred A. Knopf, 1984), esp. part 1.

89 *"But the great security"*: Federalist No. 51, in Alexander Hamilton, James Madison, and John Jay, *The Federalist*, Benjamin Fletcher Wright, ed. (Harvard University Press, 1961), pp. 355–59, quoted at p. 356.

90 *"If a majority"*: ibid., pp. 358, 359, 358, respectively.

90 *Jefferson on majority rule:* letter of December 20, 1787, in Smith, *Republic of Letters*, vol. 1, pp. 511–15, quoted at p. 514.

90 *"restriction against monopolies"*: see letter to Madison of December 20, 1787, in *ibid.*, vol. 1, p. 512.

91 *"a group of elites"*: Sharp, p. 10.

91 *"mass of people"*: Madison, "A Candid State of Parties," September 26, 1792, in Madison, *Writings*, Gaillard Hunt, ed. (G. P. Putnam's Sons, 1900–10), vol. 6, pp. 106–19, quoted at pp. 119, 115, respectively.

91 *"mutual checks"*: Madison, "Parties," January 23, 1792, in *ibid.*, vol. 6, p. 86.

92 *"general interest"*: Madison, "Candid State of Parties," pp. 118, 119.

92 *"faithfully served"*: quoted in Sharp, p. 87.

93 *"contempt or disrepute"*: Sedition Act, July 14, 1798, reprinted in Henry Steele Commager and Milton Cantor, eds., *Documents of American History*, 10th ed. (Prentice-Hall, 1988), vol. 1, pp. 177–78, quoted at p. 178.

Parties—the People's Constitution

James MacGregor Burns, *The Vineyard of Liberty* (Alfred A. Knopf, 1982), esp. ch. 4.

James MacGregor Burns and Stewart Burns, *A People's Charter: The Pursuit of Rights in America* (Alfred A. Knopf, 1991), ch. 2.

William N. Chambers, "Parties and Nation-Building in America," in Joseph LaPalombara and Myron Weiner, eds., *Political Parties and Political Development* (Princeton University Press, 1966), pp. 79–106.

Saul Cornell, *The Other Founders: Anti-Federalism and the Dissenting Tradition in America, 1788–1828* (University of North Carolina Press, 1999).

Stanley Elkins and Eric McKitrick, *The Age of Federalism* (Oxford University Press, 1993).

Morton Grodzins, "Political Parties and the Crisis of Succession in the United States: The Case of 1800," in LaPalombara and Weiner, pp. 303–27.

Richard Hofstadter, *The Idea of a Party System: The Rise of Legitimate Opposition in the United States, 1780–1840* (University of California Press, 1969).

Roger G. Kennedy, *Burr, Hamilton, and Jefferson: A Study in Character* (Oxford University Press, 2000).

Seymour Martin Lipset, *The First New Nation: The United States in Historical and Comparative Perspective* (Basic Books, 1963), esp. part 1.

Edmund S. Morgan, *Inventing the People: The Rise of Popular Sovereignty in England and America* (W. W. Norton, 1988).

James Roger Sharp, *American Politics in the Early Republic: The New Nation in Crisis* (Yale University Press, 1993).

Robert H. Wiebe, *The Opening of American Society* (Alfred A. Knopf, 1984).

93   *"voluntary, peaceful transfer"*: Grodzins, p. 317.

94   *"destitute of every moral principle"*: quoted in Elkins and McKitrick, p. 738.

95   *"contemptible hypocrite"*: letter to James A. Bayard, January 16, 1801, in Hamilton, *Papers,* Harold C. Syrett, ed. (Columbia University Press, 1961–87), vol. 25, pp. 319–24, quoted at pp. 319, 320.

95   *"most unfit man"*: letter to Bayard, December 27, 1800, in *ibid.,* vol. 25, pp. 275–77, quoted at p. 277.

95   "extreme *&* irregular *ambition"*: Hamilton, letter to Bayard, January 16, 1801, in *ibid.,* vol. 25, p. 320.

96   *Wiebe on parties:* Wiebe, p. 89.

96   *"critical community"*: Thomas R. Rochon, *Culture Moves: Ideas, Activism, and Changing Values* (Princeton University Press, 1998), esp. pp. 25–30.

6 FRANCE: TRIALS OF LEADERSHIP

William Doyle, *The Oxford History of the French Revolution* (Oxford University Press, 1989), pp. 121–23.

George Rudé, *The Crowd in the French Revolution* (Oxford University Press, 1959), ch. 5.

Simon Schama, *Citizens* (Alfred A. Knopf, 1989), pp. 456–70.

99   *"tear out the heart"*: quoted in Schama, p. 467.

99   *"more like prisoners"*: quoted in Doyle, p. 123.

99   *"band of cruel ruffians"*: Burke, *Reflections on the Revolution in France,* Conor Cruise O'Brien, ed. (Penguin, 1986), pp. 164, 165.

99   *"foul scum"*: Taine, *The Origins of Contemporary France,* Edward T. Gargan, ed., and John Durand, trans. (University of Chicago Press, 1974), pp. 152, 153.

99   *"disembodied abstraction"*: Rudé, p. 4.

100   *"fixed abode"*: see *ibid.,* pp. 186–89.

Crown Rule and Crowd Leadership

Keith Michael Baker, "On the Problem of the Ideological Origins of the French Revolution," in Dominick LaCapra and Steven L. Kaplan, eds., *Modern European Intellectual History* (Cornell University Press, 1982), pp. 197–219.

William Doyle, *Origins of the French Revolution,* 3rd ed. (Oxford University Press, 1999).

William Doyle, *The Oxford History of the French Revolution* (Oxford University Press, 1989).

Susan Dunn, *Sister Revolutions: French Lightning, American Light* (Faber and Faber, 1999).

Michael P. Fitzsimmons, *The Remaking of France: The National Assembly and the Constitution of 1791* (Cambridge University Press, 1994).

François Furet, *Revolutionary France, 1770–1880,* Antonia Nevill, trans. (Blackwell, 1992), esp. chs. 1–2.

François Furet and Mona Ozouf, eds., *A Critical Dictionary of the French Revolution,* Arthur Goldhammer, trans. (Harvard University Press, 1989).

Jack A. Goldstone, *Revolution and Rebellion in the Early Modern World* (University of California Press, 1991), ch. 3.

Norman Hampson, *Prelude to Terror: The Constituent Assembly and the Failure of Consensus, 1789–1791* (Basil Blackwell, 1988).

Colin Lucas, "The Crowd and Politics," in Lucas, ed., *The French Revolution and the Creation of Modern Political Culture: The Political Culture of the French Revolution* (Pergamon Press, 1988), pp. 259–85.

George Rudé, *The Crowd in the French Revolution* (Oxford University Press, 1959).

Anne Sa'adah, *The Shaping of Liberal Politics in Revolutionary France* (Princeton University Press, 1990), esp. ch. 2.

Simon Schama, *Citizens* (Alfred A. Knopf, 1989), esp. parts 2–3.

William H. Sewell, Jr., "Le citoyen/la citoyenne: Activity, Passivity and the Revolutionary Concept of Citizenship," in Lucas, pp. 105–23.

Gilbert Shapiro and John Markoff, *Revolutionary Demands: A Content Analysis of the Cahiers de Doléances of 1789* (Stanford University Press, 1998).

Timothy Tackett, *Becoming a Revolutionary: The Deputies of the French National Assembly and the Emergence of a Revolutionary Culture (1789–1790)* (Princeton University Press, 1996).

Renée Waldinger, Philip Dawson, and Isser Woloch, eds., *The French Revolution and the Meaning of Citizenship* (Greenwood Press, 1993).

100 *Queen as king's only man:* see François Furet, "Louis XVI," in Furet and Ozouf, p. 240. The remark was made by Mirabeau.

102 *"Third Estate is the People":* quoted in Schama, p. 301.

103 *"National Assembly entirely destroys":* quoted in Doyle, *History,* p. 117; Doyle on "fundamental principle" at *ibid.*

103 *"natural, imprescriptible":* reprinted in A. I. Melden, ed., *Human Rights* (Wadsworth Publishing, 1970), pp. 140–42, quoted at p. 140.

104 *"Membership in the nation":* Fitzsimmons, "The National Assembly and the Invention of Citizenship," in Waldinger et al., pp. 29–41, quoted at p. 32.

104 *"voice of the nation":* *Révolutions de Paris,* July 12–17, 1789, quoted in Pierre Rétat, "The Evolution of the Citizen from the Ancien Régime to the Revolution," in *ibid.,* pp. 1–15, quoted at p. 5.

104 *"truly desire":* quoted in *ibid.,* p. 7.

104 *"canvas of bad citizens"*: Camille Desmoulins, *Révolutions de France et de Brabant,*
       December 19, 1789, quoted in *ibid.,* p. 8.
104 *"susceptible to the influence"*: Fitzsimmons, "National Assembly," p. 37.

The Rule of Terror

Richard Cobb, *The People's Armies,* Marianne Elliott, trans. (Yale University Press,
    1987).
Richard Cobb, *The Police and the People: French Popular Protest, 1789–1820* (Oxford Uni-
    versity Press, 1970).
Richard Cobb, "Some Aspects of the Revolutionary Mentality: April 1793–Thermidor,
    Year II," in Jeffry Kaplow, ed., *New Perspectives on the French Revolution* (John Wiley
    & Sons, 1965), pp. 305–37.
William Doyle, *The Oxford History of the French Revolution* (Oxford University Press,
    1989), esp. ch. 11.
Susan Dunn, *Sister Revolutions: French Lightning, American Light* (Faber and Faber,
    1999).
Ferenc Fehér, *The Frozen Revolution: An Essay on Jacobinism* (Cambridge University
    Press, 1987), esp. ch. 4.
François Furet and Mona Ozouf, eds., *A Critical Dictionary of the French Revolution,* Arthur
    Goldhammer, trans. (Harvard University Press, 1989).
Norman Hampson, "The Heavenly City of the French Revolution," in Colin Lucas,
    ed., *Rewriting the French Revolution* (Oxford University Press, 1991), pp. 46–68.
Norman Hampson, *Saint-Just* (Basil Blackwell, 1991).
Patrice Higonnet, *Goodness Beyond Virtue: Jacobins During the French Revolution* (Harvard
    University Press, 1998).
P. M. Jones, *The Peasantry in the French Revolution* (Cambridge University Press, 1988),
    esp. ch. 7.
Frank A. Kafker and James M. Laux, eds., *The French Revolution,* 3rd ed. (Robert E.
    Krieger, 1983), esp. chs. 5–6.
Arno J. Mayer, *The Furies: Violence and Terror in the French and Russian Revolutions*
    (Princeton University Press, 2000).
Gordon H. McNeil, "Robespierre, Rousseau, and Representation," in Richard Herr
    and Harold T. Parker, eds., *Ideas in History* (Duke University Press, 1965),
    pp. 135–56.
R. R. Palmer, *Twelve Who Ruled: The Year of the Terror in the French Revolution* (Princeton
    University Press, 1970).
George Rudé, *The Crowd in the French Revolution* (Oxford University Press, 1959).
George Rudé, *Robespierre: Portrait of a Revolutionary Democrat* (Viking, 1976).
Anne Sa'adah, *The Shaping of Liberal Politics in Revolutionary France* (Princeton Univer-
    sity Press, 1990), esp. ch. 3.
Simon Schama, *Citizens* (Alfred A. Knopf, 1989), esp. part 4.
Albert Soboul, *The Sans-Culottes: The Popular Movement and Revolutionary Government,
    1793–1794,* Rémy Inglis Hall, trans. (Anchor, 1972).

Isser Woloch, "The Contraction and Expansion of Democratic Space during the Period of the Terror," in Kenneth Michael Baker, ed., *The French Revolution and the Creation of Modern Political Culture: The Terror* (Pergamon Press, 1994), pp. 309–25.

105 *"becoming to the rights"*: quoted in Doyle, p. 156.

106 *Fehér on hunger:* Fehér, p. 87.

106 *"Foreign Plot was a myth"*: Palmer, p. 113.

106 *"completely contemptible"*: Cobban, *A History of Modern France* (Penguin, 1957–61), vol. 1, pp. 227–28, quoted at p. 228.

107 *"we will have bread"*: quoted in Patrice Higonnet, "Sans-culottes," in Furet and Ozouf, p. 396.

107 *"not a state"*: quoted in Rudé, *Robespierre,* p. 190.

107 *"increasingly narrow"*: Cobban, vol. 1, pp. 178–79.

108 *"manifest leader"*: Schama, p. 577.

108 *"It's not enough"*: Jacques Alexis Thuriot, quoted in Doyle, p. 277.

Napoleonic Rulership

Franklin L. Ford, *Europe, 1780–1830* (Longmans, 1970), ch. 8.

François Furet, "Napoleon Bonaparte," in Furet and Mona Ozouf, eds., *A Critical Dictionary of the French Revolution,* Arthur Goldhammer, trans. (Harvard University Press, 1989), pp. 273–86.

Pieter Geyl, *Napoleon, For and Against,* Olive Renier, trans. (Jonathan Cape, 1949).

J. Christopher Herold, *The Age of Napoleon* (Houghton Mifflin, 1987).

Robert B. Holtman, *Napoleonic Propaganda* (Louisiana State University Press, 1950).

Robert B. Holtman, *The Napoleonic Revolution* (J. B. Lippincott, 1967).

Martyn Lyons, *Napoleon Bonaparte and the Legacy of the French Revolution* (St. Martin's Press, 1994).

John McManners, *Lectures on European History, 1789–1914: Men, Machines and Freedom* (Basil Blackwell, 1966), ch. 6.

Jean Tulard, *Napoleon: The Myth of the Saviour,* Teresa Waugh, trans. (Methuen, 1985).

Isser Woloch, *The New Regime: Transformations of the French Civic Order, 1789–1820s* (W. W. Norton, 1994).

110 *Tocqueville on Napoleon:* quoted in McManners, p. 78.

110 *"I alone"*: quoted in Woloch, p. 50.

110 *1802 plebiscite:* text quoted in Lyons, p. 112, results in *ibid.,* Table 9.1, p. 113.

110 *"Jacobins, royalists"*: Herold, p. 126, Napoleon quoted at p. 127.

111 *"instrument of French conquest"*: Lyons, pp. 102–103.

112 *"cornerstone of the new civic order"*: Woloch, pp. 433, 432, respectively.

112 *"creating everywhere"*: quoted in Herold, p. 291.

113 *"health of His Majesty"*: text of December 3, 1812, *Bulletin* reprinted in Lyons, pp. 180–81.

The Gaullist Brand of Leadership

Maurice Agulhon, *The French Republic, 1879–1992,* Antonia Nevill, trans. (Blackwell, 1993).

Raymond Aron, "The Political 'System' of the Fourth Republic," in James Friguglietti and Emmet Kennedy, eds., *The Shaping of Modern France* (Collier-Macmillan, 1969), pp. 527–36.

Philippe Bernard and Henri Dubief, *The Decline of the Third Republic, 1914–1938,* Anthony Forster, trans. (Cambridge University Press, 1985).

D. W. Brogan, *The Development of Modern France (1870–1939)* (Hamish Hamilton, 1940).

Edward Whiting Fox, "The Third Force, 1897–1939," in Edward Mead Earle, ed., *Modern France: Problems of the Third and Fourth Republics* (Princeton University Press, 1951), pp. 124–36.

Robert Gildea, *France Since 1945* (Oxford University Press, 1996).

Frank Giles, *The Locust Years: The Story of the Fourth French Republic, 1946–1958* (Carroll & Graf, 1994).

John Girling, *France: Political and Social Change* (Routledge, 1998).

Anthony Hartley, *Gaullism: The Rise and Fall of a Political Movement* (Outerbridge & Dienstfrey, 1971).

Stanley Hoffmann, *Decline or Renewal?: France Since the 1930s* (Viking, 1974).

Julian Jackson, *The Popular Front in France: Defending Democracy, 1934–38* (Cambridge University Press, 1988).

Douglas Johnson, "The Political Principles of General De Gaulle," in Friguglietti and Kennedy, pp. 559–66.

Jean Lacouture, *De Gaulle: The Ruler, 1945–1970,* Alan Sheridan, trans. (W. W. Norton, 1992).

Daniel J. Mahoney, *De Gaulle: Statesmanship, Grandeur, and Modern Democracy* (Praeger, 1996).

Jean-Pierre Rioux, *The Fourth Republic, 1944–1958,* Godfrey Rogers, trans. (Cambridge University Press, 1987).

Philip Thody, *The Fifth French Republic: Presidents, Politics and Personalities* (Routledge, 1998), esp. chs. 1–2.

Eugen Weber, *The Hollow Years: France in the 1930s* (W. W. Norton, 1994).

Philip M. Williams and Martin Harrison, *Politics and Society in De Gaulle's Republic* (Doubleday, 1972).

115 *"perfect broker"*: Hoffmann, pp. 74, 75.

115 *"confusion of powers"*: quoted in Dorothy Pickles, *The Fifth French Republic: Institutions and Politics,* rev. ed. (Praeger, 1962), p. 33.

116 *"government of Public Safety"*: quoted in Lacouture, p. 167.

116 *"ready to assume"*: quoted in Rioux, p. 305.

116 *"whatever measures"*: quoted in Lacouture, p. 195.

116 *"guide of France"*: quoted in Gildea, p. 46.

117 *"poor France"*: P. M. de la Gorce, cited in Agulhon, p. 416; and Agulhon on social inequality at *ibid.*

117 *"in microcosm"*: Gildea, p. 52.

117 *"moral and social crisis"*: Serge Berstein, quoted in Girling, p. 120.

117 *"student bedwetting"*: quoted in Lacouture, p. 535.

118 *Hartley on de Gaulle's system:* Hartley, p. 287.

118 *"no longer had any hold"*: quoted in *ibid.*, p. 288.

118 *"depart immediately"*: quoted in Lacouture, p. 573.

118 *"great people brought together"*: quoted in Hartley, p. 304.

118 *1969 referendum as "absurd":* see Lacouture, p. 573. The characterization was André Malraux's.

118 *"ideological emptiness"*: Hoffmann, p. 217.

118 *"exalted and exceptional destiny"*: de Gaulle, *War Memoirs: The Call to Honour, 1940–1942,* Jonathan Griffin, trans. (Viking, 1955), p. 1.

7 LEADERSHIP AS CONFLICT

James MacGregor Burns, *Leadership* (Harper & Row, 1978), pp. 228–39.

Jerome Ch'ên, *Mao and the Chinese Revolution* (Oxford University Press, 1965).

Arthur A. Cohen, *The Communism of Mao Tse-tung* (University of Chicago Press, 1964).

Roger B. Jeans, ed., *Roads Not Taken: The Struggle of Opposition Parties in Twentieth-Century China* (Westview Press, 1992).

Peter R. Moody, *Opposition and Dissent in Contemporary China* (Hoover Institution Press, 1977).

Stuart R. Schram, ed., *The Political Thought of Mao Tse-tung,* rev. ed. (Praeger, 1969).

Philip Short, *Mao* (Henry Holt, 2000).

John Bryan Starr, *Continuing the Revolution: The Political Thought of Mao* (Princeton University Press, 1979).

Brantly Womack, *The Foundations of Mao Zedong's Political Thought, 1917–1935* (University Press of Hawaii, 1982).

120 *"in China's central"*: Mao Tse-tung, "Report of an Investigation into the Peasant Movement in Hunan," in Mao, *Selected Works* (International Publishers, 1954–62), vol. 1, pp. 21–59, quoted at pp. 21–22.

121 *"not everybody"*: Mao, "On the Historical Experience of the Dictatorship of the Proletariat" (1956), excerpted in Schram, pp. 303–304, quoted at p. 304.

121 *"thinking is relatively incorrect"*: *ibid.*

121 *"Marxism develops"*: quoted in Moody, p. 41.

His Majesty's Opposition

Stanley Ayling, *Edmund Burke* (St. Martin's Press, 1988).

Terence Ball, "Party," in Ball et al., eds., *Political Innovation and Conceptual Change* (Cambridge University Press, 1989), pp. 155–76.

Bolingbroke, *The Idea of a Patriot King,* Sydney W. Jackman, ed. (Bobbs-Merrill, 1965).

Bolingbroke, *Political Writings: The Conservative Enlightenment,* Bernard Cottret, ed. (St. Martin's Press, 1997).

John Brewer, *Party Ideology and Popular Politics at the Accession of George III* (Cambridge University Press, 1976), esp. ch. 4.

Shelley Burtt, *Virtue Transformed: Political Argument in England, 1688–1740* (Cambridge University Press, 1992).

H. T. Dickinson, *Bolingbroke* (Constable, 1970).

Archibald S. Foord, *His Majesty's Opposition, 1714–1830* (Oxford University Press, 1964).

Ian Gilmour, *Riot, Risings and Revolution: Governance and Violence in Eighteenth-Century England* (Pimlico, 1993).

J. A. W. Gunn, ed., *Factions No More* (Frank Cass, 1972).

Jeffrey Hart, *Viscount Bolingbroke: Tory Humanist* (Routledge & Kegan Paul, 1965).

B. W. Hill, *British Parliamentary Parties, 1742–1832: From the Fall of Walpole to the First Reform Act* (George Allen & Unwin, 1985).

B. W. Hill, *The Growth of Parliamentary Parties, 1689–1742* (Archon, 1976).

Richard Hofstadter, *The Idea of a Party System: The Rise of Legitimate Opposition in the United States, 1780–1840* (University of California Press, 1969), ch. 1.

Ivor Jennings, *Party Politics* (Cambridge University Press, 1960–62), vol. 2, esp. parts 1–2.

Isaac Kramnick, *Bolingbroke and His Circle: The Politics of Nostalgia in the Age of Walpole* (Harvard University Press, 1968).

William Thomas Laprade, *Public Opinion and Politics in Eighteenth Century England: To the Fall of Walpole* (Macmillan, 1936).

Harvey C. Mansfield, Jr., *Statesmanship and Party Government: A Study of Burke and Bolingbroke* (University of Chicago Press, 1965).

L. G. Mitchell, *Charles James Fox* (Oxford University Press, 1992).

Roy F. Nichols, *The Invention of the American Political Parties* (Macmillan, 1967), ch. 1.

Frank O'Gorman, *The Rise of Party in England: The Rockingham Whigs, 1760–82* (Allen & Unwin, 1975).

Frank O'Gorman, *The Whig Party and the French Revolution* (Macmillan, 1967).

Caroline Robbins, "'Discordant Parties': A Study of the Acceptance of Parties by Englishmen," *Political Science Quarterly*, vol. 73, no. 4 (December 1958), pp. 505–29.

Quentin Skinner, "The Principle and Practice of Opposition: The Case of Bolingbroke versus Walpole," in Neil McKendrick, ed., *Historical Perspectives: Studies in English Thought and Society* (Europa, 1974), pp. 93–128.

123 *"certain housemaid"*: letter to Thomas Coke, October 16, 1704, quoted in Dickinson, p. 6.

123 *"stand sullen"*: quoted in Foord, p. 116.

123 *"watch over"*: ibid., p. 322.

124 *"great principles"*: Bolingbroke, *Idea of a Patriot King*, pp. 21, 51, 49, 46, respectively.

124 *"one of the great documents"*: Gunn, p. 263; pamphlet reprinted in *ibid.*, pp. 187–91, quoted at p. 187.

125 *"narrow, bigoted"*: Burke, "Thoughts on the Cause of the Present Discontents," in Burke, *Pre-Revolutionary Writings*, Ian Harris, ed. (Cambridge University Press, 1993), pp. 116–92, quoted at pp. 185, 184, respectively.

125 *"body of men united"*: ibid., p. 187.
126 *"generous contention"*: ibid., p. 188.
126 *"first broad party association"*: Foord, p. 406.

Irrepressible Conflict?

Antebellum:

William R. Brock, *Parties and Political Conscience: American Dilemmas, 1840–1850* (KTO Press, 1979).

James MacGregor Burns, *The Vineyard of Liberty* (Alfred A. Knopf, 1982), parts 4–5 passim.

William J. Cooper, Jr., *The South and the Politics of Slavery, 1828–1856* (Louisiana State University Press, 1978).

Eric Foner, *Free Soil, Free Labor, Free Men: The Ideology of the Republican Party Before the Civil War* (Oxford University Press, 1970).

Eric Foner, *Politics and Ideology in the Age of the Civil War* (Oxford University Press, 1980), esp. ch. 3.

William E. Gienapp, "The Republican Party and the Slave Power," in Robert H. Abzug and Stephen E. Maizlish, eds., *New Perspectives on Race and Slavery in America* (University Press of Kentucky, 1986), pp. 51–78.

Michael F. Holt, *The Rise and Fall of the American Whig Party: Jacksonian Politics and the Onset of the Civil War* (Oxford University Press, 1999).

Alan M. Kraut, ed., *Crusaders and Compromisers* (Greenwood Press, 1983).

Roy F. Nichols, *The Disruption of American Democracy* (Macmillan, 1948).

Thomas H. O'Connor, *Lords of the Loom: The Cotton Whigs and the Coming of the Civil War* (Charles Scribner's Sons, 1968).

David M. Potter, *The Impending Crisis, 1848–1861,* Don E. Fehrenbacher, ed. (Harper & Row, 1976).

Kenneth M. Stampp, *America in 1857: A Nation on the Brink* (Oxford University Press, 1990).

Kenneth M. Stampp, *The Imperiled Union* (Oxford University Press, 1980), esp. chs. 1, 4.

James L. Sundquist, *Dynamics of the Party System: Alignment and Realignment of Political Parties in the United States* (Brookings Institution, 1973), esp. chs. 4–5.

Roosevelt:

James MacGregor Burns, *The Crosswinds of Freedom* (Alfred A. Knopf, 1989), part 1.

James MacGregor Burns, *Roosevelt: The Lion and the Fox* (Harcourt, Brace, 1956).

Kenneth S. Davis, *FDR: Into the Storm, 1937–1940* (Random House, 1993), ch. 9.

Richard Kirkendall, "The New Deal and American Politics," in Harvard Sitkoff, ed., *Fifty Years Later: The New Deal Evaluated* (Temple University Press, 1985), pp. 11–36.

William E. Leuchtenburg, "Franklin D. Roosevelt: The First Modern President," in Fred I. Greenstein, ed., *Leadership in the Modern Presidency* (Harvard University Press, 1988), pp. 7–40.

Sidney M. Milkis, "The Presidency and Political Parties," in Michael Nelson, ed., *The Presidency and the Political System,* 2nd ed. (CQ Press, 1988), pp. 331–49.

Sidney M. Milkis, *The President and the Parties: The Transformation of the American Party System Since the New Deal* (Oxford University Press, 1993), esp. part 1.

David K. Nichols, "Partisan Realignment and Presidential Leadership," paper prepared for delivery at the annual meeting of the American Political Science Association, Washington, D.C., August 1997.

David Plotke, *Building a Democratic Political Order: Reshaping American Liberalism in the 1930s and 1940s* (Cambridge University Press, 1996).

Sean Savage, *Roosevelt the Party Leader, 1932–1945* (University Press of Kentucky, 1991).

Sundquist, *Dynamics of the Party System,* esp. chs. 10–12.

Clyde P. Weed, *The Nemesis of Reform: The Republican Party During the New Deal* (Columbia University Press, 1994).

128 *"by common consent"*: Preston King, quoted in Foner, *Free Soil,* p. 152.

129 *"set himself to suppress"*: Rufus Choate, quoted in Brock, p. 326.

129 *"irrepressible conflict"*: quoted in Foner, *Free Soil,* pp. 69–70.

129 *"compromisers sacrificed"*: Brock, p. 327.

129 *"put our action"*: Salmon P. Chase, quoted in Foner, *Free Soil,* p. 131.

129 *"active, life-giving"*: Speech at Beloit, Wisconsin, October 1, 1859, in Lincoln, *Collected Works,* Roy P. Basler, ed. (Rutgers University Press, 1953), vol. 3, pp. 482–84, quoted at p. 482.

130 *"without any organized opposition"*: reported by Turner Catledge, quoted in Milkis, *The President and the Parties,* p. 75.

130 *"continuous liberal government"*: Radio Address on Electing Liberals to Public Office, November 4, 1938, in Roosevelt, *Public Papers and Addresses,* Samuel I. Rosenman, comp. (Random House, 1938–50), vol. 7, pp. 584–93, quoted at p. 585.

131 *"elimination committee"*: see Milkis, *The President and the Parties,* pp. 85–86.

131 *"willing to stand up"*: Address at Barnesville, Georgia, August 11, 1938, in Roosevelt, *Public Papers,* vol. 7, pp. 463–71, quoted at p. 466.

131 *"definite choice"*: Roosevelt, "Introduction," in *ibid.,* vol. 7, p. xxix.

131 *"evaporate into thin air"*: Radio Address on Electing Liberals, p. 585.

132 *"merely Tweedledum"*: Roosevelt, "Introduction," pp. xxxii, xxviii, respectively.

The Russian Oppositionists

Carol Barner-Barry and Cynthia A. Hody, *The Politics of Change: The Transformation of the Former Soviet Union* (St. Martin's Press, 1995).

Archie Brown, ed., *Contemporary Russian Politics* (Oxford University Press, 2001).

Timothy J. Colton and Jerry F. Hough, eds., *Growing Pains: Russian Democracy and the Election of 1993* (Brookings Institution Press, 1998).

Alexander Dallin and Gail W. Lapidus, eds., *The Soviet System in Crisis* (Westview Press, 1991).

Judith Devlin, *The Rise of the Russian Democrats: The Causes and Consequences of the Elite Revolution* (Edward Elgar, 1995).

M. Steven Fish, *Democracy from Scratch: Opposition and Regime in the New Russian Revolution* (Princeton University Press, 1995).

Graeme Gill and Roger D. Markwick, *Russia's Stillborn Democracy?: From Gorbachev to Yeltsin* (Oxford University Press, 2000).

Ronald J. Hill, "Parties and the Party System," in Stephen White et al., eds., *Developments in Russian and Post-Soviet Politics*, 3rd ed. (Duke University Press, 1994), pp. 88–108.

Samuel P. Huntington, *Political Order in Changing Societies* (Yale University Press, 1968).

John Löwenhardt, ed., *Party Politics in Post-Communist Russia* (Frank Cass, 1998).

Alexander Lukin, *The Political Culture of the Russian "Democrats"* (Oxford University Press, 2000).

Michael McFaul, *Russia's Unfinished Revolution: Political Change from Gorbachev to Putin* (Cornell University Press, 2001).

G. D. G. Murrell, *Russia's Transition to Democracy: An Internal Political History, 1989–1996* (Sussex Academic Press, 1997).

Richard Sakwa, *Russian Politics and Society,* 2nd ed. (Routledge, 1996).

Michael Urban, Vyacheslav Igrunov, and Sergei Mitrokhin, *The Rebirth of Politics in Russia* (Cambridge University Press, 1997).

David Walsh et al., *Governing Through Turbulence: Leadership and Change in the Late Twentieth Century* (Praeger, 1995), ch. 6.

133 *"new kind of mass mobilization"*: Bonnell, "Voluntary Associations in Gorbachev's Reform Program," in Dallin and Lapidus, pp. 151–60, quoted at p. 153.

133 *"first outright opposition party"*: Devlin, p. 95.

133 *"complete democratization"*: Andrey Voznesensky, quoted in *ibid.,* p. 121.

133 *"parties of the intelligentsia"*: *ibid.,* p. 212.

134 *"Timid, creeping reforms"*: quoted in Barner-Barry and Hody, p. 52.

134 "Perestroika *has already"*: Gorbachev interview, *Time,* vol. 135, no. 23 (June 4, 1990), pp. 27–34, quoted at p. 28; for Gorbachev as *Time*'s "Man of the Decade," see *ibid.,* vol. 135, no. 1 (January 1, 1990).

134 *"initiative and creativity"*: Gorbachev, quoted in Barner-Barry and Hody, p. 54.

134 *"socialist pluralism"*: see Thomas Remington, "A Socialist Pluralism of Opinions: *Glasnost* and Policy-Making Under Gorbachev," in Dallin and Lapidus, pp. 97–115, esp. pp. 99–101.

134 *"With hindsight"*: Barner-Barry and Hody, p. 52.

134 *"eventful" or "event-making":* see Hook, *The Hero in History: A Study in Limitation and Possibility* (John Day, 1943), esp. ch. 9.

135 *"people's tsar"*: George W. Breslauer, "Boris Yeltsin as Patriarch," in Brown, pp. 70–81, quoted at p. 76.

136 *"responsible and irreconcilable"*: quoted in Peter Reddaway and Dmitri Glinski, *The Tragedy of Russia's Reforms: Market Bolshevism Against Democracy* (United States Institute of Peace Press, 2001), p. 578.

8 THE ANATOMY OF MOTIVATION

James MacGregor Burns, *Roosevelt: The Lion and the Fox* (Harcourt, Brace, 1956).
Robert S. McElvaine, *Down & Out in the Great Depression: Letters from the "Forgotten Man"* (University of North Carolina Press, 1983).

140 *"freedom from want"*: Annual Message to the Congress, January 6, 1941, in Roosevelt, *Public Papers and Addresses,* Samuel I. Rosenman, comp. (Random House, 1938–50), vol. 9, pp. 663–72, quoted at p. 672.
140 *"ill-housed"*: Second Inaugural Address, January 20, 1937, in *ibid.,* vol. 6, pp. 1–6, quoted at p. 5.
140 *"If we do not have"*: Address at the Democratic Victory Dinner, March 4, 1937, in *ibid.,* vol. 6, pp. 113–21, quoted at p. 121.

Sheer Want

Joel Aronoff, *Psychological Needs and Cultural Systems: A Case Study* (Van Nostrand Reinhold, 1967).
James MacGregor Burns, *Leadership* (Harper & Row, 1978), esp. part 2.
Alan R. Buss, "Humanistic Psychology as Liberal Ideology: The Socio-Historical Roots of Maslow's Theory of Self-Actualization," *Journal of Humanistic Psychology,* vol. 19, no. 3 (Summer 1979), pp. 43–55.
James C. Davies, "The Existence of Human Needs," in Roger A. Coate and Jerel A. Rosati, eds., *The Power of Human Needs in World Society* (Lynne Rienner, 1988), pp. 23–33.
James C. Davies, *Human Nature in Politics: The Dynamics of Political Behavior* (John Wiley and Sons, 1963).
James C. Davies, "Maslow and Theory of Political Development: Getting to Fundamentals," *Political Psychology,* vol. 12, no. 3 (1991), pp. 389–420.
James C. Davies, "The Priority of Human Needs and the Stages of Political Development," in J. Roland Pennock and John W. Chapman, eds., *Human Nature in Politics* (New York University Press, 1977), pp. 157–96.
Germann Diligensky, "Problems of the Theory of Human Needs," *Social Science Information,* vol. 20, no. 1 (1981), pp. 169–85.
Amitai Etzioni, "A Creative Adaptation to a World of Rising Shortages," *Annals of the American Academy of Political and Social Science,* no. 420 (July 1975), pp. 98–110.
Ross Fitzgerald, "Abraham Maslow's Hierarchy of Needs—An Exposition and Evaluation," in Fitzgerald, ed., *Human Needs and Politics* (Pergamon Press, 1977), pp. 36–51.
Ross Fitzgerald, "Introduction," in Fitzgerald, pp. viii–xvi.
Arnold S. Kaufman, "Wants, Needs, and Liberalism," *Inquiry,* vol. 14 (1971), pp. 191–212.
C. B. Macpherson, "Needs and Wants: An Ontological or Historical Problem?," in Fitzgerald, pp. 26–35.

Abraham H. Maslow, "'Higher' and 'Lower' Needs," *Journal of Psychology,* vol. 25 (1948), pp. 433–36.

Abraham H. Maslow, *Motivation and Personality* (Harper & Brothers, 1954).

Abraham H. Maslow, *Toward a Psychology of Being,* 2nd ed. (D. Van Nostrand, 1968).

Andrew Neher, "Maslow's Theory of Motivation: A Critique," *Journal of Humanistic Psychology,* vol. 31, no. 3 (Summer 1991), pp. 89–112.

Ramashray Roy, "Three Visions of Needs and the Future: Liberalism, Marxism, and Gandhism," in Coate and Rosati, pp. 59–76.

Robert Shaw and Karen Colimore, "Humanistic Psychology as Ideology: An Analysis of Maslow's Contradictions," *Journal of Humanistic Psychology,* vol. 28, no. 3 (Summer 1988), pp. 51–74.

M. Brewster Smith, "Comment on Davies's 'Maslow and Theory of Political Development,'" *Political Psychology,* vol. 12, no. 3 (1991), pp. 421–23.

M. Brewster Smith, "Metapsychology, Politics, and Human Needs," in Fitzgerald, pp. 124–41.

Patricia Springborg, *The Problem of Human Needs and the Critique of Civilisation* (George Allen & Unwin, 1981), esp. ch. 2.

Mahmoud A. Wahba and Lawrence G. Bridwell, "Maslow Reconsidered: A Review of Research on the Need Hierarchy Theory," *Organizational Behavior and Human Performance,* vol. 15 (1976), pp. 212–40.

141 *"unrestricted individualism"*: quoted in Roy, pp. 72, 71, respectively.

142 *Davies on needs:* see Davies, *Human Nature,* esp. pp. 9–11, quoted at p. 9.

143 *"effectance"*: see White, "Motivation Reconsidered: The Concept of Competence," *Psychological Review,* vol. 66, no. 5 (September 1959), pp. 297–333, esp. pp. 321–23.

143 *"their own potentialities"*: Maslow, *Motivation and Personality,* p. 214.

143 *"to a value or a purpose"*: Heller and Fehér, *The Postmodern Political Condition* (Columbia University Press, 1988), p. 37.

143 *"leading by being led"*: see Burns, *Leadership,* p. 117.

143 *"to become everything"*: Maslow, *Motivation and Personality,* p. 92.

143 *"contingency into destiny"*: Heller and Fehér, p. 27.

Real Need

John W. Burton, "Human Needs Versus Societal Needs," in Roger A. Coate and Jerel A. Rosati, eds., *The Power of Human Needs in World Society* (Lynne Rienner, 1988), pp. 34–58.

David J. Carroll, Jerel A. Rosati, and Roger A. Coate, "Human Needs Realism: A Critical Assessment of the Power of Human Needs in World Society," in Coate and Rosati, pp. 257–74.

James C. Davies, *Human Nature in Politics: The Dynamics of Political Behavior* (John Wiley and Sons, 1963).

Germann Diligensky, "Problems of the Theory of Human Needs," *Social Science Information,* vol. 20, no. 1 (1981), pp. 169–85.

Ian Fraser, *Hegel and Marx: The Concept of Need* (Edinburgh University Press, 1998).

Erich Fromm, *The Sane Society* (Rinehart, 1955).

Carol C. Gould, *Marx's Social Ontology: Individuality and Community in Marx's Theory of Social Reality* (MIT Press, 1978).

Agnes Heller, *The Theory of Need in Marx* (St. Martin's Press, 1976).

David Lethbridge, *Mind in the World: The Marxist Psychology of Self-Actualization* (MEP Publications, 1992).

C. B. Macpherson, "Needs and Wants: An Ontological or Historical Problem?," in Ross Fitzgerald, ed., *Human Needs and Politics* (Pergamon Press, 1977), pp. 26–35.

Karl Marx, "Economic and Philosophic Manuscripts of 1844," in Marx and Frederick Engels, *Collected Works* (International Publishers, 1975–), vol. 3, pp. 229–346.

David McLellan, "Marx's View of the Unalienated Society," *Review of Politics,* vol. 31, no. 4 (October 1969), pp. 459–65.

John O'Manique, "A Marxian View of the Fundamentals of Political Development," *Political Psychology,* vol. 15, no. 2 (June 1994), pp. 277–305.

John Plamenatz, *Karl Marx's Philosophy of Man* (Clarendon Press, 1975).

Jean-Jacques Rousseau, *The* Discourses *and Other Early Political Writings,* Victor Gourevitch, ed. and trans. (Cambridge University Press, 1997).

Jean-Jacques Rousseau, The Social Contract *and Other Later Political Writings,* Victor Gourevitch, ed. and trans. (Cambridge University Press, 1997).

Patricia Springborg, "Karl Marx on Human Needs," in Fitzgerald, pp. 157–73.

Patricia Springborg, *The Problem of Human Needs and the Critique of Civilisation* (George Allen & Unwin, 1981).

145 *"fewness of his needs"*: Rousseau, *Émile,* Barbara Foxley, trans. (Dent, 1911), pp. 174–75.

145 *Springborg on Marx:* Springborg, *Problem of Human Needs,* p. 101.

145 *"bestial barbarisation"*: Marx, pp. 307, 304, respectively.

146 *"deprivation of human needs"*: Roger A. Coate and Jerel A. Rosati, "Human Needs in World Society," in Coate and Rosati, pp. 1–20, quoted at p. 8.

147 *"be achieved or satisfied"*: Burton, p. 50.

147 *"conflicts between"*: Carroll, Rosati, and Coate, p. 261.

Empowering Motives

Joel Aronoff and John P. Wilson, *Personality in the Social Process* (Lawrence Erlbaum Associates, 1985).

Albert Bandura, *Self-Efficacy: The Exercise of Control* (W. H. Freeman, 1997).

Albert Bandura, ed., *Self-Efficacy in Changing Societies* (Cambridge University Press, 1995).

Roy F. Baumeister, "The Self," in Daniel T. Gilbert et al., eds., *The Handbook of Social Psychology,* 4th ed. (McGraw-Hill, 1998), vol. 1, pp. 680–740.

Sharon S. Brehm and Jack W. Brehm, *Psychological Reactance: A Theory of Freedom and Control* (Academic Press, 1981).

James C. Davies, *Human Nature in Politics: The Dynamics of Political Behavior* (John Wiley and Sons, 1963).

Edward L. Deci and Richard M. Ryan, *Intrinsic Motivation and Self-Determination in Human Behavior* (Plenum Press, 1985).

Erik H. Erikson, *Childhood and Society* (W. W. Norton, 1950), esp. ch. 7.

Erich Fromm, *The Sane Society* (Rinehart, 1955), esp. ch. 3.

Viktor Gecas, "The Self-Concept as a Basis for a Theory of Motivation," in Judith A. Howard and Peter L. Callero, eds., *The Self-Society Dynamic: Cognition, Emotion, and Action* (Cambridge University Press, 1991), pp. 171–87.

Viktor Gecas, "The Social Psychology of Self-Efficacy," *Annual Review of Sociology*, vol. 15 (1989), pp. 291–316.

Peter M. Gollwitzer and John A. Bargh, eds., *The Psychology of Action: Linking Cognition and Motivation to Behavior* (Guilford Press, 1996).

Abraham H. Maslow, *Motivation and Personality* (Harper & Brothers, 1954).

David C. McClelland, *Human Motivation* (Scott, Foresman, 1985).

David C. McClelland, *Power: The Inner Experience* (Irvington, 1975).

David C. McClelland, ed., *Studies in Motivation* (Appleton-Century-Crofts, 1955).

Thane S. Pittman, "Motivation," in Gilbert et al., vol. 1, pp. 549–90.

Stanley A. Renshon, "Human Needs and Political Analysis," in Ross Fitzgerald, ed., *Human Needs and Politics* (Pergamon Press, 1977), pp. 52–73.

Wallace A. Russell, ed., *Milestones in Motivation: Contributions to the Psychology of Drive and Purpose* (Appleton-Century-Crofts, 1970).

Martin E. P. Seligman, *Helplessness: On Depression, Development, and Death* (W. H. Freeman, 1975).

Richard M. Sorrentino and E. Tory Higgins, eds., *Handbook of Motivation and Cognition*, 3 vols. (Guilford Press, 1986–96).

Gifford Weary et al., eds., *Control Motivation and Social Cognition* (Springer-Verlag, 1993).

Daniel M. Wegner and James W. Pennebaker, eds., *Handbook of Mental Control* (Prentice Hall, 1993).

Robert W. White, "Motivation Reconsidered: The Concept of Competence," *Psychological Review*, vol. 66, no. 5 (September 1959), pp. 297–333.

150 *"People strive"*: Bandura, "Exercise of Personal and Collective Efficacy in Changing Societies," in Bandura, *Self-Efficacy in Changing Societies*, pp. 1–45, quoted at p. 1.

150 *"An understanding of motivation"*: Cantor et al., "On Motivation and the Self-Concept," in Sorrentino and Higgins, pp. 96–121, quoted at p. 96.

9 CREATIVE LEADERSHIP

Walter Allen, ed., *Writers on Writing* (Phoenix House, 1948).

Teresa M. Amabile, *The Social Psychology of Creativity* (Springer-Verlag, 1983), esp. ch. 1.

Ronald W. Clark, *Einstein* (World Publishing, 1971).

I. Bernard Cohen, *Revolution in Science* (Belknap Press, 1985), esp. chs. 2, 9, 27, 28.

Howard Gardner, *Creating Minds* (Basic Books, 1993), esp. chs. 1, 4, 7.

Stanley Goldberg, "Albert Einstein and the Creative Act: The Case of Special Relativity," in Rutherford Aris et al., eds., *Springs of Scientific Creativity* (University of Minnesota Press, 1983), pp. 232–53.

Gerald Holton, *The Advancement of Science, and Its Burdens* (Cambridge University Press, 1986), esp. part 1.

Gerald Holton, *Thematic Origins of Scientific Thought: Kepler to Einstein,* rev. ed. (Harvard University Press, 1988), part 2, and passim.

Arthur I. Miller, "Imagery and Intuition in Creative Scientific Thinking: Albert Einstein's Invention of the Special Theory of Relativity," in Doris B. Wallace and Howard E. Gruber, eds., *Creative People at Work* (Oxford University Press, 1989), pp. 171–87.

152 *Descartes and Galileo's condemnation:* see Stephen Gaukroger, *Descartes* (Clarendon Press, 1995), pp. 290–92.

152 *Galois:* see Laura Toti Rigatelli, *Evariste Galois, 1811–1832,* John Denton, trans. (Birkhäuser Verlag, 1996), esp. chs. 2, 5.

152 *"hellish agony":* letter to A. N. Maikov, January 12, 1868, in Dostoyevsky, *Selected Letters,* Joseph Frank and David I. Goldstein, eds., and Andrew R. MacAndrew, trans. (Rutgers University Press, 1987), pp. 260–67, quoted at p. 260.

153 *Dickens on "penalties":* letter to Mrs. Winter, April 3, 1855, in Dickens, *Letters,* Graham Storey et al., eds. (Clarendon Press, 1965–2002), vol. 7, pp. 583–84, quoted at p. 584.

153 *"ticket to one's funeral":* quoted in Peter Ackroyd, *T. S. Eliot* (Simon and Schuster, 1984), p. 290.

153 *Wolfe and good reviews:* see Wolfe, *The Story of a Novel* (Charles Scribner's Sons, 1936).

153 *Plath and Sexton:* see Lynda K. Bundtzen, *Plath's Incarnations: Women and the Creative Process* (University of Michigan Press, 1983), esp. ch. 1; Diane Wood Middlebrook, *Anne Sexton* (Houghton Mifflin, 1991); Diana Hume George, ed., *Sexton: Selected Criticism* (University of Illinois Press, 1988); Amabile, pp. 8–12.

153 *"Some people see things":* quoted in Theodore H. White, *The Making of the President 1968* (Atheneum, 1969), p. 171; see also Shaw, *Back to Methuselah* (Brentano's, 1921), p. 6 (Part 1, Act 1).

Liberating Ideas

Joan V. Bondurant, *Conquest of Violence: The Gandhian Philosophy of Conflict* (Princeton University Press, 1958).

Judith M. Brown, *Gandhi and Civil Disobedience: The Mahatma in Indian Politics, 1928–34* (Cambridge University Press, 1977).

Dennis Dalton, *Mahatma Gandhi: Nonviolent Power in Action* (Columbia University Press, 1993).

Erik H. Erikson, *Gandhi's Truth: On the Origins of Militant Nonviolence* (W. W. Norton, 1969).

Mohandas K. Gandhi, *An Autobiography: The Story of My Experiments with Truth,* Mahadev Desai, trans. (Beacon Press, 1957).

Homer A. Jack, ed., *The Gandhi Reader* (Indiana University Press, 1956).

Kenneth Keele, *Leonardo da Vinci's Elements of the Science of Man* (Academic Press, 1983).

Roger D. Masters, *Fortune Is a River: Leonardo da Vinci and Niccolò Machiavelli's Magnificent Dream to Change the Course of Florentine History* (Free Press, 1998).

Hyman Muslin and Prakash Desai, "The Transformations in the Self of Mahatma Gandhi," in Charles B. Strozier and Daniel Offer, eds., *The Leader: Psychohistorical Essays* (Plenum Press, 1985), pp. 111–32.

Arne Naess, *Gandhi and Group Conflict: An Exploration of* Satyagraha (Universitetsforlaget, 1974).

C. D. O'Malley, ed., *Leonardo's Legacy* (University of California Press, 1969).

Ladislao Reti, ed., *The Unknown Leonardo* (McGraw-Hill, 1974).

A. Richard Turner, *Inventing Leonardo* (Alfred A. Knopf, 1993).

Alessandro Vezzosi, *Leonardo da Vinci: The Mind of the Renaissance,* Alexandra Bonfante-Warren, trans. (Harry N. Abrams, 1997).

154 *"wonders of the courts"*: Vezzosi, p. 54.

154 *"empirical observation"*: Ackerman, "Science and Art in the Work of Leonardo," in O'Malley, pp. 205–25, quoted at p. 209.

155 *"Leonardo's art"*: Butterfield, "The Breakthrough" (review of David Alan Brown, *Leonardo da Vinci: Origins of a Genius*), *New Republic,* vol. 221, no. 1 (July 5, 1999), pp. 41–45, quoted at p. 41.

155 *"passive resistance"*: Gandhi, *Satyagraha in South Africa* (1924–25), in Gandhi, *Collected Works* (Publications Division, Ministry of Information and Broadcasting, Government of India, 1958–94), vol. 29, quoted at p. 92.

155 *"banyan tree"*: Speech at Preparatory Meeting for Hindi Conference, Bombay, before April 18, 1919, in *ibid.,* vol. 15, pp. 240–45, quoted at p. 244.

155 *"disciplined rule"*: Interview to Journalists, March 6, 1931, in *ibid.,* vol. 45, pp. 263–67, quoted at p. 263.

155 *"swaraj of a people"*: quoted in R. K. Prabhu and U. R. Rao, eds., *The Mind of Mahatma Gandhi,* rev. ed. (Navajivan Publishing House, 1967), p. 321.

156 *"greatest necessity"*: Gandhi, "Salt Tax," February 27, 1930, in Gandhi, *Collected Works,* vol. 42, pp. 499–501, quoted at p. 499.

157 *"sanity returns"*: quoted in Dalton, p. 155.

157 *"we shall never allow"*: *ibid.,* p. 158.

The Springs of Creativity

Alfred Adler, "The Fundamental Views of Individual Psychology," *International Journal of Individual Psychology,* vol. 1 (1935), pp. 5–8.

Alfred Adler, *The Practice and Theory of Individual Psychology,* P. Radin, trans. (Harcourt, Brace, 1927).

Teresa M. Amabile, *The Social Psychology of Creativity* (Springer-Verlag, 1983).

Harold H. Anderson, ed., *Creativity and Its Cultivation* (Harper & Brothers, 1959).

Heinz L. Ansbacher and Rowena R. Ansbacher, eds., *The Individual Psychology of Alfred Adler* (Harper Torchbooks, 1964).

Silvano Arieti, *Creativity: The Magic Synthesis* (Basic Books, 1976).

John S. Dacey and Kathleen H. Lennon, *Understanding Creativity: The Interplay of Biological, Psychological, and Social Factors* (Jossey-Bass, 1998), esp. parts 3–5.

William James, "Great Men and Their Environment," in James, The Will to Believe, *and Other Essays in Popular Philosophy,* Frederick H. Burkhardt et al., eds. (Harvard University Press, 1979), pp. 163–89.

Abraham H. Maslow, *The Farther Reaches of Human Nature* (Penguin/Arkana, 1993), esp. part 2.

R. Ochse, *Before the Gates of Excellence: The Determinants of Creative Genius* (Cambridge University Press, 1990).

Otto Rank, *The Myth of the Birth of the Hero, and Other Writings,* Philip Freund, ed. (Vintage, 1959).

Albert Rothenberg and Carl R. Hausman, eds., *The Creativity Question* (Duke University Press, 1976).

Mark A. Runco and Steven R. Pritzker, eds., *Encyclopedia of Creativity,* 2 vols. (Academic Press, 1999).

Dean Keith Simonton, *Origins of Genius: Darwinian Perspectives on Creativity* (Oxford University Press, 1999).

Steven M. Smith, Thomas B. Ward, and Ronald A. Finke, eds., *The Creative Cognition Approach* (MIT Press, 1995).

Andrew Steptoe, ed., *Genius and the Mind: Studies of Creativity and Temperament* (Oxford University Press, 1998).

Robert J. Sternberg, ed., *Handbook of Creativity* (Cambridge University Press, 1999).

Robert J. Sternberg, ed., *The Nature of Creativity* (Cambridge University Press, 1988).

Robert J. Sternberg and Janet E. Davidson, eds., *The Nature of Insight* (MIT Press, 1995).

Thomas B. Ward, Steven M. Smith, and Jyotsna Vaid, eds., *Creative Thought: An Investigation into Conceptual Structures and Processes* (American Psychological Association, 1997).

Robert Paul Weiner, *Creativity & Beyond: Cultures, Values, and Change* (State University of New York Press, 2000).

158 *"inherent creativeness"*: Sinnott, "The Creativeness of Life," in Anderson, pp. 12–29, quoted at pp. 28, 13, 28, 19, respectively.

159 *"biopsychosocial"*: see Dacey and Lennon, ch. 12, quoted on "biological elements" at p. 9.

159 *"excessively powerful"*: Freud, *Introductory Lectures on Psychoanalysis,* lecture no. 23, in Freud, *Complete Psychological Works,* James Strachey, ed. and trans. (Hogarth Press, 1981), vol. 16, pp. 358–77, quoted at p. 376.

159 *"artist of his own personality"*: Ansbacher and Ansbacher, p. 177; see also Ochse, pp. 17–18.

159 *"fundamental characteristic"*: Maslow, *Motivation and Personality* (Harper & Brothers, 1954), p. 223.

Golden Ages

Teresa M. Amabile, *The Social Psychology of Creativity* (Springer-Verlag, 1983).

Silvano Arieti, *Creativity: The Magic Synthesis* (Basic Books, 1976).

Charles David Axelrod, *Studies in Intellectual Breakthrough: Freud, Simmel, Buber* (University of Massachusetts Press, 1979).

Joanne Bentley, *Hallie Flanagan: A Life in the American Theatre* (Alfred A. Knopf, 1988).

Augusto Boal, *Games for Actors and Non-Actors,* Adrian Jackson, trans. (Routledge, 1992).

Augusto Boal, *Legislative Theatre: Using Performance to Make Politics,* Adrian Jackson, trans. (Routledge, 1998).

August Boal, *Theater of the Oppressed,* Charles A. and Maria-Odilia Leal McBride, trans. (Theatre Communications Group, 1985).

Edward Braun, *Meyerhold: A Revolution in Theatre* (University of Iowa Press, 1995).

Yolanda Broyles-González, *Teatro Campesino: Theater in the Chicano Movement* (University of Texas Press, 1994).

Randall Collins, *The Sociology of Philosophies: A Global Theory of Intellectual Change* (Belknap Press, 1998).

Richard S. Crutchfield, "Conformity and Creative Thinking," in Howard E. Gruber et al., eds., *Contemporary Approaches to Creative Thinking* (Atherton Press, 1962), pp. 120–40.

John S. Dacey and Kathleen H. Lennon, *Understanding Creativity: The Interplay of Biological, Psychological, and Social Factors* (Jossey-Bass, 1998), part 2, and passim.

J. M. B. Edwards, "Creativity, Social Aspects," in David L. Sills, ed., *International Encyclopedia of the Social Sciences* (Macmillan/Free Press, 1968), vol. 3, pp. 442–57.

Hallie Flanagan, *Arena* (Duell, Sloan and Pearce, 1940).

Hallie Flanagan, *Dynamo* (Duell, Sloan and Pearce, 1943).

Hallie Flanagan, *Shifting Scenes of the Modern European Theatre* (George G. Harrap, 1929).

Jorge A. Huerta, *Chicano Theater: Themes and Forms* (Bilingual Press, 1982).

Vytautas Kavolis, "Community Dynamics and Artistic Creativity," *American Sociological Review,* vol. 31, no. 2 (April 1966), pp. 208–17.

Vytautas Kavolis, "Political Dynamics and Artistic Creativity," *Sociology and Social Research,* vol. 49 (July 1965), pp. 412–24.

Jane De Hart Mathews, *The Federal Theatre, 1935–1939: Plays, Relief, and Politics* (Princeton University Press, 1967).

Robert K. Merton, *The Sociology of Science,* Norman W. Storer, ed. (University of Chicago Press, 1973).

R. Ochse, *Before the Gates of Excellence: The Determinants of Creative Genius* (Cambridge University Press, 1990).

John O'Connor and Lorraine Brown, eds., *Free, Adult, Uncensored: The Living History of the Federal Theatre Project* (New Republic Books, 1978).

Barbara Rogoff, *Apprenticeship in Thinking: Cognitive Development in Social Context* (Oxford University Press, 1990).

Albert Rothenberg and Carl R. Hausman, eds., *The Creativity Question* (Duke University Press, 1976).

Mark A. Runco and Steven R. Pritzker, eds., *Encyclopedia of Creativity*, 2 vols. (Academic Press, 1999).

Dean Keith Simonton, *Genius, Creativity, and Leadership: Historiometric Inquiries* (Harvard University Press, 1984).

Robert J. Sternberg, ed., *Handbook of Creativity* (Cambridge University Press, 1999).

Robert J. Sternberg, ed., *The Nature of Creativity* (Cambridge University Press, 1988).

E. Paul Torrance, *Guiding Creative Talent* (Prentice-Hall, 1962).

Luis Valdez, *Early Works* (Arte Publico Press, 1990).

Robert Paul Weiner, *Creativity & Beyond: Cultures, Values, and Change* (State University of New York Press, 2000).

Willson Whitman, *Bread and Circuses: A Study of Federal Theatre* (Oxford University Press, 1937).

160   *Velleius Paterculus on creative epochs:* see Arieti, p. 294.

161   *"by standing on the sholders"*: letter to Robert Hooke, February 5, 1675, in Newton, *Correspondence,* H. W. Turnbull, ed. (Cambridge University Press, 1959–77), vol. 1, pp. 416–17, quoted at p. 416.

161   *James on creative community:* James, "Great Men and Their Environment," in James, The Will to Believe, *and Other Essays in Popular Philosophy,* Frederick H. Burkhardt et al., eds. (Harvard University Press, 1979), pp. 163–89, quoted at pp. 181–82.

162   *"75 percent of a group"*: Ochse, p. 73.

162   *"vicious, inflexible"*: quoted in Arthur Koestler, *The Watershed: A Biography of Johannes Kepler* (Anchor, 1960), p. 22.

162   *"Hatred of one parent"*: Vidal, "The Great World and Louis Auchincloss," in Vidal, *United States* (Random House, 1993), pp. 364–74, quoted at p. 370.

162   *"Schools suppress creativity"*: Dacey and Lennon, p. 69.

163   *"drama of remembrance"*: Flanagan, *Shifting Scenes,* pp. 119, 121, 111, respectively.

163   *"equal to the gigantic task"*: Flanagan, *Arena,* p. 45.

163   *"free, adult"*: Harry Hopkins, quoted in Mathews, p. 33.

164   *"influence human thought"*: Flanagan and Philip Davis, "The Word Became Flesh," *New Republic,* vol. 87, no. 1121 (May 27, 1936), pp. 65–67, quoted at p. 67.

164   *"apoplexy"*: quoted in Mathews, p. 177.

164   *"ill-housed"*: Second Inaugural Address, January 20, 1937, in Roosevelt, *Public Papers and Addresses,* Samuel I. Rosenman, comp. (Random House, 1938–50), vol. 6, pp. 1–6, quoted at p. 5.

164   *"Join the union"*: Huerta, p. 16.

164   *"mass struggle"*: Valdez, "Notes on Chicano Theatre," in Valdez, pp. 6–10, quoted at pp. 8–9.

165   *"political theatre"*: Boal, *Legislative Theatre,* pp. 16, 15, respectively.

165 *"best of all possible worlds"*: Boal, "Categories of Popular Theatre" (1971), reprinted in *ibid.,* pp. 209–46, quoted at pp. 211–12.
165 *"transformation-oriented"*: *ibid.,* pp. 213, 211, 217, 20, 219, respectively.

The Transforming Vision

D. E. Berlyne, *Conflict, Arousal, and Curiosity* (McGraw-Hill, 1960).

Randall Collins, *The Sociology of Philosophies: A Global Theory of Intellectual Change* (Belknap Press, 1998).

Donatella della Porta and Mario Diani, *Social Movements* (Blackwell, 1999), esp. ch. 3.

Lewis A. Dexter, "Some Strategic Considerations in Innovating Leadership," in Alvin W. Gouldner, ed., *Studies in Leadership: Leadership and Democratic Action* (Harper & Brothers, 1950), pp. 592–600.

Douglas B. Emery, "Self, Creativity, Political Resistance," *Political Psychology*, vol. 14, no. 2 (1993), pp. 347–62.

Ron Eyerman, "Intellectuals and Progress: The Origins, Decline, and Revival of a Critical Group," in Jeffrey C. Alexander and Piotr Sztompka, eds., *Rethinking Progress: Movements, Forces, and Ideas at the End of the 20th Century* (Unwin Hyman, 1990), pp. 91–105.

Ron Eyerman and Andrew Jamison, *Social Movements: A Cognitive Approach* (Pennsylvania State University Press, 1991), ch. 4, and passim.

Brian Fay, *Critical Social Science: Liberation and Its Limits* (Cornell University Press, 1987).

Leon Festinger, "The Motivating Effect of Cognitive Dissonance," in Gardner Lindzey, ed., *Assessment of Human Motives* (Rinehart, 1958), pp. 65–86.

Paulo Freire, *Pedagogy of the Oppressed,* Myra Bergman Ramos, trans. (Herder and Herder, 1970).

Howard Gardner, *Leading Minds: An Anatomy of Leadership* (Basic Books, 1995).

Luther P. Gerlach and Virginia H. Hine, *People, Power, Change: Movements of Social Transformation* (Bobbs-Merrill, 1970), ch. 6.

Erving Goffman, *Frame Analysis: An Essay on the Organization of Experience* (Northeastern University Press, 1986).

Howard E. Gruber, "Creativity and Human Survival," in Doris B. Wallace and Gruber, eds., *Creative People at Work* (Oxford University Press, 1989), pp. 278–87.

Howard E. Gruber, *Darwin on Man: A Psychological Study of Scientific Creativity* (E. P. Dutton, 1974), ch. 12.

Bert Klandermans, *The Social Psychology of Protest* (Blackwell, 1997), esp. ch. 2.

Nan Lin and Gerald Zaltman, "Dimensions of Innovations," in Zaltman, ed., *Processes and Phenomena of Social Change* (John Wiley & Sons, 1973), pp. 93–115.

Alberto Melucci, *Challenging Codes: Collective Action in the Information Age* (Cambridge University Press, 1996), esp. ch. 18.

Michael D. Mumford and Mary S. Connelly, "Leaders as Creators: Leader Performance and Problem Solving in Ill-Defined Domains," *Leadership Quarterly*, vol. 2, no. 4 (Winter 1991), pp. 289–315.

Harry C. Payne, *The Philosophes and the People* (Yale University Press, 1976).

Robert Richards, "Theories of Scientific Change," in Alfred I. Tauber, ed., *Science and the Quest for Reality* (New York University Press, 1997), pp. 203–30.

Neal Riemer, *Creative Breakthroughs in Politics* (Praeger, 1996).

Thomas R. Rochon, *Culture Moves: Ideas, Activism, and Changing Values* (Princeton University Press, 1998).

Peter C. Sederberg, *The Politics of Meaning: Power and Explanation in the Construction of Social Reality* (University of Arizona Press, 1984).

David A. Snow and Robert D. Benford, "Master Frames and Cycles of Protest," in Aldon D. Morris and Carol McClurg Mueller, eds., *Frontiers in Social Movement Theory* (Yale University Press, 1992), pp. 133–55.

David A. Snow et al., "Frame Alignment Processes, Micromobilization, and Movement Participation," in Doug McAdam and Snow, eds., *Social Movements* (Roxbury Publishing, 1997), pp. 235–51.

Sidney Tarrow, *Power in Movement: Social Movements, Collective Action and Politics* (Cambridge University Press, 1994), esp. ch. 7.

Göran Therborn, *The Ideology of Power and the Power of Ideology* (Verso, 1980).

Arnold Toynbee, "Is America Neglecting Her Creative Minority?," in Calvin W. Taylor, ed., *Widening Horizons in Creativity* (John Wiley & Sons, 1964), pp. 3–9.

Robert Paul Weiner, *Creativity & Beyond: Culture, Values, and Change* (State University of New York Press, 2000).

Sheldon S. Wolin, "Paradigms and Political Theories," in Gary Gutting, ed., *Paradigms and Revolutions* (University of Notre Dame Press, 1980), pp. 160–91.

Sheldon S. Wolin, *Politics and Vision: Continuity and Innovation in Western Political Thought* (Little, Brown, 1960).

166 *"explanatory collapse"*: Sederberg, p. 181.

166 *"by a profound belief"*: Wolin, "Paradigms," p. 182.

167 *"motivating state"*: Festinger, p. 69.

167 *"The deeper the experience"*: Havel, *Disturbing the Peace*, Paul Wilson, trans. (Alfred A. Knopf, 1990), p. 201.

167 *"institutionalization of hypocrisy"*: Keniston, "Youth, Change and Violence," *American Scholar*, vol. 37, no. 2 (Spring 1968), pp. 227–45, quoted at p. 239.

167 *"new spaces"*: della Porta and Diani, p. 72.

167 *Rochon's modes of values-change:* Rochon, pp. 54, 55.

168 *"fabricated out of whole cloth"*: Tarrow, p. 130.

168 *"intimately tied"*: Mumford and Connelly, p. 308.

168 *"ideal of an order"*: Wolin, *Politics and Vision*, p. 21.

168 *"not simply to alter"*: Wolin, "Paradigms," p. 179.

168 *"experience something"*: Sederberg, p. 185.

169 *"reflective participant"*: see Freire, p. 52.

169 *"as they grow"*: Weiner, p. 264.

169 *"closed world"*: Freire, p. 34.

10 THE LEADER-FOLLOWER PARADOX

170 *"sown in the nature"*: Madison, "The Federalist X," in Bernard Bailyn, ed., *The Debate on the Constitution* (Library of America, 1993), part 1, pp. 404–11, quoted at p. 406.

170 *"thousands of books"*: Wills, *Certain Trumpets: The Call of Leaders* (Simon & Schuster, 1994), p. 13.

Followers as Leaders

Edwin Amenta et al., "A Hero for the Aged?: The Townsend Movement, the Political Mediation Model, and U.S. Old-Age Policy, 1934–1950," in Doug McAdam and David A. Snow, eds., *Social Movements* (Roxbury Publishing, 1997), pp. 494–510.

David H. Bennett, *Demagogues in the Depression: American Radicals and the Union Party, 1932–1936* (Rutgers University Press, 1969).

Irving Bernstein, *Turbulent Years: A History of the American Worker, 1933–1941* (Houghton Mifflin, 1969).

Alan Brinkley, *Voices of Protest: Huey Long, Father Coughlin, and the Great Depression* (Alfred A. Knopf, 1982).

James MacGregor Burns, *Roosevelt: The Lion and the Fox* (Harcourt, Brace, 1956), esp. part 3.

John A. Crampton, *The National Farmers Union: Ideology of a Pressure Group* (University of Nebraska Press, 1965).

E. P. Hollander, "Leadership, Followership, Self, and Others," *Leadership Quarterly*, vol. 3, no. 1 (1992), pp. 43–54.

Abraham Holtzman, *The Townsend Movement: A Political Study* (Bookman Associates, 1963).

Theodore Saloutos, *The American Farmer and the New Deal* (Iowa State University Press, 1982).

Arthur M. Schlesinger, Jr., *The Coming of the New Deal* (Houghton Mifflin, 1958), esp. parts 1, 2, and 5.

Arthur M. Schlesinger, Jr., *The Politics of Upheaval* (Houghton Mifflin, 1960), esp. part 1.

John L. Shover, *Cornbelt Rebellion: The Farmers' Holiday Association* (University of Illinois Press, 1965).

Raymond Gram Swing, *Forerunners of American Fascism* (1935; reprinted by Books for Libraries Press, 1969).

Charles J. Tull, *Father Coughlin and the New Deal* (Syracuse University Press, 1965).

T. Harry Williams, *Huey Long* (Alfred A. Knopf, 1970).

171 *"All initiatives"*: Hollander, p. 44.

172 *"need for enlightened"*: Euchner, *Extraordinary Politics: How Protest and Dissent Are Changing American Democracy* (Westview Press, 1996), p. 135.

173 *"grass will grow"*: Address at Madison Square Garden in New York City, October 31, 1932, in Hoover, *Public Papers: 1932–33* (U.S. Government Printing Office, 1977), pp. 656–80, quoted at p. 669.

173 *"Roosevelt wants* you": quoted in Burns, p. 216.

174 *"scarcity economics"*: *ibid.,* p. 194.

174 *"what we have overproduction of"*: John A. Simpson, president of the Farmers' Union, quoted in Gilbert Fite, "Farm Opinion and the Agricultural Adjustment Act, 1933," *Mississippi Valley Historical Review,* vol. 48, no. 4 (March 1962), pp. 656–73, quoted at p. 665.

174 *"working fer him"*: quoted in Brinkley, p. 64.

174 *"After an average broadcast"*: *ibid.,* p. 169.

174 *"Roosevelt or Ruin!"*: quoted in *ibid.,* p. 108.

Leaders as Followers

Edwin Amenta et al., "Stolen Thunder? Huey Long's 'Share Our Wealth,' Political Mediation, and the Second New Deal," *American Sociological Review,* vol. 59, no. 5 (October 1994), pp. 678–702.

David H. Bennett, *Demagogues in the Depression: American Radicals and the Union Party, 1932–1936* (Rutgers University Press, 1969).

Daniel J. Boorstin, "Selling the President to the People: The Direct Democracy of Public Relations," *Commentary,* vol. 20 (November 1955), pp. 421–27.

Alan Brinkley, *Voices of Protest: Huey Long, Father Coughlin, and the Great Depression* (Alfred A. Knopf, 1982).

James MacGregor Burns, *The Crosswinds of Freedom* (Alfred A. Knopf, 1989), esp. ch. 2.

James MacGregor Burns, "Empowerment for Change: A Conceptual Working Paper," prepared for the Kellogg Leadership Studies Project, September 1996.

James MacGregor Burns, *Roosevelt: The Lion and the Fox* (Harcourt, Brace, 1956), part 3 passim.

Elmer E. Cornwell, Jr., *Presidential Leadership of Public Opinion* (Indiana University Press, 1965), esp. ch. 6.

Kenneth S. Davis, *FDR: The New Deal Years, 1933–1937* (Random House, 1986), esp. part 2.

Glen Jeansonne, ed., *Huey at 100* (McGinty Publications, 1995).

Glen Jeansonne, *Messiah of the Masses: Huey P. Long and the Great Depression* (HarperCollins, 1993).

J. Craig Jenkins and Barbara J. Brents, "Social Protest, Hegemonic Competition, and Social Reform: A Political Struggle Interpretation of the Origins of the American Welfare State," *American Sociological Review,* vol. 54, no. 6 (December 1989), pp. 891–909.

J. T. Salter, *The Pattern of Politics: The Folkways of a Democratic People* (Macmillan, 1940), ch. 5.

Arthur M. Schlesinger, Jr., *The Politics of Upheaval* (Houghton Mifflin, 1960).

Richard W. Steele, "The Pulse of the People: Franklin D. Roosevelt and the Gauging of American Public Opinion," *Journal of Contemporary History,* vol. 9, no. 4 (October 1974), pp. 195–216.

Leila A. Sussmann, "FDR and the White House Mail," *Public Opinion Quarterly,* vol. 20, no. 1 (Spring 1956), pp. 5–16.

Charles J. Tull, *Father Coughlin and the New Deal* (Syracuse University Press, 1965), esp. chs. 3–5.

T. H. Watkins, *The Hungry Years* (Henry Holt, 1999).

Graham J. White, *FDR and the Press* (University of Chicago Press, 1979).

T. Harry Williams, *Huey Long* (Alfred A. Knopf, 1970).

Ann Ruth Willner, *The Spellbinders: Charismatic Political Leadership* (Yale University Press, 1984).

Betty Houchin Winfield, *FDR and the News Media* (University of Illinois Press, 1990).

George Wolfskill, *The Revolt of the Conservatives: A History of the American Liberty League, 1934–1940* (Houghton Mifflin, 1962).

175 *"Once more"*: quoted in *Time,* vol. 25, no. 11 (March 18, 1935), p. 13.

175 *"genuine period"*: Annual Message to the Congress, January 4, 1935, in Roosevelt, *Public Papers and Addresses,* Samuel I. Rosenman, comp. (Random House, 1938–50), vol. 4, pp. 15–25, quoted at p. 25.

176 *"because of human weakness"*: letter to Ray Stannard Baker, March 20, 1935, in Roosevelt, *Personal Letters, 1928–1945,* Elliott Roosevelt, ed. (Duell, Sloan and Pearce, 1947–50), vol. 3, pp. 466–67.

176 *1935 Democratic National Committee poll:* see Brinkley, pp. 207–209, 284–86; entry of October 30, 1935, in Harold L. Ickes, *The Secret Diary* (Simon and Schuster, 1953–54), vol. 1, p. 462.

177 *Supreme Court NIRA decision: Schechter Poultry Corp. v. United States,* 295 U.S. 495 (1935); see also Peter H. Irons, *The New Deal Lawyers* (Princeton University Press, 1982), ch. 5.

177 *"pathetic appeals"*: Press Conference, May 31, 1935, in Roosevelt, *Public Papers,* vol. 4, pp. 200–22, quoted at pp. 201, 221.

178 *FDR's support in July 1936 poll:* Davis, p. 638.

179 *"Government by organized* money": Campaign Address at Madison Square Garden, October 31, 1936, in Roosevelt, *Public Papers,* vol. 5, pp. 566–73, quoted at p. 568. Emphases based on a recording of the speech at the Franklin D. Roosevelt Library, Hyde Park, New York.

179 *"news sense"*: quoted in White, p. 10.

180 *"with imagination"*: Einaudi, *The Roosevelt Revolution* (Harcourt, Brace, 1959), p. 60.

180 *"just about everybody"*: Edwin E. Witte, quoted in Cornwell, p. 133.

From Engagement to Empowerment

Bruce J. Avolio and Tracy C. Gibbons, "Developing Transformational Leaders: A Life Span Approach," in Jay A. Conger et al., eds., *Charismatic Leadership: The Elusive Factor in Organizational Effectiveness* (Jossey-Bass, 1988), pp. 276–308.

Bernard M. Bass, *Bass & Stogdill's Handbook of Leadership,* 3rd ed. (Free Press, 1990), chs. 12, 18.

Stephen D. Brookfield, "What It Means to Think Critically," in J. Thomas Wren, ed., *The Leader's Companion* (Free Press, 1995), pp. 379–88.

Joanne B. Ciulla, "Leadership and the Problem of Bogus Empowerment," in Ciulla, ed., *Ethics, the Heart of Leadership* (Quorum Books, 1998), pp. 63–86.

Richard A. Couto, "Grassroots Policies of Empowerment," paper prepared for delivery at the annual meeting of the American Political Science Association, Chicago, September 3–6, 1992.

James C. Davies, *Human Nature in Politics: The Dynamics of Political Behavior* (John Wiley and Sons, 1963).

James V. Downton, *Rebel Leadership: Commitment and Charisma in the Revolutionary Process* (Free Press, 1973).

John W. Gardner, *On Leadership* (Free Press, 1990), esp. chs. 16–17.

Viktor Gecas, "The Self-Concept as a Basis for a Theory of Motivation," in Judith A. Howard and Peter L. Callero, eds., *The Self-Society Dynamic: Cognition, Emotion, and Action* (Cambridge University Press, 1991), pp. 171–87.

Viktor Gecas, "The Social Psychology of Self-Efficacy," *Annual Review of Sociology,* vol. 15 (1989), pp. 291–316.

Kenneth J. Gergen and Matthew Ullman, "Socialization and the Characterological Basis of Political Activism," in Stanley Allen Renshon, ed., *Handbook of Political Socialization* (Free Press, 1977), pp. 411–42.

E. P. Hollander, "Leadership, Followership, Self, and Others," *Leadership Quarterly,* vol. 3, no. 1 (1992), pp. 43–54.

Robert J. House and Philip M. Podsakoff, "Leadership Effectiveness: Past Perspectives and Future Directions for Research," in Jerald Greenberg, ed., *Organizational Behavior: The State of the Science* (Lawrence Erlbaum Associates, 1994), pp. 45–82.

Jane M. Howell, "Two Faces of Charisma: Socialized and Personalized Leadership in Organizations," in Conger et al., pp. 213–36.

Robert W. Hunt and M. Lal Goel, "Unconventional Political Participation," in David Horton Smith et al., eds., *Participation in Social and Political Activities* (Jossey-Bass, 1980), pp. 133–52.

Rabindra N. Kanungo and Manuel Mendonca, *Ethical Dimensions of Leadership* (Sage, 1996).

Robert E. Kelley, *The Power of Followership* (Currency/Doubleday, 1992).

Stanley Allen Renshon, *Psychological Needs and Political Behavior: A Theory of Personality and Political Efficacy* (Free Press, 1974).

David C. Schwartz, "A Theory of Revolutionary Behavior," in James C. Davies, ed., *When Men Revolt and Why* (Transaction, 1997), pp. 109–32.

Peter C. Sederberg, *The Politics of Meaning: Power and Explanation in the Construction of Social Reality* (University of Arizona Press, 1984), ch. 6.

Boas Shamir, "The Charismatic Relationship: Alternative Explanations and Predictions," *Leadership Quarterly,* vol. 2, no. 2 (Summer 1991), pp. 81–104.

Boas Shamir, Robert J. House, and Michael B. Arthur, "The Motivational Effects of Charismatic Leadership: A Self-Concept Based Theory," *Organization Science,* vol. 4, no. 4 (November 1993), pp. 577–94.

Neil J. Smelser, *Theory of Collective Behavior* (Free Press, 1971).

Robert C. Solomon, "Ethical Leadership, Emotions, and Trust: Beyond 'Charisma,'" in Ciulla, *Ethics,* pp. 87–107.

Robert C. Tucker, "The Theory of Charismatic Leadership," *Daedalus,* vol. 97, no. 3 (Summer 1968), pp. 731–56.

182 *"I accept the commission":* June 27, 1936, in Roosevelt, *Public Papers and Addresses,* Samuel I. Rosenman, comp. (Random House, 1938–50), vol. 5, pp. 230–36, quoted at p. 236.

183 *"high self-efficacy":* Gecas, "The Social Psychology of Self-Efficacy," p. 310.

184 *"confidence, competence":* Ciulla, pp. 63, 64.

184 *"intrinsic value":* Shamir, "Charismatic Relationship," p. 92, summarizing the findings of Shamir, House, and Arthur, "Motivational Effects."

184 *"socialized leaders":* see Howell, pp. 223–24.

184 *"moral commitments":* Ciulla, pp. 84, 83, 64, respectively.

184 *Couto on two forms of empowerment:* see Couto, p. 10.

11 CONFLICT: THE ARMING OF LEADERSHIP

187 *"man of war":* Exodus, 15:3.

187 *"do good to them":* Matthew, 5:44, 10:34, 10:21, respectively.

The Conflict over Conflict

Howard Becker and Harry Elmer Barnes, *Social Thought from Lore to Science,* 3 vols., 3rd ed. (Dover, 1961).

Jessie Bernard, "Some Current Conceptualizations in the Field of Conflict," *American Journal of Sociology,* vol. 70, no. 4 (January 1965), pp. 442–54.

Thomas J. Bernard, *The Consensus-Conflict Debate: Form and Content in Social Theories* (Columbia University Press, 1983).

T. B. Bottomore, "Sociological Theory and the Study of Social Conflict," in John C. McKinney and Edward A. Tiryakian, eds., *Theoretical Sociology* (Appleton-Century-Crofts, 1970), pp. 137–53.

John Burton, *Deviance Terrorism & War* (St. Martin's Press, 1979).

Randall Collins, *Conflict Sociology* (Academic Press, 1975).

Randall Collins, *Four Sociological Traditions,* rev. ed. (Oxford University Press, 1994), esp. ch. 1.

Lewis A. Coser, *The Functions of Social Conflict* (Free Press, 1956), esp. ch. 1.

Ralf Dahrendorf, *Class and Class Conflict in Industrial Society* (Stanford University Press, 1959).

Ralf Dahrendorf, "Out of Utopia: Toward a Reorientation of Sociological Analysis," in N. J. Demerath III and Richard A. Peterson, eds., *System, Change, and Conflict* (Free Press, 1967), pp. 465–80.

Ralf Dahrendorf, "Toward a Theory of Social Conflict," *Journal of Conflict Resolution*, vol. 2, no. 2 (June 1958), pp. 170–83.

N. J. Demerath III and Richard A. Peterson, eds., *System, Change, and Conflict* (Free Press, 1967).

Graeme Duncan, *Marx and Mill: Two Views of Social Conflict and Social Harmony* (Cambridge University Press, 1973).

Robert W. Friedrichs, *A Sociology of Sociology* (Free Press, 1970).

Ludwig Gumplowicz, *The Outlines of Sociology*, Frederick W. Moore, trans. (American Academy of Political and Social Science, 1899).

Han Fei Tzu, *Basic Writings*, Burton Watson, trans. (Columbia University Press, 1964).

John Horton, "Order and Conflict Theories of Social Problems as Competing Ideologies," *American Journal of Sociology*, vol. 71, no. 6 (May 1966), pp. 701–21.

Charles H. Kahn, ed., *The Art and Thought of Heraclitus* (Cambridge University Press, 1979).

Robert H. Lauer, *Perspectives on Social Change* (Allyn and Bacon, 1973), esp. chs. 4, 8.

Herbert Marcuse, *One-Dimensional Man* (Beacon Press, 1964).

Elton B. McNeil, ed., *The Nature of Human Conflict* (Prentice-Hall, 1965).

James H. Meisel, ed., *Pareto & Mosca* (Prentice-Hall, 1965).

C. Wright Mills, *The Sociological Imagination* (Oxford University Press, 1959).

Anthony Oberschall, *Social Conflict and Social Movements* (Prentice-Hall, 1973), esp. chs. 1–2.

Vilfredo Pareto, *The Mind and Society*, Arthur Livingston, ed., Livingston and Andrew Bongiorno, trans., 4 vols. (Harcourt, Brace, 1935).

Vilfredo Pareto, *The Rise and Fall of the Elites* (Bedminster Press, 1968).

Talcott Parsons, *The Social System* (Free Press, 1951).

Talcott Parsons, *The Structure of Social Action* (McGraw-Hill, 1937).

Talcott Parsons, *The System of Modern Societies* (Prentice-Hall, 1971).

John Plamenatz, *Karl Marx's Philosophy of Man* (Clarendon Press, 1975), esp. ch. 14.

Anatol Rapoport, *Conflict in Man-Made Environment* (Penguin, 1974), esp. part 2.

Georg Simmel, *Conflict, and The Web of Group Affiliations*, Kurt H. Wolff and Reinhard Bendix, trans. (Free Press, 1955).

William Graham Sumner, *Essays*, Albert G. Keller and Maurice R. Davie, eds., 2 vols. (Yale University Press, 1934).

William Graham Sumner, *Folkways* (Ginn, 1906).

William Graham Sumner, *What Social Classes Owe to Each Other* (Yale University Press, 1925).

Jonathan H. Turner, *The Structure of Sociological Theory*, 5th ed. (Wadsworth, 1991), esp. parts 1–2.

Lester F. Ward, *Applied Sociology* (Ginn, 1906).

Lester F. Ward, *Dynamic Sociology*, 2nd ed., 2 vols. (D. Appleton, 1897).

Lester F. Ward, *Pure Sociology* (Macmillan, 1903).

Lester F. Ward, "The Sociology of Political Parties," *American Journal of Sociology*, vol. 13, no. 4 (January 1908), pp. 439–54.

S. L. Washburn, "Conflict in Primate Society," in Anthony de Reuck and Julie Knight, eds., *Conflict in Society* (Little, Brown, 1966), pp. 3–15.

187 *"madness of the multitude"*: Plato, *Republic,* Paul Storey, trans., in Plato, *The Collected Dialogues,* Edith Hamilton and Huntington Cairns, eds. (Princeton University Press, 1961), p. 732 (6.496).

187 *"They wish"*: Aristotle, *The Nicomachean Ethics,* Book 9, ch. 6, as translated in Bernard, p. 37.

188 *"every man is enemy"*: Hobbes, *Leviathan,* J. C. A. Gaskin, ed. (Oxford University Press, 1996), pp. 84 (13.9) and 115 (17.15).

189 *"sudden spurts"*: Pareto, *Mind and Society,* vol. 4, p. 1556 (§2227).

189 *"competition of life"*: Sumner, *Folkways,* p. 16.

189 *"perpetual and vigorous struggle"*: Ward, *Pure Sociology,* p. 184.

189 *"deviant tendencies"*: Parsons, *Social System,* p. 298.

190 *"terrorized masses"*: Mills, pp. 42, 43.

190 *"all that is creativity"*: Dahrendorf, *Class and Class Conflict,* pp. 208, 162, respectively.

190 *"peace of utopia"*: Dahrendorf, "Out of Utopia," pp. 471, 472, 480, 474, 479, respectively.

The Leadership of Conflict

William Sheridan Allen, *The Nazi Seizure of Power: The Experience of a Single German Town, 1922–1945,* rev. ed. (Franklin Watts, 1984).

Hannah Arendt, *The Origins of Totalitarianism,* 2nd ed. (Harcourt Brace Jovanovich, 1979), ch. 10, and passim.

Leonard Binder et al., *Crises and Sequences in Political Development* (Princeton University Press, 1971).

Taylor Branch, *Parting the Waters: America in the King Years, 1954–1963* (Simon and Schuster, 1988).

Taylor Branch, *Pillar of Fire: America in the King Years, 1963–1965* (Simon and Schuster, 1998).

James MacGregor Burns and Stewart Burns, *A People's Charter: The Pursuit of Rights in America* (Alfred A. Knopf, 1991), ch. 10, and passim.

John Burton, ed., *Conflict: Human Needs Theory* (St. Martin's Press, 1990).

Lewis A. Coser, *The Functions of Social Conflict* (Free Press, 1956).

Lewis A. Coser, "Some Social Functions of Violence," *Annals of the American Academy of Political and Social Science,* vol. 364 (March 1966), pp. 8–18.

Michael Crowder, ed., *Cambridge History of Africa: From c. 1940 to c. 1975,* vol. 8 (Cambridge University Press, 1984).

Robert A. Dahl, ed., *Regimes and Oppositions* (Yale University Press, 1973).

John Darwin, *The End of the British Empire* (Basil Blackwell, 1991).

Steven I. Davis, *Leadership in Conflict: The Lessons of History* (Macmillan, 1996).

Morton Deutsch, "Conflicts: Productive and Destructive," *Journal of Social Issues,* vol. 25, no. 1 (1969), pp. 7–41.

Henry F. Dobyns and Paul L. Doughty, *Peru* (Oxford University Press, 1976), esp. ch. 10.

Harry Eckstein, ed., *Internal War* (Free Press, 1964).

Murray Edelman, *Politics as Symbolic Action: Mass Arousal and Quiescence* (Academic Press, 1971).

Clinton F. Fink, "Some Conceptual Difficulties in the Theory of Social Conflict," *Journal of Conflict Resolution,* vol. 12, no. 4 (December 1968), pp. 412–60.

Luther P. Gerlach and Virginia H. Hine, *People, Power, Change: Movements of Social Transformation* (Bobbs-Merrill, 1970), esp. chs. 6–7.

Prosser Gifford and Wm. Roger Louis, eds., *Decolonization and African Independence: The Transfers of Power, 1960–1980* (Yale University Press, 1988).

Partha Sarathi Gupta, *Imperialism and the British Labour Movement, 1914–1964* (Holmes & Meier, 1975).

Sandor Halebsky, *Mass Society and Political Conflict* (Cambridge University Press, 1976).

Denyse Harari and Jorge Garcia-Bouza, *Social Conflict and Development* (OECD, 1982), ch. 9, and passim.

William Kornhauser, *The Politics of Mass Society* (Free Press, 1959).

Louis Kriesberg, *The Sociology of Social Conflicts* (Prentice-Hall, 1973).

Emil Lederer, *State of the Masses: The Threat of the Classless Society* (W. W. Norton, 1940).

Norrie Macqueen, *The Decolonization of Portuguese Africa* (Longman, 1997).

Gary T. Marx, ed., *Racial Conflict: Tension and Change in American Society* (Little, Brown, 1971).

Elton B. McNeil, ed., *The Nature of Human Conflict* (Prentice-Hall, 1965).

Aldon D. Morris, *The Origins of the Civil Rights Movement: Black Communities Organizing for Change* (Free Press, 1984).

Minion K. C. Morrison, *Black Political Mobilization: Leadership, Power, and Mass Behavior* (State University of New York Press, 1987).

Malyn Newitt, *Portugal in Africa: The Last Hundred Years* (C. Hurst, 1981).

H. L. Nieburg, "Uses of Violence," *Journal of Conflict Resolution,* vol. 7, no. 1 (March 1963), pp. 43–54.

Anthony Oberschall, *Social Conflict and Social Movements* (Prentice-Hall, 1973).

F. LaMond Tullis, *Lord and Peasant in Peru: A Paradigm of Political and Social Change* (Harvard University Press, 1970).

F. LaMond Tullis, *Politics and Social Change in Third World Countries* (John Wiley and Sons, 1973), ch. 11, and passim.

William Foote Whyte and Giorgio Alberti, *Power, Politics, and Progress: Social Change in Rural Peru* (Elsevier, 1976).

I. William Zartman, ed., *Governance as Conflict Management: Politics and Violence in West Africa* (Brookings Institution Press, 1997).

192 *"readily available"*: Kornhauser, p. 39.

192 *Hanover town in 1932:* Allen, pp. 16–20, quoted at p. 20; see also Oberschall, p. 108.

194 "*strong man*": quoted in Tullis, *Politics and Social Change,* p. 247.
195 "*nebulous cultural policy*": Oberschall, p. 275.

The Power of Leadership

Peter Ackerman and Christopher Kruegler, *Strategic Nonviolent Conflict: The Dynamics of People Power in the Twentieth Century* (Praeger, 1994).

Bernard M. Bass, *Bass & Stogdill's Handbook of Leadership,* 3rd ed. (Free Press, 1990), ch. 9, part 3 passim, and chs. 21–22.

Bernard M. Bass, *Leadership, Psychology, and Organizational Behavior* (Harper & Row, 1960), esp. part 5.

Peter M. Blau, *Exchange and Power in Social Life* (John Wiley & Sons, 1964), esp. ch. 9.

Joan V. Bondurant, ed., *Conflict: Violence and Nonviolence* (Aldine-Atherton, 1971).

Dorwin Cartwright, "Influence, Leadership, Control," in Roderick Bell et al., eds., *Political Power* (Free Press, 1969), pp. 123–65.

Dorwin Cartwright and Alvin Zander, eds., *Group Dynamics,* 3rd ed. (Harper & Row, 1968), esp. part 4.

Michel Crozier and Erhard Friedberg, *Actors and Systems: The Politics of Collective Action,* Arthur Goldhammer, trans. (University of Chicago Press, 1980).

Jo Freeman, "Resource Mobilization and Strategy: A Model for Analyzing Social Movement Organization Actions," in Mayer N. Zald and John D. McCarthy, eds., *The Dynamics of Social Movements: Resource Mobilization, Social Control, and Tactics* (Winthrop Publishers, 1979), pp. 167–89.

John R. P. French, Jr., and Bertram Raven, "The Bases of Social Power" (1959), in Cartwright and Zander, pp. 259–69.

William A. Gamson, *Power and Discontent* (Dorsey Press, 1968).

Carl F. Graumann, "Power and Leadership in Lewinian Field Theory: Recalling an Interrupted Task," in Graumann and Serge Moscovici, eds., *Changing Conceptions of Leadership* (Springer-Verlag, 1986), pp. 83–99.

Joseph S. Himes, "The Functions of Racial Conflict," in Gary T. Marx, ed., *Racial Conflict: Tension and Change in American Society* (Little, Brown, 1971), pp. 449–60.

Edwin P. Hollander, "Intimacy, Power, and Influence: A Perspective on the Relational Features of Leadership," in Martin M. Chemers and Roya Ayman, eds., *Leadership Theory and Research* (Academic Press, 1993), pp. 29–47.

Richard L. Hughes et al., "Power, Influence, and Influence Tactics," in J. Thomas Wren, ed., *The Leader's Companion* (Free Press, 1995), pp. 339–51.

Robert W. Jackman, *Power Without Force: The Political Capacity of Nation-States* (University of Michigan Press, 1993).

Kenneth F. Janda, "Towards the Explication of the Concept of Leadership in Terms of the Concept of Power," in Glenn D. Paige, ed., *Political Leadership* (Free Press, 1972), pp. 45–68.

Elizabeth Janeway, *Powers of the Weak* (Alfred A. Knopf, 1980).

Nicholas N. Kittrie, *The War Against Authority: From the Crisis of Legitimacy to a New Social Contract* (Johns Hopkins University Press, 1995).

David Knoke, "Power Structures," in Samuel L. Long, ed., *The Handbook of Political Behavior* (Plenum Press, 1981), vol. 3, pp. 275–332.

Michael Lipsky, "Protest as a Political Resource," *American Political Science Review*, vol. 62, no. 4 (December 1968), pp. 1144–58.

David C. McClelland, *Power: The Inner Experience* (Irvington, 1975).

Andrew S. McFarland, *Power and Leadership in Pluralist Systems* (Stanford University Press, 1969).

Jean B. Miller, "Domination/Subordination," in Wren, pp. 222–30.

Marvin E. Olsen and Martin N. Marger, eds., *Power in Modern Societies* (Westview Press, 1993).

Leroy H. Pelton, *The Psychology of Nonviolence* (Pergamon Press, 1974).

Robert Prus, *Beyond the Power Mystique: Power as Intersubjective Accomplishment* (State University of New York Press, 1999).

Bertram H. Raven and Arie W. Kruglanski, "Conflict and Power," in Paul Swingle, ed., *The Structure of Conflict* (Academic Press, 1970), pp. 69–109.

Thomas R. Rochon, *Culture Moves: Ideas, Activism, and Changing Values* (Princeton University Press, 1998), esp. part 2.

James C. Scott, *Domination and the Arts of Resistance: Hidden Transcripts* (Yale University Press, 1990).

Gene Sharp, *The Politics of Nonviolent Action*, 3 vols. (Porter Sargent, 1973).

Gene Sharp, *Social Power and Political Freedom* (Porter Sargent, 1980).

Sidney Tarrow, *Power in Movement: Social Movements, Collective Action and Politics* (Cambridge University Press, 1994), esp. part 2.

Dennis H. Wrong, *Power: Its Forms, Bases, and Uses* (1979; reprinted by University of Chicago Press, 1988).

Stephen Zunes et al., eds., *Nonviolent Social Movements: A Geographical Perspective* (Blackwell, 1999).

196   *Arendt on power:* Arendt, *On Violence* (Harcourt, Brace & World, 1970), p. 44.

196   *"power is a gift"*: Boulding, "Nonviolence and Power in the Twentieth Century," in Zunes et al., pp. 9–17, quoted at p. 11.

196   *"afraid of Caesar"*: Epictetus, *Discourses,* Book 4, ch. 1, quoted in Chester G. Starr, *Civilization and the Caesars: The Intellectual Revolution in the Roman Empire* (W. W. Norton, 1965), p. 144 (emphasis added).

196   *"possession of things"*: Pascal, *Discourses on the Condition of the Great,* in Pascal, *Thoughts, Letters, and Minor Works,* O. W. Wight, trans. (Derby & Jackson, 1859), pp. 473–80, quoted at p. 479.

196   *"opportunity to dispense"*: Bass, *Leadership, Psychology,* p. 222.

198   *Crozier and Friedberg on leadership and power:* Crozier and Friedberg, pp. 248–49.

198   *"symbolic and intangible"*: Lipsky, p. 1148.

12 THE POWER OF VALUES

Peter Brown, *The Making of Late Antiquity* (Harvard University Press, 1978).

Peter Brown, *The Rise of Western Christendom: Triumph and Diversity, AD 200–1000* (Blackwell, 1997).

Norbert Brox, *A Concise History of the Early Church,* John Bowden, trans. (Continuum, 1995).

E. R. Dodds, *Pagan and Christian in an Age of Anxiety* (Cambridge University Press, 1965), esp. ch. 4.

Everett Ferguson, ed., *Encyclopedia of Early Christianity,* 2nd ed., 2 vols. (Garland, 1997).

Robin Lane Fox, *Pagans and Christians* (Alfred A. Knopf, 1987).

Kenneth Scott Latourette, *A History of the Expansion of Christianity* (Harper & Brothers, 1937–45), vols. 1–2.

Jacques Waardenburg, "The Early Period, 610–650," in Waardenburg, ed., *Muslim Perceptions of Other Religions* (Oxford University Press, 1999), pp. 3–17.

Robert L. Wilken, "The Christians as the Romans (and Greeks) Saw Them," in E. P. Sanders, ed., *Jewish and Christian Self-Definition* (Fortress Press, 1980–83), vol. 1, pp. 100–25.

201 *"by what means"*: Gibbon, *The Decline and Fall of the Roman Empire,* J. B. Bury, ed. (Heritage Press, 1946), vol. 1, p. 348.

202 *"equally—and totally"*: Brown, *Rise of Western Christendom*, p. 50.

202 *"Jesus, the son of Mary"*: Sura 4:171.

What Values for Leaders?

Bernard M. Bass, *Bass & Stogdill's Handbook of Leadership,* 3rd ed. (Free Press, 1990), ch. 10.

Bernard M. Bass, "The Ethics of Transformational Leadership," in Joanne B. Ciulla, ed., *Ethics, the Heart of Leadership* (Quorum Books, 1998), pp. 169–92.

Bernard M. Bass and Paul Steidlmeier, "Ethics, Character, and Authentic Transformational Leadership Behavior," *Leadership Quarterly,* vol. 10, no. 2 (Summer 1999), pp. 181–217.

Wendell Bell, *Foundations of Futures Studies,* vol. 2, *Values, Objectivity, and the Good Society* (Transaction, 1997).

James MacGregor Burns and Stewart Burns, *A People's Charter: The Pursuit of Rights in America* (Alfred A. Knopf, 1991), ch. 13.

Joanne B. Ciulla, "Leadership Ethics: Mapping the Territory," in Ciulla, *Ethics,* pp. 3–25.

Yael Danieli et al., eds., *The Universal Declaration of Human Rights: Fifty Years and Beyond* (Baywood Publishing, 1999).

Jack Donnelly, *The Concept of Human Rights* (St. Martin's Press, 1985).

Jack Donnelly, *Universal Human Rights in Theory and Practice* (Cornell University Press, 1989).

Asbjørn Eide et al., eds., *The Universal Declaration of Human Rights: A Commentary* (Scandinavian University Press, 1992).

Gilbert W. Fairholm, *Values Leadership: Toward a New Philosophy of Leadership* (Praeger, 1991).

Tom Farer, "The United Nations and Human Rights: More Than a Whimper, Less Than a Roar," *Human Rights Quarterly*, vol. 9, no. 4 (1987), pp. 550–86.

Thomas M. Franck, "Are Human Rights Universal?," *Foreign Affairs*, vol. 80, no. 1 (January–February 2001), pp. 191–204.

Mary Ann Glendon, *A World Made New: Eleanor Roosevelt and the Universal Declaration of Human Rights* (Random House, 2001).

Jill W. Graham, "Leadership, Moral Development, and Citizenship Behavior," *Business Ethics Quarterly*, vol. 5, no. 1 (1995), pp. 43–54.

Michael Hechter, "Should Values Be Written Out of the Social Scientist's Lexicon?," *Sociological Theory*, vol. 10, no. 2 (Fall 1992), pp. 214–30.

Michael Hechter, "Values Research in the Social and Behavioral Sciences," in Hechter et al., eds., *The Origin of Values* (Aldine de Gruyter, 1993), pp. 1–28.

Ronald A. Heifetz, *Leadership Without Easy Answers* (Belknap Press, 1994), esp. ch. 1.

Jeanne Hersch, "Is the Declaration of Human Rights a Western Concept?," in Howard E. Kiefer and Milton K. Munitz, eds., *Ethics and Social Justice* (State University of New York Press, 1970), pp. 323–32.

Edwin P. Hollander, "Ethical Challenges in the Leader-Follower Relationship," in Ciulla, *Ethics*, pp. 49–61.

M. Glen Johnson, "The Contributions of Eleanor and Franklin Roosevelt to the Development of International Protection for Human Rights," *Human Rights Quarterly*, vol. 9, no. 1 (1987), pp. 19–48.

Joseph P. Lash, *Eleanor: The Years Alone* (W. W. Norton, 1972), ch. 3.

Paul Gordon Lauren, *The Evolution of International Human Rights: Visions Seen* (University of Pennsylvania Press, 1998).

H. J. McCloskey, "Human Needs, Rights and Political Values," *American Philosophical Quarterly*, vol. 13, no. 1 (January 1976), pp. 1–11.

Richard McKeon, "Philosophy and History in the Development of Human Rights," in Kiefer and Munitz, pp. 300–22.

Johannes Morsink, *The Universal Declaration of Human Rights: Origins, Drafting, and Intent* (University of Pennsylvania Press, 1999).

A. Glenn Mower, Jr., *The United States, the United Nations, and Human Rights: The Eleanor Roosevelt and Jimmy Carter Eras* (Greenwood Press, 1979), chs. 1–4.

Milton Rokeach, *The Nature of Human Values* (Free Press, 1973).

Joseph C. Rost, *Leadership for the Twenty-First Century* (Praeger, 1991), esp. ch. 7.

Edward Schwartz, "Traditional Values, Moral Education, and Social Change," in Richard W. Wilson and Gordon J. Schochet, eds., *Moral Development and Politics* (Praeger, 1980), pp. 221–36.

Shalom H. Schwartz, "Are There Universal Aspects in the Structure and Contents of Human Values?," *Journal of Social Issues,* vol. 50, no. 4 (Winter 1994), pp. 19–45.

James L. Spates, "The Sociology of Values," *Annual Review of Sociology,* vol. 9 (1983), pp. 27–49.

Carroll Underwood Stephens et al., "The Moral Quandary of Transformational Leadership: Change for Whom?," *Research in Organizational Change and Development,* vol. 8 (1995), pp. 123–43.

United Nations, *"These Rights and Freedoms"* (United Nations, Department of Public Information, 1950).

Marisa Zavalloni, "Values," in Harry C. Triandis and Richard W. Brislin, eds., *Handbook of Cross-Cultural Psychology: Social Psychology,* vol. 5 (Allyn and Bacon, 1980), pp. 73–120.

203 *Roosevelt on the aim of peace:* see Annual Message to the Congress, January 6, 1941, in Roosevelt, *Public Papers and Addresses,* Samuel I. Rosenman, comp. (Random House, 1938–50), vol. 10, pp. 651–72, esp. p. 672.

203 *"Nothing is more likely":* quoted in Lauren, p. 95.

204 *"life of dignity":* Donnelly, *Universal Human Rights,* p. 17.

204 *"carbon copy":* James P. Hendrick, quoted in Lash, p. 62.

204 *"no personal liberty":* quoted in Glendon, p. 115.

205 *"everyone has the right":* "Universal Declaration of Human Rights," in *Human Rights: A Compilation of International Instruments of the United Nations* (United Nations, 1973), pp. 1–3, quoted at pp. 1 (Articles 3, 4), 2 (Article 23).

205 *"criteria for selection":* Robin M. Williams, Jr., "The Concept of Values," in David L. Sills, ed., *International Encyclopedia of the Social Sciences* (Macmillan/Free Press, 1968), vol. 16, pp. 283–87, quoted at p. 283.

206 *"summative construct":* Albert, "Value Systems," in *ibid.,* vol. 16, pp. 287–91, quoted at p. 288.

206 *"value laden":* Gini, "Moral Leadership and Business Ethics," in Ciulla, *Ethics,* pp. 27–45, quoted at p. 36.

206 *"higher moral ground":* Rost, p. 165.

207 *"necessarily vary":* quoted in Glendon, p. 116.

207 *Heifetz on leadership and values:* Heifetz, pp. 13–14.

207 *"To differentiate":* Friedrich, "Political Leadership and the Problem of the Charismatic Power," *Journal of Politics,* vol. 23, no. 1 (February 1961), pp. 3–24, quoted at p. 19.

Transforming Values

Reinhard Bendix, *Kings or People: Power and the Mandate to Rule* (University of California Press, 1978).

Michael K. Briand, *Practical Politics: Five Principles for a Community that Works* (University of Illinois Press, 1999), ch. 4.

Stuart Hampshire, *Morality and Conflict* (Harvard University Press, 1983), esp. ch. 7.

Rabindra N. Kanungo and Manuel Mendonca, *Ethical Dimensions of Leadership* (Sage, 1996).

Nicholas N. Kittrie, *The War Against Authority: From the Crisis of Legitimacy to a New Social Contract* (Johns Hopkins University Press, 1995), esp. ch. 6.

Bert Klandermans, *The Social Psychology of Protest* (Blackwell, 1997), esp. ch. 2.

G. Mollat, *The Popes at Avignon, 1305–1378,* Janet Love, trans. (Thomas Nelson and Sons, 1963).

George L. Mosse, *The Nationalization of the Masses: Political Symbolism and Mass Movements in Germany from the Napoleonic Wars through the Third Reich* (H. Fertig, 1975).

Anthony Oberschall, *Social Conflict and Social Movements* (Prentice-Hall, 1973), ch. 4, and passim.

Yves Renouard, *The Avignon Papacy, 1305–1403,* Denis Bethell, trans. (Archon, 1970).

Peter C. Sederberg, *The Politics of Meaning: Power and Explanation in the Construction of Social Reality* (University of Arizona Press, 1984).

Neil J. Smelser, *Theory of Collective Behavior* (Free Press, 1971), ch. 10, and passim.

Sidney Tarrow, *Power in Movement: Social Movements, Collective Action and Politics* (Cambridge University Press, 1994).

Michael Walzer, "Welfare, Membership and Need," in Michael J. Sandel, ed., *Liberalism and Its Critics* (New York University Press, 1984), pp. 200–18.

Bernard Williams, *Moral Luck: Philosophical Papers, 1973–1980* (Cambridge University Press, 1981), esp. ch. 5.

Diana Wood, *Clement VI: The Pontificate and Ideas of an Avignon Pope* (Cambridge University Press, 1989).

Robert Wuthnow, "State Structures and Ideological Outcomes," *American Sociological Review,* vol. 50, no. 6 (December 1985), pp. 799–821.

208 *"successor of St. Peter"*: Renouard, p. 48.

208 *"inalienable rights"*: reprinted in John Hall Stewart, ed., *A Documentary Survey of the French Revolution* (Macmillan, 1951), pp. 113–15, quoted at p. 114.

209 *"the People having"*: Wordsworth, *The Prelude* (*Text of 1805*), Ernest de Selincourt, ed. (Oxford University Press, 1933), p. 165 (Book 9, lines 530–32).

209 *"rulers who neither see"*: Shelley, "Sonnet: England in 1819," in Shelley, *Complete Poems* (Modern Library, 1994), p. 613 (lines 4–5).

209 *"Rise like Lions"*: Shelley, "The Mask of Anarchy," in *ibid.,* pp. 366–73, quoted at p. 373 (lines 368–72).

210 *"Egyptians, Persians"*: Oberschall, p. 3.

211 *Parliamentary campaigns in Qum:* Susan Sachs, "Iran Holy City Doubles as Hotbed of Reform Politics," *New York Times,* February 16, 2000, p. A3; see also John F. Burns, "In Islam's State, an Islamic Cry for Change," *ibid.,* January 30, 2000, sect. 4, pp. 1, 4.

Empowering Values

Robert D. Benford and Scott A. Hunt, "Dramaturgy and Social Movements: The Social Construction and Communication of Power," *Sociological Inquiry*, vol. 62, no. 1 (February 1992), pp. 36–55.

Kenneth E. Boulding, *Conflict and Defense* (Harper & Brothers, 1962), esp. ch. 14.

Alison Brysk, "'Hearts and Minds': Bringing Symbolic Politics Back In," *Polity*, vol. 27, no. 4 (Summer 1995), pp. 559–85.

Douglas E. Emery, "Self, Creativity, Political Resistance," *Political Psychology*, vol. 14, no. 2 (1993), pp. 347–62.

Charles C. Euchner, *Extraordinary Politics: How Protest and Dissent Are Changing American Democracy* (Westview Press, 1996).

Myra Marx Ferree and Frederick O. Miller, "Mobilization and Meaning: Toward an Integration of Social Psychological and Resource Perspectives on Social Movements," *Sociological Inquiry*, vol. 55, no. 1 (Winter 1985), pp. 38–61.

Gary Alan Fine and Kent Sandstrom, "Ideology in Action: A Pragmatic Approach to a Contested Concept," *Sociological Theory*, vol. 11, no. 1 (March 1993), pp. 21–38.

Paulo Freire, *Pedagogy of the Oppressed*, Myra Bergman Ramos, trans. (Herder and Herder, 1970).

Jill W. Graham, "Leadership, Moral Development, and Citizenship Behavior," *Business Ethics Quarterly*, vol. 5, no. 1 (1995), pp. 43–54.

Eric L. Hirsch, "Sacrifice for the Cause: Group Processes, Recruitment, and Commitment in a Student Social Movement," *American Sociological Review*, vol. 55, no. 2 (1990), pp. 243–54.

Ronald Inglehart, "Values, Ideology, and Cognitive Mobilization in New Social Movements," in Russell J. Dalton and Manfred Kuechler, eds., *Challenging the Political Order: New Social and Political Movements in Western Democracies* (Oxford University Press, 1990), pp. 43–66.

Chalmers Johnson, *Revolutionary Change* (Little, Brown, 1966).

Rabindra N. Kanungo and Manuel Mendonca, *Ethical Dimensions of Leadership* (Sage, 1996).

Bert Klandermans, *The Social Psychology of Protest* (Blackwell, 1997).

David McLellan, *Ideology*, 2nd ed. (University of Minnesota Press, 1995), ch. 1, and passim.

Anthony Oberschall, *Social Conflict and Social Movements* (Prentice-Hall, 1973).

James C. Scott, *Weapons of the Weak: Everyday Forms of Peasant Resistance* (Yale University Press, 1985), chs. 6, 8, and passim.

Peter C. Sederberg, *The Politics of Meaning: Power and Explanation in the Construction of Social Reality* (University of Arizona Press, 1984).

Eric Selbin, "Revolution in the Real World: Bringing Agency Back In," in John Foran, ed., *Theorizing Revolutions* (Routledge, 1997), pp. 123–36.

Neil J. Smelser, *Theory of Collective Behavior* (Free Press, 1971), ch. 9, and passim.

Göran Therborn, *The Ideology of Power and the Power of Ideology* (Verso, 1980).

13 THE PEOPLE, YES?

The X Factor

Warren G. Bennis et al., eds., *The Planning of Change*, 2nd ed. (Holt, Rinehart and Winston, 1969).

Guy Benveniste, *Mastering the Politics of Planning* (Jossey-Bass, 1989).

James MacGregor Burns, "Empowerment for Change: A Conceptual Working Paper," prepared for the Kellogg Leadership Studies Project, September 1996.

Dudley J. Burton and M. Brian Murphy, "Democratic Planning in Austerity," in Pierre Clavel et al., eds., *Urban and Regional Planning in an Age of Austerity* (Pergamon, 1980), pp. 177–205.

Philip G. Cerny, *The Changing Architecture of Politics: Structure, Agency, and the Future of the State* (Sage, 1990).

William U. Chandler, *The Myth of TVA: Conservation and Development in the Tennessee Valley, 1933–1983* (Ballinger, 1984).

Stuart Chase, *Rich Land, Poor Land: A Study of Waste in the Natural Resources of America* (Whittlesey House, 1936), esp. ch. 15.

Elisabeth S. Clemens, "To Move Mountains: Collective Action and the Possibility of Institutional Change," in Marco G. Giugni et al., eds., *From Contention to Democracy* (Rowman & Littlefield, 1998), pp. 109–23.

Randall Collins, "The Romanticism of Agency/Structure versus the Analysis of Micro/Macro," *Current Sociology*, vol. 40, no. 1 (Spring 1992), pp. 77–97.

Walter D. Conner and Piotr Ploszajski, eds., *The Polish Road from Socialism: The Economics, Sociology, and Politics of Transition* (M. E. Sharpe, 1992).

Richard A. Couto, "TVA and Democratic Aspirations," paper prepared for delivery at the Southern Humanities Conference, Nashville, February 5, 1982.

Walter L. Creese, *TVA's Public Planning: The Vision, the Reality* (University of Tennessee Press, 1990).

Michel Crozier and Erhard Friedberg, *Actors and Systems: The Politics of Collective Action*, Arthur Goldhammer, trans. (University of Chicago Press, 1980).

Harry Eckstein, "On the Etiology of Internal Wars," *History and Theory*, vol. 4, no. 2 (1965), pp. 133–63.

David J. Finlay et al., *Enemies in Politics* (Rand McNally, 1967), esp. ch. 1.

John Forester, *Planning in the Face of Power* (University of California Press, 1989).

Gil Friedman and Harvey Starr, *Agency, Structure, and International Politics: From Ontology to Empirical Inquiry* (Routledge, 1997).

John Friedmann, *Planning in the Public Domain: From Knowledge to Action* (Princeton University Press, 1987).

Luther P. Gerlach and Virginia H. Hine, *People, Power, Change: Movements of Social Transformation* (Bobbs-Merrill, 1970), esp. ch. 7.

Anthony Giddens, *The Constitution of Society: Outline of the Theory of Structuration* (University of California Press, 1984).

Peter M. Gollwitzer, "The Volitional Benefits of Planning," in Gollwitzer and John

A. Bargh, eds., *The Psychology of Action: Linking Cognition and Motivation to Behavior* (Guilford Press, 1996), pp. 287–312.

Lawrence Goodwyn, *Breaking the Barrier: The Rise of Solidarity in Poland* (Oxford University Press, 1991).

Stephen Grabow and Allan Heskin, "Foundations for a Radical Concept of Planning," *Journal of the American Institute of Planners*, vol. 39, no. 2 (March 1973), pp. 106, 108–14.

Otis L. Graham, Jr., *Toward a Planned Society: From Roosevelt to Nixon* (Oxford University Press, 1976), esp. ch. 1.

Nancy L. Grant, *TVA and Black Americans: Planning for the Status Quo* (Temple University Press, 1990).

Erwin C. Hargrove, *Prisoners of Myth: The Leadership of the Tennessee Valley Authority, 1933–1990* (Princeton University Press, 1994).

Erwin C. Hargrove and Paul K. Conkin, eds., *TVA: Fifty Years of Grass-Roots Bureaucracy* (University of Illinois Press, 1983).

William C. Havard, Jr., "Images of TVA: The Clash over Values," in Hargrove and Conkin, pp. 297–315.

Patsy Healey, "Planning Through Debate: The Communicative Turn in Planning Theory," in Frank Fischer and John Forester, eds., *The Argumentative Turn in Policy Analysis and Planning* (Duke University Press, 1993), pp. 233–53.

George C. Homans, "Bringing Men Back In," *American Sociological Review*, vol. 29, no. 5 (December 1964), pp. 809–18.

Ghita Ionescu, ed., *The Political Thought of Saint-Simon* (Oxford University Press, 1976).

Thomas S. Langston, *Ideologues and Presidents: From the New Deal to the Reagan Revolution* (Johns Hopkins University Press, 1992), esp. ch. 3.

David E. Lilienthal, *Journals: The TVA Years, 1939–1945* (Harper & Row, 1964).

David E. Lilienthal, *TVA: Democracy on the March*, 20th anniversary ed. (Harper & Brothers, 1953).

Frank E. Manuel, *The New World of Henri Saint-Simon* (Harvard University Press, 1956).

Robert Mayer et al., *Centrally Planned Change: A Reexamination of Theory and Experience* (University of Illinois Press, 1974).

Thomas K. McGraw, *Morgan vs. Lilienthal: The Feud Within the TVA* (Loyola University Press, 1970).

Steven M. Neuse, *David E. Lilienthal: The Journey of an American Liberal* (University of Tennessee Press, 1996).

David Ost, *Solidarity and the Politics of Anti-Politics: Opposition and Reform in Poland Since 1968* (Temple University Press, 1990).

Noel Parker, *Revolutions and History* (Polity Press, 1999).

Jaroslaw Piekalkiewicz, "Poland: Nonviolent Revolution in a Socialist State," in Jack A. Goldstone et al., eds., *Revolutions of the Late Twentieth Century* (Westview Press, 1991), pp. 136–61.

Eric Selbin, "Revolution in the Real World: Bringing Agency Back In," in John Foran, ed., *Theorizing Revolutions* (Routledge, 1997), pp. 123–36.

Philip Selznick, "Dilemmas of Leadership and Doctrine in Democratic Planning," in Alvin W. Gouldner, ed., *Studies in Leadership: Leadership and Democratic Action* (Harper & Brothers, 1950), pp. 560–91.

Stephen Skowronek, *The Politics Presidents Make: Leadership from John Adams to George Bush* (Belknap Press, 1993).

Piotr Sztompka, "Agency and Progress: The Idea of Progress and Changing Theories of Change," in Jeffrey C. Alexander and Sztompka, eds., *Rethinking Progress: Movements, Forces, and Ideas at the End of the 20th Century* (Unwin Hyman, 1990), pp. 247–63.

Piotr Sztompka, *Society in Action: The Theory of Social Becoming* (University of Chicago Press, 1991).

R. H. Tawney, *Equality* (Harcourt, Brace, 1931).

Ronald C. Tobey, *Technology as Freedom: The New Deal and the Electrical Modernization of the American Home* (University of California Press, 1996).

Bruce G. Trigger, *Sociocultural Evolution: Calculation and Contingency* (Blackwell, 1998), ch. 10.

Diane Raines Ward, *Water Wars: Drought, Flood, Folly, and the Politics of Thirst* (Riverhead Books, 2002).

Aaron Wildavsky, *Speaking Truth to Power: The Art and Craft of Policy Analysis* (Little, Brown, 1979).

Richard Wilson, *Labyrinth: An Essay on the Political Psychology of Change* (M. E. Sharpe, 1988), esp. ch. 5.

Gerald Zaltman et al., eds., *Creating Social Change* (Holt, Rinehart and Winston, 1972), part 3 passim.

215 *Homans on functionalism:* Homans, pp. 817, 816, respectively.

216 *Tawney on inequality:* Tawney, pp. 44, 45, 83, 12, 125, 137, 88, respectively; see also my *Uncommon Sense* (Harper & Row, 1972), p. 82, on whose commentary I have drawn.

218 *"Chamber of* Invention": Saint-Simon, *The Organizer* ("Sixth Letter"), in Ionescu, pp. 147–52, quoted at pp. 147 and 148 footnote 1.

218 *"feasts of* expectation": *ibid.,* p. 148.

218 *"relatively simple wants":* Chase, p. 267.

219 *Hargrove on Arthur Morgan:* Hargrove, *Prisoners of Myth,* p. 25.

219 *"make vital concessions":* quoted in *ibid.,* p. 34.

219 *"contumacious" behavior:* quoted in Neuse, p. 104.

219 *Hargrove on Lilienthal:* Hargrove, *Prisoners of Myth,* p. 41.

220 *"reconstruct the total pattern":* Schlesinger, *The Politics of Upheaval* (Houghton Mifflin, 1960), pp. 375–76.

"Life, Liberty, and ..."

Albert Bandura, "Exercise of Personal and Collective Efficacy in Changing Societies," in Bandura, ed., *Self-Efficacy in Changing Societies* (Cambridge University Press, 1995), pp. 1–45.

Albert Bandura, *Self-Efficacy: The Exercise of Control* (W. H. Freeman, 1997), ch. 11, and passim.

James MacGregor Burns, "Empowerment for Change: A Conceptual Working Paper," prepared for the Kellogg Leadership Studies Project, September 1996.

Richard A. Couto, "Grassroots Policies of Empowerment," paper prepared for delivery at the annual meeting of the American Political Science Association, Chicago, September 3–6, 1992.

Richard A. Couto, *Lifting the Veil: A Political History of Struggles for Emancipation* (University of Tennessee Press, 1993).

Charles C. Euchner, *Extraordinary Politics: How Protest and Dissent Are Changing American Democracy* (Westview Press, 1996).

Sara M. Evans and Harry C. Boyte, *Free Spaces: The Sources of Democratic Change in America* (Perennial, 1987).

Ron Eyerman, "Intellectuals and Progress: The Origins, Decline, and Revival of a Critical Group," in Jeffrey C. Alexander and Piotr Sztompka, eds., *Rethinking Progress: Movements, Forces, and Ideas at the End of the 20th Century* (Unwin Hyman, 1990), pp. 91–105.

Ron Eyerman and Andrew Jamison, *Social Movements: A Cognitive Approach* (Pennsylvania State University Press, 1991), esp. ch. 4.

Brian Fay, *Critical Social Science: Liberation and Its Limits* (Cornell University Press, 1987).

Paulo Freire, *Pedagogy of the Oppressed,* Myra Bergman Ramos, trans. (Herder and Herder, 1970).

Viktor Gecas, "The Self-Concept as a Basis for a Theory of Motivation," in Judith A. Howard and Peter L. Callero, eds., *The Self-Society Dynamic: Cognition, Emotion, and Action* (Cambridge University Press, 1991), pp. 171–87.

Kenneth J. Gergen and Matthew Ullman, "Socialization and the Characterological Basis of Political Activism," in Stanley Allen Renshon, ed., *Handbook of Political Socialization* (Free Press, 1977), pp. 411–42.

Judith A. Howard, "From Changing Selves Toward Changing Society," in Howard and Callero, pp. 209–37.

Chalmers Johnson, *Revolutionary Change* (Little, Brown, 1966).

Thomas R. Rochon, *Culture Moves: Ideas, Activism, and Changing Values* (Princeton University Press, 1998).

James N. Rosenau, *Turbulence in World Politics: A Theory of Change and Continuity* (Princeton University Press, 1990).

Piotr Sztompka, *Society in Action: The Theory of Social Becoming* (University of Chicago Press, 1991).

Tom R. Tyler and Heather J. Smith, "Social Justice and Social Movements," in Daniel T. Gilbert et al., eds., *The Handbook of Social Psychology,* 4th ed. (McGraw-Hill, 1998), vol. 2, pp. 595–629.

222 *"When a society"*: Johnson, p. 60.

223 *Tocqueville and Davies on frustrated expectations:* Tocqueville, *The Old Régime and the French Revolution,* Stuart Gilbert, trans. (Doubleday Anchor, 1955), esp.

pp. 169–79 (part 3, ch. 4), quoted at p. 177; Davies, "Toward a Theory of Revolution," *American Sociological Review*, vol. 27, no. 1 (February 1962), pp. 5–19.

224 *"Who can better understand"*: Freire, p. 29.

224 *"critical communities"*: Rochon, esp. chs. 2, 6, quoted at p. 29.

225 *"Shaping the social future"*: Bandura, *Self-Efficacy: The Exercise of Control*, p. 500.

225 *Organizing at Rock Hill, South Carolina:* Burgess, *Fighting for Social Justice* (Wayne State University Press, 2000), ch. 9, mill owner quoted at pp. 74, 75.

225 *Yellow Creek, Kentucky:* Sherry Cable, "From Fussin' to Organizing: Individual and Collective Resistance at Yellow Creek," in Stephen L. Fisher, ed., *Fighting Back in Appalachia: Traditions of Resistance and Change* (Temple University Press, 1993), pp. 69–83.

226 *Morristown, Tennessee:* Eve S. Weinbaum, "Transforming Democracy: Women, Appalachian Communities and Economic Inequality," paper prepared for delivery at the 1996 annual meeting of the American Political Science Association, San Francisco, quoted at p. 14.

227 *"informed participant citizen"*: quoted in Rosenau, p. 374.

227 *"new outlets"*: *ibid.*, p. 380.

". . . The Pursuit Of Happiness"

Vernon L. Allen, ed., *Psychological Factors in Poverty* (Academic Press, 1970).

Michael Argyle, *The Psychology of Happiness,* 2nd ed. (Routledge, 2001).

James MacGregor Burns and Stewart Burns, *A People's Charter: The Pursuit of Rights in America* (Alfred A. Knopf, 1991), part 1.

Ralf Dahrendorf, *Life Chances* (University of Chicago Press, 1979).

Bernard P. Dauenhauer, "Hope and Its Ramifications for Politics," *Man and World,* vol. 17, nos. 3–4 (1984), pp. 453–76.

John Patrick Diggins, *On Hallowed Ground: Abraham Lincoln and the Foundations of American History* (Yale University Press, 2000), esp. chs. 1–2.

Deal W. Hudson, *Happiness and the Limits of Satisfaction* (Rowman and Littlefield, 1996), esp. ch. 5.

Francis Hutcheson, *Collected Works,* 7 vols. (Georg Olms Verlag, 1990).

Howard Mumford Jones, *The Pursuit of Happiness* (Harvard University Press, 1953).

Stanley N. Katz, "Thomas Jefferson and the Right to Property in Revolutionary America," *Journal of Law & Economics,* vol. 19, no. 3 (October 1976), pp. 467–88.

Oscar Lewis, *The Children of Sánchez: Autobiography of a Mexican Family* (Random House, 1961).

James Moore, "The Two Systems of Francis Hutcheson: On the Origins of the Scottish Enlightenment," in M. A. Stewart, ed., *Studies in the Philosophy of the Scottish Enlightenment* (Clarendon Press, 1990), pp. 37–59.

Charles Murray, *In Pursuit Of Happiness and Good Government* (Simon and Schuster, 1988).

Roy Porter, *The Creation of the Modern World: The Untold Story of the British Enlightenment* (W. W. Norton, 2000), esp. ch. 11.

Caroline Robbins, "'When It Is That Colonies May Turn Independent': An Analysis of the Environment and Politics of Francis Hutcheson (1694–1746)," *William and Mary Quarterly*, 3rd series, vol. 11, no. 2 (April 1954), pp. 214–51.

William B. Scott, *In Pursuit of Happiness: American Conceptions of Property from the Seventeenth to the Twentieth Century* (Indiana University Press, 1977).

Julian L. Simon, ed., *The State of Humanity* (Blackwell, 1995).

Wladyslaw Tatarkiewicz, *Analysis of Happiness,* Edward Rothert and Danuta Zielińskn, trans. (Martinus Nijhoff/Polish Scientific Publishers, 1976).

Ursula M. von Eckardt, *The Pursuit of Happiness in the Democratic Creed: An Analysis of Political Ethics* (Praeger, 1959).

Garry Wills, *Inventing America: Jefferson's Declaration of Independence* (Doubleday, 1978).

228 *"all of us desire"*: Plato, *Euthydemus,* in Plato, *Dialogues,* B. Jowett, trans. (Random House, 1937), vol. 1, pp. 133–70, quoted at p. 140 (279).

228 "our moral Sense": Hutcheson, *An Inquiry into the Original of our Ideas of Beauty and Virtue,* 2nd ed. (1726), pp. 177–78.

228 *Hutcheson on rights:* see Hutcheson, *A System of Moral Philosophy,* in Hutcheson, *Collected Works,* vol. 5, bk. 2, ch. 5.

228 *"excluded from the enjoyment"*: ibid., vol. 5, p. 226.

228 *1774 Continental Congress declaration:* see "The Bill of Rights [and] a List of Grievances," in James H. Hutson, ed., *A Decent Respect to the Opinions of Mankind: Congressional State Papers, 1774–1776* (Library of Congress, 1975), pp. 52–56, esp. p. 53.

228 *"our natural wants"*: letter to Pierre Samuel Dupont de Nemours, April 24, 1816, in Jefferson, *Writings,* Paul Leicester Ford, ed. (G. P. Putnam's Sons, 1892–99), vol. 10, pp. 22–25, quoted at p. 24.

229 *"greatest degree of happiness"*: letter to Francis Adrian van der Kemp, March 22, 1812, in Jefferson, *Works,* H. A. Washington, ed. (Townsend Mac Coun, 1884), vol. 6, pp. 44–46, quoted at p. 45.

229 *"happiness of the people"*: Jefferson, "Hints to Americans Travelling in Europe" (1788), in Jefferson, *Papers,* Julian P. Boyd, ed. (Princeton University Press, 1950–   ), vol. 13, pp. 264–75, quoted at p. 269.

229 *"lived like that"*: quoted in Tamara K. Hareven, *Eleanor Roosevelt: An American Conscience* (1968; reprinted by Da Capo Press, 1975), p. 10.

229 *"world of violence"*: Lewis, p. xii.

EPILOGUE
GLOBAL POVERTY: PUTTING LEADERSHIP TO WORK

Vernon L. Allen, *Psychological Factors in Poverty* (Academic Press, 1970).

Lauren D. Applebaum, "The Influence of Perceived Deservingness on Policy Decisions Regarding Aid to the Poor," *Political Psychology,* vol. 22, no. 3 (September 2001), pp. 419–42.

Mabelle Arole, "Jamkhed," in Carl E. Taylor et al., eds., *Partnerships for Social Develop-ment* (Future Generations, 1995), pp. 24–31.

Christian Bay, *Strategies of Political Emancipation* (University of Notre Dame Press, 1981).

Arthur Bonner, *Averting the Apocalypse: Social Movements in India Today* (Duke Univer-sity Press, 1990).

Ashish Bose, "Population: The Quest for Stabilization," in Hiranmay Karlekar, ed., *In-dependent India: The First Fifty Years* (Oxford University Press, 1998), pp. 314–32.

Pierre Bourdieu et al., *The Weight of the World: Social Suffering in Contemporary Society*, Priscilla Parkhurst Ferguson et al., trans. (Stanford University Press, 1999).

Elizabeth Bumiller, *May You Be the Mother of a Hundred Sons: A Journey Among the Women of India* (Random House, 1990).

Robert Cassen et al., *Does Aid Work?* (Clarendon Press, 1986).

John Clark, *Democratizing Development: The Role of Voluntary Organizations* (Kumarian Press, 1991).

Giovanni Andrea Cornia and Sheldon Danziger, eds., *Child Poverty and Deprivation in the Industrialized Countries, 1945–1995* (Clarendon Press, 1997).

Barbara Ehrenreich, *Nickel and Dimed: On (Not) Getting By in America* (Metropolitan Books, 2001).

Ross Fitzgerald, ed., *Human Needs and Politics* (Pergamon Press, 1977).

Paulo Freire, *Pedagogy of the Oppressed*, Myra Bergman Ramos, trans. (Herder and Herder, 1970).

George H. Gallup, "Human Needs and Satisfactions: A Global Survey," *Public Opin-ion Quarterly*, vol. 40 (1976), pp. 459–67.

Nandita Gandhi and Nandita Shah, *The Issues at Stake: Theory and Practice in the Con-temporary Women's Movement in India* (Kali For Women, 1992), esp. ch. 4.

Bronislaw Geremek, *Poverty: A History*, Agnieszka Kolakowska, trans. (Blackwell, 1994).

"Globalism and the World's Poor," special supplement to *The American Prospect* (Win-ter 2002).

Pranay Gupte, *Mother India: A Political Biography of Indira Gandhi* (Charles Scribner's Sons, 1992), ch. 19.

Douglas A. Hicks, "Inequality, Globalization, and Leadership: 'Keeping Up with the Joneses' Across National Borders," *Annual of the Society of Christian Ethics*, vol. 21 (2001), pp. 63–80.

Robin Jeffrey, *Politics, Women, and Well-Being: How Kerala Became "a Model"* (Macmillan, 1992).

A. M. Khusro, *The Poverty of Nations* (St. Martin's Press, 1999).

Üner Kirdar and Leonard Silk, eds., *People: From Impoverishment to Empowerment* (New York University Press, 1995).

Robert E. Lane, "Self-Reliance and Empathy: The Enemies of Poverty—and of the Poor," *Political Psychology*, vol. 22, no. 3 (September 2001), pp. 473–92.

Anthony Lewis, "The Inescapable World," *New York Times*, October 20, 2001, p. A23.

Jeff Madrick, "Economic Scene," *New York Times*, August 2, 2001, p. C2.

Mahmood Mamdani, *The Myth of Population Control: Family, Caste, and Class in an Indian Village* (Monthly Review Press, 1972).

George Martine et al., eds., *Reproductive Change in India and Brazil* (Oxford University Press, 1998).

George McGovern, "The Healing in Helping the Poor," *New York Times,* January 1, 2002, p. A21.

Rekha Mehra and K. Saradamoni, *Women and Rural Transformation* (Concept Publishing, 1983).

Kusum Nair, *Blossoms in the Dust: The Human Element in Indian Development* (Gerald Duckworth, 1961).

Deepa Narayan et al., *Voices of the Poor: Can Anyone Hear Us?* (Oxford University Press, 2000).

Deepa Narayan et al., *Voices of the Poor: Crying Out for Change* (Oxford University Press, 2000).

Lucile F. Newman et al., eds., *Hunger in History: Food Shortage, Poverty, and Deprivation* (Basil Blackwell, 1990).

A. S. Oberai, *Population Growth, Employment and Poverty in Third-World Mega-Cities* (St. Martin's Press, 1993).

S. L. Ogale, *The Tragedy of Too Many,* 2nd ed. (Academic Books, 1970).

V. A. Pai Panandiker and P. K. Umashankar, "Fertility Control and Politics in India," in Jason L. Finkle and C. Alison McIntosh, eds., *The New Politics of Population: Conflict and Consensus in Family Planning* (Oxford University Press, 1994), pp. 89–104.

Alwyn R. Rouyer, "Political Capacity and the Decline of Fertility in India," *American Political Science Review,* vol. 81, no. 2 (June 1987), pp. 453–70.

Alan Schwartz, "Getting at the Roots of Arab Poverty," *New York Times,* December 1, 2001, p. A27.

Amartya Sen, *Development as Freedom* (Alfred A. Knopf, 1999).

Abusaleh Shariff, *India: Human Development Report* (Oxford University Press, 1999).

Julian L. Simon, ed., *The State of Humanity* (Blackwell, 1995).

Richard Sokolsky and Joseph McMillan, "Foreign Aid in Our Own Defense," *New York Times,* February 12, 2002, p. A27.

Alexander Stille, "Grounded by an Income Gap," *New York Times,* December 15, 2001, pp. A17, 19.

Finn Tarp, ed., *Foreign Aid and Development: Lessons Learnt and Directions for the Future* (Routledge, 2000).

Gracious Thomas, *People's Participation in Community Development* (Uppal Publishing, 1992).

Josh Tyrangiel, "Bono," *Time,* vol. 159, no. 9 (March 4, 2002), pp. 62–72.

Marion den Uyl, *Invisible Barriers: Gender, Caste and Kinship in a Southern Indian Village* (International Books, 1995).

Joachim von Braun et al., *Famine in Africa: Causes, Responses, and Prevention* (Johns Hopkins University Press, 1998).

Steven R. Weisman, "Where Births Are Kept Down and Women Aren't," *New York Times,* January 29, 1988, p. A4.

231 *"ideas are weapons"*: Max Lerner, *Ideas Are Weapons: The History and Uses of Ideas* (Viking, 1939), esp. ch. 1.

231 *Bennis on corporate leadership:* Bennis, "A Corporate Fear of Too Much Truth," *New York Times,* February 17, 2002, sect. 4, p. 11.

232 *Country poverty ratios:* Khusro, p. 7.

232 *"experiences the highest level"*: Hicks, p. 64.

232 *World income distribution: ibid.*

232 *"sometimes just get sick"*: quoted in Narayan et al., *Crying Out for Change,* p. 91; see also Norman E. Whitten, Jr., *Sacha Runa: Ethnicity and Adaptation of Ecuadorian Jungle Quichua* (University of Illinois Press, 1976), pp. 82–85.

233 *Brown's proposal:* Joseph Kahn, "Britain Urges U.S. to Expand Worldwide Anti-poverty Programs," *New York Times,* December 18, 2001, p. A7; Kahn, "U.S. Rejects Bid to Double Foreign Aid to Poor Lands," *ibid.,* January 29, 2002, p. A11.

233 *American aid, as GNP ratio:* Peter Hjertholm and Howard White, "Foreign Aid in Historical Perspective: Background and Trends," in Tarp, pp. 80–102, cited at p. 89 (Figure 3.2).

234 *Aid decline, by 1990s: ibid.,* p. 86 (Figure 3.1).

234 *Voices of the poor:* quoted in Narayan et al., *Crying Out for Change,* pp. 80, 84, 95, 98, 107–8, respectively.

235 *"rich descriptions"*: Narayan et al., *Can Anyone Hear Us?,* pp. 3, 8.

235 *"basic unit of work"*: Mamdani, pp. 21, 103.

236 *"uneducated, ignorant"*: Ogale, p. 22.

236 *Gandhi on "drastic" steps:* quoted in Panandiker and Umashankar, p. 90.

236 *"police and other officials"*: Bonner, p. 161.

236 *Sanctions against villages and children:* Gandhi and Shah, p. 119.

236 *8 million sterilizations:* Bonner, p. 161.

237 *"bold and confident"*: Arole, p. 29.

239 *Democracy as conducive to pursuits of happiness:* see Benjamin Radcliff, "Politics, Markets, and Life Satisfaction: The Political Economy of Happiness," *American Political Science Review,* vol. 95, no. 4 (December 2001), pp. 939–52, and sources cited therein.

240 *"desire for self-fulfillment"*: Maslow, *Motivation and Personality* (Harper & Brothers, 1954), pp. 91, 201.

240 *"Bearing yet not possessing"*: Lao-Tsu, *Tao Te Ching,* Gia-Fu Feng and Jane English, trans. (Vintage, 1972), ch. 10.

ACKNOWLEDGMENTS

Milton Djuric has given me indispensable aid, advice, and support at every stage of this work. I want to thank also my colleagues at the Jepson School of Leadership Studies at the University of Richmond and at the Leadership Studies Program at Williams College for intellectual stimulation and encouragement. I am grateful to Georgia Sorenson and Gill Hickman for providing crucial institutional support. Joanne Ciulla and James C. Davies made many valuable comments on the manuscript in their areas of expertise. Douglas Hicks helped me think through tough questions regarding global poverty. I appreciate the advice and encouragement I received from both Morgan Entrekin and Eric Price at Grove/Atlantic, and editors Brendan Cahill and Brando Skyhorse offered excellent suggestions and support. For unfailing assistance at Williams, I thank the Faculty Secretarial Office and the staff of Sawyer Library. David, Stewart, Deborah, and Mecca Antonia Burns gave me the benefit of their insights and ideas. Antonia conducted extensive research on womanhood and transforming leadership in India; my treatment of this subject in the Epilogue, as well as of creative leadership in the theater, is based on her efforts.

Warmest thanks to Susan Dunn, my coauthor in history at Williams, for reading the manuscript and providing critical and loving support throughout.

INDEX